THE COMMITTEE OF ONE MILLION

"CHINA LOBBY" POLITICS, 1953–1971

STANLEY D. BACHRACK

NEW YORK   COLUMBIA UNIVERSITY PRESS   1976

THE COMMITTEE OF ONE MILLION

"CHINA LOBBY" POLITICS,

1953–1971

Library of Congress Cataloging in Publication Data

Bachrack, Stanley D. 1927–
    The Committee of One Million: "China Lobby" politics, 1953-1971 / Stanley D. Bachrack.–
    Bibliography: p.349-356.
    Includes index.
    1. United States—Foreign relations—China.
2. China—Foreign relations—United States.
3. Committee of One Million (against the Admission
of Communist China to the United Nations) New York.
4. United Nations—China. I. Title
JX1428.C6B3   327.73'051   76-18117
    ISBN 0-231-03933-6

Columbia University Press
New York   Guildford, Surrey
Copyright © 1973, 1976 Columbia University Press
Printed in the United States of America

FOR MARILYN
MY COMMITTEE OF ONE

CONTENTS

Research on this book began in the winter of 1971, before the first flush of rapprochement with China, before the break-in at the Watergate, before the long series of official and unofficial disclosures about secret American intelligence operations at home and abroad—remarkable events of contemporary history which bear on this work in different ways.

Clandestine debris continues to surface from the depths of the cold war. This story, part of that flotsam and jetsam, is itself incomplete in one critical detail: the exact origins of the group founded in the immediate aftermath of the Korean War and later known as The Committee of One Million Against the Admission of Communist China to the United Nations. A Freedom of Information Act lawsuit filed to clarify this matter (see chapter 3) was dismissed by a federal judge in United States District Court on April 26, 1976.

The word *documentary* best describes the pages that follow, for this account is based almost entirely on documents. My primary source materials on The Committee of One Million were the organization's own files, maintained and later donated to the Hoover Institution on War, Revolution, and Peace at Stanford University by Marvin Liebman, the group's longtime secretary as well as publicist and fund raiser until early 1969 for many anti-Communist and conservative political organizations. (Liebman's various files also became available for research at the Hoover Institution Archives in 1969.) Other primary sources included the White House files of three Presidents, official records and publications of Congress and the Department of State, and public records of the New York State Department of Social Welfare. This documentary approach has necessitated extensive use of footnotes which, thanks to Columbia University Press, are readily discoverable in the Notes section without being obtrusive in the text.

A final academic note: my 1973 Ph.D. dissertation, on which this work is based, comprised eight chapters, the first of which, "Group Theory and Foreign Policy," is not included here. In addition to five new chapters in this volume, the seven originally included in my dissertation have been completely or substantially rewritten.

An author, I've discovered, is constantly asking for favors—from friends, relatives, acquaintances, librarians, archivists, editors, lawyers, colleagues. Even as I write these final lines I realize this process will continue until some unknown point in the future. I am, therefore, eager to acknowledge some, if not all, of those people who have helped in one way or another and may continue to do so: Patrick Breslin, Mollie Copeland, Jack Goldsmith, Sadelle Hershey-Miller, W. L. Holland, E. William Johnson, Richard Kagan, Crone C. Kernke, Paul Kircher, Franz G. Lassner, Paul Marsh, Ernest T. Nash, Charles R. Nixon, Charles O. Porter, Frances Rose, Stanley K. Sheinbaum, Donald J. Simon, John R. Sisson, Bob Tilley, Joyce Toscan, Robert C. Toth, and John E. Wickman.

Richard G. Berry deserves a special note of thanks for lawyering my Freedom of Information Act lawsuit with considerable patience and skill for which he was not richly remunerated. I am also grateful to my father, Herman A. Bachrack, and to my friend, Thomas J. McDermott Jr., for their valuable legal counsel.

The manuscript was read in whole or in part and commented upon at various stages by Herman A. Bachrack, Richard Baum, Donald A. Marchand, Robert P. Newman, Joel Rapp, Harry M. Scoble, Eli Sobel, H. Arthur Steiner, Laurence Vittes, and Roberta Wohlstetter. Professors Baum, Scoble, and Sobel approved the original dissertation and encouraged me to seek publication. I especially wish to thank Rick Baum and Laurence Vittes for their ceaseless support, suggestions, and editing. Also, I am pleased to record my appreciation to Arthur Steiner, who rescued me from many difficulties while offering encouragement and humor. Bernard Gronert and Joan McQuary of Columbia University Press eased the anxieties of authorship while immeasurably improving the manuscript, a double contribution.

Finally I salute Max Elden and my wife Marilyn, both of whom shared the rough going (although the former slipped off to Norway, leaving the latter my indispensable Committee of One).

Naturally, none of the above need share my responsibility for errors of fact or judgment.

STANLEY D. BACHRACK
LOS ANGELES, CALIFORNIA
JULY 1976

BACKGROUND

Origins of the "China Lobby"

Although the exact origins of the "China Lobby" catchphrase are some-what dubious, the expression received widespread attention in the spring of 1950, when America's China policy became engulfed in national hys-teria over the "loss of China to the Reds" in the fall of 1949. To this day, large chunks of the U.S. China policy record, including the "China Lobby" fragment, remain in dispute. This book examines part of that fragment, an organization founded in 1953 and known as The Committee for One Million Against the Admission of Communist China to the United Nations.* The time was that immediately following the Korean War, literally within days of the armistice and thus at a critical psychological juncture in the embattled relations between the United States and China—like the first seconds following a fist fight when bleeding and emotionally drained opponents pause momentarily before deciding whether to settle their differences or continue the struggle. By then, with a new Republican administration in Washington and with the Chinese Communist Party (CCP) in clear control of the mainland, the once vocal domestic debate over China policy had quieted.

Actually, between the end of World War II and the Nixon adminis-trations, there were three major debates over relations with China. The first focused on the proper course for the United States to follow in China after 1945: initially, whether to continue mediation efforts in search of a Chinese coalition government, then whether (and to what ex-tent) to continue aiding the Nationalist government of President Chiang

---

* Throughout the book this organization will be referred to as The Committee for One Million or simply the Committee. Similarly, the group reconstituted in 1955 as The Committee of One Million Against the Admission of Communist China to the United Nations will be called The Committee of One Million or the Committee.

Kai-shek. The second debate—more a brawl than a debate—concerned acceptance of the State Department's White Paper in 1949 on U.S. relations with China, released in August in anticipation of the complete takeover of the mainland by the CCP. The third followed the Korean War and centered on the twin questions of whether the United States should recognize the People's Republic of China and accept its membership in the United Nations.

All three debates took place within the wider context of the cold war, were characterized by frequent clashes within and between Congress and the Executive branch, and were peopled in part by an amorphous yet ubiquitous agglomeration of individuals and groups collectively called the "China Lobby."

The Committee for One Million was organized to direct and dominate the third debate, a task for which it was uniquely prepared by a steering committee controlled by important members of Congress. Indeed, as we shall see, the Committee was born—if not totally conceived—in a congressional subcommittee. Key Committee activists recruited their congressional colleagues as members, authorized a New York-based public relations operation to solicit public support, then exerted their influence publicly and privately to hold successive national administrations to a hard line on China policy. A handful of the Committee's congressional leaders thus functioned as an insider-type lobby, conducting Committee business from their own offices on Capitol Hill. It is not surprising, then, that for eighteen years, from 1953 to 1971, "The Committee *for* One Million" and its successor, "The Committee *of* One Million" comprised the "China Lobby" in American politics.

The Catchphrase Emerges

Specialists will recognize in the previous sentence the title of Ross Y. Koen's pioneering *The China Lobby in American Politics,* a work victimized by its own disclosures and withdrawn from circulation—i.e., *suppressed*—immediately after printing and distribution in 1960 to remain legally unpublished until 1974.[1] (An account of this dismal incident is provided in chapter 7.) As Koen made clear, confusion surrounded the expression "China Lobby" from the beginning.

Originally, the term referred to Chinese agents of the Kuomintang who sought to combat pressures by American leftists to discredit Chiang Kai-shek's government. A "Chinese lobby in Washington" became the subject of a program memorandum on China policy by the Communist Party of New York State in January 1949 which called for a congressional investigation of its activities.[2] But in the wake of the White Paper and the collapse of the Nationalists on the mainland, the "China Lobby" label matured and flourished in the context of partisan recriminations over past China policies.

While Senator Joseph R. McCarthy and one of his principal targets, Professor Owen Lattimore, traded charges before a Senate hearing called to investigate the Republican senator's accusations that State Department officials had been responsible in part for a Communist conspiracy to influence China policy, another Republican senator wrapped the "China Lobby" phrase in a Communist mantle.[3] Reading from the same New York State Communist Party's program memorandum on China policy, California's William F. Knowland said on the Senate floor that any lobbies not complying with the law ought to be investigated but that a bipartisan foreign policy would be made more difficult "if the inference is drawn, either by the Lattimores or by any others interested in this subject, that men who are deeply concerned that the security of their country and the welfare of the world are being disturbed by the debacle in the Far East are motivated by anything other than their desire to protect their Nation." [4]

Two weeks later, on April 30, the *New York Times* took up the question: **"Is There a China Lobby?"** headlined a story by Cabell Phillips. The question had come up, reported Phillips, because McCarthy's series of charges about pro-Communist State Department policies in China raised the further question of "Who's feeding McCarthy his stuff?" No one was certain, but "that such a thing as a 'China lobby' exists is indisputable in the minds of most observers." Rather than a "tight and tangible conspiracy of possible sinister intent," however, it was more accurately a "loose conglomeration of persons and organizations which for various reasons are interested in China." Moreover, the lobby drew its strength from people "who passionately believe American policy to be wrong; who think that American withdrawal from

China has caused a needless and dangerous break in the dike against the spread of communism.'' Their moral, intellectual, and financial backing created ''both the lobby and the political climate in which it flourishes.''

Phillips identified Alfred Kohlberg and William J. Goodwin as the only two people who clearly seemed to have ''any visible connection with Senator McCarthy and his crusade against the State Department and Professor Lattimore.'' Kohlberg was described as ''a man of great vigor and greater volubility. He owns a prosperous New York importing firm that does a $1,000,000 business a year in linens and other fine Chinese textiles.'' Goodwin was said to have had ''pre-war connections with many militantly right-wing organizations.'' Until several weeks before the article he was ''a highly paid publicist in this country for the Nationalist Government of China.'' A third man, Frederick C. McKee of Pittsburgh, was reported to be a wealthy casket manufacturer who had ''no personal axes to grind by being a member of the pro-Nationalist group.'' Additionally, the Nationalist cause had been ''effectively promoted in the United States by members of two of China's wealthiest families, those of T. V. Soong and H. H. Kung. Both men have held high positions in the Nationalist government, are respected and well connected throughout the Western world and now live near New York.'' Both were related to Madame Chiang Kai-shek. Also mentioned in the article were Dr. Wellington Koo, the Chinese ambassador; Chen Chih-mai, counselor of the Embassy; and David B. Charnay, a New York public relations man, all said to be active on behalf of Nationalist China. The most effective pleaders in Congress for the Nationalists, said Phillips, were Representative Walter H. Judd and Senators McCarthy, Knowland, Kenneth S. Wherry, and Styles H. Bridges, all Republicans.

The budding debate broke out on the floor of the Senate a week later on May 10. Following Senator Knowland's insertion in the *Congressional Record* of an exchange of correspondence between Alfred Kohlberg and two Chinese mentioned in the *Times* story, the Californian was interrupted by Texas Democrat Tom Connally: ''Is this the same Kohlberg who has been mentioned frequently in the press lately as the head of the so-called China lobby?'' [5] To which Knowland replied:

. . . this is the same Mr. Kohlberg who has been charged in the Communist paper, the *Daily Worker,* as being a part of the so-called "China lobby"—in quotation marks as they put it. It is the same Mr. Kohlberg who has been attacked by the Communist Party in the United States. It is the same Mr. Kohlberg who has been subjected to attack by the left-wing press of this country.

One month before the outbreak of war in Korea, the Senate subcommittee investigating McCarthy's charges ended its hearings. With the war came the 1950 mid-term elections and exploitation of the "loss of China" theme popularized during the hearings. (The GOP gained 28 seats in the House, 5 in the Senate, and 7 new governors.) By mid-1951, the *Congressional Quarterly* would describe the "China Lobby" as "[p]robably the most variously interpreted term now in the news" and *Reporter* magazine, the following April, would publish a sensational, two-part exposé.[6] Additionally, the 1951 Senate inquiry into the dismissal of General Douglas MacArthur from his Far Eastern commands produced new charges and countercharges about the "China Lobby" in American politics.[7] However the term came to be used—descriptively, pejoratively, polemically, casually or mockingly—by the outbreak of the Korean War the catchphrase had captured a place in the nation's political rhetoric.

The "China Lobby" Defined

Irrespective of its linguistic origins on the left, "China Lobby" became a convenient expression for characterizing Chiang Kai-shek's supporters on the right. Like the newspaper and magazine accounts before him, Ross Koen found no centralized or formal organization directing their collective efforts. "It is probably more accurate to say," he concluded, "that what is usually termed the China lobby in the United States was no more than a series of individuals and groups which had a common interest and were more or less closely knit to form, in its collective capacity, a pressure group." [8] Nonetheless, Koen offered an operational definition which included two distinct categories of individuals and organizations: ". . . (I) an inner 'core' which consistently supported and pursued the interests of Chiang Kai-shek and the Kuomintang party, and (II) . . . affiliates who were increasingly allied to the Chiang regime in their sympathies.'' In the first category were Chinese and Americans whose personal interests were dependent on continued American aid to Chiang Kai-shek; in the second were those who supported the Chinese leader for political or ideological reasons. Named were a ''kaleidoscopic array'' of individuals and organizations, including many identified earlier in the *Times,* the *Congressional Quarterly,* and the *Reporter.*

These people, Koen argued, gradually succeeded in eliminating from positions of influence on U.S. China policy critics of the Kuomintang regime. Mainly, this was accomplished by the publicity resulting from the series of congressional investigations, background material for which was supplied to sympathetic congressmen by Chiang's agents and propagandists acting through their American friends. Their basic approach was based on the assumption ''that no negotiation or agreement with the Communists is possible except on terms which will lead inevitably to their aggrandizement and to the defeat of the West. This assumption is not peculiar to the China lobby. It has long been held by Russophobes and extreme anti-communist groups. Such a premise cannot be readily disproved. On the other hand, neither can it be confirmed on the basis of past experience.'' The 1974 paperback edition of Koen's book includes the following addition: ''. . . the basic fear of communism, abroad and at home, enabled Chiang's agents and their American friends to exploit issues and events to marshall support for Chiang Kai-shek and attack those critical of his regime.'' (p. 55)

The ''American friends'' are the subject of this book. Chapters 3 through 11 examine post-Korean War dimensions of ''China Lobby'' behavior in the American political system; chapter 12 offers an appraisal of their work. Although the focus is China policy, the frame of reference is American politics. Emphasis will be placed on that aspect of the Committee's operations which intended to influence American policy.

Because The Committee *for* One Million and The Committee *of* One Million were centralized, formal organizations publicly identified with anti-People's Republic and pro-Nationalist foreign policy sentiment in this country, they can justifiably be called successors to the ''China

Lobby" label. Still, to emphasize the distinction between the amorphous group of people and organizations analyzed by Koen and his journalistic predecessors, and those who comprised the Committee(s) under study, the "China Lobby" expression will remain in quotations throughout this book.

The "China Lobby" Heritage

Certain historical, attitudinal, and biographical factors may have made inevitable the mid-century formation of an American "China Lobby." The roots of a conservative lobby group go back at least as early as 1844, when the first Chinese-American treaty opened up U.S. trade and extraterritorial rights on a most-favored-nation basis. But the "China Lobby" of the 1950s was concerned with policy that differed in character and degree from earlier expressions of American interest in China, which included pressures to exclude Chinese immigrants, missionary efforts to subvert Chinese culture (under the guise of religion), and governmental policies designed to maintain American primacy over maritime commerce.[9]

Distilling fact from fancy has preoccupied virtually every observer of Chinese-American relations. Even before the Manchu Dynasty was toppled in 1911, Americans had never developed a clear understanding of what the Chinese were like. From 1844 to 1868, the American view of China was that of a backward society that could be manipulated to serve American interests. Not until 1868, when a treaty extended most-favored-nation status for Chinese nationals in the United States (but excepted the right of naturalization) was China accorded even the nominal appearance of equal treatment. American attitudes took form in a manner that would ill prepare the American public to understand the nature of the changes that would revolutionize China in the twentieth century. To be sure, there would not have been a "China Lobby" had there not been a Chinese Communist Party—for how Americans interpreted and reacted to the Chinese revolution that began in 1911 ultimately became the linchpin for emotional national debates over China policy.

Generally, the fabled "Open Door" notes are credited with starting

America's China policy down a road of high-sounding principles and sacred doctrines mixing expectations of future power and interest with existing realities.[10] Often overlooked among the factors which turned the "Open Door" ploy into sacrosanct policy was the role of The Committee of American Interests in China, "the first organization formed by American businessmen for the express purpose of effecting a change in Far Eastern policy." [11] Founded in January 1898 to "arouse the administration" to a defense of Far Eastern business interests (viewed by the American minister to China, Charles Denby, and others as threatened by discriminatory commercial policies if the shaky great power balance collapsed into a partitioned China), the group was spurred to action by the *Journal of Commerce* newspaper, the cotton industry, and the American-China Development Company, incorporated in 1895 to procure railway, mining, and other China concessions.[12] Representatives of the Standard Oil Company, Frazar and Company (an American trading house), Deering, Milliken and Company (cotton exporters), Bethlehem Iron Company, and the *Journal of Commerce* helped organize this committee, which enjoyed modest influence at first but later developed into a powerful pressure group. Soon, in fact, it reorganized as the American Asiatic Association, whose roster in 1900 listed almost 250 individuals and firms, including those which represented the largest financial interests in China. "Open Door" diplomacy had the "complete acceptance" of the Association, which sent an expression of "profound satisfaction" to Secretary of State Hay.

The American public accepted the "Open Door" actions as a major diplomatic achievement. "Its imagination was fired, its admiration won," George Kennan has written. "Hay was established in its affections as a great statesman. The popularity of the administration's foreign policy was materially improved just at the time of the coming presidential elections." [13] And the first domestic American pressure group on China policy was satisfied.

Some Americans were singularly equipped by background to lead future American pressure groups.

One Presbyterian missionary's son whom we shall meet from time to time in the pages that follow was born at Tengchow in eastern

Shantung province on April 3, 1898, and christened Henry Robinson Luce. His father, newly ordained and married, had sailed to the Far East the year before aboard *The Empress of China,* a large ocean liner named after the first American sailing vessel to reach China in 1784. The elder Luce devoted himself to philanthropic and religious endeavors and played a role, under J. Leighton Stuart, in the building of Yenching University. His good works are chronicled by a devoted biographer and fellow missionary educator, Dr. B. A. Garside, who years later would help organize China relief causes as well as later lobbying groups.[14] On the Chinese mainland in the year 1900, when the Boxer Rebellion occurred, American holdings amounted to only $24.7 million, including $17.5 million in business investments and $5 million in mission properties, which at the time comprised thirty-one missionary societies and about 1,000 missionaries.[15] But the missionaries, who were delighted with the 1898 annexation of the Philippines and "Open Door" diplomacy, remained politically important "out of all proportion to their numbers." [16]

On the American mainland, meanwhile, the image of China at the turn of the century "was formed in a crucible of hostility and resentment fired by the heat of unreasoning fear and inflamed prejudice." [17] Hatred toward "slopies" and the "Chinaman" who were originally encouraged to immigrate had turned into angry cries for their expulsion. Antagonism had mounted with the slackening demand in the 1870s for cheap "coolie" labor, resulting in the series of Exclusion Acts beginning in the 1880s. Implicit in the exclusion legislation was the specter of a "yellow peril," which became a more powerful image in determining domestic attitudes than the work of missionary propagandists and other Americans who sought to stimulate interest in China.[18] Emotional debates over the exclusion laws further marred the Chinese image. "In almost every instance," writes one observer, "the issue of the presence of the Chinese was raised because some special interest group sought to profit by stirring up feelings of animosity against the Chinese." [19]

So early twentieth-century American attitudes toward China and the Chinese amounted to a hodgepodge of governmental concern for special trading privileges, businessmen's visions of a vast China market, missionary zeal for saving souls, and public antipathy toward the Chinese immigrant.

In 1915, 28-year-old Alfred Kohlberg fell in love with a Chinese display of laces and silks at the Panama Pacific Exposition in his native San Francisco (where the great earthquake and fire of 1906 abruptly had ended his undergraduate days at Berkeley and launched him in the printing business until he joined his father as a dry-goods salesman). For the remaining forty-five years of his life, Kohlberg's fascination for China and preoccupation with his own country's relations there earned him the title legitimized by an idolatrous biographer: *The China Lobby Man*. [20] His personal fortune was made selling fine handkerchiefs ("Kohlkerchiefs"): patterns were designed in the United States while Irish linen was purchased in Belfast and shipped to contractors throughout southeastern China where women provided the delicate embroidery. But Kohlberg's public reputation was made as a controversial gadfly of Chinese causes in America, an energetic organizer and China traveler, a prolific epistolizer and polemicist, a tireless scrapper in most if not all of the nation's scuffles over China policy.

Kohlberg had traveled to the Far East at least twice by 1925, the year Dr. Walter Henry Judd, a young medical missionary from Rising City, Neb., first landed in southeastern China. [21] As a high school senior attending a YMCA conference, Walter Judd had felt impassioned by a plea for "taking Christ to the benighted heathen of foreign lands." For Judd, China became a lifelong crusade.

A Congregationalist, physician, and Phi Beta Kappa from the University of Nebraska, Judd began his years on the Chinese mainland treating everything from leprosy to malaria at a hospital in northwestern Fukien province which came under harassment from Communist guerrilla bands. Once mistaken for an English "colonialist," he was taken to a river bank and nearly executed before being recognized as an American. Forced by an attack of malaria to return home in 1931, Judd returned to Fenchow in Shansi province by 1934. Two years later, his family was evacuated prior to a Communist attack, but Judd stayed through the siege, ministering to Communist Chinese ills (including a Lin Piao ulcer) during the brief period of CCP-KMT coalition which followed the Japanese invasion. Rejoining his family in the United States five months after the Japanese captured Fenchow, Judd toured the country lecturing on the immediate dangers of Japanese imperialism and the longer threat of Asian communism. During a two-year span from 1939 to 1941, when he moved to Minneapolis and resumed practicing medicine, Judd delivered some 1,400 lectures on behalf of the American Committee for Non-Participation in Japanese Aggression, a group seeking to prevent scrap iron from being shipped to Japan for use in China. Strongly anti-Japanese and pro-Chinese at this time, the China he perceived was a free and independent society liberated from Confucian and imperial traditions.

Dr. Judd's twenty-year legislative career was launched in 1943, boosted by friends who thought his Asian credentials would serve a wartime Congress well. His maiden speech deplored the discriminatory Exclusion Acts, whose repeal he championed. It also included a lecture on oriental "face," observations for understanding the Japanese enemy, a plea for keeping both Russia and China in the war, and denunciations of American diplomacy of the 1920s and 1930s: "I believe that the chief reason for such errors has been because we have tended to project our own ideas and our own reactions over into the minds of people who have not had our background and who, therefore, naturally do not have many of our ideas and our reactions." [22] Left unsaid was whether Walter Judd counted himself among those Americans who had pressed their private missions on the minds of Chinese they ministered.

American Far Eastern diplomacy of the 1920s and 1930s was carried out—if not always conceived—by a mere handful of State Department officials. In 1925, for example, the Department listed only five Foreign Service officers, an acting chief, and five clerks in the entire Division of Far Eastern Affairs. Several years later, early in 1928, Stanley K. Hornbeck was appointed chief of this division. Born in Franklin, Mass., in 1883, Dr. Hornbeck had earned a Ph.D. in political science from the University of Wisconsin in 1911. In China he taught at the Chekiang Provincial College and the Fengtien (Mukden Law) College from 1909 to 1913 before returning to Wisconsin as an assistant professor and writing a book on Far Eastern politics. The Manchus were driven from their tottering throne, wrote Hornbeck five years before the founding of the Chinese Communist Party, "by the irresistible force of crystallizing popular discontent. The sages of China have taught that a ruler should hold the throne only so long as he governs well and is a true and honest 'father' to his people." [23]

Dr. Hornbeck later acted in various academic, military, and advisory capacities, often on matters dealing with the Far East, where he had again traveled in the early 1920s. His reign as chief of the Far Eastern desk lasted ten years before he was named an Adviser on Political Relations to the Secretary of State in 1937. In July 1928, several months after he had taken control of the Far Eastern Division, the U.S. government decided the Kuomintang leadership of General Chiang Kai-shek had achieved "a degree of unity" (as the "White Paper" would remark years later) and recognized the Nationalist government, signing an accompanying treaty which restored tariff autonomy to China.

The Hoover administration had two opportunities to stand by the "Open Door" principles embodied in the 1928 treaty: first, in mid-1929, during the Sino-Soviet dispute over the Chinese Eastern Railway in Manchuria; and second, in the fall of 1931 with the Japanese invasion of Manchuria. American diplomacy under Secretary of State Henry L. Stimson failed to stem the forcible expansions in both cases. Instead, Stimson later promulgated the famous "nonrecognition doctrine" by sending identical notes to Japan and China which said, in effect, that the United States would refuse to recognize territorial changes brought about by force but would not take other relevant action. [24]

The man destined to become the central figure in the China policy "conspiracy thesis" after World War II disagreed with Stimson's nonrecognition doctrine in the Far East. Patrick J. Hurley, soldier-businessman-politician from Oklahoma and Hoover's Secretary of War when Japan attacked Manchuria, told a Cabinet meeting after his return from a trip to the Orient that notes and diplomatic representations were not going to do much good unless backed by force; the Japanese had a far-flung plan of imperial expansion which only a war could stop. [25] (Soon, Hurley was himself responsible for a controversial use of domestic force, issuing an order in the summer of 1932 which directed General Douglas MacArthur, Army Chief of Staff whom Hurley had recommended for the post, to use troops for clearing camps set up in Washington, D.C. by the Bonus Expeditionary Force of veterans. Hurley and MacArthur, both accused of exceeding presidential orders in connection with the Army's crossing of a bridge to pursue the retreating veterans, thus were linked to a political controversy which quickly became an election issue in the Hoover vs. Roosevelt campaign.) [26]

The Hoover administration's rhetorical response to the Manchurian takeover had dramatized the gap between "Open Door" principles and the government's unwillingness to defend them. Before full-scale, undeclared war broke out between Japan and China, the main question about Japanese aggression for American policy makers centered on whether U.S. interests in China were sufficiently important to risk antagonizing Japan.

The Roosevelt administration continued the policy of noninterference in China and nonprovocation of Japan. "The United States has not much to lose," Dr. Hornbeck wrote in 1933 as the Japanese advanced in north China. "The principles of our Far Eastern policy and our ideals . . . may be further scratched and dented . . . and our trade prospects may be somewhat further impaired; but from the point of view of material interests there is nothing there that is vital to us." [27] Shared by all senior officials responsible for Far Eastern matters, this "hands off" policy remained the American position toward Japanese expansion through Roosevelt's first term, coming under strong question only later.

Fresh Japanese aggression provided the Nationalist government with evocative symbols for publicizing its plight. Yet only 44.6 percent of Americans responded affirmatively in 1937 when asked whether they sympathized with China or Japan: still, of those, 93.5 percent said they sympathized with China and only 6.5 percent with Japan. [28] The Chinese cause received added support from reports of Japanese atrocities and the bombing of helpless civilians. Pro-Chinese action groups sprouted, many under the guidance of former mission leaders whose allegiances to the Kuomintang had been strengthened by Chiang Kai-shek's marriage to Soong Mei-ling, an American-educated Methodist, and his conversion in 1931 to Christianity. Moreover, many American missionaries had returned home from a war-ravaged China with communism's challenge to Christianty very much on their minds.[29] Among the earliest groups was the one that sponsored Dr. Judd's national speaking tour, the American Committee for Non-Participation in Japanese Aggression, organized in 1938. Its vice-chairman from 1938 to 1941 was the senior Luce's biographer, Dr. B. A. Garside, who had returned to the United States in the late 1920s from various missionary assignments in China to become secretary of the China Union University Central Office in New York City and then executive secretary of the Association of Boards of Christian Colleges in China.[30]

On the executive committee of the American Committee for Non-Participation in Japanese Aggression was industrialist Frederick C. McKee. Born in Pittsburgh in 1891, McKee became general manager of his father's business interests in 1912, which included the Winfield Railroad and enterprises in sand, minerals, limestone, and cement.[31] Then, in 1939, he became treasurer of the National Casket Company. Active as a campaign contributor for various congressional candidates, McKee also was associated with other foreign policy interest groups in the late 1930s and 1940s: as an organizer in 1939 of the Non-Partisan Committee for Revision of the Neutrality Act; as national treasurer in 1940 of the Committee to Defend America by Aiding the Allies; as treasurer of the League of Nations Association (later the American Association for the United Nations); and as national chairman in 1942 and 1943 of Citizens for Victory.

China relief causes and agencies, each vying for funds to aid specialized appeals, proliferated as the Sino-Japanese War continued. There was the Committee for Chinese War Orphans, China Emergency Relief, China Famine Relief, Churches Committee for China Relief, Aid to China Committee, and, among still others, the American Bureau for Medical Aid to China (ABMAC), of which B. A. Garside later served as executive director. To redirect this clear duplication of effort, Garside proposed combining the major agencies into one large organization—United China Relief (UCR), which eventually pulled together eight different agencies and raised millions of dollars. The man Garside solicited for help, the "real boss" of UCR, was Henry Robinson Luce, who agreed to put up $60,000, loaned Garside two *Time* publicity men, persuaded several business leaders to join the board, and sent out a personal appeal to *Time* subscribers which brought in some $240,000 and helped turn UCR into a powerful propaganda organization.[32]

For four full decades beginning in 1927—in what must be regarded as a truly remarkable example of American journalistic puffery on behalf of a foreign political leader—the Luce empire zealously promoted Chiang Kai-shek and the Nationalist government. China's heroism, her importance to America's defense, her traitorous enemies (Japanese and "Chinese Reds"), and her gallant leader, Generalissimo Chiang, became celebrated themes. By 1945 the Chinese leader had been honored by his sixth *Time* cover story, till then the largest number conferred on any mortal. Luce's adulation of Chiang, part of his own grand scheme for "Christianizing and Americanizing China," was personal and total. The Generalissimo was "the greatest ruler Asia has seen since Emperor Kang Hsi, 250 years ago," Luce himself wrote in *Life* in 1941 after his initial meeting with "The Man Himself." [33]

There is no available absolute measure of "Lucepress" influence on pre-World War II American attitudes toward China, Chiang, and the Nationalist government. Part of the Generalissimo's stature in this country before the war resulted from the stimulation of sympathetic public opinion by returning missionaries; part came from the propagandizing of his own agents sent abroad to drum up support for the war against the Japanese; and part could be attributed to the widespread feeling in government and diplomatic circles that Chiang Kai-shek was singularly responsible for holding together the Nationalist government, that in the person of Chiang "lay the greatest strengths and weaknesses of the Nanking government." [34] But the greatest concentration of mass media attention on the themes that Chiang embodied—a democratic, united, and free China—came from the holdings of Henry Luce. Swanberg estimates that a Luce theme communicated through all of his outlets may have reached *"at least a third and perhaps considerably more of the total literate adult population of the country."* [35] To be sure, not all reports of Chiang and the Nationalists reaching the American people were uncritical, but unfavorable opinion largely was confined to books and esoteric journals, not the mass media.[36] Indeed, by the time the

United States entered World War II, the vast majority of Americans probably accepted Chiang Kai-shek as this country's foremost ally in the Far East. The vicissitudes of war would strengthen this image.

Henry Luce's awestruck appraisal of Chiang Kai-shek in *Life* was published in the summer of 1941 as newly authorized Lend Lease aid for China got underway. The Chinese received Lend Lease assistance at this time, according to the U.S. Army's official history of World War II, because in Washington "there was a myth and a hope about China. An ardent, articulate, and adroit Sinophile faction claimed that the Chinese were courageously and competently resisting the Japanese and needed only arms to drive them to the sea. The services were too well informed to share that belief, but they hoped that if the Chinese were rearmed, reorganized, and trained they might cause the Japanese such concern as to bar any adventures in the South Seas." [37] That fall, an American military mission to China headed by Brigadier General John A. Magruder, a former language officer with prior China service, was organized. Magruder wrote the War Department in February 1942 about reports from Chinese diplomatic sources referring to "the marvelous achievements and abilities of the Chinese Army. Such reports are absolutely without foundation," he said. "They are largely due to the . . . Chinese love of symbolism, or else can be attributed to nothing other than a downright desire to achieve certain specific objectives by clever deception." This spirit of Chinese symbolism was deep rooted in the United States, he added, "mainly because of Chinese propagandists in America, and because of the sponsorship accorded such propaganda on the part of many outstanding individuals, including missionaries as well as adherents to radical and liberal viewpoints." [38]

Not all government officials, of course, shared Magruder's pessimism about the Chinese Army. "The Chinese have fought for four and one-half years," answered Maxwell M. Hamilton, Hornbeck's longtime assistant and by then successor as head of the Far Eastern Division.

> They have suffered tremendously in blood, in treasure, in forced removal from their accustomed homes. They have done some remarkably good fighting and some remarkably heroic things. . . .
>
> Chiang Kai-shek's determination, his persistence, his on the whole

broad-gauge outlook constitute perhaps the most important element in China as a fighting force.

This sentiment was echoed by Dr. Hornbeck, then an adviser to the Secretary of State on Political Relations: "Should it not be remembered," he wrote in another context, "that Chiang Kai-shek has for four and one-half years successively carried on defensive operations which most of the military experts . . . thought and said at the outset . . . could not be continued beyond a few weeks or at the utmost a few months; . . . that Chiang has reason to believe that his military judgment is at least as good as that of any of the British or American generals and admirals (with the possible exception of MacArthur)." [39]

Thus differing perceptions of Chinese capabilities complicated the key wartime problem of dealing with the Generalissimo: whether to apply a *quid pro quo* bargaining tactic by "exchanging American aid for Chinese action and conditioning American activities upon Chinese performance." [40] General Joseph W. Stilwell, the ranking American officer on the scene, opted for *quid pro quo*. Stilwell first had set foot on Chinese soil six weeks after the outbreak of revolution in 1911. By the time he returned thirty-one years later, "Vinegar Joe" had logged three separate Army tours in China which spanned ten years and thousands of diary-filled miles as a language officer, battalion commander, and military attaché. Stilwell was one of many Americans destined by the fortunes of war to revisit China. Another was his new political officer, John Paton Davies, a Chinese-speaking diplomat born in Kiating in Szechwan province.[41] Another was Dr. David Nelson Rowe, born in Nanking in 1905 and raised mostly in central China before he began a scholarly and consulting career in the 1920s. A student of Chinese language, history, and politics, Dr. Rowe returned to China in the fall of 1941 as special assistant to the director of the research and analysis staff of the Coordinator of Information—soon to become the Office of Strategic Services (OSS). In Chungking from November 1941 to May 1942, he was special assistant to the American ambassador.[42]

An episode as meaningless to the outcome of the war in the Far East as it was meaningful to the maturation of "China Lobby" perspec-

labyrinthine sub-plots and intrigues, the tug-of-war between Stilwell and Chiang had raged from mid-1942 to the spring of 1943 as Stilwell sought to comply with War Department directives to break the blockade of China and reform the Chinese Army. American policy had advanced along three separate levels by late 1943: making China a great power "in form if not in substance" at the Moscow Conference; modernizing the Nationalist Army and Air Force; and averting a Chinese civil war by advocating a political settlement between the KMT and the CCP.[49] Up to this point in the war, Roosevelt, threatened by intermittent Chinese hints of a separate peace with Japan had tended to reject Stilwell's *quid pro quo* approach to Chinese problems, feeling this was not the way to deal with Chiang Kai-shek.[50] But the Japanese in 1944 launched a major offensive against Chinese positions, shattering them, scattering Chinese forces, and driving through central China to threaten U.S. air bases in the south, which had to be abandoned. Faced with a grave military situation, Roosevelt recommended to Chiang that Stilwell in effect be given full command of the Chinese armies with authority to coordinate "all Allied military resources in China, *including the Communist forces*" (italics added).[51] The proposal was prepared by the Joint Chiefs of Staff after a spring trip to Chungking by Vice-President Henry A. Wallace, who had explored possibilities for consolidating the Chinese war effort. Chiang equivocated, agreeing in principle, and renewed a request that Roosevelt send a trusted emissary who could collaborate with him on political and military questions. Acquiescing, Roosevelt gave the assignment to his wartime Republican troubleshooter, Patrick J. Hurley.

General Hurley's China tour under Presidents Roosevelt and Truman spanned a sixteen-month period that was crucial in terms of substantive China policy decisions and incipient "China Lobby" perspectives. Practically every major decision starting with his appointment in August 1944 and ending with his dramatic public resignation in November 1945 became the subject of controversy. Hurley's letter of resignation charging subversion, disloyalty, and China policy sabotage on the part of Foreign Service officers and State Department officials triggered the China policy explosions. Quintessentially, Hurley isolated the issues, set the tone, and generated initial public interest in a conspiratorial explanation for the country's deteriorating policies in China. Although it would be four years before the "loss of China" was exploited to rationalize events on the mainland, Hurley's sudden blast, repeated in congressional and public forums, established him both as discoverer and leading GOP prosecutor of a China policy conspiracy. Hurley's charges quickly became gospel for those already predisposed toward conspiratorial explanations of fading Far Eastern fortunes—for example, the founders of the emerging American China Policy Association (ACPA). Prior to Hurley's resignation, Alfred Kohlberg, soon to be ACPA's foremost spokesman, mailed him press clippings which had divulged items from the ambassador's China reports (leaks that may have helped convince Hurley not to return to China).[52]

The Hurley period of Sino-American relations merits a brief overview. What is salient here, in the narrow context of postwar "China Lobby" politics, is not an evaluation of Hurley's ambassadorial performance but rather, in reverse order, a summary of his later charges and how he came to make them.

Hurley had served Roosevelt throughout the war as a special emissary in the Middle East, Southwest Pacific, East Asia, India, and the Soviet Union. Virtually ignorant of Chinese history, language, politics, or wartime problems, he began his China assignment as Roosevelt's special emissary; the American ambassador, Clarence E. Gauss, remained at his post for the time being.[53] (After Gauss resigned, following the removal of Stilwell, Hurley was appointed American ambassador to China.) Written orders directed Hurley to promote harmonious relations between General Chiang and General Stilwell and to facilitate the latter's exercise of command over the Chinese armies placed under his direction. Unrecorded oral instructions from Roosevelt were interpreted by Hurley as authorization for seeking a military unification of the CCP-KMT armies—a policy reaffirmed in substance by American officials, some of whom came to question his negotiating tactics. Another problem facing the President's emissary was the question of who would control allocation of Lend-Lease supplies. Because Hurley soon reported to Roosevelt that Stilwell and Chiang were "incompatible personalities," when Stilwell was recalled and replaced by General Alfred C. Wedemeyer, Hurley believed the biggest problem in Sino-American relations was solved.[54]

The first round in Hurley's mediation efforts between the Chinese Communists and the Kuomintang—negotiations whose handling featured prominently in the later domestic furor—took place between October 1944 and February 1945. Hurley first drew up a general "Basis for Agreement" which acknowledged the need for military unification to defeat Japan; the supremacy of Chiang Kai-shek as China's political and military leader; the pursuit of democratic processes of government; the legality of the CCP and all other Chinese political parties; and the legitimacy of one national government and one army in China. Accepted by the Kuomintang with slight modifications, this document was carried by Hurley to CCP headquarters in Yenan. There, the Communist leaders drafted their own five-point proposal including reorganization of the Nationalist government into a "Coalition National government." Hurley accepted this concept, offered improvements, negotiated the rephrasing of various points, and signed, along with Mao Tse-tung, a proposed CCP-KMT agreement.[55] Returning to Chungking, Hurley discovered the agreement was unacceptable to Chiang Kai-shek. Nationalist government counterdrafts dropped the proposal for a coalition government; Chinese Foreign Minister T. V. Soong told Hurley the Communists had duped him.[56] Yet Hurley still insisted the CCP's offer represented a basis for constructing a settlement and urged acceptance. Thereafter the Nationalists presented a three-point counterproposal which excluded provisions for a coalition government. The CCP rejected this.

After persistent efforts by the American mediator to find a path toward Chinese unity, the CCP hardened its negotiating positions. Hurley later claimed the stiffer attitude by the Communists resulted from their being informed that General Wedemeyer's chief of staff had proposed a plan for military cooperation between American and Communist forces which Hurley knew about but did not want divulged before Chiang approved.[57] Hurley interpreted this incident as an effort to subvert his role and arm the Communists. At the same time, he learned of other CCP attempts to achieve their goals by trying to by-pass him.[58]

By mid-February of 1945 an impasse in the negotiations was reached, so Hurley returned to Washington without an agreement. Success for him, concludes Buhite, "meant the achievement of a plan for the unification of Chinese fighting forces. . . . Even though interpreting his instructions as a directive to seek unification through Chiang Kai-shek, evidence indicates that Hurley was not working to prevent the Communists from achieving power. He did not see the CCP as a truly Communist organization." [59]

It was during Hurley's Washington consultations that an intra-State Department squabble which eventually led to a national obsession—fear of Communist subversion in government—broke out. Following Hurley's departure for Washington, the embassy's political officers in Chungking drafted and sent the Department a long telegram which argued, in effect, that the policy of attempting to negotiate unity in China was correct but that American concessions and assurances to Chiang Kai-shek left the Generalissimo unwilling to compromise. [60] The officers recommended the United States exert some leverage on Chiang by telling him the American government was ready to offer military supplies and cooperation to the Communists and other Chinese groups willing to help fight Japan. Vehemently opposed to arming the Communists and believing this matter already settled, Hurley was incensed at what he considered a disloyal act—going "behind his back." Rejecting the argument that the men simply were doing their jobs, Hurley demanded the removal and transfer of the embassy's political officers. Hurley's already strained relations with the Department's officials, many of whom had become at odds with him over the years, exacerbated the situation. [61] But the fundamental problem was disagreement between Hurley and many officials over how to deal with the CCP and the KMT on the question of Chinese unification, which all agreed was necessary.

Basically, the political reporting of the career diplomats in wartime China underscored three major themes: 1) that the Communists were efficient, honest, committed, militarily strong, actively fighting the Japanese, and would control north China after the war; 2) that the Nationalist government was weak, corrupt, inefficient, and led by a man losing support because of his inability to effect reforms, to fight the Japanese, and to reach a solution with the Communists; and 3) that the United States should adopt a realistic policy in China by effecting political gains with the Chinese Communists and not allowing the Chinese to become completely tied to the Russians.[62]

Hurley resisted the flexible approach; indeed, his inflexibility—especially on the question of arming the Communists—was a major source of friction between him and his political officers. This became apparent during the second round of CCP-KMT negotiations which resumed in June 1945 following Hurley's return to Chungking.[63] The second and third rounds—the third beginning after the Pacific War ended—were conducted against a background of intense international diplomatic activity; moreover, Hurley's mediating role was complicated by the uncertain intentions of the major powers toward the political dispute in China. The Nationalist government began treaty negotiations with the Soviet Union before the war ended. Immediately after V-J Day, with both the CCP and the KMT maneuvering for position upon Japan's defeat, armed clashes between the two sides occurred. The final round of negotiations, which started at Chungking in September, included Chiang Kai-shek, Mao Tse-tung, and Chou En-lai. As the talks stalled, the Nationalist government received verbal assurance from President Truman that the United States was prepared to help China develop a moderately sized armed force in order to maintain internal peace and security—on the condition the materials not be used for "fratricidal warfare or to support undemocratic administration." Partially through Hurley's efforts the talks lingered on, but the ambassador left China on September 22. "The spirit between the negotiators is good," he reported. "The rapprochement between the two leading parties of China seems to be progressing, and the discussion and rumors of civil war recede as the conference continues." [64]

Analysts remain fascinated by Hurley's envoyship and ambassadorship in China. Among the many questions still under debate, however, by far the most urgent in domestic political terms is Hurley's charge that China policy was consciously subverted by American officials.[65] Hurley's resignation blast was both unprecedented and shocking. He accused then unnamed Foreign Service officers of siding with the Chinese Communists and advising them "that my efforts in preventing the collapse of the Nationalist government did not represent the policy of the United States. These same professionals openly advised the Communist armed party to decline unification of the Chinese Communist Army with the National Army unless the Chinese Communists were given control." [66] Hurley left no doubt about his opinion that career diplomats in Washington and Chungking had stifled his mission: "The Hydraheaded direction and confusion of our foreign policy in Washington during the late war is chargeable to the weakness of our Foreign Service." America's foreign policy officials were "divided against themselves," thus leaving the country "prey to the nations that give lip service to our ideals and principles in order to obtain our material support." (No nation was identified by name here, but surely he was not referring to the Chinese Nationalist government.)

Ironically for America's Far Eastern affairs, Hurley buttressed his charges against former colleagues by condemning a bureaucratic practice destined for far greater use and controversy a score of years later during another Asian policy dilemma: *government secrecy*. Charging that information was all too often leaked to the public in "distorted, garbled, or partial" form (while admitting wartime secrecy was necessary and expedient), Hurley said that "an informed public opinion would do much to give intelligent direction and implementation to our international objectives." He wanted his own China reports released along with those of the Foreign Service officers. "The blessings of factual publicity," he wrote the President, "would be manifold."

Suddenly, amid the vicissitudes of postwar domestic politics, America's relations with China surfaced as a potentially partisan issue. Embellishing on his serious accusations, names of alleged conspirators in hand, Patrick Hurley took his charges to Capitol Hill. Thus the Senate Foreign Relations Committee became the first in a long line of congressional forums to forward what would gradually mature from a personal search for scapegoats to a full-fledged national conspiracy—America's "loss of China."

2

The "China Lobby" and the "Loss of China"

Ambassador Hurley's resignation performance, it now seems clear, helped create an hypothesis around which both disciples and subsequent events would combine to produce a self-fulfilling prophecy. The disciples came to be known in their collective capacity as the "China Lobby." They emerged first from a mélange of Americans (some of whom were introduced earlier) whose lives and fortunes—and hence perceptions—had been touched by China somewhere between the 1911 revolution and World War II and, second, from Ross Koen's "inner core" of Chinese and Americans whose immediate economic, political, and ideological interests were more directly tied to the fate of Chiang Kai-shek and the Kuomintang Party of Nationalist China. Mushrooming events on both mainlands, Chinese and American, highlighted the ultimately futile efforts of the United States government to effect the outcome of the civil war in China. The public evolution of the "loss of China" theme, which began with Hurley's outbursts and peaked after the Truman administration's 1949 White Paper, offers one backdrop for summarizing the swirl of activity circumscribed by the "China Lobby" label. Disciples and events converged to test for the last time an American myth born early in the twentieth century and found wanting—that China's administrative and territorial integrity was an essential element of U.S. Far Eastern policy. Many individuals and groups, in and out of government, were motivated to political action. What they shared in common was a desire to "save" China from communism. Logically, from their perspective, what could not be saved was necessarily lost.

America's wartime and postwar China policy politics have been described and analyzed from diverse perspectives and viewpoints, including exhaustive studies by Herbert Feis, Tang Tsou, and Anthony Kubek.[1] While Ross Koen focused on *The China Lobby in American Politics,* other writers have examined selected and important aspects of the problem—notably H. Bradford Westerfield, Felix Greene, A. T. Steele, Robert P. Newman, Earl Latham, Joseph Keeley, Kenneth E. Shewmaker, Ronald J. Caridi, Barbara W. Tuchman, Ross Terrill, and James Peck.[2] Still other recent and closely related titles comprise this divergent literature.[3] The discussion that follows offers a brief overview of the "loss of China" theme from its "Hurleyed" inception several years before the Nationalist Chinese were driven from the mainland to its inexorable institutionalization by The Committee *for* One Million and The Committee *of* One Million.

The Conspiracy Thesis Matures

Conspiracies, by definition, breed in secrecy, then usually mature in public in the process of becoming political issues. Actually, the maturing of the "loss of China" thesis, as Koen's research demonstrates, ultimately revolved around six events. Three had their beginnings in 1945—the Yalta Agreement, the Amerasia Affair,[4] and Hurley's resignation—and three occurred later: in January 1947, the recall of General Marshall from China, marking the failure of his special mission; in July 1948, the start of congressional hearings featuring testimony by ex-Communists concerning charges of prewar and wartime "espionage activities" in the United States; finally, in June 1950, the outbreak of the Korean War. Each of these easily exploitable events raised sufficient questions and doubts to provide a rationale for people who sensed—or *sought*—an American conspiracy as the explanation for the deterioration and collapse of the Nationalist cause on the Chinese mainland.

Even before these events, moreover, the intellectual groundwork for such a conspiracy had been laid. During World War II, for example, two authors, Rodney Gilbert and the Right Reverend Monsignor George Barry O'Toole, deplored what they read as a rising tide of anti-Nationalist literature. In 1943, Gilbert told readers of the New York

Herald Tribune that Communist propagandists and misguided U.S. military officers were largely responsible for discrediting the Kuomintang regime. Monsignor O'Toole, first editor, in 1939, of the staunchly pro-Nationalist *China Monthly,* compiled a list of "Red Snipers," identified international communism as the source of anti-KMT attacks, and is credited by Kenneth Shewmaker as responsible for "the most explicit articulation of the conspiratorial viewpoint prior to 1945." [5]

(As a brief aside, milestone events occurred that year in the lives of two individuals whose later careers would cross on the steering committee of a China policy pressure group. Joseph C. Grew, Undersecretary of State, retired after fifty years of government service and was replaced by Dean G. Acheson, who soon appointed longtime China Service officer John Carter Vincent as director of the Office of Far Eastern Affairs. Grew, descendant of a pre-revolutionary family of wealth and prominence, served a decade-long ambassadorship in Japan from 1932 to the day of the Pearl Harbor attack. Optimistic up to that fateful day that war with Japan could be avoided, Grew "never lost his conviction that he had been robbed of his historic role as 'the peacemaker.' " [6] Also in 1945, far removed from State Department matters, 22-year-old Marvin Liebman, a pivotal figure in the chapters that follow, quit the Communist Party.) [7]

Probably because the entire record of the Yalta Conference, containing understandings about Soviet entry in the Pacific war and related references to China, was not made public until 1955 and because investigations and developments in the Amerasia case failed to prove any overarching (or even miniscule) conspiracies, Ambassador Hurley's explosive charges made the most noise in the early postwar era. Yet his desire to spread the "blessings of factual publicity" on the China-related documents of the war, the release of which he felt would vindicate his mission, was frustrated. Moreover, President Truman's immediate appointment of General Marshall as his special representative in China (complete with accompanying fanfare of a presidential China policy statement reiterating American interest in "the development of a strong, united and democratic China"—words Hurley himself had popularized) [8] quieted public debate over charges of official treason. Thus, early in 1946, as Hurley went off to New Mexico to launch the first of three unsuccessful tries for a U.S. Senate seat, the conspiracy stirrings began.

A diverse and disparate collection of individuals and groups, Chinese as well as Americans, including militantly anti-Communist organizations and, beginning with the Republican controlled 80th Congress in 1947, a "China bloc" of legislators, later came to be identified with the "China Lobby" catchphrase. Initially, however, insofar as the postwar maturation of a conspiracy hypothesis, the original disciples came together early in 1946 as the American China Policy Association (ACPA). After an attempt by author Christopher Emmet Jr. failed to start a similar group late in 1945, newspaper correspondent J. B. Powell, teacher Helen Loomis, and Alfred Kohlberg, among others, met "to form a committee to warn the country of the dangerous policy we were following in China," as Kohlberg later would relate to a Senate subcommittee investigating the Institute of Pacific Relations (IPR).[9] The three had had extensive experiences in China: Powell as the dean of American newspaper correspondents and editor of *China Weekly Review;* Loomis as a missionary teacher; and, of course, Kohlberg—the peripatetic importer, epistolarian, and publisher. Still a member of the IPR at this time, Kohlberg shared his membership on the new ACPA's board of directors with Clare Booth Luce (who became president for a year after Powell's death in 1947), Irene Corbally Kuhn, and Dr. Maurice William. Within weeks the organization got its first major publicity break, the release of a "Manchurian Manifesto." Signed by "65 leading Americans," including Admiral Harry E. Yarnell, Congressman Walter Judd, Henry and Clare Booth Luce, Sidney Hook, Norman Thomas, Max Eastman, Christopher Emmet Jr., John Earl Baker, Felix Morley, General David P. Barrows, and Clarence Streit, the document was issued as a protest to Secretary of State Byrnes over a remark by Dean Acheson promising U.S. material and training support to Chinese Communist fighting forces that joined the Nationalist Army of China.[10] Moreover, as a foretaste of the bitter charges to follow release of the Yalta Protocol, the "Manifesto" said the Yalta agreement "was not only made behind China's back, but . . . America was pledged to deliver the promised concessions in Manchuria and Mongolia to Soviet Russia, whether the Chinese Government agreed or not.''

Kohlberg's printing facilities, mailing lists, and even stamps were kept busy. In the fall of 1946, weeks before the mid-term elections, Kohlberg personally delivered to Charles Ross, Truman's press secretary, a document purporting to be a translation of a Chinese Communist Party (CCP) document revealing that the Russians *still* controlled the CCP. In an example of Kohlberg's blunt style, a covering letter to the President was said to have urged "that Russia be told to keep hands off China." [11] Although the ACPA lasted for fourteen years, until Kohlberg's death in 1960, the organization was one among myriad other Kohlberg activities devoted to China policy causes and anti-Communist themes. In 1946, for example, with the assistance of Reverend John Cronin, secretary of the Catholic Welfare Conference in Washington, and ex-Communist Benjamin Mandel, then research director of the House Committee on Un-American Activities, Kohlberg helped establish *Plain Talk,* a pocket-sized monthly edited by Isaac Don Levine. [12] The first issue carried an "inside story" by one of the men implicated in the Amerasia case. The managing editor of the magazine, before it folded in 1950, was author Ralph de Toledano, whose wife Nora would play a role several years later in publicizing The Committee for One Million. Kohlberg also was briefly involved in a successor magazine, *The Freeman,* which enjoyed a short run under editors John Chamberlain, Henry Hazlitt, and Suzanne LaFollette.

Throughout the duration of the Marshall Mission, until the first few days of 1947, ACPA publicity concentrated on Marshall's lack of understanding of the China problem. Thereafter, simultaneous with convening of the 80th Congress, Kohlberg and others, especially *China Monthly* for which he was a frequent contributor, switched to "sins of Yalta" themes. During this period, says Koen, epithets such as "traitors" and "betrayal" became standard. [13] Also during this period, the Truman administration's China policy came under increasingly bitter attack. Among the reasons was the suppression of General Alfred C. Wedemeyer's report following his return from a fact-finding mission to China in the summer of 1947. Dispatched both to convince the Chinese they could not waste American aid and to convince Washington of the need for such aid, Wedemeyer later said that newly appointed Secretary of State Marshall persuaded him to go because "pressure in Congress (from Congressman Walter Judd, Senator Styles Bridges, and others) and from other sources accusing the administration of pursuing a negative policy in China were compelling a reappraisal of United States policy." [14]

Wedemeyer's recommendation for a Manchurian guardianship or trusteeship, considered by the administration as impractical and highly offensive to Chinese sensitivities, was later given as the major reason for suppression of the report. But Tang Tsou has called this administration action "one of the most unnecessary as well as most unfortunate . . . ," adding:

> Had the report been published, the public debate evoked would have clarified many of the basic issues. If the public had shown its unwillingness to assume the costs of a positive policy in China and to risk eventual American participation in the Chinese civil war, the administration would have obtained some sort of endorsement of its passive policy. If the administration had lost the debate, it would not have been too late to inaugurate a new policy in China. *In any event, the administration would not have been vulnerable to charges of concealing vital information from the Congress and the American people.* [15]

Within weeks of the decision on the Wedemeyer report, moreover, *Life* magazine published an explosive article by William C. Bullitt, a former ambassador to Russia and France who had visited China before the war as Roosevelt's personal representative. "Can China be kept out of the hands of Stalin?" Bullitt asked. "Certainly—and at a cost to ourselves which will be small compared to the magnitude of our vital interest in the independence of China." [16] Punctuated by subheads and captions reading "Yalta—disgraceful document," "China was shamelessly betrayed into Stalin's hands at the Yalta Conference," and "Cynical indecency," Bullitt himself said, "No more unnecessary, disgraceful and potentially disastrous document has ever been signed by a President of the U.S." He outlined a reform program for China plus a $1.35 billion price tag for keeping the mainland from falling to the Russians. Bullitt concluded that one American with the military, political, and personal know-how could "fly to China to organize with the Generalissimo a joint plan to prevent subjugation of China by the Soviet Union"—that American was General Douglas MacArthur.

Bullitt's missive elevated the conspiratorial hypothesis from *China Monthly* and the ACPA's publicity releases to the pages of Henry Luce's national pastime—*Life*. Moreover, the article had consequences in Congress, then in debate on the China aid question.

The conspiracy thesis, it should be noted, attracted the attention of others who went on to organize China policy interest groups. In 1951, *Congressional Quarterly News Features* published the first press roundup of American (and Chinese) groups pursuing pro-Nationalist policies. Among them, in addition to ACPA, were committees whose officers would provide leadership for an even later China policy organization: [17]

The China Emergency Committee
Chairman: Frederick C. McKee
National Advisory Council: Representative Walter H. Judd (R., Minn.) Representative B. Carroll Reece (R., Tenn.) Irene Corbally Kuhn

The Committee to Defend America by Aiding Anti-Communist China
Chairman pro tem: Frederick C. McKee
Vice-Chairman: Charles Edison
Vice-Chairman: General William S. Donovan
Vice-Chairman: Bishop Herbert Welch
Treasurer: James G. Blaine
Board of Directors: Arthur H. Burling, Arthur Bliss Lane, David Dubinsky, Matthew Woll, James A. Farley, Jay Lovestone, Peter Grimm, Arthur J. Goldsmith, Clare Booth Luce, Mrs. Wendell Willkie, Dr. George A. Fitch

Committee on National Affairs
Chairman: Frederick C. McKee
Secretary: Arthur J. Goldsmith
Executive Committeemen: George Fielding Eliot, Cord Meyer, Dr. L. M. Birkhead

The Free Trade Union Committee (AFL)
   Honorary President: William Green
   President: Matthew Woll
   Vice-President: David Dubinsky
   Honorary Secretary: George Meany
   Executive Secretary: Jay Lovestone

Committee for Constitutional Government
   Rev. William R. Johnson

Additionally, *Congressional Quarterly* named fourteen active or terminated foreign agents of the Nationalist government as having registered with the Department of Justice since 1942. The agents were listed in five separate categories—finance, trade, political party, information, and education. One, under information, was the Chinese News Service, the official information office of Nationalist China, whose director some years later would maintain close ties to The Committee of One Million. Another, under education, was the China Institute of America, created in 1926, an educational foundation which aimed at promoting "culture between the United States and China." Head of the board of directors in 1951 was Henry R. Luce.

Before moving briefly to Capitol Hill and the "China bloc," the conspiracy thesis needs to be placed in a wider context. To be sure, the gradual build-up of a clandestine plot to account for the later "loss of China" was part of a larger outlook on U.S. foreign policy which emerged in the disillusioning aftermath of World War II. Differing rational perspectives for evaluating America's national interests and policies gave way to the country's growing "anti-Communist impulse" (Michael Parenti's graphic aphorism). With the emergence of Russian "satellites" where independent countries once flourished, with the advent of spy trials and loyalty checks, Americans soon were engulfed in clouds of conspiratorial conjecture. If, indeed, an American or international conspiracy to deliberately destroy the effectiveness of the Chinese Nationalist government or to elevate the Chinese Communists to power did exist, as writers would continue to allege,[18] the conspiracy never was clearly defined, let alone proven. "Propounders," as Shewmaker has written, "nebulously interpreted it to include espionage, the promotion of a naive view of Chinese communism, the spreading of calculated lies, the undermining of government policy, and the praising of Chinese Communists at the expense of Chinese Nationalists.'' [19]

Shewmaker, who focuses here mainly on intellectual appraisals of the Chinese Communists, sees the conspiracy thesis as serving the purpose of discrediting favorable appraisals written between 1936 and 1945. ''From the militantly anti-Communist perspective,'' he writes, ''the Chinese Communists, like all other Communists, were part of an international plot against the 'free world'. Individuals who wrote friendly assessments of the CCP thereby became objects of suspicion— probably perpetrators of an enormous artifice.'' [20] Increasingly, beginning in 1947, these suspicions and other more immediate fears tended to be centered in the halls of Congress.

The "China Bloc" in Congress

Interestingly, the "China bloc" label, long a fixture of the literature, first was used to describe the pro-Nationalist critics of the Truman administration after Truman left office. Even at that, H. Bradford Westerfield employed the term rather offhandedly by way of addressing the question of why China policy became a partisan political issue after World War II.[21] Westerfield found three answers to his question: the GOP's historical interest in the Far East (''Asia First''), the influence within the Republican party of General Douglas MacArthur, and the failure of the Truman administration to associate prominent Republicans with China policy. Few if any Republicans, Westerfield noted, had been consulted by the State Department in the creation of postwar China policy. Moreover, General Marshall's return home coincided with the convening of the 80th Congress, whose incoming Republican chairman of the Senate Foreign Relations Committee, Michigan's Arthur H. Vandenberg, had told an audience early in January he would no longer support U.S. attempts to achieve a coalition government in China.[22]

Proclamation on March 12 of the Truman Doctrine plus deteriorating events on the Chinese mainland prompted Chinese officials in Washington, using the encroaching danger of communism as their weapon, to seek American aid. The requests, says Tang Tsou, ''confronted officials in the State Department with new complications in working out a policy toward China because they had to be weighed in the light of the administration's global program and Republican demands for a change in China policy." [23] Yet the administration also was losing patience with Chiang Kai-shek. "In the final analysis," the new Secretary of State Marshall wrote the Generalissimo in July, "the fundamental and lasting solution of China's problems must come from the Chinese themselves. The United States cannot initiate and carry out the solution of those problems and can only assist as conditions develop which give some beneficial results." [24]

Shortly after this message was sent to China, General Wedemeyer was similarly dispatched, partially, at Dr. Judd's instigation. This concession to the GOP was accompanied by two others, Tsou claims—lifting of the arms embargo to China and replacement of John Carter Vincent by Walton Butterworth as director of the Office of Far Eastern Affairs—all three aimed at conciliating Republican China policy critics in order to win their support for the administration's proposed European economic assistance program. Indeed, Tsou argues, after Marshall's renunciation of further U.S. mediation in China, the ensuing struggle in Congress over aid to the Nationalists, which lasted well into the presidential election year, immobilized the administration's China position by forcing a policy of limited aid to Chiang Kai-shek. [25] The fight was led by two representatives and a senator: Walter Judd and John M. Vorys (who once served with Yale-in-China), both members of the House Committee on Foreign Affairs, and Senator Styles H. Bridges, the New Hampshire Republican. In the process, Dr. Judd kept the conspiracy thesis alive by lashing out at the Far Eastern Affairs desk of the State Department. The campaign to discredit the Nationalists abroad while the Chinese Communists made progress against them at home was largely led in the United States, Judd said, "by about 20 or 30 writers and lecturers and commentators, and by some men who became Far Eastern advisers to our State Department," which included "what has become widely known as the 'Red Cell' in the State Department, the Far Eastern office." [26] Tsou's conclusion follows: "Thus, the far Eastern experts' accurate appraisal of Chiang's weaknesses, their moral revulsion against aiding a corrupt, oppressive regime, and their underestimation of the Chinese Communist threat was turned into a partisan issue."

Westerfield's analysis pinpoints intra-party differences in the House and intricate compromises between the administration and the Senate as significant factors as well. Initially, skirmishing between economy-minded Republicans on the House Appropriations Committee (especially Chairman John Taber, the conservative New York Republican) and China-minded GOP lawmakers like Judd and Vorys of the Foreign Affairs Committee, prevented any large-scale "interim aid" assistance to the Nationalists.[27] In mid-February 1948, however, the administration sent to Capitol Hill an upwardly revised Marshall compromise proposal of $570 million in aid. At one point, $463 million was authorized, with $125 million understood as set aside for vaguely stated military purposes. Ultimately, as a result of Taber's further cutting, a final appropriation of $400 million emerged in June 1948. Thereafter, says Westerfield, bureaucratic delays held up implementation of military assistance for some months. Arms shipments in substantial quantities did not begin until November. During this period, moreover, the Chinese Communists took Manchuria and readied themselves for the final push south. "By indifference if not by intention," Westerfield concludes, "the administration had utterly bungled its chance to show that an aid program of 'GOP proportions' could not save Chiang. It would still be possible for Republicans to claim that they had done their best to save China but that the Democratic administration had sabotaged their efforts. Even State Department-minded Republicans were hardly likely to offer any public defense of this failure to implement effectively the delicate compromise they had effected on China aid to placate both Walter Judd and General Marshall."[28]

Although Tsou singles out Judd, Vorys, and Bridges in his assessment of "China bloc" machinations in Congress (at one point saying Judd was "one of the more responsible and level-headed members of the China bloc . . . ," p. 537), other legislators were mentioned either in the context of individual assaults on the administration's China policy positions or in connection with initiatives aiding the Nationalist cause.

They included: Senators William F. Knowland (R., Calif.), H. Alexander Smith (R., N.J.), Pat McCarran (D., Nev.), Kenneth S. Wherry (R., Neb.), and Owen Brewster (R., Me.); and Representatives James G. Fulton (R., Pa.), Robert B. Chiperfield (R., Ill.), and Donald L. Jackson (R., Calif.).

Another analyst of America's relations with the Chinese Communists, Foster Rhea Dulles, identifying Judd, Vorys, Knowland, Bridges, Wherry, and McCarran from Tsou's list, adds four Republican senators—Ferguson of Michigan, Jenner of Indiana, Wiley of Wisconsin, and John M. Butler of Maryland—while observing that senatorial support for Chinese Nationalists "grew more out of a rabid anti-Communism and reactionary opposition to everything about the Truman administration than from any great concern for China." [29]

Conspicuously absent from these lists is the name of Senator Joseph R. McCarthy of Wisconsin, whose discovery of China would come later.

Coincident with the denouement of the China Aid Act in mid-1948 was the July start of the "espionage activities" hearings of the House Committee on Un-American Activities. A parade of former Communists took the stand to allege, in essence, that countless American Communists had infiltrated the United States government before and during World War II. Aside from the immediate implications for the presidential election only four months away, the hearings had important implications for the "loss of China" theme as well. Ross Koen identifies two in particular: the charges, once made, could not be disproved; and virtually anyone could be named. Thus began the technique of associating an official named by an ex-Communist as having responsibility for China policy followed by the allegation that the individual had been identified as a Communist or Communist tool. This technique became prevalent, Koen avers, "to convince Americans that China was conquered by the forces of Mao Tse-tung because of American traitors." [30]

By all accounts of the 1948 election, the Republicans did not run on foreign policy. Instead, the thrust of their campaign was an attack on New Deal domestic policies and principles; China policy failed, despite the urgings of Alfred Kohlberg, to become a major issue in the campaign. Like everyone else, Kohlberg was optimistic about Thomas E. Dewey's chances. Unlike others, apparently, he tried on many occasions to persuade the New York governor "to take a strong stand on China." [31]

Scoffing at a bipartisan foreign policy, the "China Lobby Man" nonetheless offered both major parties identical planks for their 1948 platforms, which, it might be noted, stopped short of suggesting the use of American troops in China:

> "The _____ Party reaffirms the principles of the Open Door Policy and pledges support to the National Government of China in its efforts to regain sovereignty over all China, including Manchuria with its ports of Dairen and Port Arthur. To attain these objectives we promise to that Government adequate financial aid, military supplies, advice and training."

Kohlberg was among a small delegation of "outstanding anti-Communists" who met with Dewey after his nomination and urged him to take a positive stand on communism and foreign policy (the others: George S. Schuyler, author of *Black and Conservative;* Senator Styles Bridges; William Loeb, publisher of the *Manchester Union Leader;* Isaac Don Levine; and Louis Waldman).

After Dewey's defeat, Kohlberg refused to attend a GOP fund-raising dinner, extending his regrets: "Because there is nowhere else to go, I shall have to remain a Republican. I cannot, however, support the present timid leadership of the Party, subservient as it is to Democratic initiative in foreign affairs." On December 1, 1948, in the aftermath of the unexpected election outcome, Madame Chiang Kai-shek arrived in Washington to plead for $3 billion in aid over a three-year period and to request that another American military mission be sent to China. Before she left China, however, discussion already had gotten underway in the American government toward a document on Sino-American relations.

The White Paper

The project was not officially launched until early in 1949. Six weeks before its August 5 release, sixteen Republican senators and five

Democrats signed a letter to Truman, circulated by Senator Knowland, which expressed concern over reports the United States might recognize the Communist regime.[32] Among the first to react to the White Paper, a 1,054-page history of Sino-American relations, which concentrated on the 1944–1949 period, was former Ambassador Hurley. "What the white paper does not show," he said in a publicity release, "is that I was called on the carpet with a full array of the pro-Communists of the State Department as my judges and questioners, to defend the American policy in China against 'every official of the American Embassy in China' " [33] Hurley called the document "a smooth alibi for the pro-Communists in the State Department who have engineered the overthrow of our ally . . . and aided in the Communist conquest of China." It failed "to really tell what happened in China," he added, saying "the Yalta secret agreement is the blueprint for Communist conquest of China." (Hurley had included this attack on the Yalta accords in a draft of his 1945 resignation letter, but had deleted all mention of Yalta, according to one source, at the instigation of Senator Vandenberg.) [34]

Secretary of State Acheson's answer to the "smooth alibi" charge was contained in his "Letter of Transmittal" accompanying the White Paper. Seeking to place blame for the Nationalist government's demise squarely on Kuomintang political, economic, and military failures, Acheson said, in an oft-quoted passage:

> The unfortunate but inescapable fact is that the ominous result of the civil war in China was beyond the control of the government of the United States. Nothing that this country did or could have done within the reasonable limits of its capabilities could have changed that result; nothing that was left undone by this country has contributed to it. It was the product of internal Chinese forces, forces which this country tried to influence but could not. A decision was arrived at within China, if only a decision by default.[35]

The only alternative open to the United States, he said—gigantic, full-scale American intervention in the Chinese civil war—would have been "resented" by the mass of Chinese people and "condemned" by the American people.

Allegations against the White Paper mounted. Senators Knowland,

Bridges, Wherry, and McCarran called it a "whitewash of a wishful, do-nothing policy" that placed Asia in danger of Soviet conquest.[36] But the most damaging charge—that sixteen key documents had been omitted from the vast compilation of papers—came from Dr. Judd. Demanding "these missing pieces of evidence," Judd struck what would become a familiar rhetorical note in the years ahead: "We have not tried to win the war in China. We have tried to end it. But the only way to end the war with communism—anywhere—is to win it." [37]

Judd was quickly supported by his ACPA colleague, Kohlberg, who charged that the State Department's purpose, "whether they knew it or not, was to make clear in official documents the fact that while China was our fighting ally we were preparing its betrayal." [38] Two 1945 Army intelligence reports Judd insisted should have been included in the White Paper later were obtained, reproduced, and made available by ACPA, although Acheson also made them available to the press on August 24 when he released a point-by-point analysis of Judd's 16 "missing" items.[39]

The government's huge compendium also raised questions among commentators not given to bruiting charges of betrayal or conspiracy. Columnist Walter Lippmann, for one, was not prepared to accept uncritically the propositions that the outcome in China was beyond American control and that U.S. policy had been essentially correct.[40] There was no indication in the documents, he pointed out, that any other friendly allied power had been consulted over the possibility of sharing responsibility for China's future. Nor was there an explanation for why the American government had been unable to negotiate with the Nationalists. American policy, Lippmann concluded, had become so irrevocably and rigidly committed to Chiang Kai-shek that "Chiang's destiny became our destiny in China and so, when he went down, he took us down with him."

A colloquy in *Far Eastern Survey,* a publication of the soon-to-be-skewered IPR, raised similar questions. Lawrence K. Rosinger noted that Acheson's summary of the three policy alternatives available to American diplomacy after the war failed to include a fourth option: "to seek to avoid civil war by working for compromise, but to keep the United States in a flexible position, basically uncommitted to the extension of Nationalist, or any other, power in China and ready to adjust it-self to the further evolution of that country." And John K. Fairbank commented that the real criticisms of American policy involved the na-tion's lack of strategy and planning "when confronted with the threat-ened Communist domination of China." Failure in China came, he said, "because we were forcing the pace of history, seeking to foster a mo-dernity of which Chinese political life was incapable. . . . We sought to foster a Western-style society in Kuomintang China, but in the end found ourselves unwillingly supporting just another third-rate bureau-cratic despotism." [41]

Finally, Paul M. A. Linebarger wondered how citizens of a democ-racy could comment on foreign policy "when the policy is shrouded in secrecy until *after* the decisions are made and is then presented in elabo-rate apologetic documents, neatly edited after the fact?" [42] The question was destined to reoccur in other contexts in the future of America's Far Eastern relations.

McCarthyism and Korea

Joseph R. McCarthy discovered China in February 1950—after Dewey's defeat, after the White Paper, after the collapse of the Nation-alists on the mainland and the birth of "Communist China," and imme-diately after Alger Hiss, a high State Department aide, had been found guilty of perjury at a second sensational trial.

McCarthy analysts are in almost universal agreement about his striking some sensitive nerve in the American body politic. "From Feb-ruary through May and June of 1950," Richard Rovere writes, "from the Lincoln Day lecture series through the Tydings hearings—the dollar bills and the five-dollar bills came tumbling in, accompanied by a few checks and postal notes for ten, twenty-five, and a hundred dollars (as well as some odd sums like $2.70 and $38); the money came from Washington, New York, Chicago, Los Angeles, Philadelphia, Houston—and from Columbia City, Ind.; Fort Lee, N.J.; Hayward, Calif.; Akron, Colo.; Princeton, Minn.; Centerville, Ala.; and Brown-ing, Mont." [43]

The major points to be made here about the McCarthy phenomenon are first, that the senator launched his campaign of reckless accusations about Communists in government with faulty data vis-à-vis China relations and quickly called on Alfred Kohlberg as his research assistant of sorts ("a staunch American," McCarthy later would write, "without whose indefatigable efforts to expose the truth we might already have been totally lost in Asia"; [44] and second, that the McCarthy approach dramatically changed the China policy debate—and other issues as well—from foreign policy questions to front-page charges of domestic subversion and disloyalty.

McCarthy first met Kohlberg in late March, after Senate subcommittee hearings began on the loyalty of State Department employees (the Tydings hearings). Over dinner in Washington, the senator asked him for the step-by-step story of the "China sellout." That was the beginning of their relationship. [45] McCarthy refused a $500 Kohlberg donation because he did not want the press to get the notion he was being backed by "an imaginary China Lobby," but he used Kohlberg's data (in part leftover from Kohlberg's wartime IPR episode) both in his testimony before the Tydings Committee and in later accusations on the Senate floor. [46] Amid the confusion and sensationalism preceding the Tydings investigation, Dean Acheson went before the Senate Foreign Relations Committee to clarify his position on the Alger Hiss case and Judith Coplon was convicted of conspiracy in another widely publicized "spy trial." Moreover, the Tydings hearings, with McCarthy as the first witness, quickly became disorderly affairs in which a numbers game of McCarthy's "cases" tended "to defeat clarity and discovery." Indeed, as Earl Latham continues, although subversion of China policy by a pattern of conspiracy was the theory of McCarthy's attack, of the nine people specifically charged by McCarthy, six had no connection with China policy. [47]

It is beyond the scope of this introductory section to mention in anything but cursory fashion the handful of additional congressional investigations which erupted in the aftermath of the outbreak of the Korean War. Each of these heralded inquiries (of General MacArthur's dismissal, the IPR, the nomination of Philip C. Jessup as ambassador to the United Nations, and the activities of tax-exempt foundations [48]) rediscovered the "loss of China." Yet Senator McCarthy had co-opted "China Lobby" perspectives and scapegoats during the pre-Korean period of Sino-American relations. He did so, moreover, with the blessings of the Republican leader in the Senate, Ohio's Robert A. Taft. "If one case doesn't work," Taft told McCarthy, "try another." [49]

After creation of the Central People's Government of China in October 1949, pro-Nationalist forces knew the question of U.S. recognition of the new regime would become closely tied to the defense of Formosa, to which the Nationalists had fled. The American position on recognition first was stated during a press conference by Acheson on October 12. There were three conditions: that the new rulers effectively control what they claimed to govern, recognize their international obligations, and govern with the consent of the people. Acheson had at least two private opportunities to elaborate these criteria before executive sessions of the Senate Foreign Relations Committee.[50] "In essence," a committee staff study later concluded, "it was the American position that the Communists would have to meet the necessary 'international obligations' before obtaining Western recognition." [51] But in 1949 and early 1950 the term was stretched, this study continues, "to include the observation of treaty commitments made by the Ch'ing dynasty and the Nationalist government which protected private American property interests as well as American diplomats and diplomatic property." At any rate, in January 1950, the Chinese Communists "requisitioned" and took over, at Peking, a compound containing the premises and residence quarters of the American consulate general—thus signaling they were not interested in recognition.

This "final blow" triggered an anti-recognition campaign in the American press, which took the form of emphasizing Formosa's importance to American security—a campaign bolstered in January by former President Hoover's support for a U.S. naval defense of the island and by Senator Taft's quick concurrence. Hoover's statement had been arranged by Senator Knowland.[52]

After Korea erupted but before the Chinese entered the conflict, American officials were greatly concerned about the danger of Chinese involvement, as Acheson made clear before a joint executive session of the Senate Committee on Foreign Relations and the House Committee on Foreign Affairs. He also said the question of Chinese representation at the United Nations had not been worked out "with all of our allies." Acheson thought the Russians might press for a quick vote on the question, which prompted Congressman Walter Judd to ask on what basis the Chinese Nationalists could be removed from the United Nations. The argument probably would revolve around the question of which people represent the member known as China, Acheson answered. To which Judd replied:

> I think there are three ways people tend to look at how to keep the Chinese Communists out of the war in Korea, which I think is one of our No. 1 objectives, second only to keeping Russia out. One group says we have got to go to war. Another group represents the policy of appeasement, which is to say, "We will seat the Chinese Communists as the Chinese Representatives in the U.N. We will abandon the Chinese National Government on Formosa, and thereby we will persuade the Chinese Communists not to enter the war in Korea against us."
>
> I hope that won't be followed, because I am convinced it will produce the opposite result. Every time we have appeased and tried to buy them off, from before Yalta on through, by sacrificing other people's rights, it has backfired. I am convinced that is the surest way of getting the Communists into Korea. If we remove Formosa as a thorn in their side, which ties up a lot of their strength, they are much freer to go into Korea and into Indochina. . . .
>
> The third policy is the same policy we followed in Greece, to give firm assistance to the Chinese on Formosa, the same as in the Philippines and in Indochina. I think that is the best way for us to assist those opposing Communism in Asia.[53]

As noted, there were abundant congressional opportunities during the Korean War period for "China Lobby" themes to be exploited. There were also electoral opportunities. In the 1950 mid-term elections, which saw Republicans make modest gains in both Houses (including Richard Nixon's Senate triumph over Helen Gahagan Douglas), the GOP National Committee's candidate handbook emphasized that a dark conspiracy overshadowed America's international problems.[54] As Ronald J. Caridi has written,

The Republican party at last had at its disposal the weapons for a full-scale dissent. The most vocal elements within the party interpreted their election gains as an indication of widespread distrust of Administration policy. There was now proof of Truman's unwillingness to endorse MacArthur's plans to escalate the war. And finally, with the intervention of Chinese troops, there was dramatic evidence that once again Democratic policy had led to disaster in the Far East.[55]

Most of the political fallout to come followed Truman's relief of MacArthur and the latter's monumental welcome back to America. The long series of hearings that explored the "Military Situation in the Far East" and the facts surrounding the general's dismissal regurgitated volumes of additional perceptions about America's relations with China. Included was the first attempt by a nationally known senator, Oregon's then Republican Wayne Morse, to raise the possibility of an investigation of those working for Nationalist Chinese interests in the country: "Although the vicious operations of the Communists have been widely exposed . . . there never has been, however, a thorough public investigation of the so-called China lobby." [56] Morse asked Acheson a long, involved question, the point of which was to inquire whether the Secretary felt a "China Lobby" existed. "Senator Morse," Acheson began, "I am not able to answer the question as to whether I do or do not feel that the facts are as represented in those statements."

Several weeks later, *Congressional Quarterly* published its special supplement, "The China Lobby: A Case Study." The following April, the *Reporter* ran a two-part exposé treatment.[57] A half century after formation of the Committee on American Interests in China, the "China Lobby" was getting some overdue attention.

As a catchphrase, "China Lobby" has evoked intense emotional responses: positive from those who objected, for whatever reasons, to America's long guardianship of Chiang Kai-shek; negative from those who saw the Nationalists, irrespective of flaws, as the only salvation for the China of *their* perceptions. More importantly, however, especially for U.S.-China relations, as Ross Koen first observed, the administration's loss of initiative on China policy placed Congress in a vastly superior power position. After the outbreak of war in Korea, the pro-Chiang bloc, greatly strengthened both by events and by the rapidly increasing acceptance of China lobby views, could block any program requested by the Administration unless Congress were allowed to dictate policy toward China. Capitulation was therefore the only course open to the Executive branch.[58]

China, many have commented, was never "ours" to lose. China policy, on the other hand, was.

PRESSURES ON CHINA POLICY, 1953–1971

3

The Formation and Organization of The Committee for One Million

At his death in 1964 at the age of 62, Nicholas de Rochefort was identified by the *New York Times* as a writer, linguist, research analyst, faculty member, and "expert on psychological warfare," [1] but the obituary omitted what may have been the former Frenchman's foremost claim to expertness—the idea behind The Committee for One Million Against the Admission of Communist China to the United Nations.

Four years after his arrival in 1949, as Count de Rochefort, on a lecture tour of the United States, and one year before renouncing his French citizenship in 1954 to become an American, de Rochefort contacted the White House. He telephoned, then wrote to C. D. Jackson, special assistant to President Eisenhower and a former vice-president of Time Inc., who had been loaned to the 1952 Eisenhower campaign as a speechwriter by Henry Luce. The letter, dated June 17, 1953, was written nine days after delegates to the Panmunjom truce talks had signed a prisoners-of-war agreement and six weeks before an armistice ended three years of war in Korea.

Typed in French and datelined Washington D.C., the letter came directly to the point: "If the armistice is concluded in Korea, the question of the admission of the Chinese Communist government will be raised in the UN." [2] All members of the Commonwealth, most European nations, and nearly all Asian ones favored Chinese Communist admission, the letter stated, but the United States opposed this action and should therefore anticipate being placed in a delicate and disadvantageous position with respect to her domestic politics and international prestige. "It seems to me," the graduate of St. Cyr and School of Law, University of

Paris added, "that there might still be time to ameliorate this position by an offensive action of psychological warfare."

What de Rochefort had in mind would be patterned after the 1950 Stockholm Appeal to ban the atom bomb, a propaganda campaign mounted by the Soviet Union which allegedly resulted in 500 million signatures being collected throughout the world.

> It would thus be a question of provoking a vast movement of international character opposed to the entry of Red China to the U.N., somewhat analogous to the "Petition for Peace" of Stockholm instigated by the Soviets. Directed by an international organization with chapters in each country, such a campaign of petitions and protest meetings would be able to a certain degree to influence the respective governments. In every case, it would have the effect of demonstrating that, far from being alone, the United States has, in their resistance, the support of public opinion throughout the world which would reinforce their international prestige.[3]

Then, after commenting that "we have always left the psychological initiative to the Soviets . . ." de Rochefort solicited Jackson's aid by requesting introductions to people who might help him launch such a campaign.

Jackson's June 22, 1953 reply demurred:

> I quite agree with your statement about the importance of an informed public opinion on the question of the admission of Communist China to the United Nations, and as you know that is indeed the official position of this Government . . . As to your suggestion about a possible movement to promote this result, I feel that it is not something I could possibly become interested or involved in, since any action or opinion I might express would inevitably be considered official in view of my position with the Administration. Under these circumstances, I do not feel that it would be appropriate for me to appear to sponsor such a plan.[4]

But de Rochefort persisted. Seven weeks later he sent a second letter to Jackson, this one laboriously typed in English:

> You may remember my suggestion of a campaign against the admission of Red China to the UN. About one month ago, I succeeded in interesting in it Dr. Judd, Representative from Minnesota, who asked me to present

my plan at a meeting of the Sub-Committee for the Far East of the House For. Aff. Committee. As a consequence, a group was formed headed by Dr. Judd and assisted by Mr. F. C. McKee from Pittsburgh. This group will launch a public appeal signed by a certain number of prominent citizens . . ." [5]

The letter went on to mention a proposed petition drive in which various religious, professional, and veterans organizations would be asked to win over their counterparts abroad to American policy and then "exercise a pressure on their respective Governments." As to his own participation, the former French army captain who served in the First French Armored Division when the allies invaded the continent during World War II, had this to say:

> I am participating in this campaign for my modest part, namely in attempting to assure a liaison between the agencies of the Administration which ought to inconspicuously coordinate the action and the organizers of the campaign. The necessity of this coordination seems to be entirely overlooked by both sides.

Indeed, de Rochefort was not optimistic:

> In my opinion, the striking fact is the extreme conventionalism of our organization of propaganda, lack of planning and non-existence of operational facilities. My statement may sound blunt and impertinent, but you know which spirit inspires it.

He closed with a final appeal:

> I earnestly request you to grant me an appointment. I am assured that I could supply you with important information, perhaps with some not entirely useless suggestions.

The White House files do not include a Jackson response to this letter but do contain a memorandum from Jackson to then Under-Secretary of State Walter Bedell Smith, Director of the Central Intelligence Agency (CIA) from 1950 to 1953, Ambassador to the Soviet Union from 1946 to 1949, and General Eisenhower's Chief of Staff during World War II:

Count N. de Rochefort, who has been quite active in anti-communist work but who for some reason unknown to me did not enjoy particularly good standing in your former outfit, is spearheading with Congressman Judd and one or two others, a public petition drive against the inclusion of Red China in the United Nations.

This drive is different from the normal one in that the target is not American public opinion but Western European public opinion.

Congressman Judd is fairly enthusiastic and de Rochefort is very energetic.

de Rochefort wants to come and see me to talk about this matter and I wonder if you have any advice for me.[6] (Italics added)

Handwritten across the bottom of this document: "9/9—Smith advised best not to get W.H. [White House] involved in any way."

In his second letter to Jackson, de Rochefort had suggested an appearance before the Far East and Pacific subcommittee of the House Committee on Foreign Affairs to present his plan. He did testify before that subcommittee—five days after the Korean War armistice was signed following more than two years of truce talks. The date was July 31, 1953, the day Senate Majority Leader Robert A. Taft died and several days before the first session of the 83rd Congress adjourned.

Dr. de Rochefort (his doctorate from l'École Libre des Sciences Politique) testified in executive session before the House subcommittee, whose chairman was, indeed, Dr. Walter H. Judd. Exactly what Witness de Rochefort had to say remains unknown, at least to this writer, after five unsuccessful attempts to read the transcripts—locked away for fifty years, *perhaps to the year 2003,* under a House secrecy rule protecting executive session testimony.[7]

Other than his attempt to enlist Jackson's support and his testimony before Congressman Judd's subcommittee, there is no further evidence of de Rochefort's direct activities on behalf of the Committee. That he was nonetheless active for the balance of the year is suggested by part of the closing paragraph of the Committee's minutes of a steering committee meeting held in Washington, D.C. on December 30, 1953: "It was also agreed to discontinue the full-time services of Dr. Nicholas de Rochefort, so as to carry on activities outside the Committee. The gratitude of all present was expressed for the splendid work of Dr. deRochefort.'' [8] The *Times*'s obituary, which said de Rochefort was a member of one of France's oldest families, with the ancestral house in Auvergne, listed his employment at death as a faculty member of American University and research analyst at the Library of Congress for the Agency for International Development.

Nicholas de Rochefort: A Caveat

My unsuccessful attempts to read Nicholas de Rochefort's July 1953 testimony before Dr. Judd's subcommittee have kept hidden important details of the Committee's exact origins. Initially, speculation focused around three points: 1) C. D. Jackson's September 2 memorandum to former CIA Director Walter Bedell Smith and his comment that de Rochefort "did not enjoy particularly good standing in your former outfit," plus the cryptic handwritten line across the bottom of this document: "9/9—Smith advised best not to get W.H. involved in any way"; 2) de Rochefort's definition of his own role in the campaign, i.e., to assure a "liaison between the agencies of the Administration which ought to inconspicuously coordinate the action and the organizers of the campaign."; and 3) de Rochefort's brief employment by the Committee's organizers and his year-end severance "so as to carry on activities outside the Committee." Together, these points raise several critical questions: Had Dr. de Rochefort been a member of the OSS (Office of Strategic Services, the World War II predecessor to the CIA) and/or the CIA? If so, over what period of time? Still a French citizen in 1953, was he employed by the CIA during the Committee's inception? Finally—and crucially—did he act alone in his initiatives—first to Jackson, then to Dr. Judd's subcommittee—or was he working with direction or guidance at some level of the nation's Central Intelligence Agency?

To wit: Was the formation of The Committee for One Million Against the Admission of Communist China to the United Nations an early example of a covert CIA domestic political operation?

It is, perhaps, a small measure of the post-Watergate revelations about domestic surveillance and clandestine operations that the above question seemed too farfetched to raise in the early stages of this research. Soon, of course, nothing in domestic politics seemed farfetched. The denouement of Watergate, two books about CIA operations, and the series of explosive disclosures about the Agency's domestic spying activities, which began in the *New York Times* in December 1974 and continued unremittingly through various investigations well into 1976, had legitimized the reexamination of every cold war occurrence.[9]

Several days before the original revelations in the *Times,* I began a correspondence with the CIA that lasted until June 1975 and coincided, beginning in February 1975, with the newly available provisions of the Freedom of Information Act (amended in 1974 and passed by Congress over one of President Ford's early vetos). The CIA refused to reveal any information about de Rochefort, claiming statutory exemption from FOIA disclosure requirements. On June 5, 1975, after reviewing my final appeal (as required before judicial review can take place), the chairman of the Agency's Information Review Committee wrote that "The fact of a relationship of any individual with OSS or this Agency could be classified and some of any such relationships might also involve information relating to intelligence sources and methods. Pursuant to sections b(1) and b(3) of the Freedom of Information Act, the existence of any such relationship with Mr. de Rochefort therefore is neither confirmed nor denied." [10]

Neither confirmed nor denied.

In November 1975, with the able and underpaid assistance of my lawyer, Richard G. Berry of Los Angeles, I filed a Freedom of Information Act lawsuit in the United States District Court for the Central District of California: *Stanley D. Bachrack vs. Central Intelligence Agency, William Colby;* Case No. CIV 75-3727-WPG.

A preliminary pre-trail hearing was held in the Los Angeles chambers of U.S. District Court Judge William P. Gray on February 10, 1976. At that conference the government indicated it would file a motion to dismiss the case, which it did on March 11, 1976. Our response, on April 9, was a motion for *in camera* inspection by the Court of any documents or files relating to Dr. de Rochefort.

The motions were argued before Judge Gray on the morning of April 26, 1976—by coincidence, the same day that the Senate Select Committee studying intelligence activities released the first reports of its fifteen-month inquiry (which includes a brief but fascinating section on the CIA's Allen W. Dulles era, from 1953 to 1961, that concludes: "Dulles's marked orientation toward clandestine activities, his brother's position as Secretary of State, and cold war tensions combined to maximize the Agency's operational capability. In terms of policymakers' reliance on the CIA, allocation of resources, and the attention of the Agency's leadership, clandestine activities had overtaken intelligence analysis as the CIA's primary mission").[11]

Judge Gray granted the government's motion for dismissal and denied our motion for *in camera* inspection. In essence, he agreed with the CIA's contention that the disclosure requirements of the Freedom of Information Act did not apply to matters specifically exempted from disclosure by prior statutes governing the Agency.

Before ruling, however, Gray acknowledged "a substantial dilemma here from the standpoint of public interest," as recorded by the official court reporter's transcript of the proceedings. He expressed "a lot of sympathy" for the plaintiff's effort "to study the manner and extent, if he can, of the involvement of intelligence agencies in seeking to mold public opinion with respect to matters that have a domestic connotation."

"This is something that intelligence agencies have no business getting into. And if they are trying to mold public opinion, like helping this man to foment his agency of A Million to keep Red China out of the UN—if the CIA is mixed up in that, why, the public has an interest in finding out about it. I am mindful of that horn of the dilemma, but there is another horn of the dilemma, and that is, we must protect the identities of CIA personnel. That thing over in Greece pointed that out, if anything needed to be pointed out in that respect [the murder in December 1975 of acknowledged CIA agent Richard S. Welch].

"If the CIA says, 'All right, this man is not involved,' well, that's fine as far as this case is concerned. We could stop worrying about it. But then the next time somebody makes an inquiry, if the CIA says anything other than 'He's not involved,' it's the same thing as saying, 'We did have a relationship with him.' And under those circumstances, I can see very clearly how the CIA must take the position it can neither confirm nor deny, because if they do anything else, it gives information, and the same thing is true with respect to the Court.''

The CIA's insistence on secrecy, meanwhile, magnifies congressional reluctance to release the testimony of Dr. de Rochefort. Here, the secrecy problem may be twofold: The House of Representatives' fifty-year rule on executive session testimony and Congressman Thomas E. Morgan (D., Pa.), chairman of the House Committee on Foreign Affairs since 1959 (now the Committee on International Relations) and a member of the steering committee of The Committee of One Million from January 1965 at least through January 1969.[12]

Petitioning the President

Nicholas de Rochefort's attempt on August 11 to see Jackson followed his subcommittee appearance by less than two weeks and preceded by ten weeks the presentation of the original petition to the President.

Five men, including Dr. Judd, spearheaded the pre-presentation organizational effort. Their goal, according to Liebman, was to utilize the anticipated publicity from a White House meeting to alert the American people on the issue, and provide what they saw as ''the facts.'' [13] Congressman Judd requested the appointment with the President, acted as spokesman for the delegation on October 22, wrote the follow-up letter to Eisenhower, and took credit, on behalf of his subcommittee, for developing the ''original idea'' for the ''movement.'' The other four were Governor Charles Edison, Frederick C. McKee, Dr. B. A. Garside, and Marvin Liebman.

The President's appointment calendar notes that at 9:30 A.M., between a 9:15 call by Lt. Gen. Jean Valluy of NATO and a 10:00 meeting of the National Security Council, six men were scheduled to see the President and that ''Congressman Judd requested this appointment in order that this group might present to the President a petition against the admission of Communist China to the United Nations.'' [14] Judd had been an early supporter of Eisenhower for the 1952 GOP presidential nomination, coming out for him in 1951 and hailing his nomination after the 1952 Republican convention as a ''rising up of the rank and file of the party members against the old guard leadership.''

That Judd acted as spokesman for the petitioners in the eyes of the President is confirmed by a ''Dear Walter'' letter acknowledging receipt of the petition:

> Since you appeared to be the spokesman of the group that came to my office the other day to present the petition against admission of Communist China to the United Nations, I am writing to make a record of my receipt of the petition.
>
> After your visit, *I spoke to the Secretary of State and learned that he is already in possession of a copy of the same document.*
>
> As I indicated to your group, existing international facts, in my view, preclude the seating of the Chinese Communist regime to represent China in the UN.
>
> We have every reason to fear that the Chinese Communist regime in fact now seeks representation in the UN in order to promote the objectives of international Communism by creating dissension among the nations of the world, rather than to become a partner in seeking just and peaceful solutions for the world's problems.
>
> With warm regards . . .[15] (Italics added)

Judd's follow-up letter to the President expressed his own sense of urgency about the need for heading off pressures from the Communist bloc on the admission question and justified the personal meeting. Additionally, the letter included a point Judd had forgotten to mention to the President:

> Your receiving us gave us an invaluable boost as we start the second stage of our developing effort. I forgot to mention that we have just organized a ''Committee For One Million'' (Against the Admission of Communist China to the United Nations). Mr. Warren Austin is serving as the Honorary Chairman, dramatizing the conviction that, contrary to the impression

of some, the admission of Communist China would gravely injure the UN rather than strengthen it.[16]

Dr. Judd also neglected to say that the "original idea" for the Committee came from his own House subcommittee, a view revealed two and one half weeks later in a letter to fellow petitioner and Committee organizer, Charles Edison. Judd was replying to an Edison letter of October 27, 1953, written the day after the Committee's first office opened on West 44th Street, New York City, which enclosed a bank form, dated October 22, 1953, from the Marine Midland Trust Company, that required signatures of two other Committee members so that Edison could act as treasurer. In response to Edison's comment

> The Press is certainly catching fire on this *crusade*. . . . just how the Press got the impression that I was the one who did the presenting and appear to be taking the lead in the *crusade*, I cannot understand. It is embarrassing to me and I want to assure you that I am doing everything I can, when the opportunity presents itself, to emphasize that you are the real inspiration of the whole movement.[17] (Italics added)

Congressman Judd replied:

> . . . You need not be in the least embarrassed about being given proper recognition as the leader in this movement. *The original idea developed in my Sub-committee in Congress*, but you have done more work on it than anybody else and the influence of your name and blessing have been incalculable.[18] (Italics added)

This admission by Judd that the Committee's concept had been spawned in his congressional subcommittee was mailed to Governor Edison's Waldorf Towers Suite 38A residence in New York City. Not far away was the Committee's new headquarters, where Marvin Liebman was beginning an almost sixteen-year reign as the China policy group's secretary. An appropriate introduction to Marvin Liebman, born in Brooklyn on July 21, 1923, is found in his own compilation of anti-Communist and/or conservative organizations he represented—listed in a February 5, 1969, letter to the Hoover Institution at Stanford University immediately prior to his leaving the public relations business and depositing his records and files there.

American-African Affairs Association
American Conservative Union
American Emergency Relief Committee on the Panama Canal
Businessman's Committee on China
Clergyman's Emergency Committee on China
American Committee for Aid to Katanga Freedom Fighters
Committee of One Million Against the Admission of Communist China to
    the UN
Communications Distribution, Inc.
Council for American Foreign Policy
Council on Communist Anti-Semitic Policy and Practice
International Youth Crusade
National Review Fifth Anniversary Dinner
National Committee for Justice for (Senator Thomas J.) Dodd
Young Americans for Freedom
American Emergency Committee for Aid to Tibetan Refugees
Draft Goldwater Movement
Judd (Walter H.) for Vice-President Committee
New York Republican Education and Action Program
People's Emergency Committee on Vietnam
Tshombe Emergency Committee
Public Action Committee
Buckley For Mayor (William F. Jr.)
Buckley For Senator (James L.)
World Youth Crusade For Freedom
Student Committee for a Free China.[19]

Said journalist Richard Dudman about Liebman: "the best single action-group organizer on the far right today." [20] Dudman provides other biographical details on Liebman: first a member of the Young Communist League in 1938 and later a member of the Communist Party of the United States, he quit communism after leaving the army in 1945. The expulsion of party head Earl Browder, he later said, was unfair. After World War II, Liebman visited Italy and France and found adventure in the Mediterranean, including a brief internment in Cyprus after a voyage to Palestine aboard a ship belonging to the Jewish terrorist organization *Irgun Zvai Leumi*. He worked for the International Rescue Committee in 1951, "came to see the Soviet Union as a world danger," and helped start, in 1952, Aid to Refugee Chinese Intellectuals. According to Dudman, in 1961 the building directory on the ninth floor of Liebman's office at 79 Madison listed, in addition to the "Committee of 1,000,000" and "American-Asian Educational Exchange," the "American Committee for Aid to Katanga," and the "McGraw-Edison Co. Committee for Public Affairs." The 'Greater New York School of Anti-Communism,' Fred C. Schwarz's project, also operated out of Liebman's office."

Marvin Liebman worked, in 1953 (and until 1958 when he started Marvin Liebman Associates, Inc.), for Harold L. Oram, Inc., a New York public relations and fund-raising organization.

The Petition and the Petitioners

The document President Eisenhower took in hand October 22, 1953 contained a cover page listing the names of the petition's seven sponsors,[21] a one-sentence statement of "our opposition to the admission of the so-called Chinese People's Republic to the United Nations," eight brief reasons for this stand, a three-sentence summary appeal to the President, and the names, in alphabetical order without titles, of 210 American citizens.

The first (and longest) paragraph of reasons dealt with the effect of admission on the United Nations Organization. Not only would admission of the People's Republic of China (PRC) "destroy the purposes, betray the letter, and violate the spirit of the law" of the United Nations, but the mainland Chinese government was "constitutionally unable" to carry out the obligations of the UN Charter because "it officially declares itself to be a 'dictatorship' based on 'democratic centralism' " and therefore excludes "freedom of discussion or criticism of government."

Second, to admit "the so-called Chinese People's Republic" (this identification appears eight times) would mean expelling a charter member of the United Nations and "the duly constituted government of China," an action of "unthinkable outrage against human decency and international justice." Moreover, in the language of paragraph three, the

Peking regime "has shown its unwillingness to carry out the obligations of the Charter by systematically disregarding every human right and violating every freedom," and, in paragraph four, has proved itself an aggressor state "by aiding in aggression upon South Korea and making war on the United Nations."

Admission would "destroy the prestige and the position of the United States and of the Free World in Asia," (paragraph five), in turn encouraging Asian nations to "make fatal compromises with the Communist bloc." Paragraph six accused the People's Republic of violating "the most elemental laws of war in mistreating, torturing, and murdering United Nations soldiers who were prisoners of war, in an unlawful war which they waged against the very organization in which their supporters now claim membership for them."

On a different theme, paragraph seven claimed that admission "would restore the prestige and authority of the Soviet Government . . . at a time when Communist dictatorship seems to be badly shaken inside the USSR and in its satellite Empire." Finally, admission would encourage "subversive totalitarian movements in the free nations of the world" and thus, "the danger of a new war would be vastly increased by the rewards offered to aggressors."

Next, the President was requested "to defend the freedom and the decency of the Free World by continuing to firmly oppose the admission" of the People's Republic to the United Nations.

Although the petition unequivocally rejected any appeasement of the People's Republic, it ignored the questions of whether future policy should remain unalterable and under what conditions China policy should change. There is evidence, moreover, even in the Committee's files, that the President held flexible views on the subject which may have been expressed to the visiting petitioners. In Judd's follow-up letter to Eisenhower, for example, he said that his group thoroughly agreed with the President's view that if and when the new Chinese regime demonstrated its intention to live according to civilized international rules and become representative of the people, the situation would be totally changed.[22] At that time, however, the regime represented the Kremlin, he added, and not the Chinese people.

Additionally, materials in the Committee's files suggest that a paragraph reflecting the potential for future flexibility in Sino-American relations was written into, then removed from, an early draft of the petition. The possibility is deduced from handwritten notes in the margin of one copy of a letter from China-policy gadfly Alfred Kohlberg to former Ambassador Warren R. Austin, then the honorary chairman of the emerging Committee for One Million. This November 1953 letter, indicating copies to the petition's six sponsors and Marvin Liebman, includes a handwritten underline beneath the name "Gov. Charles Edison," and handwritten margin notes dated "Dec. 1/53," suggesting that the notations are in Edison's handwriting. Kohlberg's letter called attention to an editorial entitled "Red China and the U.N." from that morning's (November 27) *New York Times.* The editorial, Kohlberg noted, though favorable to the petition, implied that "your petition means that the signers are only opposed to the admission of Red China to the U.N. as of now; and that if the Red Chinese regime reforms in its actions, they would not be so opposed." [23] To which Kohlberg added:

> This, I believe, misrepresents the viewpoint of the signers of your petition, as I met them. Most of them are not closely informed of the Red China regime, but they do know that it is a disciplined part of the World Communist Movement, and they are unalterably opposed to it now, have been so in the past, and will be so in the future. They feel that the brand of Cain is indelibly stamped on it and they, I feel sure, would refute the view expressed by the New York TIMES on their behalf.

Kohlberg proposed that the Committee

> . . . state that there was no thought in the mind of those who prepared the petition that the Communist tyranny in China could ever change in such a way as to make it properly admissible to the U.N. in the opinion of the drafters of the petition.
>
> I fear that if this is not done, the TIMES editorial will seem to be an accepted interpretation of your petition, which may very well be called to the attention of the President by his advisers at the time your petition is presented, and may very well mislead the President as to the sentiment of the signers.

The marginal notes handwritten on this copy of Kohlberg's letter (taken to be Edison's) read:

> Dec 1/53 I called Al Dec 1 & explained the background on this—*that some members & Ike had suggested the policy remain flexible*—that I had managed to have the [symbol for paragraph inserted here] omitted from the petition that would indicate that if conditions changed we might then let them in. Explained that it was not the right time for the Com. itself to make an issue of the point Al raised in this letter but I was glad he had done so to Austin etc. When a volume of names are in then may be the time for the Com. to say something about it. (Italics added)

As events unfolded, however, the Committee would not alter its hard line position on the admission question for eighteen years—until the closing days of the 1971 debate preceding the historic turnaround.

The original of Kohlberg's letter was sent to Warren R. Austin, America's first ambassador to the United Nations, in his capacity as honorary chairman of the newly formed Committee. Mistakenly, however, the Committee's first letterhead,[24] from a West 44th Street address in New York City, listed Austin as "Chairman," an error for which Congressman Judd apologized, in a long letter to Austin at his Vermont home that also makes clear Judd's role as the ambassador's immediate recruiter.[25]

Among the original petition's seven sponsors (Austin was not a sponsor), another was former President Herbert Hoover. An unsuccessful effort by Governor Edison to conscript Hoover into signing a letter to a national magazine will be taken up later, but there is no evidence that Hoover attended any meetings or otherwise engaged himself in Committee business.

Similarly, with the exception of an important steering committee meeting on February 26, 1954 (about which, more later), there is little to suggest that, during the Committee's first few months, prominent roles were played by House Minority Whip John W. McCormack (D., Mass.), Senator John Sparkman (D., Ala.), or Senator H. Alexander Smith (R., N.J.), chairman of the Far East subcommittee of the Senate

Foreign Relations Committee. None of these men attended the December 30, 1953, steering committee meeting in Washington.[26]

Yet another original sponsor, former Ambassador to Japan Joseph C. Grew, was one of the three petitioners at the White House to see Eisenhower on October 22d.[27] Additionally, Grew contributed his time, name, and other initiatives to be identified in the pages that follow.

Who else petitioned the President? Table 3.1 offers an overview of the 210 other signers by occupation and professional status. Table 3.2 identifies the 49 congressional signers (plus 4 congressional sponsors).

TABLE 3.1

Identification by Occupation or Professional Status of Persons Who Signed October 22, 1953 Petition to President Eisenhower

PROFESSION/OCCUPATION	NUMBER	PERCENT OF TOTAL
Members of Congress (excluding sponsors) Representatives (21) Senators (28)	49	23.3
Governors of states	12	5.7
Retired military officers Generals (11) Admirals (9)	20	9.5
Retired diplomats and ambassadors	7	3.3
Former officials of executive, legislative, and judicial branches	11	5.2
Scientists and educators	22	10.4
Publishers, journalists	18	8.5
Business, industry, and finance executives	33	15.7
Religious leaders, clerical and lay	14	6.7
Labor leaders	4	1.9
Arts, entertainment, sports	7	3.3
NA	13	6.1
Total	210	99.6 *

* The total is less than 100% because of rounding.

TABLE 3.2

53 Members of 83rd Congress Who Signed or Sponsored October 22, 1953 Petition to President Eisenhower

HOUSE OF REPRESENTATIVES (23)

DEMOCRATS (9)	REPUBLICANS (14)
Battle, Laurie C. (Ala.)	Chiperfield, Robert B. (Ill.) *
Hays, Brooks (Ark.)	Church, Marguerite S. (Ill.)
Gordon, Thomas S. (Ill.)	Hope, Clifford R. (Kan.)
McCormack, John W. (Mass.) †	Bentley, Alvin M. (Mich.)
McCarthy, Eugene J. (Minn.)	Judd, Walter H. (Minn.) †
Addonizio, Hugh J. (N.J.)	Short, Dewey (Mo.)
Kelly, Edna F. (N.Y.)	Auchincloss, James C. (N.J.)
Teague, Olin E. (Tex.)	Wolverton, Charles A. (N.J.)
Zablocki, Clement J. (Wisc.)	Javits, Jacob K. (N.Y.)
	Radwan, Edmund P. (N.Y.)
	Vorys, John M. (Ohio)
	Fulton, James G. (Pa.)
	McConnell, Samuel K. Jr. (Pa.)
	Scott, Hugh D. Jr. (Pa.)

SENATE (30)

DEMOCRATS (14)	REPUBLICANS (16)
Sparkman, John J. (Ala.) †	Knowland, William F. (Calif.) ‡
Douglas, Paul H. (Ill.)	Williams, John J. (Del.)
Gillette, Guy M. (Iowa)	Welker, Herman (Ida.)
Humphrey, Hubert H. (Minn.)	Payne, Frederick G. (Me.)
Eastland, James O. (Miss.)	Smith, Margaret C. (Me.)
Hoey, Clyde R. (N.C.)	Ferguson, Homer (Mich.)
Monroney, A. S. Mike (Okla.)	Potter, Charles E. (Mich.)
Maybank, Burnet R. (S.C.)	H. Alexander Smith (N.J.) †
Daniel, Price (Tex.)	Ives, Irving M. (N.Y.)
Robertson, A. Willis (Va.)	Young, Milton R. (N.D.)
Magnuson, Warren G. (Wash.)	Bricker, John W. (Ohio)
Kilgore, Harley M. (W. Va.)	Martin, Edward (Pa.)
Neely, Matthew M. (W. Va.)	Flanders, Ralph E. (Vt.)
Hunt, Lester C. (Wyo.)	Bennett, Wallace F. (Utah)
	Watkins, Arthur V. (Utah)
	Wiley, Alexander (Wisc.) §

* Chairman, House Committee on Foreign Affairs.

† Sponsors.

‡ Senate Majority Leader after Senator Taft's death on July 31, 1953.

§ Chairman, Senate Foreign Relations Committee.

Of the twelve petition-signing governors, Frank Clement (Tenn.) was the only Democrat. The eleven Republicans: Sigurd Anderson (S.D.), J. Hugo Aronson (Mont.), George Craig (Ind.), John S. Fine (Pa.), Hugh Gregg (N.H.), Walter J. Kohler (Wisc.), J. Bracken Lee (Utah), Howard Pyle (Ariz.), Charles H. Russell (Nev.), William G. Stratton (Ill.), and Dan Thornton (Colo.).

The eleven retired generals included: David P. Barrows, Lewis H. Brereton, Claire L. Chennault, Lucius D. Clay, Robert L. Eichelberger, George C. Kenney, George C. Marshall, James Van Fleet, Albert C. Wedemeyer, James H. Doolittle, and John R. Hodge. The nine admirals were: Oscar C. Badger, Charles M. Cooke, John L. Hall, Thomas C. Hart, Leland P. Lovette, Chester W. Nimitz, William H. Stanley, Emory D. Stanley, and Harry E. Yarnell.

Seven retired diplomats and/or ambassadors were included: Warren Austin, Robert W. Bliss, Joseph E. Davies, Stanley K. Hornbeck, Nelson T. Johnson, Richard C. Patterson, and J. Leighton Stuart, the latter a missionary-educator in China from 1905 to 1946, when he became Ambassador to China, a post he held to 1950.

Of the eleven former nationally known politicians, two were ex-senators, Tom Connally (D., Tex.), and Herbert R. O'Conor (D., Md.); one a former Supreme Court Justice, Owen J. Roberts; three onetime cabinet secretaries, John W. Snyder, Jesse Jones, and Louis A. Johnson; one ex-Navy Secretary, Dan Kimball; plus the following other officials: Dr. Frank L. Meleney, Evelyn Merz, Elizabeth Luce Moore, and Meir Steinbrink.

Four labor leaders were represented: George Meany, Sal B. Hoffmann, Jay Lovestone, and Matthew Woll.

The seven persons identified under the heading of ''Arts, Entertainment, Sports'' included author John Dos Passos, actors Adolphe Menjou and Robert Montgomery, poets Conrad Aiken, Newton Arvin, Merian Cooper, and boxer Gene Tunney.[28]

Fourteen church leaders were signers of the petition: Fr. Dennis J. Comey, S.J.; Rev. Theodotus DeWitow; J. Roswell Flower; Bishop L. R. Marston; Rev. Frederick A. McGuire, C.M.; Archbishop Michael; Theodore W. Anderson; C. J. O'Malley, C.M.; Rev. Daniel Poling; [29]

Bishop Herbert Welch; John R. Mott; Charles E. Scott; J. W. Storer; and James E. Wagner.

Among the signers were eighteen identified here as publishers or journalists: Ralph de Toledano, Manchester Boddy, Norman Chandler, Frank E. Gannett, William R. Hearst Jr., H. V. Kaltenborn, William Loeb, Robert S. Allen, Demaree Bess, John Chamberlain, William H. Chamberlain, Max Eastman, Robert W. Johnson, Frank Kluckhohn, Eugene Lyons, George S. Schuyler, William L. White, and William B. Ziff.

The list comprised twenty-two scientists and educators: George Counts, Horace M. Kallen, Roscoe Pound, Arthur M. Schlesinger, Robert Gordon Sproul, Wallace Sterling, Karl Wittfogel, James Burnham, Roy Chapman Andrews, Karl T. Compton, Horace Albright, C. Suydam Cutting, Magnus I. Gregersen, Philip K. Hitti, Emil Lengyel, Aura Severinghaus, Leslie Severinghaus, Wendell M. Stanley, George E. Taylor, Kenneth Colegrove, Richard L. Walker, and Max Yergan.

The thirty-three executives from business, industry, and finance were:

> Harold L. Bache, James G. Blaine, H. M. Bixby, Lee H. Bristol, George Bucher, Harry Bullis, L. M. Cassidy, Arthur M. Connell, J. Cheever Cowdin, Cleveland Dodge, Harold Falk, Frank Folson, John Fox, J. P. Grace Jr., Albert Greenfield, Carroll R. Harding, Conrad Hilton, Charles E. Johnson Jr., R. Roy Keaton, Eli Lilly, P. W. Litchfield, Frederick C. McKee, Harley V. McNamara, Eleanor Pillsbury, James H. Rand, Philip D. Reed, J. Louis Reynolds, Igor Sikorsky, Juan Trippe, W. H. Wheeler Jr., Robert E. Wood, Howard I. Young, Jack Frye.

Only thirteen signers were not identified by occupation or profession.[30]

The "53" in the 83rd Congress

The 83rd Congress—Eisenhower's first as President—was Republican controlled by the narrowest of margins: 48 Republicans to 47 Democrats and 1 Independent in the Senate; 221 Republicans to 213 Democrats, with 1 other, in the House. Hardly had it gotten underway, moreover, when the President, in his State of the Union message, touched off a national debate about Far Eastern policy in general and the Korean War in particular by ordering what became popularly known as the "unleashing" of Chiang Kai-shek's military forces on Formosa.[31]

Argument in Congress over the wisdom of the President's order continued through the spring, receding after the resumption of truce talks at Panmunjom on April 26, 1953. Thereafter, concern over rumors and reports of growing support for PRC membership in the United Nations prompted congressional activity in the form of various resolutions, amendments to bills, and riders to amendments. Overall, however, to put this issue in congressional perspective, these activities remained rather subdued compared with the simultaneous emergence in the 83rd Congress of two highly partisan, vexing, and headline-grabbing domestic issues: the so-called Bricker Amendment and the case of Senator Joseph R. McCarthy (R., Wisc.).

Together, these controversial problems preoccupied the 83rd Congress throughout 1953 and 1954. Deeply involved in both situations (each of which, incidentally, had China policy undertones), the President and his advisers fell into protracted negotiations with legislative leaders, particularly Senators John W. Bricker (R., Ohio), who signed the Committee's original petition to Eisenhower, and petition sponsor William F. Knowland, the California Republican who took over the Majority Leader's post after the death on July 31, 1953 of Senator Robert A. Taft (R., Ohio). Briefly, the Bricker Amendment reflected the view that the American Constitution was being threatened by treaty law and international executive understandings symbolized by the tarnished Yalta agreements and heightened by various later international agreements, including those with the United Nations and NATO. The proposed constitutional amendment, introduced in January 1953, before Eisenhower took the oath of office, turned on a highly technical legal question. The amendment would have had the effect of abrogating treaties which denied or abridged any constitutional rights—either individual or those reserved to the states. Together with the evolving debate over this issue came the furor over the person and conduct of Senator

McCarthy, whose slashing attacks in the name of anti-Communism assaulted numerous Old China Hands among many others. These two hassles, in the words of one journalist close to the administration, "aroused deep political passions in America and set right against left, Old Guard against the new, liberal against conservative, internationalist against isolationist. In the final analysis both issues bore a threat to the Presidential power and prerogative." [32]

So the Committee's petition-bearing ceremony at the White House occurred amidst these swirling events—indeed, midway between the end of the first session of the 83rd Congress on August 3 and the beginning of the second session on January 6, 1954.

In Congress, the opportunity to exercise leadership tends toward those who control—or share the views of those who control—the routine legislative processes, the most important of which is the work done in committee. For leadership on any issue, therefore—foreign or domestic—one naturally looks to the membership of the appropriate committee or committees.

Before he became Senate Majority Leader, Knowland was chairman of the Senate's Majority Policy Committee and a member of both the Appropriations Committee and the Committee on Foreign Relations. Appointed in August 1945 by California Governor Earl Warren to fill the vacancy caused by the death of Hiram W. Johnson, the then 45-year-old assistant publisher of the Oakland *Tribune* ranked 21st in terms of continuous senatorial service during most of the first session of the 83rd Congress. In but eight years time, the onetime chairman of the executive committee of the Republican National Committee had moved into the Senate hierarchy, his frequent anti-Communist speeches and outspoken support for the leadership of Chiang Kai-shek receiving widespread coverage in the press.

On May 19, 1953, about five weeks before Nicholas de Rochefort's first letter to C. D. Jackson, Knowland remarked on the Senate floor that "in the past few weeks there has been apparently a growing pressure on the United Nations, at New York and elsewhere, to admit Communist China as a member of the United Nations either before or after a cease fire in Korea." Knowland included in the *Record* two 1950

UN resolutions and two 1951 congressional resolutions—all variously hostile to the People's Republic—and introduced two identical resolutions calling for U.S. withdrawal from the United Nations if the Chinese were admitted.[33]

Two weeks later, on June 3, 1953, an amendment to the appropriations bill, falling far short of the Knowland proposal, passed the Senate, 76 to 0, after Senator Styles Bridges (R., N.H.), President Pro Tempore and Chairman of the Senate Appropriations Committee, assured his colleagues that the language had been discussed and approved at the White House and had the full endorsement of the President: "It is the sense of Congress that the Communist Chinese Government should not be admitted to membership in the United Nations as the representatives of China." [34] Between Knowland's resolution, which did not have substantial support, and the June 3 vote, other attempts to stiffen the Senate's stand more along the Knowland lines had failed. Press speculation attributed the final wording to Eisenhower's active resistance to congressional attempts, mainly by GOP leaders, to maneuver him into a rigid position on future relations with the mainland Chinese.[35]

The House ultimately followed the Senate's lead, on July 21, 1953, by another unanimous margin. Earlier, however, a handful of resolutions were submitted to the House Committee on Foreign Affairs. The first, by Representative Charles J. Kersten (R., Wisc.), on June 17, began with a long indictment of Communist ideology and practice and concluded with an appeal to the President to help bring about the "liberation" of the Chinese people by various political, moral, educational and diplomatic means.[36] On June 26, Representative Alvin M. Bentley (R., Mich.), introduced H. J.Res. 286, urging the United States to reexamine its policy toward the United Nations if Communist China were admitted.[37] Again, on July 2, four separate but similar resolutions reached the Foreign Affairs Committee: two by its chairman, Representative Robert B. Chiperfield (R., Ill.), and one each by Representatives Laurie C. Battle (D., Ala.), and Marguerite Stitt Church (R., Ill.).[38]

The difference in language between the Senate's resolution and the one later passed, 379 to 0, by the House was explained by Dr. Judd, who brought H. Con. Res. 129 to the floor. "Mr. Speaker," he said, "I believe the language of the above resolution is more complete and precise because it states the indisputable reason why the Chinese Communists must be prevented from taking China's seat in the United Nations, namely, they are not entitled to it." [39] The House Concurrent Resolution read: "That it is the sense of the Congress that the Chinese Communists are not entitled to and should not be recognized to represent China in the United Nations."

This language, stronger than the Senate's, had been recommended by Dr. Judd's subcommittee, a fact made clear by a report, also submitted by Judd, accompanying the resolution and placed in the *Record* before the vote—by Judd. The report reviewed congressional concern over China's UN seat and over Communist China's adherence to "the Kremlin line," adding: "This concern is presently heightened by the truce negotiations that may be followed by an armistice and a political settlement. It is reasonable to expect that the Chinese Communists may hold out for a seat in the United Nations as a quid pro quo for an armistice or a political settlement." The report also discussed the genesis of H. Con. Res. 129, mentioning the two resolutions introduced by Representatives Battle and Church, both similar in language to the Senate-passed resolution, and continued:

> The Subcommittee . . . under the chairmanship of the Honorable Walter H. Judd, considered both resolutions and recommended to the full committee a concurrent resolution with a slightly altered language. After a complete exploration by the full committee of the different issues involved, House Concurrent Resolution 129 was unanimously approved and introduced as a committee resolution by the Honorable Robert C. Chiperfield . . .

The report's arguments subsumed moral, legal, practical, and psychological issues. Morally, its tone reflected Dr. Judd's introductory remarks in explaining why the People's Republic was not *entitled* to admission: "It is bad enough to have some in it [the U.N.] from the start who later proved themselves unworthy. It would be plain hypocrisy to admit, under the guise of a peace-loving nation . . . the Communist regime in China which brazenly went to war with the U.N. itself."

On the legal issues, the report quoted portions of the UN Charter's preamble and first two articles, adding that measured against these criteria the Chinese Communists did not meet the standards for membership. Admission "would violate both the letter and the spirit of the charter." Both the moral and legal issues were said to be in conflict with the main practical issue, i.e., giving a permanent Security Council seat to those engaged in open hostilities against the United States, an occurrence which "would enhance their prestige, give courage to their sympathizers, and weaken those who are resisting Communist aggression from without and Communist subjugation from within. It would imply an acceptance of their permanent conquest of China and give them an air of respectability."

Finally, the psychological consequences would be "disastrous." Seating the People's Republic "would be a reward to the enemies of the United Nations and the United States." The organization's prestige would suffer "irreparably."

The arguments, rhetoric, and catchwords in the committee's report would shortly reappear in the petition to the President—albeit in slightly different form and with an added point or two. Unquestionably, as the resolutions showed, the views and sentiments expressed in the report were shared, in varying degrees and for different reasons, by the overwhelming majority of representatives and senators in the first session of the 83rd Congress. Soon-to-be Committee sponsor John W. McCormack, the Minority Whip, sounded congressional unanimity in the waning days of the session. Referring to conflicting foreign statements about Communist China's admission to the United Nations, he asked rhetorically, "Does anyone doubt that the people of America are overwhelmingly opposed to that?" [40]

Between the first and second sessions of the 83rd Congress, four House members conducted a six-week "Special Study Mission to Southeast Asia and the Pacific." The foursome left Washington D.C. on November 9, 1953. Included were three members who by that time either had sponsored or signed the Committee's anti-P.R.C. petition: Dr. Judd, the Mission's chairman, Marguerite Stitt Church (R., Ill.), and Clement J. Zablocki (D., Wisc.). The non-signing member was Congressman E. Ross Adair (R., Ind.). Interestingly, the four did not comprise the members of Judd's Far East Subcommittee; only Judd and Church were subcommittee members.[41]

The purpose of the "Special Study Mission to Southeast Asia and the Pacific" was spelled out in its subsequent report to the Committee on Foreign Affairs:

> When the Korean truce was under negotiation in the spring of 1953, the Committee on Foreign Affairs discussed the desirability of some of its members visiting the Pacific area to make a first-hand assessment of United States problems, policies, and programs. The signing of the truce in late July only accentuated the importance of such a study. The focus shifted from military action to complex political, economic, and psychological factors, whose magnitude was increased by the dilatory tactics and divisive efforts of the Communists.[42]

On the day the Mission departed, Dr. Judd dictated several letters, signed in his absence. One, to "Dear President Ike," reported that the petition against the admission to the U.N. of Communist China was moving along "with a bang." [43] More on the Mission's report will follow. First, by way of summarizing the identities and congressional roles of the "fifty-three" in the first session of the 83rd Congress, twenty were members of either the Senate Foreign Relations Committee or the House Committee on Foreign Affairs. Of the Foreign Relations Committee's fifteen total members, seven would be sponsors or signers of the petition: sponsors—Senators John Sparkman and H. Alexander Smith, the latter, chairman of the Committee's Far East subcommittee; signers—Chairman Alexander Wiley and Senators Ferguson, Gillette, Humphrey, and Knowland. Of the Foreign Affairs Committee's thirty total members, thirteen would be sponsors or signers of the October petition: sponsors—Representatives Judd and McCormack; signers— Chairman Chiperfield and Representatives Battle, Bentley, Church, Gordon, Hays, Kelley, Javits, Fulton, Vorys, and Zablocki. Six legislators from the two congressional foreign policy committees (Judd, Chiperfield, Bentley, Battle, Church, and Knowland) initiated some action on the admission question, either by introducing or bringing resolutions to the floor during the first session of the 83rd Congress. Others who missed signing the Committee's first petition later would associate themselves with its purposes. Some had simply left the nation's capital during the long recess from August to January.

The Committee at Year's End

At the December 30, 1953, steering committee meeting which discontinued Dr. de Rochefort's services, Secretary Marvin Liebman gave a progress report of the public petition campaign and Dr. Judd reported "off-the-record" on his mission to the Far East. Also, the Committee's finances were reviewed and its public relations management contract with Harold L. Oram, Inc. renewed on a month-to-month basis, the fee left unspecified. Harold Oram attended this meeting, as he did another in Washington on February 26, 1954. (According to *Newsweek,* the Oram firm once handled the public relations work in the United States for Vietnam during an undisclosed six-year period prior to 1962.) [44] There are virtually no references to Oram after The Committee *for* One Million went into "hibernation" in the summer of 1954 and before The Committee *of* One Million got underway early in 1955. Another "consultative" participant at the December 30 meeting was Dr. Garside, joining Judd, Liebman, Oram, Ambassador Grew, and, by both proxy and through the telephone, Governor Edison. Liebman was the first to report on the campaign's progress. Over 180,000 petition forms had been distributed, approximately 100,000 signatures received, $22,000 contributed, and $17,000 disbursed. Although an indebtedness of approximately $7,500 and a deficit of $2,500 existed, the campaign was "still gathering momentum," and should "be continued and expanded until every possible source of signatures and publicity were utilized."

Concerning Dr. Judd's "off-the-record" remarks about his recently concluded (December 17, 1953) congressional "Special Study Mission to Southeast Asia and the Pacific," the minutes read:

> His findings in that area of the world convinced him that the campaign of The Committee For One Million was of paramount importance and should be continued for its great moral support to our friends in the Far East. *He also stressed that it would be of value if a full scale campaign were in ef-*

fect when the question of the admission of Communist China is brought before the United Nations—probably in March. [45] (Italics added)

(The Committee Print of the "Special Study Mission's" report, dated January 29, 1954, includes Judd's referral letter to Foreign Affairs Committee Chairman Chiperfield, dated February 1, 1954. Hence it would appear that Dr. Judd's "off-the-record" report during this steering committee meeting of The Committee for One Million probably preceded presentation of the official "Special Study Mission's" findings to Judd's congressional colleagues.) [46]

At this point in the meeting, "Those present were in full agreement with Dr. Judd and Mr. Liebman." Treasurer Edison (whether by proxy or telephone is not indicated) next reported on the difficulties of gaining adequate finances, estimating that an "expanded campaign" would cost approximately $7,500 per month. If such funds could be raised, he wanted to continue.

> Mr. Harold L. Oram, whose organization is managing the campaign, stated that his experience showed that it would be possible to raise the necessary financing to cover all costs, in addition to taking full advantage of the public's interest in the issue in the actual gathering of the signatures. The Committee agreed on this basis to continue the life of the Committee For One Million on a month-to-month basis, *aiming at a full completion of the effort sometime in March.* [47] (Italics added)

The final item in the minutes, as previously quoted, mentioned the decision to discontinue Dr. de Rochefort's services and thanked him for his "splendid work."

Campaigning for Signatures

The Committee's first office on 44th Street opened on October 26, 1953, four days after the petition its originators had counted on to launch the national publicity campaign was presented to President Eisenhower. Two weeks later, on November 5, an announcement on the group's new letterhead (the one erroneously listing Warren R. Austin as chairman instead of honorary chairman) was sent to the original 210 pe-

tition signers. It noted that the undersigned (Edison, Grew, Judd, Mc-
Cormack, Smith, Sparkman) had formed The Committee for One Million in order to obtain "upwards of one million signatures to the petition
for presentation to the President." [48] This step was taken, the letter
explained, to mobilize public support while interest was high. Response
to the story of the petition, the letter continued, had resulted in widespread press coverage throughout the country. Hundreds of requests for
petitions were being received. A minimum $50,000 was required to put
together an effective campaign. Contributions were needed from those
who wished to add financial support to their "invaluable moral support."

Some idea of how the Committee turned to the task of generating
national publicity follows.

As President Eisenhower had been the publicity catalyst for launching The Committee for One Million, former President Hoover, a Committee sponsor, would play a similar role in the quest for public signatures.

Before the Hoover publicity appeal was initiated, letters were sent
by John D. Venable, Governor Edison's business associate (Assistant to
the Chairman of the Board, Thomas A. Edison Company), to numerous
businessmen and others, informing them of Governor Edison's current
activities on behalf of the Committee and soliciting support.[49] Edison
himself wrote many appeals for funds and publicity.[50] On January 22,
letters signed by Edison and enclosing a statement by President Hoover
were mailed to publishers and newsmen across the country. "Dear Colonel McCormick," one began,

> Former President Herbert Hoover has made the statement enclosed
> for release Monday, January 25, which I felt would be of especial interest
> to you and the Chicago *Tribune* in view of the vital importance of the sub-
> ject.
>
> My personal view is that there is no more important issue before the
> American people today than this question of admitting or not admitting
> Communist China to the United Nations. If international pressures and the
> campaign now being waged in this country in favor of admission should
> succeed in sabotaging the avowed policy of the United States to keep

them out, I believe the free world, so-called, would be about washed up.
. . . In this country the people would be so outraged that they would rise
up and throw the United Nations and all its works into the ocean.

This Petition is not just another petition. It is rather a device by
which the American people can speak forcefully and unequivocally to the
other peoples of the world, to their governments, and in support of our
own government's position.

Timing is important. They must speak *now* before the die is cast and
the damage is done.

Whatever assistance the *Tribune* could give, the letter closed, "would
be tremendously helpful." [51]

On release day, January 25, the *New York Times* ran a three-
paragraph story on page three under the headlines: **"Drive Against Red
China** Hoover Asks Signatures to Plea to Bar Nation From U.N." The
article reported that Hoover had asked every American to join the petition campaign and had opposed admission of the Communist Chinese
from the day they conquered China. The petition-signing campaign was
being conducted, said the story, by The Committee for One Million,
headed by former Ambassador Warren Austin. (Untrue, as noted; Austin was a figurehead.)

One publisher receiving the Edison appeal, Jack R. Howard, President of Scripps-Howard Newspapers, replied to Edison on January 27:
The Committee could count on the continued support of his newspapers.[52] To follow-up Howard's reply and develop a publicity story for
the Scripps-Howard chain, the Committee sent him a letter signed by
Mrs. Ralph (Nora) de Toledano, who worked on Committee publicity
projects early in the campaign.[53] Her letter offered several publicity
angles to approach the story. One sought to emphasize the emotional involvement of people, proposing a story about a POW's mother who had
collected several thousand signatures. Another was about a young boy
of thirteen who did not want to get killed later in a war and thus was
circulating the petition.

Another letter from Nora de Toledano went to William Randolph
Hearst Jr., thanking the publisher for giving such wonderful support to
the petition campaign.[54] Several months later, prior to public announce-

ment of the millionth signature, Edison got a letter from Hearst, saying that he would publish an editorial and a coupon in all papers around the theme "Let's get the million signatures to show Mr. Churchill and Mr.· Eden how we here in America feel." [55]

Pierre Huss, an INS reporter, approached the Committee, according to a draft letter prepared for Charles Edison's signature by Mrs. de Toledano, with a publicity idea: a signed article by Warren Austin critically discussing the arguments against Communist China's admission to the United Nations.[56] Coming from Austin, the draft continued, the article would be deeply significant. Handwritten marginal notes on de Toledano's January 26 memo to Edison accompanying the draft indicate that Edison instead telephoned Austin, that Austin agreed to write the article if Huss first would write him with the request, mentioning what points to emphasize.[57]

Another attempt to capitalize on President Hoover's name started with an item in the March 29 "Periscope" section in *Newsweek:* Onetime Republican presidential candidate Alf Landon "had taken on the Republican Party's elder statesman, Herbert Hoover, in a fight over foreign policy." [58] Landon was speaking against the petition drive, the story added, because he felt the President "should have a free rein in the field of diplomacy."

That same day, Edison dispatched a letter to Hoover and a suggested reply from Hoover to the magazine. *Newsweek* had given the Committee "the silent treatment," Edison said, so the reply letter had a twofold purpose: To get Hoover off the hook in a matter he may not want to be involved in and to get the magazine to mention The Committee for One Million.[59]

The Liebman Collection is short on publicity materials for this developmental period of The Committee for One Million. (Liebman did not start his own firm until 1958 and thus probably did not bring with him from the Oram firm all the Committee-related materials for the 1953–1958 period.) A quick survey of the *New York Times,* however, reveals some of the publicity pegs used during the formative period. Stories mentioning the Committee began with a November 27, 1953, editorial supporting the signature campaign (to which Alfred Kohlberg had expressed reservations) and continued with stories on January 25 (the Herbert Hoover appeal for signatures), February 22, March 17, April 9, June 25, and July 9.

The February story, under the headline, **"Mayor Appeals On China,"** a three-paragraph item on page 8, said that Mayor Robert Wagner, in a Washington's birthday proclamation, had urged all residents to sign the Committee's petition. It added that the New York City Council had adopted a resolution calling on residents to sign the petition. In March, the page 22 story was pegged to Charles Edison's announcement that 500,000 signatures had been obtained. Three of Edison's points were included in the item: that admission of Communist China would be an indication the U.S. was not in a position to enforce its policies; that admission was the most vital part of Russia's plan for world domination; and that admission would discourage Asian friends of the free world and would wreck the United Nations.

A "whispering campaign" to sabotage the Committee's goal of a million signatures was the *Times*'s lead on April 9 for a page 12 story reporting Marvin Liebman's expectations for receiving the millionth signature by April 26, which coincided with the convening of the upcoming peace conference in Geneva.

The committee made page 2 of the *Times* on June 25 in a three-paragraph story telling of its telegram to President Eisenhower urging him to seek an expression of U.S.-British unity on the admission question from visiting Prime Minister Winston Churchill and Foreign Secretary Anthony Eden. The telegram itself produced a reply to Edison from Presidential assistant Sherman Adams.[60]

Finally, a story in the *Times* of July 9 reported on a telegram sent to the President by Edison and Judd on behalf of the Committee. The message had endorsed the chief executive's stand, taken at a July 7 news conference, against the admission of Communist China to the United Nations. The telegram added that the Committee collected its millionth signature at 3:56 P.M. on July 6, although the story in the *Times* failed to mention the point.[61] (A pamphlet published some years later by The Committee of One Million said that receipt of the millionth signature was announced on July 17, four days before the Geneva armistice agreements were signed on July 21.) [62]

4

"Watchdog" Over the Geneva Conference

Early in 1954 the Committee altered its tactics. Less than three months after Nicholas de Rochefort testified in executive session before Walter Judd's congressional panel, the Committee's public campaign for a million signatures had been launched by using President Eisenhower as a publicity peg. Its organizational and fund-raising routines quickly established, the new group soon broadened its China policy interests beyond the United Nations question. The main purpose of this chapter is to show how this came about, how the Committee perceived the administration's developing China policy and acted on these perceptions.

The Policy Background

Two of the earliest dated documents among the Pentagon Papers throw a revealing light on underlying China policy assumptions during the formative period of The Committee for One Million. Large-scale Chinese Communist military intervention in Southeast Asia, for example, was felt to be a danger "inherent in the existence of a hostile and aggressive Communist China" in the final year of the Truman administration, according to a 1952 National Security Council policy statement.[1] An overt attack by the Chinese Communists should be "vigorously opposed." Likewise, to prevent the loss of Indochina in the event of an overt Chinese Communist attack, one recommendation (among many) was the utilization, "as desirable and feasible, of anti-Communist Chinese forces, including Chinese Nationalist forces in military operations in Southeast Asia, Korea, or China proper." Later, in

August 1953 (immediately following de Rochefort's testimony), the National Security Council decided that any negotiated settlement in Indochina would mean the eventual loss to Communism of the whole of Southeast Asia. Moreover, the "loss of Indochina would be critical to the security of the U.S." This decision was updated in January 1954 in a NSC paper approved by President Eisenhower. "The domino theory and the assumptions behind it were never questioned," the *Times* quoted from the Pentagon study of the Eisenhower years. "The result was that the Government's internal debate usually centered more on matters of military feasibility than on questions of basic national interests," the newspaper added.[2]

Meanwhile, following the Korean armistice—as diplomats sought to convene a political conference on Korea—intensification of the war between the Vietminh and the French in Indochina prompted a meeting of the President's Special Committee on Indochina to consider urgent French requests for military aid. The meeting was held on January 29, 1954, its recommendations for assisting the French passed along the next day in a memorandum by Brigadier General Charles H. Bonesteel 3d.[3] Already, the administration had focused public attention on the question of aiding the French military effort. The date was January 12. Secretary of State Dulles' memorable "massive retaliation" challenge to the Communist world also included this warning to the People's Republic of China: "I have said in relation to Indochina that, if there were open Red Chinese aggression there, that would have grave consequences which might not be confined to Indochina."[4]

Within a day or two of these somber words, the *Department of State Bulletin* published the Eisenhower administration's first exclusive statement on U.S. China policy, "China in the Shadow of Communism," by Walter P. McConaughy, then Director of the Office of Chinese Affairs.[5] Aside from its timing, the article was noteworthy for the rhetoric used both to defend the Chinese Nationalist government on Formosa and to denigrate the People's Republic.

Support for the Nationalist government was forcefully advocated. There was even "reason to hope that the government at Taipei will continue to grow in strength, in devotion to the cardinal principles of democracy, and in international prestige." McConaughy acknowledged and deplored "intemperate abuse heaped on the Chinese Government and its head," abuse based "on shortcomings which are no longer relevant." Still, "If there was ever any excuse for overlooking the faults of the enemy and magnifying the alleged faults of the friend, it abruptly ended in November 1950 when the Chinese Communists without warning or warrant hurled their forces against the U.N. defenders of Korea. . . . There is no doubt that the overwhelming majority of the American people do see this issue in proper perspective."

The case against recognition of the Chinese government on the mainland was argued on grounds of international law based on four "generally accepted criteria" of acceptance. The Chinese Communists were "subservient to Moscow and international communism" and therefore did not meet the criterion of "sovereign independence"; they imposed "an alien minority rule by force and falsification on an intimidated, isolated and misinformed populace," and so were not of "truly representative character"; they flouted all Chinese treaty obligations, all U.N. Charter principles, all clauses "in any reasonable formulation of human and property rights for aliens," hence they failed to accept inherited and international treaty and other obligations. Indeed, the only criterion met, "perhaps the least essential of the four," was the one governing effective control of territory.

Turning to "practical grounds," the case against recognition was equally strong. Here McConaughy broke new "psychological" ground:

> Recognition has assumed a political and psychological significance which is new. It has become a symbol. Recognition in this case would mean in the eyes of millions, especially in Asia, accommodation, and reconcilement.
>
> Nonrecognition means refusal to accept the Communist triumph as definitive. It means to many that the will to resist Communist expansion is alive. . . .
>
> Some may be unable to see why the recognition issue should signify all this; but the fact is that it does to many Asians, including numbers who are "on the fence." Many an Asian has told me that American nonrecognition of the Communist regime in Peiping has had much to do with checking the impetus of the Communist advance in Asia.

Beyond the legal, political, and psychological arguments, there were other considerations as well. First, recognition "would be an unthinkable betrayal of the Chinese Government and its people on Formosa and likewise a grave disservice to the mass of Chinese people on the mainland suffering under Communist dictatorship." Also, the Communists were "becoming increasingly aware of the immense political and psychological advantages, as well as the parliamentary advantages in the United Nations." As a result, "we are beginning to see a series of maneuvers out of Moscow and Peiping designed to force the general international acceptance of the Mao Tse-tung regime as the legitimate government of China." The maneuvers were not disclosed; but "this endeavor must be resisted." Next, the current negotiations in Korea were cited as an example of "the arrogant, incorrigible, unyielding position taken by the Chinese Communist mouthpieces wherever they appear at a conference" and of the difficulty "to negotiate even the simplest matter with them." In sum, there was "nothing to be gained from diplomatic relations with such a regime, which believes in the use of diplomacy as a weapon of propaganda and subversion rather than as a means of constructive diplomatic intercourse."

McConaughy said the Korean armistice did not change matters: "Even the aggression in Korea cannot be considered as terminated merely by an armistice. In the absence of a satisfactory settlement in a political conference, the Korean issue remains open." He concluded "that the U.S. ban on trade, shipping, and financial relations with Communist China must be maintained, in the absence of a fundamental change in the posture, the composition and the essential orientation of the regime." The objectives of this policy were clearly spelled out:

> By maintaining a policy of pressure and diplomatic isolation we can at least slow the growth of the war-making potential of Communist China and retard the consolidation of its diplomatic position. A relationship of dependence on the senior partner as complete as we can make it will not make the embrace any more congenial for either the Soviet senior partner or the Chinese Communist junior partner.

The article closed on a note of irreconcilable hostility:

It is not pleasant to have to report that nothing better than a prolonged period of tension and uncertainty may be in store for us. It is cold comfort to say that the prospects of checkmating any further encroachments of the opposition in the Far East are slowly improving . . .

. . . But let us take comfort in the assurance that we now know the nature of the enemy . . . and in the conviction that any system so violative of all the things mankind holds most dear must veritably carry within itself the seeds of its own ultimate dissolution.

Such was the administration's first major statement solely devoted to China policy.

On February 18, 1954, the Big Four Foreign Ministers, meeting in Berlin, agreed on a Far Eastern peace parley to convene on April 26 in Geneva. In all, seventeen nations, including the People's Republic, would participate in discussions concerning both Korea and Indochina. Inclusion of the mainland Chinese in a proposed five-power conference had been rejected by Dulles on January 25 when the foreign ministers first met.[6] Thus the Berlin communiqué, reflecting accommodation to a larger conference, said the upcoming Geneva meetings would not "imply diplomatic recognition in any case where it has not already been accorded."

Nonetheless, the Geneva Conference became the Committee's first genuine crisis—internal as well as external.

Setting Committee Policy

Four days after the announcement from Berlin, two steering committee members, Charles Edison and John W. McCormack, circulated a memorandum asking concurrence in the issuance of a statement expressing "apprehension" about the decision to confer with Peking:

Any such meeting with Communist China must be studied realistically. *In effect it appears to afford a degree of recognition to Communist China* that has heretofore been denied by this country. . . . At the same time that Secretary Dulles, less than three weeks ago, refused demands for such a meeting, French Foreign Minister George Bidault, supporting Mr. Dulles' refusal, noted that China was still killing French soldiers in Indo-China.[7]

Recipients were asked to reply by telegram if agreeable. Reaction was cool. Retired State Department officer Stanley K. Hornbeck regretted that he could not join in the statement at that particular moment:

> I believe that issuance at this time of a statement adding interpretation and seeming to suggest doubt regarding the integrity and skill of the (hard-put-it) negotiators would do more harm than good.[8]

A summary of the poll's results showed a mixture of apathy and uncertainty about the Committee's course of action. Approximately 250 people were polled, according to a Liebman memo, but only 89 (35.6 percent) replied.[9] Sixty-nine people approved the statement; several thought it not strong enough. Eight disapproved strongly. Seven generally agreed but chose not to go on record for one reason or another. Four were undecided. The most significant result of the Edison/McCormack memo was the calling of a steering committee meeting on the Friday after the Monday on which the memo had been mailed.

Two versions of minutes from this meeting, held on Capitol Hill and chaired by Governor Edison, are available: a draft ending with a typewritten "Marvin Liebman," and a shorter version signed by hand, "Marvin Liebman." [10] Both documents are instructive. The draft troubled over the making of committee policy (as prompted by the Edison/McCormack memo), while the Liebman-signed document focused on the substance of committee policy vis-à-vis the upcoming meetings. The opening language of the draft downplayed the importance of the Edison/McCormack memo, Edison reported as defining the purpose of the meeting to establish a policy line and give the staff authorization to turn out publicity materials without the necessity for frequent steering committee meetings. In the "Marvin Liebman" version no mention was made of the Edison/McCormack memo. Instead, Edison is reported to have noted that problems caused by the Berlin decision on Geneva meant the Committee had to establish a policy line. Accordingly, agreement was reached to extend the life of the group at least through the Geneva Conference and to pursue the goal of the million signatures, accenting publicity efforts toward emphasizing the Committee's role as a "watchdog."

With the Committee given life through the Geneva Conference, five specific "areas of operation" would guide the "watchdog" role, according to the Liebman-signed document. In essence, the guidelines for future policy announcements concerned ways to maximize support for Dulles' arguments while minimizing the weakness of his position on the Geneva gathering. The first point called for emphasis and re-emphasis of the government's official opposition to recognition of the Peking regime, i.e., simply repeating Secretary Dulles' statements that the Geneva Conference did not imply recognition and that he adhered to non-recognition and non-admission without compromise. Another point made clear that Dulles himself should not be attacked. Yet statements warning of perils inherent in the Geneva Conference could be publicized so long as the Committee's basic policy of reiterating the Government's official non-admission and non-recognition China policy was main-tained. Also, the minutes addressed the practical problems posed by release of the Edison/McCormack memo. Thereafter, statements on the Geneva Conference issued in the name of the steering committee would be submitted in advance for approval by individual members. Substan-tial agreement on controversial material would be required.

Two other points (agreed to, it should be noted, by two United States Senators and two Congressmen) established policy for statements by individual members of the steering committee and other Committee members. Statements which fell within the first guideline (i.e., empha-sizing the government's official position, etc.) could be released in the name of the Committee. (This decision, although applicable to the im-mediate circumstances, lingered on, causing internal Committee prob-lems in later years. Its effect enhanced Liebman's authority over all publicity and promotional matters.) Additionally, if any member of the steering committee wanted to speak for himself outside the policy line, he was free to act without mentioning the Committee.

Liebman's personally signed minutes merely enumerated the above decisions. But the draft offered insights to the steering committee dis-cussion. For example, Senator Smith, a close friend of John Foster Dul-les, insisted on prior consultation before any Committee statements were issued. Calling attention to his role as chairman of the subcommittee on the Far East (of the Senate Foreign Relations Committee), he noted the possible embarrassment to him of statements released without his knowledge. Congressman McCormack, the only other legislator to make the same point, according to the draft, said that he felt the necessity above all for substantial unanimity on the Committee. The Minority Whip said that measures should not be carried through by majority vote but rather by a meeting of minds.

On the Geneva problem, Dr. Judd said that the Edison/McCormack statement did not jibe with the facts on one significant point: the Geneva Conference did not constitute a meeting of the Big Five powers, including Communist China, but only the Big Four, who would listen to the Communist Chinese before deciding anything—*without* their participation. Dulles would have been placed in an untenable situation, added Judd, had he refused to talk with the Big Four about Asian problems. Agreeing, Ambassador Grew said it was imperative that Dulles be supported by the Committee in his effort to maintain Allied unity. Similarly, Senator Sparkman pointed out the Committee's most effective contribution was to reaffirm support for Dulles' statement that the Chinese Communists would not be admitted to the United Nations. The Alabaman wanted to make the Secretary of State a leader in the fight against admission through the repeated use of Dulles' own publicly expressed statements.

All members of the steering committee but Senator Smith were explicitly on record in the draft as favoring the continuance of the Committee. McCormack is reported to have said that to break up the Committee at that point would bring about unfortunate public repercussions. The Committee should continue, he felt, through the Geneva Conference—"at least through the Geneva Conference," the draft said in summarizing the views of Judd, Grew, and Sparkman.

As reported in the draft, Governor Edison's summation noted that the Edison/McMormack memo would not be issued. Affirming the Committee's broad policy line to back up Dulles' stand against P.R.C. admission to the United Nations, Edison is said to have affirmed that the one million signatures of American signers to the petition would be given to the Secretary of State before his flight to Geneva. Finally, the draft included Harold L. Oram's assessment of the Committee's financial situation. In sum: the group had started with no funds and no angels. Enough public interest had been generated to sustain reasonable activity levels. There was a $5,000 or $6,000 deficit, but the programs for the next couple of months would be taken care of by public contributions. The average contribution, however, was very small. The Committee merited no tax exemption. Thus the $38,000 raised till then comprised many small contributions. None exceeded $1,000, of which there were only three.

With the Edison/McCormack approach to the Geneva Conference rejected by the steering committee, Liebman dispatched a mailing to initial petition signers and other friends summarizing results both of the February 22 poll and the steering committee's decisions.[11] He acknowledged that the original intentions of the group had been to wind up activities by March 15, but that the Berlin decisions on Geneva and the subsequent threat of French concessions in Indochina had prompted a policy meeting. About 500,000 signatures were in hand, he reported, with perhaps that many not yet turned in; but the petitions would continue to circulate. The Committee felt, Liebman concluded, that the mere accumulation of signatures was not enough. The signatures proved that the American people would not tolerate concessions toward the People's Republic. Communists could not bully or shoot their way into the United Nations. The Committee would continue to act as a "watchdog."

How long that role would last Liebman did not say. But the Committee's original role clearly had been changed by the Big Four decision in Berlin to convene a conference on Asian problems.

Implementing Policy: Congressional Roles

After the steering committee's decision to make Dulles, through his own public statements, the leader in the fight against UN admission for the mainland Chinese, some supporters of the Committee in the second session of the 83rd Congress became more vocal.

One of the 210 initial signers of the original petition was Senator Ralph Flanders (R., Vt.), a 74-year-old former machine-tool industry executive whose Senate committee assignments included armed services and finance. Senator Flanders, as an initial signer, presumably had received a copy of the February 22 Edison/McCormack memo. Regardless, the following day, February 23, he became the first senator to make a direct appeal to his colleagues on the Senate floor to join the Committee. Warning of "strong influences at work in this country looking to the recognition of Communist China," Flanders answered a colleague's suspicion that the public was being deliberately softened up for recognition: "I suggest that the Senator from Nevada [George W. Malone, R., Nev.] and I, and everyone else so minded, join the Committee of (sic) One Million, which has hundreds of thousands of signatories already and see if we cannot stem the undertow . . . at work." Flanders then inserted in the *Record* an article copyrighted by the International News Service, "Why I Am Opposed to Recognition of Red China," by Ambassador Joseph C. Grew, which mentioned the Committee and its petition drive.[12]

Among the first participants at the February 26 steering committee meeting to discuss the Geneva Conference on the floor of Congress were Senator H. Alexander Smith and Representative John W. McCormack. Both spoke on March 3. Smith, the New Jersey lawyer, onetime lecturer at Princeton's Department of Politics, and future delegate to the Ninth Session of the General Assembly of the United Nations, took "strong exception" to a March 2 column by Walter Lippmann entitled "A Booby Trap for Geneva." The columnist had written that "Sen. Knowland and his friends," by insisting on an "absolute and unconditional refusal to admit Red China to the U.N.," would make it easier for the People's Republic "to offer terms that are more attractive to Europe and to Asia than they would, in fact, be willing to agree to." Therefore, "if there are no conditions under which we will ever agree to the Red Chinese being admitted to the U.N., then how can Secretary Dulles compel them to disclose their real conditions for peace in Indochina?"[13]

Smith denied that Knowland " 'and his friends' . . . are attempting to deprive Secretary Dulles of his 'negotiable position' at the Geneva Conference . . . and that the American position [on the admission

question] should be 'relative and conditional.' '' Dulles had ''no intention or desire,'' Smith said, ''to hold forth admission of Communist
China to the United Nations as an inducement to gain concessions from
the Soviet Union or Red China. This I state categorically,'' he added.
Moreover, Dulles himself had insisted the Berlin communiqué include
the caveat that Geneva would not imply diplomatic recognition. Negotiation on the admission issue, Smith declared, ''or the admission that
this issue was negotiable would lose us almost as much as actual admission. Face, Mr. President, remains of incalculable importance in the Far
East.''

At the other end of Capitol Hill, meanwhile, Representative Mc-
Cormack argued that Geneva was a step forward for the Chinese Communists (a ''degree of recognition,'' said the Edison/McCormack
memo) and placed the United States in a defensive position. Dr. Judd
disagreed, as he had at the February 26 meeting. ''Geneva is merely a
resumption of Panmunjom under conditions less favorable to the Communist side,'' he replied to McCormack, adding that to discuss the issue
with those waging the war does not constitute recognition.[14]

Preoccupation with the Geneva parley was not, of course, confined
to Committee activists in Congress. Among ten resolutions introduced
in the second session of the 83rd Congress expressing various degrees of
concern over these matters, only three were submitted by 'initial signers' of the Committee's petition.[15] One non-signer, Representative
Thomas J. Lane (D., Mass.), introduced a resolution suggesting ''that
the Chinese Communists are not entitled to and should not be recognized to represent China at the Geneva meeting on April 26, 1954.''
One Senate newcomer was ''somewhat apprehensive about Geneva''
and saw the meeting as ''a partial Soviet diplomatic victory since it will,
de facto, give a degree of recognition to the Chinese Communist
government.'' He was Mike Mansfield (D., Mont.), whose
March 22 speech on ''Geneva & Indochina'' needled his Republican
colleagues:

> The decision to meet with the Communists in Geneva was made by the
> administration solely on its own responsibility. There was no prior consul-

tation with Members of this side of the aisle. And judging by the reaction of . . . Mr. Knowland, when he heard the announcement of the conference, the other side of the aisle must also have been kept in the dark.[16]

Mansfield, whose name would begin to appear on The Committee Of One Million letterheads in 1955, said that Dulles faced the most difficult task of his career and needed encouragement and support.

During this period of close congressional attention to Geneva, the State Department regularly repeated the Government's position on a range of Far East questions related to Geneva. Between March 8 and August 23, no less than eleven speeches by the Secretary of State and other ranking Department spokesmen (not to mention news conference comments, articles, congressional testimony, etc.) were reprinted in the *Bulletin*. A chronological rundown of titles and authors is instructive: "Responsibilities of the U.S. in the Far East," by Walter S. Robertson, Assistant Secretary, Far Eastern Affairs; "Faith in the Future of China," by Robertson; "Significance of the Berlin Conference," by Walter P. McConaughy, Director, Office of Chinese Affairs; "The Threat of a Red Asia," by Secretary Dulles; "Considerations Underlying U.S.-China Policy," by Edwin W. Martin, Deputy Director, Office of Chinese Affairs; "Present United States Policy Toward China," by Alfred le Sesne Jenkins, Officer in Charge, Chinese Political Affairs; "The United Nations Record of Accomplishment," by Ambassador to the United Nations, Henry Cabot Lodge Jr.; "The Issues at Geneva," by Dulles; "The United States and a Divided China," by Jenkins; "Security in the Pacific," by Dulles; and "Communist Tactics in the Far East," by Robertson.[17]

The Department also was attempting, through these speeches, to allay the fears, congressional and otherwise, of a softening of American policy toward the People's Republic as a result of Geneva. For example, the first Jenkins speech, timed for publication on April 26, the day the talks convened, recited administration indictments against the Chinese government on the mainland. That the regime: did not represent the "will of the people it controls"; was dedicated (though a junior partner) "to the proposition of world Communist revolution under the leadership of the [Soviet Union]''; followed ''no recognized standards of international conduct''; and was ''a ruthless police state with all that that implies.'' For these reasons, among others,

> . . . it is hardly surprising that the firm policy of the [U.S.] is one of strong opposition to the Chinese Communist regime. We cannot recognize this regime, and we shall continue vigorously to oppose attempts to accept it in any United Nations organization as representing the Chinese people.[18]

Recognition and acceptance of the People's Republic would weaken the will of other Asians to resist Communist expansion, Jenkins continued. Nor was it a question of ''recognizing reality'': ''We do recognize reality, and much of it we do not like. But it is not in the American tradition to confuse the real with the immutable. . . .''

Political policy thus covered, Jenkins spelled out economic policy—in short, ''total embargo against Communist China''—before broaching Geneva. The United States had been committed since the Korean armistice of July 1953 to seek a ''Korean Political Conference.'' Although the Berlin conference ''laid plans for a multipower conference at Geneva . . . ,'' nevertheless:

> This will not be, as the Communists are claiming, a five-power conference. Communist China, far from attending the conference as a great power, *will not in our view even attend as a government.* . . .
>
> The time, place, and composition of the Korean Political Conference are entirely as we wanted. We do not fear this conference. . . .
>
> We will not be prepared at Geneva to allow the aggressors to achieve at the conference table what they failed to achieve in battle. This applies not only to territorial considerations but to any 'deal' which would . . . trade a United Nations seat and an end to the trade controls for an agreement by Communist China to stop supplying the Viet Minh . . .
>
> . . . [W]e do not contemplate any action at Geneva or anywhere else which would damage the cause of the Government of the Republic of China.[19]

By coincidence, the day this speech was published in the *Bulletin,* The Committee for One Million sent a cablegram, signed by Charles

Edison, to Secretary of State Dulles in Geneva, announcing that 833,867 Americans had signed the petition as of that day.[20] The message congratulated and upheld the Secretary of State "in his steadfast determination to resist any and all attempts to legalize or accept as representative the Communist dictatorship imposed by force and violence on the peoples of the Chinese mainland."

About this time, an interesting exchange of letters between a Committee worker and Secretary Dulles occurred. The letters represent the earliest dated Committee-related materials supplied to me by the State Department, which claims to have searched its files for all documents about the Committee, regardless of classification, and to have furnished all located documents.[21] Accordingly, a letter dated June 16, 1954 reached Dulles from W. Reginald (Rex) Wheeler, who identified himself as a member of a group collecting signatures for the "Committee of (sic) One Million," told a story about a cobbler who refused to sign the petition (one of the cobbler's assistants later told Wheeler the man was a member of the Communist Party), and expressed the hope that the government would resist British pressures to admit Red China to the United Nations.[22] Dulles replied on June 28, 1954, acknowledging the Committee's petition campaign, expressing the "firm view" of the government that world order would not be served by admitting to the United Nations

> a regime which is a convicted aggressor, which has not purged itself of that aggression, and which continues to promote the use of force in violation of the principles of the United Nations. *I have made this policy clear to other friendly governments beyond the possibility of any misunderstanding, but you may be sure that I will reiterate it whenever the occasion requires.*[23]

The State Department's efforts to reassure various publics on the steadfastness of American Far East policy did not, however, reduce congressional pressure. One of the more dramatic examples made national headlines on July 1 when Senator Knowland told his colleagues "the time has come for the agonizing reappraisal of our foreign policy which has previously been mentioned by our Secretary of State." The Committee supporter said he would resign his majority leadership in the

Senate the day Communist China was voted into the United Nations. Then he would devote his full efforts to terminating U.S. membership and financial support for the world organization. Later that day, referring to the Knowland "ultimatum," Senator Pat McCarran (D., Nev.), commended the majority leader's statement and offered a joint resolution (S. J.Res. 171), proposing that the United States terminate its membership in the United Nations if Communist China were admitted. Though confident that Dulles himself "does not personally favor letting the Chinese Communists into the United Nations," McCarran feared that "Mr. Dulles will not demonstrate the courage of his convictions on this point if too many others in the administration take a different viewpoint." [24]

The next day, July 2, Senate Minority Leader Lyndon B. Johnson (D., Tex.), also commended Knowland, saying the American people would refuse to support the United Nations "if Communist China shoots its way into membership" (a phrase possibly borrowed by LBJ; see p. 110). The future President stopped short of advocating withdrawal in the event. Two senators disagreed. Senator Herbert Lehman (D., N.Y.), argued against admission of the People's Republic to the United Nations but said his opposition did not mean the United States should withdraw if the mainland Chinese were allowed in "over our objections." Oregon's Independent, Wayne Morse, concurred, admitting that UN entry for the mainland Chinese would be a "terrible mistake" but that Americans would not favor withdrawal once they understood the facts.[25]

One Committee petition-signer spoke against U.S. withdrawal from the United Nations in the event of P.R.C. admission—Senator Guy Gillette (D., Ia.). During a July 8 speech in which he acknowledged his Committee membership and lauded the group's efforts ("It clearly represents a formidable public opinion in this country, one which no foreign government should underestimate"), the 75-year-old lawyer from Cherokee, Ia., gave his reasons for opposing P.R.C. membership but attacked the withdrawal proposal as

> unjustified . . . a dangerous proposition . . . almost peurile in its thoughtless petulance. . . .

In simplest terms, what this proposal means is the abandonment of the United Nations to the other great power belonging to it, the Soviet Union. It means the elimination of any American influence in the councils of the only existing world organization.[26]

That same day, July 8, Senator Flanders told his Senate colleagues he had written Ambassador Warren R. Austin (his predecessor in the Senate) and Ambassador Joseph C. Grew in an effort to get the Committee to issue "some such statement as the one that was made by the Republican floor leader, and was seconded by the Democratic floor leader, expressing legislative opposition to admission of Red China to the United Nations." But, he added, Austin and Grew had been skeptical about too much pressure: "If this were to be tied in with a statement that it would be difficult to get appropriations from the Congress for the United Nations if Red China were to be admitted, these esteemed elder statesmen felt that that would be in the nature of a threat, and would be an unwise thing to do." [27]

The House vote on H. Res. 627, which reiterated House opposition to seating the People's Republic in the United Nations, followed a debate on July 15. Although a handful of congressmen, including Representative McCormack, said the resolution did not go far enough, it passed, overwhelmingly, 381 to 0, 53 not voting.[28]

Final Senate action on the UN seating issue came on July 29, several days after debate over an incident in which two U.S. aircraft reportedly shot down two P.R.C. propeller-type planes off the China coast after the Chinese had destroyed an airplane belonging to Cathay Pacific Airlines. An amendment to the 1954 Mutual Security Act (not McCarran's S. J.Res. 171) provided the final instrument for voting. Although the amendment simply reiterated opposition to the seating of the Peking regime in the United Nations, it also stated that in the event of such entry, the President was "requested" to inform Congress of the implications of this fact, "together with any recommendations which he may have with respect to the matter." At Knowland's urging, a separate vote on the amendment was taken. Result: 91 yeas, zero nays, five not voting.[29]

"Hibernation"

On May 1st the Committee began preparations to disband the head-quarters, Marvin Liebman wrote to the steering committee and others on May 19, 1954.[30] The organization, practically speaking, was in "hibernation." If the situation demanded, however, it was prepared to return to action. Personally, Liebman was ready to remain in business, the memorandum made clear. It began with a report on the conclusion of the signature campaign and the Committee's effort to collect every signature in time for the Geneva Conference. The purpose, he said, was to maximize the signatures available in case they had to be used to back up the Committee's point of view. The memorandum reported the text of Edison's cablegram sent to Dulles in Geneva. It also provided some details on the moving of files, storing of petitions, signature counting, handling of correspondence, and the status of finances (through May 14, 1954, $61,568 had been received, $57,612 disbursed). Petition circula-tion activities around the country, it disclosed, were continuing—in par-ticular, a drive by various AFL unions and locals in response to an edi-torial circulated by the AFL News Service, plus a notable Boston effort anticipating 100,000 signatures and led by Colonel W. Bruce Pirnie.

A paragraph subheaded "Continuing Organization" outlined Lieb-man's personal views about the Committee's value, gave his conception of the group's political ideology, and suggested the need for a "continu-ing operation."

Many people wanted the Committee to continue, Liebman said, not merely to express opposition to Communist China but to express its view on other political issues as well. Because the Committee repre-sented a broad cross-section of liberal and conservative opinion—neither the "isolationist right" nor "apologist left"—it was a vehicle for such expression. It would be an error, he argued, to give up six months of goodwill, contacts, and effective operation. He had discussed the possi-bility for continuation with Dr. Judd, Governor Edison, and Freder-ick C. McKee, as well as others.

Several weeks later Liebman again raised this question in a letter to Dr. Judd, with copies sent to Governor Edison, Representative McCormack, and Frederick C. McKee.[31] He wanted some advice and assistance and mentioned his previously stated ideas for an expanded Committee operation. Responses to his earlier memo had been favorable. He stressed the urgency of getting something started, saying the country had gigantic problems; a grassroots movement was needed to provide direction and support for the nation's leaders. Neither the Americans for Democratic Action (whose program seemed to be premised on the idea that getting rid of Senator Joseph McCarthy would perform some miracle) nor a group started in Chicago by Colonel McCormick, General Wood, and the old America First people (which seemed headed toward extreme isolationism and perhaps totalitarianism) was the answer. Liebman repeated his warning about the consequences of inaction. Anti-Communists like themselves who also believed in the need for international cooperation should take the lead to prevent irresponsible organizations from defeating their purpose. The Committee represented the beginnings of a constituency that would be wasteful to scrap at such a crucial time. He closed his appeal declaring his willingness to follow Judd's suggestions.

Judd's mid-year ideas, if any, about continuing the Committee do not appear in Liebman's files. Perhaps the energetic congressman from Minnesota was too preoccupied watching international diplomatic maneuvers, as the Geneva talks switched from Korean questions to the more immediate problems in Indochina. (As we shall see, at any rate, he did make certain that his personal views about Asian policy reached the Oval Office of the White House.) During this period of intense public and intra-governmental debate over the wisdom of American intervention in Indochina, proposals for bolstering the deteriorating French military situation were actively under consideration. As the Pentagon Papers reveal, on April 5, before the Geneva Conference got underway, a special committee in Washington recommended that U.S. policy should "accept nothing short of military victory in Indo-China," should try to obtain French support for this position, and, failing this, should actively oppose any negotiated settlement in Indochina. Toward the goal of achieving some type of coalition rescue effort in Southeast Asia, Secretary Dulles cabled Douglas Dillon, U.S. Ambassador to France, that the government was doing everything possible short of actual belligerency "to prepare public, Congressional and Constitutional basis for united action in Indo-China." A later Dulles cable to Under-Secretary of State Walter Bedell Smith directed him not to deal "with the delegates of the Chinese Communist regime, or any other regime not now diplomatically recognized by the United States, on any terms which imply political recognition or which concede to that regime any status other than that of a regime with which it is necessary to deal on a de facto basis in order to end aggression or the threat of aggression, and to obtain peace." [32]

On May 26, Chairman of the Joint Chiefs of Staff Admiral Arthur W. Radford wrote a memorandum to Secretary of Defense Charles E. Wilson, "Studies With Respect to Possible U.S. Action Regarding Indochina." Indochina was devoid of decisive military objectives from the American point of view, the Joint Chiefs believed, and the allocation of other than token U.S. forces would seriously divert limited U.S. capabilities. On the assumption of a Chinese Communist intervention, however, the Joint Chiefs foresaw, among other military operations, employing atomic weapons, "whenever advantageous," against "*selected military targets in Indochina and against those military targets in China, Hainan,* and other Communist-held offshore islands which are being used by the Communists in *direct support of their operations,* or which threaten the security of the U.S. and allied forces in the area." [33]

Dr. Judd's contribution to the flurry of events took place in late June, when British Prime Minister Winston Churchill was in Washington for talks with President Eisenhower. Sometime after Churchill's arrival, Judd apparently had a conversation with Eisenhower which resulted in his writing a seven-page memorandum to the President entitled "Defections in Viet-Nam." [34]

Overall, the intent of his argument seems to have been to warn the President against making any accommodations with the British or French to the detriment of "free Asia." Judd was not surprised that defections of Vietnamese troops (those helping the French, not the Vietminh) were taking place. He did not believe these defections proved a lack of patriotism or fighting will. In essence, he blamed the problem on France, as well as other Western powers, for not granting full independence to the Vietnamese who, he said, would have developed a government with the confidence and support of the people. American aid should have gone directly to the Vietnamese rather than through the French.

Judd quoted liberally from the findings of his December 1953 congressional study mission to Southeast Asia: Asian leaders understood the dangers of Communist aggression and the Communist Chinese menace. But they were forced to exercise caution and restraint because of the absence of a clear and firm policy on the part of the free world—including the United States. Uncertainty and irresolution in the West inhibited Asian leaders from standing up against Communist China. Free Asia, Judd said, was beginning to crumble because the Asian people knew the Communists were winning. The French should have used the Vietnam government in negotiations with the Vietminh both in Indochina and at Geneva instead of dealing directly with the Vietminh. Judd quoted from a speech he said he gave before Town Hall on March 4, 1946, which argued that American interests were not identical or parallel to the interests in Asia of Britain, Holland, and France:

> . . . I see no way out except that *we will stand by the democracies in Europe; we will not support their empires in Asia.* That is the right position. If our choice is between having on our side *in Asia* the old decadent Empires, or the hearts of the billion people who live there—then by all means let us have the hearts of the people. (Italics in original)

What he had said in 1946 was still true, Judd concluded. To check the deterioration in Asia, America always had to redeclare itself toward working for freedom of all people everywhere.

The President's secretary wrote Judd that Eisenhower had seen the memorandum.[35]

In "hibernation," debate over the Committee's future drifted away. The final 1954 document on the subject in Marvin Liebman's files is a copy of an August 3 letter from Congressman McCormack to Governor Edison suggesting that Edison earlier had solicited the Minority Whip's views. Apologizing for the delay in answering Edison's May 20 letter, McCormack said he was strongly inclined to agree with one of

Edison's own statements—i.e., that when the Committee had achieved its goal it should be wound up and any further use of its resources organized by some new or different group.[36]

Still, the "hibernation" was not total. The Committee resurged briefly in September to stage a rally at New York City's Town Hall welcoming five young Chinese ex-prisoners of war who had "refused to return to their homes in Red China and chose instead to join with the Free Chinese on Formosa." [37]

Eight days before the event, Marvin Liebman, the program chairman, as identified on letterhead of The Committee for One Million, sent a letter to President Eisenhower at the summer White House in Denver, requesting "a telegraphic message of greeting from yourself to the five anti-Communist returnees. We expect to read greetings from President Chiang and President Rhee." [38] Accompanying the letter, which also listed as sponsors the American Legion and the Veterans of Foreign Wars, was a promotional circular identifying eleven other participating organizations.[39] The rally would be chaired by former Ambassador Richard C. Patterson (an initial signer of the Committee's petition); its speakers would include Ambassador Grew, Congressman Judd, Reverend Daniel A. Poling (another initial signer), and a Colonel Harold Riegelman.[40] The President complied with Liebman's request. Walter S. Robertson, Assistant Secretary, Far Eastern Affairs, approved the sending of a message, at the same time declining an invitation to attend the rally, and one was drafted at the State Department for the President.[41] Eisenhower also sent the five visitors a letter thanking them for a "blood-stained flag symbolizing the victorious struggle for freedom made by you and the 14,000 brave men whom you represent." [42]

The rally, it should be noted, coincided with the UN General Assembly's consideration on September 21 of the Chinese seating question. An American resolution postponing debate for another year passed 43 to 11 with 16 abstentions.[43]

5

Emerging from "Hibernation"

Why did the Committee reorganize? Who provided the motivation, the funds, and the organizational initiative? What was the rationale for The Committee *of* One Million? Only three Committee-related documents deal directly with the resumption of its activities. Two other communications to President Eisenhower immediately preceding the Committee's reorganization—a letter from publisher Henry R. Luce and a telegram from Dr. Judd—offer additional insights on these questions. Before examining these materials, however, some background is necessary.

The Political Setting

Major national and Far Eastern developments affecting the perceptions of those who watched China policy politics in the United States took place between the Liebman-produced rally in September and the Committee's reorganizational conference at the home of Ambassador Joseph C. Grew in Washington D.C. on February 2, 1955.

Nationally, the mid-term elections in November saw the Democrats narrowly regain leadership of Congress: 48 to 47 with one Independent in the Senate; and 232 to 203 in the House. On its last day, December 2, the 83d Congress censured Senator Joseph McCarthy in the denouement of the protracted and divisive national controversy which swirled around the junior senator from Wisconsin after his slashing and irresponsible attacks on individuals and institutions.[1] The senator assailed President Eisenhower for congratulating the chairman of the Select Committee that investigated his behavior while at the same time urging patience "with the [Chinese] Communist hoodlums who at this very moment are torturing and brainwashing American uniformed men in Communist dungeons.'' [2] McCarthy's barb referred to the report in late November that eleven U.S. Air Force personnel and two "civilian" U.S. Army employees captured by the mainland Chinese during the Korean War, John T. Downey and Richard G. Fecteau, had been sentenced as spies to long prison terms by a military tribunal.[3] This announcement, in turn, had sparked a rapid-fire series of events which quickly returned China policy to front page headlines and led to a revived Committee. In the briefest fashion, the sequence of events ran as follows:

On November 15, intercollegiate debates on the recognition of Communist China were barred for West Point cadets and Annapolis midshipmen. On November 22 came the sentencing of the American airmen and "civilians" in the People's Republic. On November 27, Senator Knowland called for a naval blockade of the Chinese mainland until the Americans were released. On November 29, Dulles cautioned that a U.S. blockade would be an act of war, but on December 1 he said it was "certainly a possibility" if all peaceful means failed to get the airmen released.

On December 2, the United States and the Republic of China announced the signing of a mutual security pact for the defense of Formosa which did not encompass the Nationalist-held islands off the Chinese coast.[4] On December 10, the General Assembly of the United Nations adopted a resolution sponsored by the sixteen Korean War allies which accused the Chinese People's Republic of violating the armistice by jailing the American fliers and called on Secretary-General Dag Hammarskjöld to negotiate their release. On December 8, Prime Minister Chou En-lai said his government was determined to liberate Taiwan and threatened the United States with "grave consequences" if American forces were not withdrawn from Formosa. On December 15, these Chinese demands received the "full support" of the Soviet Union. On December 30, Hammarskjöld left UN headquarters in New York for Peking and, on January 10, announced that talks there had been useful. Also on January 10, the Chinese Nationalists reported that the Tachen Islands under their control, 200 miles north of Formosa, had been hit by large-scale P.R.C. air attacks.

On January 14, Hammarskjöld told newsmen that he had made no deals with the Chinese Communists for the fliers but thought it would be "useful" if the Peking regime could be admitted to the United Nations. Also on January 14, there were reports from Formosa that the Chinese Nationalists had pledged not to invade the Chinese mainland without American approval beforehand. On January 18, the People's Republic invaded and captured Yikiang Island just north of the Tachen Islands, bombing the Tachens the next day and prompting Nationalist Chinese retaliatory air attacks against mainland vessels along the China coast. Thus the Nationalists and Communists once again were embroiled in open hostilities.

On January 19, President Eisenhower told a news conference he looked to the United Nations to "exercise its good offices" to get a cease-fire in the Formosa Straits.

Henry Luce and Walter Judd were displeased. Both let the President know so on January 22.

Telling the President that only once before since the 1952 election had he burdened him with an opinion on any matter (Trieste), Luce wrote that talk of cease-fire had produced consternation in the Far East among "friends of freedom." [5] Although he was sure the President was much better informed than himself on the entire China crisis, Luce felt that even the slightest softening of America's position and posture as the staunch ally in Asia of anti-Communists would produce "disastrous consequences." Adding that he hoped his opinion would be as superfluous as the one tendered on the Trieste matter and enclosing a copy of *Time* Far Eastern correspondent John Osborne's Hong Kong dispatch covering Asian reaction to Eisenhower's cease-fire remark, Luce hoped his opinion might serve as a "small counterweight" against appeasement and complacency, which he saw as recent trends in the United States.

Judd's telegram to Eisenhower the same day came right to the point: He suggested, in effect, that the United States prevent a cease-fire and thus the neutralization or sterilization of Formosa, instead permitting the Chinese Nationalists to remain a threat on the mainland's flank in order to deter the Communist Chinese from moving further into Southeast Asia. He also urged the President not to allow American relatives to visit the flier-prisoners, thereby telling the Communists that America's will could not be softened and her attention diverted from new Communist aggression.[6]

Two days later, on January 24, the President sent a special message to Congress asking for emergency authorization to employ American armed forces at his discretion to protect Formosa and the Pescadores Islands. On January 29, Congress overwhelmingly gave the Chief Executive the authority he wanted—the so-called "Formosa Resolution." On January 31, the President thanked Senator Knowland for his "effective work of last week in connection with the Formosa Resolution."[7] On February 1, Assistant to the President Sherman Adams, at the instigation of the President, wrote Walter Judd about "your thoughtful telegram of January twenty-second concerning United States policy towards Formosa and possible visits by relatives of Americans imprisoned in Communist China."[8] Adams said the President's subsequent actions had demonstrated his substantial agreement with both of Judd's suggestions.

On February 2, The Committee for One Million came out of "hibernation."

The Rationale for Reorganization

There is an agenda but no minutes for the "informal meeting" at Ambassador Grew's home that evening. Among the agenda items was consideration of a memorandum, dated January 27, 1955, on the accomplishments of The Committee for One Million.[9] This unsigned and not otherwise identifiable memorandum from Marvin Liebman's files helps illuminate the Committee's rejuvenation process. To be sure, much of what is outlined here was quickly implemented by the newly reorganized group of China policy militants. The memorandum began by stating the Committee's original purpose and emphasizing the need for bipartisanship:

> The Committee For One Million was organized to mobilize public opinion against the admission of Communist China to the United Nations. Since sentiment for a softer policy toward Communist China was concen-

trated among liberal and international-minded Republicans and Democrats, *our key problem was to secure enough distinguished and representative Democrats to make the Committee a truly bipartisan organization, while maintaining an absolutely uncompromising anti-Communist position on the China issue. In this objective we scored a spectacular success.* (Italics added)

Then the effectiveness and importance of the signer collecting campaign were reviewed. Again claiming success, the memorandum proposed that the next step be the presentation of the completed petitions to the President.[10] But the signatures were not the whole story:

> . . . More important than the collection of signatures, however, was the impact the Committee had on public opinion. During our period of activity from October, 1953, through May, 1954, our point of view was in the ascendency, with minor exceptions. The left and extreme right, both dangerous to the sensible and effective approach to the problem of how to deal with Red China, were kept in bounds.

Unfortunately, however, America's allies were not similarly restrained. Following the "military disaster in Indo-China," the statement continued, "a new wave of pressure for appeasement" came from the British and the French and helped to revive "appeasement sentiment even among some well-meaning American international-minded groups." In mid-1954, "there began a series of oblique declarations by eminent organizations hinting at the need to recognize Communist China and admit her to the United Nations for the sake of peace." The first such approach was the declaration of the American Assembly in the summer of 1954.[11] Next, "the same view was expressed by the National Planning Association." [12]

Two paragraphs warned of a "pattern" of tendencies "which may lead to accommodations with the Communists at the Republic of China's expense. . . . We believe it is not entirely a coincidence," the memo stated, "that these dangerous developments have coincided with the end of our Committee's activity." [13] The original aim of keeping Communist China out of the United Nations was in greater danger than ever. Moreover, Senator Knowland could not carry the ball all alone. Hence:

> . . . We owe it to the more than one million Americans who entrusted us
> with their signatures to represent their point of view as effectively as pos-
> sible. We must provide a non-partisan organization which can give them
> the facts around which they can rally. . . . We dare not leave the task of
> leadership to Senator Knowland alone, for he can speak only for his
> party, or one section of that party.

The document then suggested that eight steps be taken as soon as possible: Of the eight, five were totally or substantially implemented, one
partially implemented, one too vaguely stated to judge, and one apparently tried but not achieved—to wit: "Arrange an appointment
within the next two weeks with the White House to formally present the
petitions."

There is no evidence that President Eisenhower accepted the Committee's petitions at any time. Yet several documents besides the January 27 memorandum indicate that an appointment was sought.[14]

The partially implemented step concerned the Committee's proposed new name: "The Committee *of* One Million, a citizen's group
dedicated to mobilizing public opinion against appeasement of Red
China in any form". What finally emerged, however, was "The Committee of One Million Against the Admission of Communist China to
the United Nations," the original "for" changing to "of."

Another proposal argued that an important task was "to spread information among our European and Asian allies about the strength of
American opposition to Communist China." Shortly after reorganizing,
a press conference for foreign reporters was held in Washington D.C.
Also, Marvin Liebman later made a Far Eastern tour of some significance, and, the Committee began to publish its views in the International Edition of the *New York Times*.

Of the remaining steps, one recommended accepting the resignations of steering committee members unable "for any reason, to participate in an enlarged program" and replacing them with other supporters.[15] The final four recommendations (to be amplified in the
sections that follow) included: writing a statement of principles and purposes; submitting it to a selected group of initial signers for endorsement, then soliciting other sponsors and signers; advertising the state-

ment, complete with new endorsers, in the *New York Times* in an appeal
for mass support; and using the advertisement "to gain widespread financial and moral support throughout the country."

Concluding, the memorandum declared that further Committee
functions would be "conditioned by events as they occur." The broader
scope of the new Committee again was emphasized: "It will take action
on every issue that arises as it concerns Communist China. It will have
to have complete flexibility. Its greatest importance is that we will have
an organized group ready to meet crises as they arise."

A subsequent letter from Charles Edison to Walter Judd confirmed
an "oral understanding" reached at Ambassador Grew's home the night
of the reorganizational meeting: Edison resigned as treasurer.[16] He was
replaced by Frederick C. McKee, the Pittsburgh industrialist. Marvin
Liebman was requested to turn over to McKee the financial records,
audits, and related materials of The Committee for One Million and to
transfer any remaining funds to The Committee of One Million.

Implementing Reorganization

An appeal to join The Committee *of* One Million was mailed on
March 4, 1955, on a letterhead with the old The Committee *for* One
Million name but with a new address and a revamped steering commit-
tee. The address—8 West 40th Street, New York City—was the same as
Harold L. Oram, Inc., for whom Liebman still worked. Holdovers from
the old steering committee included Ambassador Grew, Congressman
Judd, and Senator H. Alexander Smith. New members were Senator
Paul Douglas and Congressman Francis E. Walter, both Democrats,
who replaced Senator Sparkman and Congressman McCormack. Absent
but soon to reappear was the name of Honorary Chairman Warren R.
Austin. Charles Edison, as noted, was replaced by Frederick C. McKee
as treasurer, but he moved to the regular steering committee as part of
the six-man leadership. Liebman remained secretary.

The appeal itself was directed to the 268 "initial signers," those
who either had signed the original petition to the President or had subsequently signed the public petitions. Their names were printed on the

reverse side of the letterhead. Accompanying the letter was a "Statement on United States Policy Against Admission of Communist China to the United Nations." Also enclosed was a signature card with the following copy:

> I am happy to join you in opposition to the admission of Communist China to the United Nations by adding my name to the Statement you sent and by becoming a member of the COMMITTEE OF ONE MILLION. My consent includes my permission to publicize my name, as a member of the Committee, on all Committee publications and letterheads until contrary written notice.

A follow-up memorandum dated March 14, from Secretary Liebman to "Friends of the Committee For One Million," included a "first proof" of an advertisement for the *New York Times*.[17]

On April 12, the full-page advertisement was published in the *Times* and in the *Los Angeles Examiner*.[18] It contained a "partial list" of 158 names, noting that the Committee was still in formation. Timed for publication the same day was a press release printed on the new letterhead of The Committee of One Million and headed: "Bi-Partisan Group Formed to Fight Appeasement of Red China. Democrats and Republicans Join Against Admission of Communist China to the United Nations." The statement excerpted in the release was said to have been signed "by 238 leading Americans representing both major political parties and every category of national life."[19] The *New York Times* published a four-paragraph story based on the release.[20]

Several themes and phrases were repeated in the March 4, 14, and April 12 materials described above. The lead sentence of the March 4 letter and the headline of the advertisement both referred to the Chinese Communist attempt to "shoot their way into the United Nations" (a phrase originated by Warren R. Austin, according to his successor in the Senate from Vermont, Ralph Flanders).[21] Five themes predominated: 1) the Committee's bipartisan composition—"non-partisan" was the expression used in the March 14 follow-up letter; 2) the "appeasement of the Chinese Reds" by other Free World governments as well as "some of the leaders of American opinion"; 3) Chinese Communist "direct and indirect aggression in Korea, Vietnam, Malaya, and Tibet"; 4) the

importance of keeping "a new aggressor from entering the U.N. with a
veto in the Security Council to strengthen the present obstructive efforts
of the Communist powers"; and 5) the cause organized in 1953 "was in
danger."

The Statement accompanying the March 4 letter was identical to
the text of the April 12 advertisement with one major exception, explained in the March 14 follow-up letter. The original Statement contained a six-point program which 1) offered other Americans a chance to
join those who had already signed the Committee's petition; 2) declared
the need for telling people of other free nations about the bipartisan nature of the movement; 3) warned against appeasement, opposed any surrender of Quemoy or Matsu Islands or the neutralizing of Formosa, and
congratulated the President and the Congress on the wording of the congressional resolution; 4) applauded the AFL's stand on increased aid to
Formosa and the necessity for trade restrictions against the People's
Republic; 5) welcomed ratification of the mutual defense treaty between
the United States and the Republic of China; and 6) emphasized that the
Committee considered Formosa "a dynamic force for the eventual freedom of the Chinese people . . . [and] a vital part of United States security against Communist aggression." Liebman's March 14 follow-up
letter, by contrast, pointed out that parts of section 3 (opposing the
cease-fire and the neutralization of Formosa) had been deleted. This was
necessary, he explained, so that the Committee would attract as broad
and non-partisan a membership as possible, which could be accomplished by consolidating the Statement behind the sole purpose of
opposing Communist China's entry in the United Nations.[22]

(Meanwhile, between the mailing of the two solicitations, Senator
Knowland wrote to President Eisenhower, enclosing a copy of a letter
he had sent to Secretary of State Dulles about reports that Chinese Communists were chartering old British tramp ships and using them to carry
supplies down the China coast to mainland ports.[23] Knowland was informed, he wrote Dulles, that the British government allowed the ships
to maintain British registration and fly British flags, which, if correct,
was a subterfuge to keep the Republic of China from attacking the
ships. Knowland wanted Dulles to supply him information.)

How productive was this coordinated effort to rejuvenate the Committee with new members and fresh funds? As will become more apparent in the chapters that follow, membership in the Committee, as reflected by changing letterheads, was frequently a function of the specific purpose for which the direct mail piece, letterhead, advertisement, declaration, news release, or solicitation was designed. Some "members" appeared, disappeared, and reappeared on Committee materials. Others remained as permanent fixtures. Sometimes, those who merely signed petitions were referred to as "members"; in other materials, those who gave money or allowed the use of their names were similarly identified. Although the Committee later came to identify "congressional endorsers" separately in most public declarations, the April 12 reorganization advertisement alphabetically listed congressmen and senators together with others as "members."

Several interesting differences stand out about the 1955 membership drive: first, between the 268 persons whose names were printed on the reverse side of the March 4 and 14 letterheads, as opposed to the 238 persons later acknowledged by the April 12 publicity release to have signed the reorganization Statement; second, between members of Congress whose names appeared on the March 4 and 14 letterheads but not in the April 12 advertisement; and third, between members of Congress whose names appeared in the April 12 advertisement though not on any earlier Committee letterheads nor as signers of the original petition to the President.

Of the 268 names printed on the reverse side of the March 4 and 14 letterheads, 59 had not been listed either as original sponsors or among the 210 signers of the petition to the President. Conversely, only two names from the original 210—Karl T. Compton and William B. Ziff— failed to appear on the March 4 and 14 letterheads (although three senators on the original list had died in 1954).[24]

Senator Paul H. Douglas (D., Ill.), a signer of the original petition, moved to the steering committee on the March 4 and 14 letterheads. He was joined by Congressman Francis E. Walter (D., Pa.), who had not signed the original petition. The names of three original sponsors— President Hoover, Senator Sparkman, and Congressman McCormack— were among the names on the reverse side of the letterheads.

The 59 new names included 4 members of Congress (Senators Richard L. Neuberger [D., Ore.], and Andrew F. Schoeppel [R., Kan.], and Congressmen Donald L. Jackson [R., Calif.], and Wint Smith [R., Kan.]), 8 show business celebrities, 6 mayors, 5 retired military officers, 3 sports celebrities, and one former diplomat.

The publicity story released by the Committee for publication on April 12 announced that "238 leading Americans representing both major political parties and every category of national life" had signed the Committee's statement.[25] (Because this list was not discovered, one cannot determine all 30 of the 268 persons who failed, for whatever reasons, to respond to the March 4 and 14 appeals—three, of course, were the deceased senators—or responded negatively.)

Nevertheless, the April 12 advertisement did publish the names of the new steering committee members plus a "partial list" of 158 'members.' " Altogether, there were 77 members of Congress listed in the advertisement.

Table 5.1 shows that 24 members of the 84th Congress, though formerly identified both on letterhead of The Committee *for* One Million and, with two exceptions, as signers of the original 1953 petition to the President, either chose not to be listed in the April 12, 1955, reorganization advertisement or were removed from the list of "members" for some other reason. Included here were the two Democrats from the original steering committee, Senator Sparkman and Congressman McCormack, who became Majority Leader of the House in the 84th Congress. Also, Table 5.1 reveals a virtual bipartisan standoff between Democrats and Republicans both in terms of total numbers and within and between each congressional body. Proportionately, however, the 13 senators whose names did not appear in the advertisement represented 13.5 percent of the Senate and the 11 representatives, 2.5 percent of the House.

Table 5.2, indicating the Committee's *new* congressional membership, identifies the 51 members of the 84th Congress who were not "members" of The Committee *for* One Million before the publication of the April 12, 1955, advertisement. Here, the 42 House "members" and the nine Senate "members" represented slightly less than 10 percent of their respective legislative bodies.

TABLE 5.1

Members of 84th Congress Whose Names Appeared on 1953 Petition, March 4 and 14, 1955 Letterheads, but Not in April 12, 1955 Committee Reorganization Advertisement in the *New York Times*

HOUSE OF REPRESENTATIVES (11)

DEMOCRATS (6)	REPUBLICANS (5)
Hays, Brooks (Ark.)	Church, Marguerite S. (Ill.)
Gordon, Thomas S. (Ill.)	Short, Dewey (Mo.)
McCormack, John W. (Mass.)	Wolverton, Charles A. (N.J.)
McCarthy, Eugene J. (Minn.)	Radwan, Edmund P. (N.Y.)
Teague, Olin E. (Tex.)	McConnell, Samuel K. Jr. (Pa.)
Zablocki, Clement J. (Wisc.)	

SENATE (13)

DEMOCRATS (7)	REPUBLICANS (6)
Sparkman, John J. (Ala.)	Williams, John J. (Del.)
Humphrey, Hubert H. (Minn.)	Welker, Herman (Ida.)
Eastland, James O. (Miss.)	Schoeppel, Andrew F. (Kan.) *
Monroney, A. S. Mike (Okla.)	Bricker, John W. (Ohio)
Neuberger, Richard L. (Ore.) *	Bennett, Wallace F. (Utah)
Robertson, A. Willis (Va.)	Wiley, Alexander (Wisc.)
Magnuson, Warren G. (Wash.)	

* Not on 1953 petition but included on March 1955 letterheads.

Table 5.3 indicates that only 6 Democrats and 18 Republicans from the 84th Congress maintained more or less continuous identification with the Committee, from the initial signing of the 1953 petition to the President through the April 12, 1955, advertisement. Among them were two original (and holdover) steering committee members, Congressman Judd and Senator Smith, their new steering committee colleague, Senator Douglas, and the new Senate Minority Leader Knowland.

Together, Tables 5.2 and 5.3 identify the 77 members of the 84th Congress listed as Committee "members" by the April 12, 1955, advertisement.

Not among the 268 was the name Alfred Kohlberg (nor was Kohlberg's among the original 210 on the 1953 petition to the President). Some days before the reorganization meeting at Grew's home, Kohlberg suffered his second coronary. His first had come in September of 1954

TABLE 5.2

**Members of 84th Congress Whose Committee Association Began
with April 12, 1955** *New York Times* **Advertisement**

HOUSE OF REPRESENTATIVES (42)

DEMOCRATS (24) | REPUBLICANS (18)

Elliott, Carl (Ala.)
Holifield, Chet (Calif.)
Dodd, Thomas J. (Conn.) *
Fascell, Dante B. (Fla.)
Sikes, Bob (Fla.)
Pfost, Gracie (Ida.)
Freidel, Samuel N. (Md.)
Macdonald, Torbet H. (Mass.)
Diggs, Charles C. Jr. (Mich.)
Dingell, John D. (Mich.)
Hayworth, Don (Mich.)
Buckley, Charles A. (N.Y.)
Donovan, James G. (N.Y.)
Hays, Wayne L. (Ohio)
Barrett, William A. (Pa.)
Byrne, James A. (Pa.)
Kelley, Augustine B. (Pa.)
Walter, Francis E. (Pa.) †
Dorn, Wm J. Bryan (S.C.)
Davis, Clifford (Tenn.)
Murray, Tom (Tenn.)
Burnside, M. G. (W. Va.)
Byrd, Robert C. (W. Va.)
Mollahan, Robert H. (W. Va.)

REPUBLICANS (18)

Teague, Charles M. (Calif.)
Younger, J. Arthur (Calif.)
Hoffman, Richard W. (Ill.)
Reed, Chauncey W. (Ill.)
Wilson, Earl (Ind.)
Hale, Robert (Me.)
Martin, Joseph W. Jr. (Mass.)
Dondero, George A. (Mich.)
Thompson, Ruth (Mich.)
Curtis, Thomas B. (Mo.)
Cole, W. Sterling (N.Y.)
St. George, Katherine (N.Y.)
Gwinn, Ralph W. (N.Y.)
Keating, Kenneth B. (N.Y.)
Latham, Henry J. (N.Y.)
Ellsworth, Harris (Ore.)
Dixon, H. A. (Utah)
O'Konski, Alvin E. (Wisc.)

SENATE (9)

DEMOCRATS (3) | REPUBLICANS (6)

Holland, Spessard L. (Fla.)
Mansfield, Mike (Mont.)
Murray, James E. (Mont.)

REPUBLICANS (6)

Goldwater, Barry (Ariz.)
Dirksen, Everett M. (Ill.)
Capehart, Homer E. (Ind.)
Thye, Edward J. (Minn.)
Bridges, H. Styles (N.H.)
Mundt, Karl E. (S.D.)

* Incorrectly identified in advertisement as Rufus J. Dodd.
† Congressman Walter's name appeared on March 1955 letterheads as a steering
committee member of the reorganized Committee.

TABLE 5.3
Members of 84th Congress Whose Names Appeared on 1953 Petition, March 4 and 14, 1955 Letterheads, and in April 12, 1955 Committee Reorganization Advertisement in the *New York Times*

HOUSE OF REPRESENTATIVES (12)

DEMOCRATS (2)	REPUBLICANS (10)
Addonizio, Hugh J. (N.J.)	Jackson, Donald L. (Calif.) *
Kelly, Edna F. (N.Y.)	Chiperfield, Robert B. (Ill.)
	Hope, Clifford R. (Kan.)
	Smith, Wint (Kan.) *
	Bentley, Alvin (Mich.)
	Judd, Walter H. (Minn.)
	Auchincloss, James C. (N.J.)
	Vorys, John M. (Ohio)
	Fulton, James G. (Pa.)
	Scott, Hugh D. Jr. (Pa.)

SENATE (14)

DEMOCRATS (4)	REPUBLICANS (10)
Douglas, Paul H. (Ill.) †	Knowland, William F. (Calif.)
Daniel, Price (Tex.)	Payne, Frederick G. (Me.)
Kilgore, Harley M. (W. Va.)	Smith, Margaret C. (Me.)
Neely, Matthew M. (W. Va.)	Potter, Charles E. (Mich.)
	Smith, H. Alexander (N.J.)
	Ives, Irving M. (N.Y.)
	Young, Milton R. (N.D.)
	Martin, Edward (Pa.)
	Watkins, Arthur V. (Utah)
	Flanders, Ralph E. (Vt.)

* Not on 1953 petition.
† Appeared as steering committee member beginning with March 4, 1955 Committee letterhead.

and had curtailed his many activities. Nonetheless, on February 25, 1955, Kohlberg wrote Eisenhower, enclosing a short treatise on international politics which he said he had composed in the hospital in late January while recovering from the attack.[26]

Sometime later in 1955 the reorganized Committee published an

"Information Bulletin" proclaiming approximately 4,000 "supporting members" and appealing for some help in recruitment: "Because of our relatively small *active* membership each one of us must become a missionary in two ways: present our point of view against admission on every possible occasion; get new supporters from among our neighbors and associates." [27]

The First Challenge

Less than two weeks after the public reemergence of the Committee, an announcement by Prime Minister Chou En-lai dropped like an atomic explosion on the diplomatic world, spreading political fallout destined to change the China policy perspectives of everyone—including The Committee of One Million. In Bandung, Java, where representatives of twenty-nine Afro-Asian nations were gathered in conference, the terse, April 23 statement read:

> The Chinese people are friendly to the American people. The Chinese people do not want to have a war with the United States of America. The Chinese Government is willing to sit down and enter into negotiations with the United States Government to discuss the question of relaxing tension in the Far East and especially the question of relaxing tension in the Taiwan area.

This dramatic initiative, totally surprising, has been described as the decisive move toward activation of the steps which lead eventually to the start of bilateral ambassadorial talks in Geneva in August between the United States and the People's Republic.[28] Reacting in Secretary Dulles' absence and without his oversight, the State Department released a negative and somewhat confusing statement.[29]

Apparently, the Committee held its fire on the issue for almost a month. Two days after Chou's initiative, on April 25, the group conducted a briefing session for members of the overseas press. Yet Liebman's report of this news briefing failed to mention whether the subject even came up.[30] Still, two prominent legislators associated with the Committee reacted—in dissimilar fashion. Senator Knowland went public, ridiculing the Chinese initiative as "another Munich." Dr. Judd waited ten days, then sent President Eisenhower a letter and a short statement explaining that Chou En-lai wanted to trick the United States into lessening American pressures on Communist China so as to avoid defeat by giving the appearance that his posture was changing out of a desire for peace.[31] Eisenhower replied several days later. Judd had reinforced his "longtime conviction that you [Judd] are one of the most articulate and forceful speakers in our public life . . . and I regret that there aren't more hours in the day so that we could fully discuss the situation as it now appears." The President continued:

> My conviction is that, given the information now before me, you would be in full accord both with what we are doing and with what we are seeking to accomplish. As a matter of fact, I do not construe your letter and enclosure as divergent from our present policies, *although you do seem to be apprehensive that we may be outfoxed one way or another. We shall do our best not to be.*[32] (Italics added)

Not until May 18 did the Committee's public response to Chou En-lai's bombshell appear. A statement was sent on May 17, accompanied by a letter from Marvin Liebman, to both Eisenhower and Dulles as well as the press.[33] The statement carefully acknowledged the Committee's full support for "the President's desire to promote a peaceful solution to the crisis in the Formosa Strait," repeating the slogan "that the Chinese Communists shall not be permitted to shoot their way into the United Nations." But then came a new Committee approach:

> Our Committee does not take the position that all negotiations with the Chinese Communists must be rejected under any circumstances, because they imply recognition. We did negotiate with Chinese Communists for years at Panmunjom. This refutes the charge so commonly heard abroad that American policy is absurdly unrealistic because we refuse to recognize the *existence* of a government which controls 600,000,000 people.

The Committee's statement went on to recognize that "certain important principles" had to be considered: first, that faith had to be kept "with our Chinese Nationalist allies, with whom we have just concluded a treaty of mutual defense''; second, Chinese Communist good faith had to be taken into account.

> . . . They broke their pledges to General Marshall during his negotiations to arrange a lasting truce in the Chinese civil war. They broke their pledges in Korea when we signed the truce, in part, to secure the release of our captive soldiers. Now the Red leaders apparently want to negotiate with us again and so extort a second purchase price for the freedom of hundreds of American prisoners, *whose release was already bought and paid for at Panmunjom.*[34]

The increasing probability of Sino-American discussions was not directly discussed in the Committee's next try for national publicity. Nonetheless, both the target of the campaign and the substance of the message suggested this issue lay just beneath the surface. As the catalyst the Committee mobilized its supporters in the religious community, releasing, on May 30, 1955, an open letter to the President signed by clergymen representing all major faiths and "answering various pacifist appeals to the President which had urged further appeasement of the Chinese Communists."[35] Taking a lead from the earlier May 18 statement on negotiations with the Chinese, the letter expressed sympathy with the President's efforts on behalf of international peace with justice and warned that "the leaders of Communism are shifting rather than relaxing their plans to seize world control." Their objective remained "the subjugation of free men to an atheistic tyranny." Appeasement was the real issue:

> . . . We view with concern the apparent feeling among certain influential fellow Americans . . . that appeasement and further withdrawal provide the answer to this sinister policy. . . .
>
> We also believe that no true peace with world security can be gained by further withdrawals in the Far East or by attempts to appease these ruthless forces. . . . we stand with you for guaranteeing the continued integrity and freedom of Formosa and against recognizing this Peiping government or receiving it into the United Nations.

The Committee's "Information Bulletin" said the statement to the President had been signed by fourteen clergymen, seven of whom had signed the original 1953 petition to the President.[36]

In June, the United Nations celebrated its tenth anniversary with commemorative meetings at its San Francisco birthplace, an event the Committee tailored to another publicity story. A message was released in San Francisco from Committee Honorary Chairman Warren Austin, America's first ambassador to the United Nations, to Secretary-General Dag Hammarskjöld, and to Dr. Eelco N. van Kleffens, president of the commemorative meetings. It advised the United Nations to oppose the admission of Communist China and requested the statement be distributed to the sixty delegations in attendance.[37]

Another Committee press release on July 7 came in response to a news conference held the previous day in New York by Prime Minister U Nu of Burma. Unpublished in the *New York Times* but included in the Appendix of the *Congressional Record* by Congressman Judd, the release disputed U Nu's quoted impression from his talks in Washington that "most of the responsible people are not against the entry of Peiping into the United Nations." [38]

Dr. Judd's White House correspondence was not always generated by him. In July he received a letter from Bryce N. Harlow, an administrative assistant to the President, asking if he would do the President a favor. Judd was asked to insert an "attached article" (not otherwise identified) from the July 5 issue of *Newsweek* into the *Congressional Record* and to add "some appropriate, typically penetrating introductory remarks." [39] Several days later, Judd wrote Eisenhower of his satisfaction in reading that the Geneva talks would not include any Far East negotiations or agreements.[40] Mistakes made by Roosevelt at Yalta, and by Marshall and Truman regarding China and the Communists, he said, would cost these men much of their places in history. Judd sometimes feared that Eisenhower's administration would misjudge the Chinese situation because of the influential people at home and abroad who failed to see two things: there were no Asian problems that could not be solved if China was "free and friendly"; there was no peaceful solution in Asia if the Chinese Reds were permitted to dig in on the mainland, grow internationally, and pressure their neighbors. The administration, Judd added, needed to continue what it had been doing because its positions were "winning." Eisenhower's "firm leadership" could and would win a "lasting peace."

Eisenhower quickly acknowledged Judd's "interesting and helpful letter" and assured him "that we shall keep on, to use your words, doing what we have been doing, given the continuing support of the Congress and our people." [41]

Another exchange between the two men took place after the Geneva talks began. Judd was especially pleased, he wrote, that Eisenhower had spoken bluntly and unequivocally at a news conference about standing in Asia and elsewhere by America's loyal friends and allies. Judd had denied to some strong administration supporters that the Government would "sell out" Free China, although there had been many insinuations about giving in to the Chinese Communists after the talks. Taking a partisan shot, Judd acknowledged that some Democratic politicians wanted the administration to undercut America's allies because that was the only way the Democrats could escape the political liability and the shame of Teheran and Yalta. Again, Eisenhower replied promptly, saying he was gratified with Judd's expression of confidence and support and believed firmly "that we can continue to uphold our convictions and still move steadily step by step toward lasting peace." [42]

Narcotics: A New Theme

On the same day that ambassadorial talks between the United States and the Chinese People's Republic began in Geneva,[43] the *Washington Post & Times Herald* printed a Committee advertisement, and the *New York Times* published a news story, both of which introduced a new (and thereafter persistent) Committee theme: Peking's complicity in international narcotics smuggling.[44] The alleged linkage between narcotics and the Chinese previously had not been mentioned in Committee memoranda. One original signer of the 1953 petition to the President, Senator Frederick G. Payne (R., Me.), whose name appeared on Committee materials throughout his Senate career, had coupled narcotics and the Chinese Communists on January 14, 1955, introducing a joint resolution (S. J.Res. 19) that sponsored a narcotics control act. Noting the increased use of narcotics by teen-agers, Payne declared on the Senate floor: "With the present strained international situation, it is no consolation to know that Communist China is the leading source of supply of the illicit drugs being used to corrupt our young people." [45] This accusation apparently stemmed from an article Payne inserted in the *Record*, "The Story Behind Red China's Dope Peddlers," from the December 20, 1954 *The New Leader*. [46]

The first use of the narcotics theme in Committee literature appeared in the updated "Information Bulletin" probably distributed between May 18 and July 24, 1955. A four-sentence paragraph subheaded "Chinese Dope Campaign" called attention to the enclosure of a reprinted article from the *American Legion Magazine* which, the Information Bulletin said, summarized "a long series of investigations and revelations by Harry J. Anslinger . . . who for thirty years has been recognized as a world authority on the dope problem." [47]

Similarly, the entire text of the August 1, 1955, Committee advertisement, including a list of "members" and a coupon, [48] contained excerpts from remarks by Commissioner Anslinger before a UN session on narcotics held in April and May 1955. Under the heading, "Dope— Communist China's Role in the International Drug Traffic," the advertisement, complete with a picture of Anslinger, began by acknowledging that mainland China had again denied the Commissioner's "documented charges made over the past several years," but that "actual conditions in Southeast Asia and other free countries refute this unsupported denial and clearly prove that mainland China is the uncontrolled reservoir supplying the worldwide illicit narcotic traffic."

Among the charges excerpted from Anslinger's statements: that "millions of dollars obtained through the sale of opium and other narcotics are used by the Communist regime of mainland China for political purposes and to finance agents who have been found actively engaged in subversive activities"; that "large quantities of high quality crude morphine . . . is processed according to pharmaceutical standards and methods, under government supervision, and not in clandestine laboratories"; that "traffic in heroin from the Communist regime of mainland China is increasing, according to enforcement authorities concerned with traffic through Canton, Bangkok, and other ports"; and that "heroin from Communist China has been seized on both coasts of the United States, as well as in the interior at St. Louis, Mo." The text of the advertisement concluded:

> The Peiping regime's part in promoting the world drug trade is only one of its many charter violations. The [Committee] publishes Commissioner Anslinger's documented testimony as further proof of Communist China's inadmissability to the United Nations.

There was no reference in this August 1 advertisement to the Geneva talks which began that day.

A recent history of the international heroin traffic considers some of Commissioner Anslinger's charges:

> Ever since the People's Republic of China was founded in 1949, official and unofficial spokesmen in the United States and Taiwan have repeatedly charged that the Chinese Communists were exporting vast quantities of heroin to earn much-needed foreign exchange. The leading American advocate of this viewpoint was the former director of the Federal Bureau of Narcotics (FBN), Harry Anslinger, who joined with Taiwanese officials in vigorously denouncing the People's Republic. . . . Now that Mr. Anslinger has retired, the U.S. Bureau of Narcotics has changed its point of view. . . . Today many federal narcotics agents are openly bitter toward Anslinger for what they now consider to have been the abuse of the bureau's name for the purposes of blatant, inaccurate propaganda. One agent serving in Southeast Asia said in a mid 1971 interview: "Everytime Anslinger spoke anywhere he always said the same thing—"The Chicoms are flooding the world with dope to corrupt the youth of America." . . . It was kind of like the "Marijuana rots your brains" stuff the old FBN put out. It really destroyed our credibility and now nobody believes us. *There was no evidence for Anslinger's accusations, but that never stopped him.*" [49] (Italics added)

Also included in this book is a 1971 interview with then chief of the Narcotics Bureau's Strategic Intelligence Office, John Warner, who gave the following explanation for why Taiwan persisted in "damning" the mainland for its alleged involvement in narcotics:

Recently we have been getting a number of congressional inquiries about Chinese Communist involvement in the Opium trade. The Taiwanese floated a series of nonattributable articles in the right-wing press, quoting statements from British police officers in Hong Kong saying "we have seized five tons of opiates in Hong Kong this year." And the article would then state that this came from Red China. Actually it comes from Bangkok. *The real object of this sudden mushrooming of this kind of propaganda is to bar China from the U.N.*[50]

Congress and the Talks

Secretary Dulles is said to have approved on July 11, prior to an upcoming Big Four summit meeting at Geneva, the completion of arrangements for Sino-American ambassadorial talks, but public announcement of the talks was withheld until July 25, after the summit conference and as Congress approached adjournment.[51] Thus congressional debate over the talks was short-lived. In the Senate, on July 26, while Dulles held a news conference to elaborate American intentions and expectations, Senator Joseph McCarthy, the first to raise the issue on the Senate floor, asked whether the smell of appeasement was in the air. "Does he [Senator Knowland] not detect the development of an insidious campaign to betray the Republic of China?" [52] Likewise, in the House that day, Congressman Robert Hale (R., Me.; listed on both the April 12 and August 1, 1955, Committee advertisements) rose "to protest against the possibility of our having any negotiations of any kind and for any purpose with the illegitimate, Communist, so-called People's Government (*sic*) of China, unless the legitimate Nationalist government is present and participating in those negotiations." [53]

But Senator Knowland commended Eisenhower and Dulles for their efforts at Geneva "to seek ways of finding peace with honor," adding that the executive branch was "fully alive to the problems confronting us." [54] Senator McCarthy pursued his attack on the impending Geneva talks ("In heaven's name . . . what is the difference between what happened at Yalta and what is about to happen at Geneva?") and then introduced a resolution which, he said, called on the administration "to invite the Republic of China to attend any discussion that may involve its territory or may affect its rights." [55]

The ambassadorial talks between Ambassadors U. Alexis Johnson and Wang Ping-nan began—and the "narcotics advertisement" appeared—the day before Congress adjourned. In the Senate, following the awaited announcement that eleven American fliers had been released by the People's Republic, McCarthy speculated that the talks might reveal "a deal made at the Big Four meeting to surrender the offshore islands to the Communists, for it has long been apparent that we would bargain for the return of our prisoners of war by making territorial concessions to Red China." [56] Yet one Committee supporter, the late Senator Karl E. Mundt (R., S.D.; his name appeared on both the April 12 and August 1, 1955, advertisements) called the summit meetings a success, saying the United States gave nothing away to the Communists for the first time in history.[57] In the House, meanwhile, Judd's successor as chairman of the subcommittee on the Far East and the Pacific, Congressman Clement J. Zablocki (D., Wisc.), read into the *Record* a statement signed by ten members of the subcommittee, warning against "unjustified optimism" because of the ambassadorial talks:

. . . Our Government has stated that [the talks] are confined to a few practical issues. . . . But even before they started, distinguished Americans have cut the ground from our negotiator by stating that we ought to discuss the Formosa issue with Red China at higher levels. . . . Only last week Secretary Dulles stated that the present talks . . . do not imply any diplomatic recognition nor will they result in arrangements that would prejudice the rights of the Republic of China on Formosa. . . . It is the height of folly to jeopardize our position and that of our allies in Asia for an illusion of accomplishment by declaring that we ought to meet with the Chinese Communists soon to settle the Formosa issue. The problem is not Formosa. It is the lawless and aggressive behavior of Communist China. . . .[58]

Of the ten subcommittee members identified with the full statement, only four had not been associated with any Committee literature through August 1, 1955. Three names (Congressmen Judd, John M. Vorys [R., Ohio], and Robert B. Chiperfield [R., Ill.]) had appeared on all 1953,

1954, and 1955 Committee materials referred to thus far; two (Representatives Marguerite S. Church [R., Ill.] and Zablocki) had appeared on the original 1953 petition as well as the reverse side of the March 14, 1955, letterhead; and one (Congressman Robert C. Byrd [D., W. Va.]) was included in the April 12 and August 1, 1955, Committee advertisements.

The day Senator Wiley inserted the Committee's August 1 advertisement in the *Congressional Record,* August 2, 1955, the first session of the 84th Congress adjourned. On September 20, four days before President Eisenhower suffered a heart attack while vacationing in Denver, a U.S. resolution to defer for another year consideration of the Chinese membership question in the United Nations was adopted by the General Assembly, 42 to 12, with 6 abstentions.

"Strengthening Eisenhower's Hand"

Although The Committee of One Million failed to regain access to the Oval Office to regenerate its reorganizational publicity in the spring of 1955, by the start of the second session of the 84th Congress in 1956 the group nevertheless was firmly established. Its bipartisan leadership had been strengthened by the replacement of Senator Sparkman with Senator Douglas. Its congressional adherents had increased; thus its appeal as a potential source of news on China policy issues had been enhanced. And its operational direction in New York was still in the hands of the same professional fund raisers and public relations men who successfully launched the original Committee.

In 1956, the revitalized group would face its first national election campaign. Could it maintain its stability and cohesion through a disruptive national election? Could it maintain bipartisanship? How would the Committee fight threats of change in China policy during the campaign and after the election? How would it react to challenges perceived to threaten its organizational interests.

Preparing for the Campaign

The first paragraph of an article headlined "Program For 1956" in the first number of the Committee's new *Newsletter,* mailed early in February, stated the 1956 campaign-year objective: "Every effort will be made to include formal opposition to the admission of Communist China to the United Nations in the platforms of both parties. A concerted effort on the part of the Steering Committee, and individual members, will be organized to achieve this." [1]

Neither the second nor third numbers of the *Newsletter* mentioned this effort to influence the party planks. But number 4, mailed after the Democratic and Republican national conventions met in August (the former in Chicago, the latter in San Francisco), printed a banner headline, **"Both Parties Go On Record Against Red China in the United Nations,"** above a story revealing at least part of the Committee's coordinated campaign to achieve identical planks in the party platforms: the planks had been approved at both conventions after a resolution was unanimously passed by both houses of Congress by July 23, 1956.[2] The party planks were made possible, the story continued, because hundreds of people contributed the "moral and financial support" which enabled the Committee to publish two full-page advertisements aimed at delegates to both conventions.[3] Additionally, Marvin Liebman's appeal that letters be sent to the respective chairmen of the platform committees—for the Republicans, Senator Prescott Bush (R., Conn.); for the Democrats, House Majority Leader McCormack—had been favorably received.

The Committee also got one of its original supporters, Stanley K. Hornbeck, to testify on its behalf before the Democratic Party's platform committee.[4] Liebman apparently was satisfied with the two planks, though he told Hornbeck the Committee failed to get exactly what it wanted. The planks shared attention in the *Newsletter* with the announcement of "the definitive handbook for Americans on the question of the admission of Red China to the United Nations"—*Invasion Alert,* by Joseph C. Grew. As the book's own foreword made clear, the Committee devised this book for the 1956 campaign:

> The purpose of this book is to persuade both national political parties to go on record formally, in their platforms and whenever additional opportunities are offered, against admission of Communist China to the United Nations. This action by delegates to the national political meetings at which our free people freely select their candidates for the Office of Chief Executive, will confirm and strengthen the action taken by the Congress.[5]

Invasion Alert was publicized between the August national conventions and the November election: The *New York Times* covered its publication on September 6; the *New York Daily News* ran a September

10 editorial, praising the book extensively, advising where it could be purchased (at Committee headquarters) and how much it cost (50¢ a copy, lower rates for quantity orders).[6] An "Author's Note" in *Invasion Alert* (p.ii) identifies Ambassador Grew as twice Under-Secretary of State, Ambassador to Turkey from 1927 to 1931, Ambassador to Japan until the Pearl Harbor attack in 1941, a "Dean Emeritus of the U.S. diplomatic corps," and a member of the Committee's steering committee. Nowhere noted in *Invasion Alert,* however, or in any subsequent Committee or public reference to it is the information that journalist Edward Lockett "ghosted" the book for Ambassador Grew. On September 12, 1956, Lockett wrote White House Press Secretary James C. Hagerty, enclosing a copy of the book—"the straight ghost job," he called it—adding that he put together all the arguments he could find against admitting the Chinese Communists to the United Nations. Hagerty thanked Lockett on September 25, saying he planned to read the book as soon as possible, perhaps even on a plane trip that day.[7]

Ambassador Grew was among eleven prominent Committee members who recorded radio broadcasts in March 1956 on the admission question which were subsequently distributed to radio stations in the United States and Canada.[8] Senator H. Alexander Smith included in the *Congressional Record* on March 14 the text of the broadcast he "and also some public spirited citizens" had recorded, in his case, "last week."[9] Neither the script of the broadcast nor Senator Smith's remarks on the Senate floor preceding inclusion of the materials mentioned the Committee. The steering committee member simply noted that he and others were

> *perturbed by rumors* . . . that at the next meeting of the Assembly of the United Nations there will be a strong movement, which has a chance of success, of recognizing the Red Communist Government. This has given some of us so much concern that we have felt it important to get the facts before the people of the United States, in order to make the situation clear and develop the support of public opinion before the matter comes up in the General Assembly.[10] (Italics added)

The "rumors" that perturbed Senator Smith again were circulated by the steering committee in a June 1, 1956, letter soliciting contributions. "The growing success of the campaign to seat Communist China in the United Nations," it began, "is emphasized in the enclosed article by Mr. Constantine Brown." The story implied that a UN decision to convene the eleventh regular session of the General Assembly after the American presidential elections instead of mid-September was taken because American policy-makers, who still strongly opposed admission of the People's Republic, felt they no longer had the votes to prevent admission. "The official explanation," said columnist Brown (on May 4 in the *Washington Evening Star*) "is that some of the American representatives might not be able to attend because they would be busy campaigning. Actually, the British, French and Soviet delegations intend to press this year for a vote on admission of Peiping to the Assembly." [11]

Another example of this campaign-year "rumor" was made public on June 29. Senator James O. Eastland (D., Miss.), inserted in the *Record* a June 28 letter he had written to Secretary Dulles, which quoted at length from testimony before Eastland's Senate Internal Security subcommittee by Dr. Judd on May 31 about "security matters" and "systematic leaks." The senator, an original signer of the Committee's 1953 petition whose name did not, however, appear on Committee letterheads or advertisements in 1955 or 1956, quoted Judd's testimony in part:

> . . . All of you have seen in the press for 6 months repeated stories, especially from certain columnists, that the United States is going to recognize Communist China, and, after the next election, the United Nations Assembly will meet and admit Communist China to the United Nations. I asked about it 2 or 3 times down at the State Department, if this is true. It has been denied completely by everybody at the top. [12]

The Liebman UN Memo

In the waning days of the 1956 election campaign but before the November 12 convening of the UN General Assembly, Marvin Liebman sent a "Confidential Memorandum—Not For Publication," to "Steering Committee and Members," [13] Subtitled a "Confidential Report on Status of Red China's Bid for a UN Seat," the memo traced the history of UN actions on the admission question, noting that each year the U.S.

delegation's resolution to postpone consideration of proposals on the China seat had passed by a "slightly smaller margin."

Liebman identified those countries leading the fight for mainland China's admission, making the point that leadership by the Soviet Union and its satellites seemed to disprove the idea that Red China could achieve national Communism and still divorce itself from the "Communist Empire." India, Yugoslavia, other "neutralists" including Indonesia and Burma were singled out as strong P.R.C. supporters. The memorandum also dealt with domestic pressures on the admission issue. The Committee, he claimed, had helped keep to a minimum public statements by those who favored a seat for Red China. Yet "powerful forces" were working for the Communists on this question. Moreover, others who believed in appeasement were in the middle. The Americans for Democratic Action (ADA), he said, was no doubt the largest pressure group favoring China's admission.[14] Additionally, there was the former ambassador to the Soviet Union, George F. Kennan, the American Association for the United Nations, the Quaker movement, lower level State Department employees, and some of the nation's largest industrial giants.

The then fifteen-month-old Geneva talks, the secretary continued, started because pro-admission and pro-recognition forces had exerted pressures. He did not elaborate. Analyzing the upcoming session of the General Assembly, he said that a reason for the post-U.S. election session was the prospect that American apathy would pave the way for Peking's entry. Liebman detailed the expected voting lineups, predicting 22 in support of admission, 44 opposed, with 10 abstentions. (He was close. The actual vote was 24 in favor, 47 opposed, with 8 abstentions.) Next, he turned to Communist strategy: in brief, to amend the U.S. resolution for postponing discussion so the question could be introduced after the first of the year, during a planned second half of the eleventh General Assembly. According to Liebman, the Communists believed they could count on a "bandwagon psychology" after having amended the U.S. resolution during the first session. Finally, he exhorted the American delegation to take the strongest possible position on the admission issue, bragging that the Committee had done its part by galvanizing a mobilized and articulate public opinion whose opposition was steadfast. He singled out for praise Ambassador Henry Cabot Lodge and noted that Senator Hubert H. Humphrey, Paul Hoffman, and Ellsworth Bunker all were on record against admission.

The final delegate appointed by the President to the eleventh regular session of the General Assembly was William F. Knowland.

"No Trade with the Enemy"

Shortly after the presidential election and the General Assembly vote (postponing for another year consideration of the China seating question) the Committee got into print on another issue: the prospect of relaxation in the American trade embargo against the People's Republic. Responding to a declaration by the president of the U.S. Chamber of Commerce favoring resumption of trade in nonstrategic goods, Marvin Liebman released a statement warning against any expansion of trade.[15] The whole front page of the Committee's fifth *Newsletter,* under the heading "Drive to Expand Red China Trade," dealt with the trade issue.[16] The pro-recognition forces having "suffered a serious defeat" at the United Nations, "they have now embarked on a long-range program" (full trade relations with the mainland). This was "more dangerous than the overt drive to admit Red China to the UN because of its subtlety and because of the many well-known American individuals and organizations who favor such proposals." Named were the American Assembly and the U.S. Chamber of Commerce president. The article attacked the very concept of nonstrategic goods: "there are no goods which are nonstrategic to a nation dedicated to building up an aggressive military machine."

Trade would be taken on in earnest by the Committee in the spring of 1957, but its unfolding as a salient issue should be considered in the context of simultaneous developments bearing on Sino-American relations.

The sequence of events ran roughly as follows: When Secretary Dulles first was asked to comment on reports of possible changes in U.S. trade policies toward the Peking regime, he also was queried about the State Department's policy of denying American reporters travel access to the mainland.[17] This issue mushroomed during the spring, understandably receiving considerable press attention, but the Committee apparently ignored it (insofar as can be determined) except for a fleeting mention in an important May memorandum to be considered below.

Then, on February 18, the chairman of the Senate Foreign Relations Committee, Senator Theodore Francis Green (D., R.I.), was quoted as saying that sooner or later the United States should recognize Red China: "We don't like their form of government, but the country is a great country and organized, and I do not myself see why we should recognize these other Communist countries and withhold recognition of China unless we are going to apply that to other Communist countries." [18] Two days later, House Majority Leader John W. McCormack, the former steering committee member, inserted in the Appendix of the *Record* a long *Wall Street Journal* article which speculated that President Eisenhower might bow to pressure from various American allies and approve an easing of trade restrictions with the Communists.[19]

In mid-March Secretary Dulles issued a statement on China policy from Canberra, Australia, where he was attending the third meeting of the Council of the Southeast Asia Treaty Organization. "The United States adheres steadfastly to the three main aspects of its China policy," the statement began, "which is to recognize the Republic of China; not to recognize the so-called People's Republic of China; and to oppose the seating of this People's Republic in the United Nations." [20] Dulles said the policy was not merely "an expression of emotional dislike of Chinese communism," although this was "repugnant to us." Rather, the policy was based on considerations both of national and international interest:

> United States diplomatic recognition of the Chinese Communist regime would serve no national purpose but would strengthen and encourage influences hostile to us and our allies and further imperil lands whose independence is related to our own peace and security. . . .
>
>   . . . We believe that United States policies are not merely in our own interest and in the interest of the free world but also that they are in

the interest of the Chinese people themselves, with whom the American people have historic ties of friendship.

On the Senate floor two days after Dulles' statement, Committee supporter Senator Styles H. Bridges (R., N.H.), repudiated presidential assistant Meyer Kestnbaum for stating (March 7), then repeating (March 13), that the Chinese Communists should be recognized by the United States and admitted to the United Nations. "He said, of course, he was expressing his personal views," Bridges added, "but nevertheless, he is a presidential assistant and has this official capacity." [21] Bridges, onetime New Hampshire governor, was troubled about a "Red China Lobby":

> Mr. President, at times in the past we have heard quite a good deal about the China lobby. Without going into the merits or demerits of such a so-called organization, it is quite clear that there now must be a Red China lobby operating in the United States and around the world. Various individuals have spoken but one of these individuals whose remarks I considered to be wholly out of place is Meyer Kestnbaum, an assistant to President Eisenhower. . . .

On April 20, the State Department announced that the United States was prepared to discuss with the fourteen other allied nations participating in the multilateral trade control system certain modifications in the trade controls against Communist China and the Soviet bloc. In response to allied pressure on the issue, the statement said, modifications in certain items "for peaceful use" would be considered. Although these items would be removed from controls and given the status of similar items traded with the European Soviet bloc, "It was emphasized to our allies that there is no change in United States policy with respect to trade with Communist China. The United States will continue its unilateral embargo on all trade." [22]

The Committee wasted no time. "The time has come," said a May 13 letter signed by the steering committee,

> when we must once again forcefully restate the opposition of the great majority of the American people to any deals with Red China. . . .

You will find attached a memorandum which presents the reasoning behind this point of view. It is, in substance, recognition of the dangers of appeasement and a refusal to join in strengthening the avowed enemies of our nation and the Free World.[23]

Attached was a thirteen-page memorandum dated May 1957 entitled "Relations between the United States and Communist China." A later Committee pamphlet called this report a "scholarly paper," saying it was based on a "careful survey . . . of the strength and influence of pro-appeasement sentiment in the United States." [24] Indeed, some passages in the polemic balanced the Committee's views against opposing arguments with uncharacteristic restraint (perhaps prompting former Ambassador Stanley K. Hornbeck to write Marvin Liebman that it was the best presentation of the situation and problem(s) he had seen anywhere.) [25]

A "concerted effort" had gotten underway in the past few months, the paper began, "to convince the American people of the desirability of closer economic and diplomatic relations with Communist China." Pressures had reached "alarming proportions" since November; the new campaign seemed based primarily on two assumptions: because the Communists firmly controlled the Chinese mainland there was nothing the United States or the "Free Chinese on Taiwan" could do to change the situation; because "Chinese Communism is somewhat different from that promoted by the Kremlin," the expansion of trade and cultural relations would "drive a wedge between the Kremlin and Peiping and perhaps even make a Tito out of Mao Tse-tung." These two assumptions were completely false, the document said. Comparing the current situation with the conditions of pre-World War II Europe and Asia, it claimed the lessons about "the fallacy of appeasement of tyranny" evidently had not been learned. Next, the paper took on "Some Advocates of This Point of View," hitting at several newly discovered targets: first, the reports of the American Assembly's November 1956 meeting at Harriman, N.Y., which had pondered the problem of "The United States and the Far East"; [26] second, a speech on December 10, 1956, by Dr. John A. Mackay, at the National Council of Churches in Indianapolis; third, an article in the April 16, 1957, issue of *Look* magazine by Edmund Stevens, with photographs by Philip Harrington "(the two American newspapermen who recently toured Red China in defiance of the official policy of their Government)"; fourth, an article in the April 1957 *Atlantic* magazine entitled "China: Time For A Policy," by Professor John K. Fairbank; and fifth, a Foreign Policy Association pamphlet entitled "Should the United States Deal With Red China?" by Professor A. Doak Barnett. In essence, the memorandum came to the conclusion that the prestige of the People's Republic would be enhanced by any closer ties with the United States. The document's conclusion called for "strong counter measures" against "the campaign to condition the American people for a deal with Communist China," but did not specify what they should be. Considering the argument "that we must be 'realistic' and 'practical,' " the statement answered "that it is precisely because we must be realistic and practical that we must not recognize Red China or accept it into civilized society."

The "strong counter measures" began to unfold after the United Kingdom announced, on May 30, that the same restrictions on trade controls with the Soviet Union thereafter would be applied to the People's Republic. Official State Department reaction: ". . . most disappointed by this action." But the statement noted that security controls on strategic exports to Communist China would be continued on the same basis as then applied to the Soviet bloc.[27]

Publicly, the Committee's response took the form of a full-page advertisement in the June 9 International Edition of the *New York Times,* distributed, in page proof, on June 6, with an accompanying brief memorandum from the steering committee.[28]

The heading screamed **"An Appeal to All Free Men—No Trade with the Enemy,"** with the text following the arguments and sometimes the language of the long memorandum described above. The ad listed 224 "members"—95 representatives and 24 senators (including the regular legislative members of the steering committee, listed separately).[29] On June 11, the steering committee released a statement to the American press opposing the lifting of trade restrictions.[30]

Behind the scenes, the Committee worked quietly but energetically. On June 13, 1957, Liebman thanked Howard P. Jones, Deputy

Assistant Secretary of State for Far Eastern Affairs, for seeing him and Treasurer McKee the previous day and enclosed a copy of both the June 9 advertisement and the May memorandum. Liebman said he had spoken to Mr. Harold Baynton of the Senate's Interstate and Foreign Commerce Committee about proposed trade hearings and had learned they would first be conducted as closed sessions beginning June 20, without a subcommittee to deal exclusively with Red China trade.[31] The secretary then reminded the official that he was planning a trip, mainly to the Far East, and would like to discuss those areas on his itinerary where he might be of service. What type of service he did not elaborate. Several days before Marvin Liebman left on his world tour—in his official capacity, as he later would reveal, as the Committee's secretary—he wrote to President Eisenhower on behalf of the steering committee, enclosing a statement signed by 176 American business leaders. "We, the undersigned businessmen," it began, "hereby strongly express our opposition to any trade relations between our country and Communist China." [32] Opposition was based on six points: 1) that the economy of Communist China would be strengthened; 2) trade relations would be the first step toward recognition and admission to the United Nations; 3) an economy based on free labor could not compete successfully in the world market with an economy based on slave labor; 4) Communist China was an avowed enemy of the United States "and the entire Free World"; 5) opening trade with the enemy would undermine America's allies' anti-Communist position and force them into the Communist orbit; and 6) trade with Communist China would have the same effect as did trade with the Axis Powers prior to World War II, building up the military power of the aggressor. "Just because some misguided nations are willing to make the same fatal mistakes of the past is no reason for the United States to follow suit in this road to national suicide."

Assistant to the President Sherman Adams responded to the Liebman letter on July 31, after the State Department had advised the White House that it "does not consider that a personal reply from the President is required. . . . However, *in view of the prominence of The Committee of One Million and of the signers to the statement transmitted by Mr. Liebman,* it is recommended that a reply be made by an appropriate member of the President's staff'' (italics added). A suggested State Department reply, slightly revised, was sent by Adams:

> On behalf of the President, I would like to thank you for your recent letter and accompanying statement on trade relations with Communist China signed by one hundred and seventy-six leaders of the American business community.
>
> It is gratifying to receive this manifestation of support for the United States position on this vital subject. [33]

The Secretary's Trip

By his own account Marvin Liebman's fourteen-country mission on behalf of the Committee had a twofold purpose: to establish ties with overseas anti-Communist individuals and groups, particularly in Asia; and to bolster their morale by carrying the word, as expressed by the Committee, that the American people remained firmly anti-Communist. As he later reflected on these goals in a long ''Confidential Report'' to the steering committee, Liebman felt he had achieved his first purpose but admitted some difficulty on the second: [34] The Committee was well known in Asia—a point emphasized throughout the report. To be sure, the Committee was considered the American public's spokesman on United States relations with the Chinese Communists. Yet the extent of America's willingness to sacrifice in Asia was under suspicion. Was American leadership weakening? Was the United States moving toward accommodation with worldwide communism. Was it heading toward ''neutralist isolationism?''

The secretary's report was based on his own observations and conclusions, he made clear. He also cautioned readers that the report contained only recollections and impressions of conversations with various Asian leaders, not verbatim quotations. Traveling in his official capacity as secretary of the Committee, he had conferred with foreign government leaders as well as ranking American diplomats and military officers. Liebman carefully listed his contacts in each country:

Japan: U.S. Ambassador Douglas MacArthur II and staff members; the Republic of China Ambassador Chin Tung-Shen; Ryozo Asano, from a leading ruling family in prewar Japan; representatives of the American-Japan Society; the Free Asia Association, and other United States aides and military personnel;

Korea: U.S. Ambassador Walter C. Dowling and staff members; President Syngman Rhee, Vice-President Chang Myon, Foreign Minister Chung Whan Cho; Kong Chin Hang, chairman of the Korean chapter of the Asian People's Anti-Communist League; and other ROK newspaper editors, students, military, and United States officials and advisors.

Taiwan: President Chiang Kai-shek and other government leaders; also hundreds of other Chinese and Americans, including U.S. Ambassador Karl L. Rankin.

Hong Kong: No names mentioned; met with many anti-communist leaders, including refugee leaders, American and British government officials, trade union anti-communists; members of the so-called third force movement, youth leaders, and local representatives of Aid Refugee Chinese Intellectuals (ARCI), of which he was still secretary.

Vietnam: President Ngo Dinh Diem; U.S. Ambassador Elbridge Durbrow, and staff members; leaders of Vietnamese anti-communist groups and the overseas Chinese community, newspapermen and Americans in private and official capacities.

Thailand: Prince Wan Waithayakon, Minister of Foreign Affairs; Pibul Songgram, former Premier; U.S. Ambassador Max Waldo Bishop and staff members; Chinese Ambassador Han Li-Wu; Plang Phloyphrom, editor of the *Bangkok Tribune* and chairman of the local chapter of the Asian People's Anti-Communist League; other Chinese and Thai leaders.

Burma: leaders of the Burma anti-communist movement, overseas Chinese community, Buddhists, and different ethnic groups, but limited contacts with Americans.

Liebman deliberately focused the report, he said, on the seven Asian countries—not even mentioning the other seven visited—because these were the key nations in the struggle against international communism. Throughout the document, moreover, he sprinkled capsulized judgments about political, economic, and social conditions, elaborating on the work of anti-communist organizations, illustrating tactics of the "communist front" organizations, discussing how communists fashioned propaganda themes from political events in the United States, and characterizing his impressions of various Asian leaders, most frequently in relation to their anti-communism. His most optimistic judgment was reserved for Taiwan, which had made the most effective use of American aid, he said, and had shown the most progress; conversely, he was most pessimistic about Burma, which was being lost to communism by default. He was enthusiastic about President Ngo Dinh Diem, finding no "effective opposition" to the Diem regime at all. But he was discouraged by Premier U Nu, whom he did not list as having visited. He thought U Nu was going with the Communists.

Liebman had paid close attention to feedback about the Committee on his trip. Everyone agreed, he said, that it was doing a marvelous job. Every U.S. ambassador applauded the Committee's efforts and said the organization was heralded in Asia to illustrate America's determination to fight against imperialism and communism. Asians apparently found the Committee necessary for strengthening and maintaining morale in their own countries. They urged its work be expanded. In fact, they told Liebman the Committee's work was of far greater political value than the American government's information programs, which were not highly regarded. Altogether, Liebman gave a glowing account of the Committee's effectiveness and potential. There was nary a word of doubt, self-criticism, or suspicion. The Committee of One Million was clearly the outstanding American organization fighting communism in Asia. It even shouldered much of the burden of convincing Asians to keep their confidence in America's will to the cause of freedom. Thus the Committee's work needed to be expanded considerably. Liebman wanted an international propaganda enterprise in concert with Asian anti-Communist groups. The Committee's responsibilities were indeed great, he wrote his steering committee colleagues. He was hopeful the challenge would be met. Self-serving rhetoric notwithstanding, Liebman's enthusiasm was boundless. Within several months of his return from the Far East, at age thirty-four, the Committee's secretary would go into business for himself.

Shortly after arriving back in New York, Marvin Liebman, along with B. A. Garside, the Committee's assistant treasurer, signed and mailed to the New York State Department of Social Welfare a report covering aspects of the Committee's financial affairs. This was the first of successive annual reports (with exceptions in 1970 and 1971 to be noted later) filed by the group with the Department's Bureau of Charitable and Proprietary Organizations. Legislation requiring annual reports from professional fund raisers in New York became effective September 1, 1954. Thus The Committee for One Million was exempted from filing, although the reconstituted group apparently missed filing its first year, 1955–1956. (More about the Committee's reports in the next chapter, pp. 158–63.)[35]

Several days after the twelfth United Nations General Assembly postponed the Chinese seating question for another year (47 for postponement, 27 against, 7 absentions), Liebman responded to a request by Assistant Secretary of State for Far Eastern Affairs Walter S. Robertson for copies of a Committee advertisement in the September 29, 1957, International Edition of the *New York Times*. Under the heading "The Case Against Red China," the full-page statement reprinted excerpts from a Robertson article appearing in the September 1957 issue of *Western World*.[36] Robertson replied that he had refused an honorarium offered by *Western World* and wanted the widest possible distribution for "our" position. He also wanted to know whether the advertisement would be carried in foreign editions.[37]

The Policy Background: An Update

As 1957 drew to a close and the Committee started its fifth year (save for the brief hibernation), Ambassador U. Alexis Johnson and Wang Ping-nan held their seventy-third and, as events developed, last meeting until ten months later. At issue on the American side before suspension of the U.S.–P.R.C. talks were: 1) arguments for the release of the remaining Americans held by the Chinese; 2) an American renunciation of force proposal; and 3) proposals for "pooled arrangements" for American newsmen to visit the mainland, without reciprocity for Chinese newsmen to visit the United States.[38] These issues had preoccupied the two ambassadors, at least since August 6, 1956, when the

People's Republic had lifted its ban on visits by American newsmen, thus prompting what became for the administration a simmering domestic political issue. The State Department rejected the Chinese initiative the next day. While it welcomed the free exchange of information between countries with differing political and social perspectives, the Department's press release said the Chinese Communist regime had created a "special impediment" by holding American citizens "in effect as political hostages." [39]

The only actual agreement between the sides (a pledge to repatriate civilians held by each) had been announced on September 10, 1955. [40]

Since that single 1955 agreement, Secretary of State Dulles had publicly discussed China policy, in an extended and exclusive context, on only two occasions: at the SEATO meetings in Canberra, Australia, on March 12, 1957, and in a San Francisco speech, "Our Policies Toward Communism in China," on June 28, 1957, in which he steadfastly defended American policy of non-recognition, opposition to UN admission, and the nonsanctioning of trading or cultural exchanges. [41] In the San Francisco speech, Dulles reviewed the circumstances under which the Soviet Union was recognized in 1933, saying that Communist China failed to pass the tests the Soviet Union had seemed to pass. Then he ticked off the consequences of recognition: many mainland Chinese "would be immensely discouraged"; millions of overseas Chinese would reluctantly accept the guidance of the People's Republic; the Republic of China would feel betrayed by its friend; the free Asian governments of the Pacific and Southeast Asia "would be gravely perplexed"; and the Communists probably would obtain the seat of China in the United Nations. Dulles also argued against trading relations. In general, the mainland needed militarily related materials and the United States "ought not build up the military power of its potential enemy"; likewise, cultural exchanges would provide an example for China's close neighbors to follow.

Diplomatic recognition "is always a privilege, never a right," the Secretary said. The "de facto argument" for recognition was not sound international law. Besides, diplomatic recognition was not inevitable: "Communist-type despotisms are not so immutable as they sometimes appear.'' Turning to the argument that assisting the Chinese Communists might help them eventually break with the Soviet Union: "No doubt there are basic power rivalries between Russia and China in Asia. But also the Russian and Chinese Communist parties are bound by close ideological ties.'' The United States sought to appraise its China policies "with an open mind and without emotion, except for a certain indignation at the prolonged and cruel abuse of American citizens in China.'' He ended with a series of rhetorical questions about the future of Americans and Chinese, concluding:

> Communism is repugnant to the Chinese people. They are above all, individualists. . . .
>
> We can confidently assume that international communism's rule of strict conformity is, in China as elsewhere, a passing and not a perpetual phase. We owe it to ourselves, our allies, and the Chinese people to do all that we can to contribute to that passing. . . .[42]

The Committee and Sino-Japanese Trade

On May 16, 1958, Marvin Liebman wrote two identical letters to the White House—one to President Eisenhower and one to Assistant to the President Sherman Adams, each enclosing a letter written the same day by Ambassador Grew regarding extension of the Reciprocal Trade Agreements Act then under congressional consideration. In Grew's letter, however, the Reciprocal Trade Agreements Act was not identified until the final paragraph. Instead, Grew wrote that the Chinese Communists had recently broken off all trade relations with Japan and that the Committee had helped bring about this outcome by publishing advertisements in the International Edition of the *New York Times* and in the *Japan Times*.[43]

At least part of the background for Grew's letter began in the Senate on February 27, 1958. Senator George W. Malone (R., Nev.), during a speech about the Trade Agreements Act, said that a trade pact between "Red China and Japan" had been reached. Indeed, an agreement between the China Committee for the Promotion of International Trade and several Japanese business groups had been signed, noted

Senator Styles H. Bridges (R., N.H.), a Committee "member," who included in his April 3 remarks the text of the trade pact as reported by an unidentified radio monitoring service. Senator Bridges said that the previous day's *Record* included a statement released by the Committee which called on the Japanese people and government to reconsider the trade pact. Steering committee member Francis E. Walter had inserted this statement by "The Committee Of One Million," an almost verbatim copy of the advertisement printed in the April 6 International Edition of the *New York Times* and the April 9 issue of the *Japan Times*.[44] On April 15, another steering committee member, Senator H. Alexander Smith, told his Senate colleagues that the Chinese had broken off further negotiations on the trade pact after the Japanese government had recognized and resisted the Peking regime's actual attempt to achieve presumptive approval. Smith agreed with an editorial in that morning's *New York Herald-Tribune,* that the Japanese government's action reflected great credit on its courage and integrity.[45]

Returning to Grew's May 16 letter, the former ambassador to Japan quoted from the Committee's April 6 advertisement which called on Japan "to think once again before entering into any agreement with a regime which could only serve to weaken our common defense against communist imperialism." Grew drew this conclusion:

> . . . Because these sentiments were expressed by the [Committee], recognized internationally as an influential and responsible bi-partisan American organization, they had substantial impact in Japan. We believe that Premier Kishi's action in refusing to grant political concessions to Communist China was a victory for the purposes of our organization and, indeed, for the entire Free World.

Accordingly, this "victory" meant the United States must face "certain responsibilities," i.e., a share of the cost that Japan was paying "for its adherence to the Free World." The cost? Passage of HR 10368, a five-year extension of the Reciprocal Trade Agreements Act.

The two identical Liebman letters to the White House enclosing the Grew appeal received two unidentical replies, one from Douglas Dillon, Deputy Under-Secretary of State for Economic Affairs, on behalf of

President Eisenhower, and one from Sherman Adams himself. Dillon acknowledged Liebman's letter to the President, adding that the "forceful support" of the Committee was greatly appreciated by those interested in the Act's renewal.[46] Adams thanked Liebman for his letter and said they were "pleased and encouraged" to receive such a positive endorsement for extension of the Act.[47]

Marvin Liebman Associates

With Charles Edison's moral and financial support, the Committee's secretary opened his own shop in January 1958: Marvin Liebman Associates, Consultants in Public Relations, Seventeen Park Avenue, New York City.[48] Destined to stay active in political public relations for eleven years—until its abrupt dissolution early in 1969—Liebman's firm had the effect of bringing the Committee's files directly under his control. Thus the materials in the Liebman Collection at the Hoover Institution Archives covering the Committee's records from 1958 to early 1969 are substantially more comprehensive than for the 1953 to 1957 period, when Liebman worked for the Oram firm. The earliest Committee document listing its new Park Avenue address at Liebman's offices was a news release (about Chinese Communist troops leaving Korea) scheduled for publication February 21.[49]

Before the United States and the mainland Chinese once again faced another "Formosan Crisis" in the Taiwan Straits during the summer of 1958, Liebman spearheaded the Committee's more conventional publicity battles against opposing China policy views. In May, for example, an ADA resolution called for an immediate start on negotiations looking toward recognition of the People's Republic by the United States.[50] Previously, in 1956, an ADA resolution had talked only about the mainland Chinese meeting certain conditions for UN admission and had avoided U.S. recognition. The ADA's new position changed substantially: recognition would be taken "not as a gesture of moral approval—which the Chinese Communists obviously do not merit—but as a means of establishing the normal channels of international communication between the two nations."

Apparently, the Committee failed to launch an immediate coun-terattack. Two months later, however, it issued a statement by Senator Paul H. Douglas opposing closer relations with the mainland.[51] Doug-las, a steering committee member, also belonged to the ADA. The state-ment, the *Times* noted, was taken from *New Leader* magazine.[52]

In the aftermath of the Douglas article the Far East returned to the front pages: On August 6, a state of emergency was declared on Matsu and the Pescadores Islands by the Chinese Nationalist Government on Formosa; on August 11, the State Department, in a memorandum rem-iniscent of Secretary Dulles' year-old San Francisco speech on China policy, reaffirmed the non-recognition policy of the government ("The United States is convinced that the Chinese regime does not represent the true will or aspirations of the Chinese people and that our policy of withholding recognition from it is in actuality in their ultimate interest. . . . The United States holds the view that communism's rule in China is not permanent and that it one day will pass. By withholding diplo-matic recognition from Peiping it seeks to hasten that passing").[53] On August 23, shelling of Quemoy, Little Quemoy, and the Tan Islands began from the mainland; on September 4, Secretary Dulles, in a state-ment "cleared by the President," said the United States would not hesi-tate to use armed force in defense of Formosa; and on September 6, Premier Chou En-lai said the Formosa question should be discussed at a resumption of the Sino-American ambassadorial talks. The United States replied that its ambassador to Poland stood ready to meet the P.R.C.'s ambassador to Poland.

A flurry of Committee activity surfaced on September 9, when the *New York Times* printed a Committee press release which revived a fa-vorite saw by terming the shelling of Quemoy and Matsu by Communist China an attempt "to shoot their way onto the United Nations." The next day, Marvin Liebman, in his capacity as secretary of the Commit-tee, made the editorial page of the paper with a letter which warned about making concessions to the Chinese Communists over Formosa, repeated the "shoot their way in" theme, and emphasized the Commit-tee's overwhelming popular support in the United States.

On the day ambassadorial talks resumed in Warsaw between U.S.

Ambassador Jacob D. Beam and P.R.C. Ambassador Wang Ping-nan—
September 15—the *New York Times* printed the Committee's call for a
UN investigation of Communist China's "consistent record of aggression against its neighbors," a charge contained in a new book distributed, the story added, to every UN delegate: *The Black Book on Red
China* by Edward Hunter.[54] The following day the *Times* reported that
Ambassador Henry Cabot Lodge Jr., permanent U.S. representative to
the United Nations, had accepted a copy of the book from retired General James A. Van Fleet, on behalf of the Committee. The Chinese
Communists would be thwarted, Lodge predicted, in trying to shoot
their way into the United Nations. A paperback, the book gave its purpose as follows: "The point at issue can be stated quite simply. Has the
Peking regime in reality the right to speak in the name of the Chinese
people?" The back cover listed the Committee's full steering committee
plus the names of 92 "members."

Also on September 16, Marvin Liebman sent Secretary Dulles
another article by Ambassador Grew, "Quemoy and Matsu—The
Spectre of Munich," a polemic arguing that the bombardment of the
offshore islands and subsequent P.R.C. threats of world war had been
timed "with one thought in mind—the admission of Communist China
to the United Nations." [55] On September 23, the General Assembly, by
a vote of 44 to 28 with 9 abstentions, again approved a U.S. proposal to
postpone the seating question for another year.

A week later, as the November mid-term elections approached,
Liebman drafted a "Personal and Confidential" fund raising letter,
using his own firm's letterhead, on behalf of Congressman Judd.[56] Written, he said, without Judd's knowledge, the appeal for contributions
evidently was sent to members of the organizations both men served in
common—the Committee, Aid Refugee Chinese Intellectuals, the
American Bureau for Medical Aid to China, and the American Asian
Educational Exchange, Inc. Liebman was quite concerned about Judd's
campaign, emphasizing his urgency by announcing a personal contribution of $250.

Although Judd won his re-election bid, the Committee lost two important senators: H. Alexander Smith, at seventy-nine, retired; and Mi-

nority Leader William Knowland, deciding to run for governor of California, lost to Edmund G. (Pat) Brown. Governor Goodwin J. Knight, forced by California Republicans to abdicate in favor of Knowland, ran for Knowland's Senate seat and was beaten by Democrat Clair Engle. The Democrats gained a 66 to 34 Senate margin and a 283 to 154 House majority. *The Black Book on Red China* had been sent to all candidates for federal office in the 1958 election.[57]

After the election, 500 delegates to the World Order Study Conference of the National Council of Churches of Christ in the U.S.A. passed a unanimous resolution, during a Cleveland gathering on November 21, in favor of U.S. recognition of the People's Republic and its admission to the United Nations. Interestingly, coverage by the *New York Times* on November 23 featured in its headline and lead a condemnation of the resolution by an original signer of the Committee's petition and consistent supporter, Reverend Daniel Poling, editor of the *Christian Herald*. Using as its lead Dr. Poling's rebuke of the conference's action, the story reported that the resolution did not constitute approval but merely the hope that resumption of diplomatic relations would help make possible restoration of the relationship between Chinese and American churches. Before the resolution was passed, the Committee had sent the conference a telegram urging its defeat. The article added that Dr. Judd felt the resolution did not represent the feelings of Protestants, only of those who endorsed it.

To counteract this publicity, the Committee conducted a poll of Protestant clergymen, an idea originating with Dr. Judd.[58] The *Times* reported that more than 7,000 clergymen had "signed a petition" opposing U.S. recognition of Communist China, only 936 approving recognition. But on February 17, 1959, a letter from the steering committee updated the poll results: 9,088 replies received to that date; 7,837 opposed to *either* recognition or admission to the United Nations; 1,042 in favor; 209 either noncommittal or divided in opinion.[59] The exact same results later were included in a Committee pamphlet (9,088 replies, 7,837 opposed, 1,042 in favor, and 209 uncertain). But the pamphlet said: The newly organized Clergymen's Committee polled *some 46,000* Protestant clergymen in the United States on the question of recognition of Red China or its admission to the UN" (italics added).[60]

Tibet

When reports from India on March 20, 1959, indicated that a major armed revolution against the Chinese Communists was taking place in Tibet, the Committee moved quickly to champion another anti-Chinese Communist cause. Within two weeks of the announcement, Marvin Liebman talked on three occasions with the State Department's Public Affairs Adviser, Bureau of Far Eastern Affairs, regarding the formation of a proposed "American Emergency Committee for Free Tibet." [61] On April 1, Liebman phoned to say that the proposed organization was proceeding quietly and would not be announced until the State Department indicated the time was propitious. He also said his group was considering asking an American member of the International Rescue Committee to proceed quickly to Kalimpong (India) to report on the Tibetan refugee situation, but the Department's official suggested an Asian might be more suitable for the trip. On April 2, Liebman reported that plans to send an American had been canceled, that the Indian representative of the *Christian Science Monitor* had been asked by his newspaper to go to Kalimpong and report on the refugees to the Rescue Committee as well as to his newspaper. Liebman said as part of its plan to exploit the incident the emerging organization might bring to the United States the former prime minister of Tibet, then in India. On April 3, Liebman reported that he and Congressman Judd were seeing the Indian ambassador at 4:15 P.M. that day and would solicit suggestions how the proposed "Emergency Committee" might help the Tibetan refugees.

> Mr. Liebman said he agreed entirely that Asian voices on the Tibetan tragedy are more useful now than American. He repeated that he and his associates were moving forward nevertheless with plans to form the nucleus of an 'Emergency Committee' to be announced when it becomes appropriate to do so, *and only after consultation with the Department*. (Italics added)

According to a later pamphlet, the Committee's leaders helped organize "an independent philanthropic effort," the "American Emergency Committee for Tibetan Refugees," under the leadership of Lowell Thomas, prominent newscaster and author.[62]

A letter of April 21 on Committee letterhead, signed by Marvin Liebman and enclosing a "Communique to the American People" about the Tibetan situation, was circulated, according to Senator Kenneth B. Keating (R., N.Y.), who identified himself as a Committee member while including the materials in the Appendix of the May 12, 1959 *Congressional Record*.[63] Among other points, the "Communique" said that "the current fight in Tibet is not a revolution but rather the latest battle in a 9-year war against communism. The fighting in Tibet is only a part of the continuous and active struggle against communism which is being carried out in all parts of China." Activity on this issue resurfaced in September. In the interim, John Foster Dulles had resigned, died, and been replaced as Secretary of State by Christian A. Herter; Walter S. Robertson had resigned, effective July 1, 1959, and been replaced as Assistant Secretary for Far Eastern Affairs by J. Graham Parsons; and the Committee had become embattled in a decision by the International Olympic Committee to replace the Republic of China with the People's Republic during the Winter Games scheduled for Squaw Valley, Calif., in February 1960. On June 3, the day he left for Seoul, Korea, to attend the annual conference of the Asian Peoples' Anti-Communist League, Marvin Liebman dispatched a "Dear Friend" letter concerning the Olympics issue, asking readers to register their protest by writing to various American members of the Olympic Committee and to their political leaders as well.[64]

In the *New York Times* on September 14, the day before the regular session of the General Assembly convened, the Committee was quoted as urging the United Nations to take whatever action necessary to preserve the "freedom and sanctity" of the Tibetan people. The *Times* quoted the Committee as declaring the government of India need not be reminded that the same regime oppressing the peaceful Tibetans was also violating the soil and sovereignty of India and other neighboring states.

When the General Assembly convened the following day, Secretary of State Christian A. Herter headed the U.S. delegation, which also included Ambassadors Henry Cabot Lodge and James J. Wadsworth, Walter S. Robertson, the retired Assistant Secretary of State for Far Eastern Affairs, and three signers of the Committee's original petition to

Eisenhower in 1953: Representative James G. Fulton (R., Pa.), listed as a "member" since 1953; Representative Clement J. Zablocki (D., Wisc.), listed as a "member" through March 14, 1955; and George Meany, President of the AFL-CIO, listed as a "member" through March 14, 1955. Additionally, an alternate member of the U.S. delegation to the fourteenth General Assembly was Harold Riegelman, the New York attorney later listed as a registered foreign agent of Nationalist China.[65] The General Assembly voted on September 16, 1959, as it had since 1953, in favor of the seemingly inevitable U.S. resolution (44 to 29 with 9 abstentions) postponing consideration of the Chinese seating question for another year.

As a postscript to the Committee's work on the Tibetan issue, five members of the steering committee wrote to Ambassador Lodge on Committee letterhead, protesting the Tibetan draft resolution then before the General Assembly.[66] As presented by Ireland and Malaya, the resolution lacked two basic points, the letter said: it failed to name Red China for the crimes against the Tibetans, and it lacked a recommendation on any specific UN action. The letter urged Ambassador Lodge to offer two amendments: that Red China be charged with genocide against the Tibetan people and that a UN commission of inquiry be organized to investigate the Tibetan situation and report back. Lodge replied, claiming the 45 to 9 passage of the Irish and Malayan resolution (the steering committee's letter reached him the day before the vote) "was certainly not a defeat for the United Nations. Indeed it was a very definite victory." [67] He would have preferred a stronger resolution, Lodge admitted, but attempts to amend it would have risked its defeat. Presumably, Lodge's little lesson in parliamentary realities was not lost on the steering committee's five journeymen politicians.

Several years later, evaluating a tactical Committee decision before the 1962 mid-term elections, Marvin Liebman reflected back on earlier China policy politics. By demonstrating widespread public support for then existing China policy, he wrote Dr. Judd, their purpose had been to "strengthen the hand" of Eisenhower and the Republican administration. Eisenhower and Dulles, he presumed, welcomed their activities.[68]

Stirrings in Congress and Elsewhere

The 86th Congress, which convened in January 1959, was the first to ask searching questions about conditions in, and American policy toward, the People's Republic of China. Most of the inquiries originated in the Senate, by individual senators or by the Senate Foreign Relations Committee, two of whose former Republican members, H. Alexander Smith and William F. Knowland, Committee of One Million stalwarts, were gone. Who initiated China policy inquiries? How did individual Committee members and the Committee as a whole react to them?

Ironically, the first to initiate an independent study of developments on the Chinese mainland was an original signer of the Committee's 1953 petition, Senator Alexander Wiley (R., Wisc.), the ranking Republican member of the Senate Foreign Relations Committee, whose name had appeared on Committee materials when he was chairman of the Foreign Relations Committee during the 83rd Congress. On January 28, 1959, Senator Wiley told his colleagues he had asked the Legislative Reference Service and the staff of the Foreign Relations Committee "to undertake an examination of tensions in Communist China." [1] The study would cover not only internal frictions but also "the extent of divergence and cleavage between China, the Soviet Union, and the European satellites."

On February 16, 1959, a contract was drawn between the Senate Foreign Relations Committee and Conlon Associates, a San Francisco research firm, calling for a study of U.S. foreign policy in Asia. (The date is noted here to provide a chronological sequence to developments in the 86th Congress; the relevant documents will be cited below in a later discussion of the study's release.)

To be sure, other senators and congressmen previously had raised questions about different aspects of China policy—notably the State Department's refusal to allow American newsmen passports for travel on the mainland—and had included in the *Record* various pleas for policy reevaluations and assessments of conditions in China.[2] One courageous man, Congressman Charles O. Porter (D., Ore.), had publicly supported U.S. recognition of the People's Republic.[3] But the first senator to speak at length in behalf of a new China policy was the new Democratic senator from California, Clair Engle. "I know there are political dangers in undertaking to discuss our China foreign policy," he began his May 21 address:

> I am aware of the fact that the State Department regards this area of our foreign policy as one that should not be touched.
>
> I do not see why our policy in China should be any more sacrosanct than our policy in Europe . . . I am convinced that our China policy needs a critical reexamination. I am prepared to dispute the premise that our present policy is adequate and that nothing about it can or should be changed.[4]

Engle's long analysis concluded with these recommendations: that the United States should 1) recognize the principle of reciprocity with respect to the exchange of newsmen; 2) discuss the possibility of placing trade with mainland China on the same basis as trade with the Soviet Union; 3) make clear that military adventures against the mainland would not be supported; 4) assume the initiative of placing the defense of Formosa on a "broader international base"; 5) consider negotiations with the People's Republic at a higher level than the ambassadorial talks in Warsaw; and 6) clarify that all negotiations should be on a quid pro quo basis and that the United States was determined to halt any Communist aggression in the Far East.

The speech prompted immediate expressions of congratulations from several senators, among them, Senator Thomas J. Dodd (D., Conn.), a frequent Committee "member" as a congressman and subsequently a steering committee member.[5] One week later on the House floor, Dr. Judd, not mentioning Engle's Senate address, attacked the strategy of containment, the prerequisites of which, he said, "do not now exist . . . . The will and capacity of captive peoples to gain their freedom are not increasing as rapidly as the parallel will and capacity of free peoples to defend their freedom are diminishing.'' [6] There had been, Judd added, ''the steady erosion of our most vital national characteristic, our will-to-win.''

On June 4, Congressman Porter proposed a trade mission to China as a first step toward ascertaining ''recent and reliable facts'' on which China policy could be based. Porter was challenged by two Committee activists, Congressman Alvin M. Bentley (R., Mich.), a consistent supporter since 1953, and Dr. Judd. On June 8, another Committee adherent, a former congressman and freshman senator from West Virginia, Robert C. Byrd, justified U.S. China policy as the policy of both political parties since the Truman administration, arguing against any change.[7] On August 17, the House debated and passed (368 to 2, 48 not voting) H. Con. Res. 369, introduced by Congressman Clement J. Zablocki (D., Wisc.). Identical resolutions also had been introduced by Dr. Judd and another original signer of the 1953 petition and longtime ''member,'' Congressman James G. Fulton (R., Pa.):

> . . . . That it is the sense of the Congress that its opposition to the seating in the United Nations of the Communist China regime as the representative of China should be as is hereby reiterated; and be it further *Resolved,* That it is hereby declared to be the continuing sense of the Congress that the Communist regime in China has not demonstrated its willingness to fulfill the obligations contained in the charter of the United Nations and should not be recognized to represent China in the United Nations.[8]

On September 2, Congressmen Zablocki and Fulton were among the delegates and alternates appointed by President Eisenhower to the upcoming fourteenth United Nations General Assembly and confirmed by the Senate.[9]

''Tensions in Communist China,'' the study initiated by Senator Wiley in January, emerged several days before Congress recessed in September.[10] Subtitled ''An Analysis of Internal Pressures Generated Since 1949,'' Wiley's foreword is noteworthy: ''This report indicates,'' he said, "that some of the factual assumptions on which our China policy is based are not static but are constantly in a state of change. Opposition to the present regime in Communist China is poorly and ineffectively organized, according to the report." Wiley concluded that an "effective China policy" must be based on the following factors: Peking's increasing military power; the impact of its "population explosion" on the world; the impact on world trade of the "growing Chinese economic might"; and "the interrelationships in the Communist league, particularly between Peking and Moscow."

Basically, the study meant three things to Wiley: that the Communist leadership had a "strong grasp on China," that "large groups of Chinese people . . . are experiencing some economic benefits under the Communist system," and that if the rate of Chinese economic expansion continued, "China may in a few years rank as one of the great powers." Thus, "our China policy cannot be based on an attitude of 'turning our heads.' We must remain alert and adequate."

The "Conlon Report"

Midway between the first and second sessions of the 86th Congress (on October 31), the Senate Foreign Relations Committee released "United States Foreign Policy in Asia," soon to be known as the "Conlon Report." [11] The document, which covered 115 substantive pages, 36 of which dealt with the People's Republic and Taiwan, concluded American policy ought to be based on the assumption that, barring a war with the United States, "the Chinese Communist Government will have a lengthy tenure." (p. 527) The authors also said: "Communist China is confident that within a decade her power and influence will demand acknowledgement, and that the basic issues involving China can then be settled on her terms, probably without war." (p. 535) One section discussed the political, economic, and social trends on Taiwan, making only one "fairly safe" prediction: "either Taiwan will be joined with mainland China or the process of Taiwanization will continue. In the concrete terms of the present, if Taiwan does not go to the Communists, it will go increasingly to the Taiwanese." (p. 539)

U.S. China policy was divided into a point-by-point analysis of three general approaches to the problem: 1) "containment through isolation" (current policy, the study indicated); 2) "normalization of relations" (i.e., recognizing the Chinese Communists and agreeing to their seating in the United Nations); and 3) "exploration and negotiation." The last, adopted as the basic recommendation of the report, would have three objectives: to test P.R.C. willingness to "coexist" with the United States; to seek an expanded, more dynamic, flexible, and positive policy; and "to make possible a greater degree of collective agreement on the China issue among the major nations of the free world." (pp. 549–51)

First stage proposals to implement this policy included exchanging journalists; conducting informal discussions with the Chinese on the mainland; and holding informal and private discussions with America's allies to solicit ideas about "the problem of China." If the first stage showed promise, the second would consist of a relaxation of trade restrictions; additional discussions with allies, including Taiwan, regarding various specific points of accommodation (e.g., UN admission for the People's Republic, U.S. recognition of—and underwriting the defense of—a "Republic of Taiwan"); and a treaty of commerce with the Peking regime which, if successful, would be followed by *de facto* recognition.

The Conlon Report was released to the press on Saturday, October 31. The *New York Times* covered the story with a UPI dispatch on page 27 of the Sunday paper, reporting that a step-by-step revision of U.S. China policy had been recommended to the Senate Foreign Relations Committee by a group of private researchers. Senator J. William Fulbright thought it "very provocative" but said he did not believe the United States should recognize the Chinese People's Republic at that time, adding that it also was unwise to ignore 600 million people.

The Committee of One Million reacted quickly. In a response scheduled for release Wednesday, November 4, but which failed to make the *Times,* the steering committee recited the history of U.S. public and private opposition to any softening of American policy toward the Chinese Communists.[12] The majority of peoples and nations backed this stand, the release added, but

> . . . there are some governments and even some leaders of American opinion who see fit to travel the road of appeasement and accommodation with an avowed enemy of our country and of universal freedom. They follow the mentality of the ostrich who has hidden his head in the sands of illusion and has not learned the bitter lesson of past appeasement of tyranny. . . .
>
> By standing strongly against the Peiping regime we will, in effect, be helping the enslaved masses of China toward the day when they may once again live in freedom and human dignity.

Next, Marvin Liebman was quoted as expressing doubts about the competence of Conlon Associates:

> To the best of my knowledge, Conlon Associates conducted no serious investigation of either the sentiment of the American people or their leaders or, more important, the sentiments of our allies in Asia. The [Committee] is the one organization in the United States dedicated to the single purpose of opposing [recognition and admission to the U.N.]. We were not consulted at any time. . . .

A letter to members and friends on November 9 from a new Committee address (343 Lexington Avenue, New York 16, New York) told how the Committee "counter-attacked immediately" in order to "keep the record straight and to show our allies in Asia that the Conlon Report represented neither the thinking of the American people nor the Government of the United States." The Committee was "the one organization in the United States that is able to take such immediate action." Then came an appeal for money:

> To carry on this type of activity and maintain our continuing program of providing factual information and material on Red China to the American people, we must have the support of all alert Americans who realize the tremendous issues at stake. . . . We hope you will see fit to continue your support by making your immediate maximum contribution. . . .[13]

This "Dear Friend" solicitation, tagged onto an attack on the Conlon Report, typified a favorite Committee fund raising technique. This subject requires elaboration.

Fund Raising and Finances

The problem of raising funds, Liebman often noted, was continuous. Undoubtedly, part of the difficulty resulted from the group's non-tax exempt status, meaning it had to rely on "hard dollar" contributions. Each year the Committee seemed to start with a financial deficit, managing to overcome it by the end of the year. Thus fund-raising appeals never ended. As suggested by the solicitation above, moreover, a broadside or propaganda piece frequently concluded with a pitch for money. So did some of the Committee's advertisements, pamphlets, and related materials. Most solicitations, however, were sent by mail over the signature of the steering committee or selected steering committee members. Thus contributions were always arriving at Committee headquarters—the offices of Marvin Liebman Associates.

Marvin Liebman was the Committee's secretary, while his firm was registered as the group's professional fund raiser. Marvin Liebman Associates, Inc. represented other politically active groups in a like manner. In 1962, for example, he wrote the Public Relations Society of America that his firm specialized largely in public interest organizational work, mainly in causes fighting communism abroad or supporting the conservative political philosophy at home.[14] He listed his clients as follows: McGraw-Edison Company Committee for Public Affairs, The Committee of One Million, American Afro-Asian Educational Exchange, Greater New York School of Anti-Communism, the Conservative Party, and American Committee for Aid to Katanga Freedom Fighters. Past clients, he said, included American Emergency Committee for Tibetan Refugees, Aid Refugee Chinese Intellectuals, Thomas Alva Edison Foundation, Committee for Freedom for All Peoples, Young Americans for Freedom, American Jewish League Against Communism, Historical Research Foundation, Alfred Kohlberg Memorial Fund, National Review Fifth Anniversary Dinner Committee, and

Emergency Committee for Chinese Refugees. Liebman said his services for these organizations included public relations counseling, fund raising, program organization and management, staff services, and complete office facilities. Remuneration, he added, was received through agreed monthly fees on a contractual basis. In short, Marvin Liebman Associates, Inc. was a central operation serving similarly funded political organizations.

The above facts should be kept in mind when considering the Committee's financial affairs. Aside from numerous random references in memoranda, minutes, reports, etc., data about the Committee's finances are derived from two basic sets of materials: 1) Liebman's own files, which include statements of the Committee's cash receipts and disbursements attached to C.P.A. examination reports for fiscal years ending March 31, 1958, 1959, 1960, 1962, and 1966; [15] and 2) annual public reports filed on behalf of the Committee with the New York State Board of Social Welfare, Bureau of Charitable and Proprietary Organizations, where the Committee, under New York law, was registered (No. 7351) as an unincorporated association (a "charitable organization," in the lexicon of the New York bureau) established in February 1955. Its stated purpose was to "mobilize bi-partisan support to back the government policy of opposition of Communist China to the UN and non-recognition of the Peiping regime through broad public educational and informational programs." [16] Consecutive reports bearing Liebman's signature as Secretary (and either B. A. Garside's or, in 1958, Frederick C. McKee's) were filed for the fiscal years ending March 31, 1957 through fiscal 1968. The Committee moved to Washington, D.C. in March 1969, after Liebman abruptly terminated his business. The fiscal 1969 report was filed and signed by Lee Edwards as Committee secretary and B.A. Garside as assistant treasurer. Subsequently, although the Committee sent in reports for 1970 and 1971, neither was signed and both were returned for signatures, which were not forthcoming, leaving New York State with no report for 1970 and an unsigned (and thereby unofficial) copy of the 1971 report—the largest year for contributions in the organization's history.

Table 7.1 shows total annual contributions as filed in the fifteen

TABLE 7.1
**Portions of Committee Annual Reports to New York State Board
of Social Welfare Covering Contributions and
Total Fund-Raising Expenses**

FISCAL YEAR ENDING MARCH 31	TOTAL CONTRIBUTIONS REPORTED	TOTAL FUND-RAISING EXPENSES INCLUDING COMPENSATION	PERCENTAGE EXPENSES TO CONTRIBUTIONS
1956 (no report filed)	—	—	—
1957 *	$ 43,861.24	$ 13,317.45	30.4
1958 *	66,997.47	20,104.86	30.0
1959 *	69,688.54	17,803.96	25.6
1960	38,689.04	7,980.14	20.6
1961 *	59,828.48	19,735.55	33.0
1962	81,907.04	23,987.71	29.3
1963 (original)	54,290.31	15,419.57	28.4
1963 (as amended)	54,290.31	23,692.77	43.6
1964	62,027.69	32,848.80	53.0
1965	54,717.13	32,490.34	59.4
1966	66,343.00	31,462.00	47.4
1967	109,430.00	44,848.00	41.0
1968 †	22,858.00	20,214.00	88.4
1969 *	46,515.00	36,596.00	78.7
1970 (unavailable)	—	—	—
1971 (unofficial because unsigned)	310,860.00	255,977.00	82.3

* indicates years in which reporting form revised.
† last report signed by Secretary Liebman.

available Committee reports; total fund-raising expenses, including compensation; and percentage of fund-raising expenses to contributions. Only the total annual contributions remained a uniform category on all fifteen sets of available New York State reports (five different sets of forms, using varying reporting categories and definitions, were in use during this period). Thus the data included under "Total Fund-Raising Expenses Including Compensation" are derived from the Committee's annual answers to differing specifications for breaking down expenditures. Nonetheless, it is apparent from these figures—especially after a

1963 New York State field audit corrected the reporting procedure for allocating expenditures and ordered an amended report for 1963—that a high percentage of dollars was expended in the process of raising funds. Part of the problem (as evidenced by the solicitation in the Conlon Report letter above) was the difficulty in separating, for accounting purposes, propaganda from fund-raising functions. The Committee was, after all, the type of informal membership organization which typically expends a relatively high percentage of income for mobilizing public opinion on a political issue.

To be sure, the problem was recognized in 1963 by the New York State Department of Social Welfare, which conducted a field audit of the records both of Marvin Liebman Associates, Inc., in its capacity as a professional fund raiser, and the Committee as a registered "charitable organization." The audit was conducted at Leibman's offices, then at 79 Madison Avenue, Suite 905. Liebman and two members of his staff were present.[17]

In reporting his findings, the auditor indicated that Liebman had said he got together groups of well known people interested in a political problem and then set up an organization. The auditor noted that periodic fund raising was accomplished through mail appeals sent to a contributors list over the signature of the steering committee.

On January 1, 1963, the auditor further indicated, Marvin Liebman Associates, Inc. and the Committee executed a written agreement whereby the former was employed by the latter to raise funds, counsel on public relations, and manage and execute the organization's program in conjunction with the steering committee. Liebman's total monthly fee was to be $2,000 ($500 for fund raising and public relations and $1,500 for program management, staff, and headquarters). Additionally, the firm was to be reimbursed for out-of-pocket expenses. The Committee was to pay directly all suppliers and services.

The auditor noted that fees actually paid to Marvin Liebman Associates, Inc., totaling $18,000, were not broken down in the cash book according to the functions of the expenditures—i.e., services rendered, administration, and fund raising. The auditor then reviewed the Committee's cash book for fiscal 1963, which showed expenditures of

$51,481,18, broken down by the Committee's own accountant into the following disbursements:

Disbursements:

Special Committee Projects:

Publications including mailing	$31,511.61	
Public information and opinion mobilization	4,500.00	
Press information service	50.00	$36,061.61

Administrative Expenses for General
Education Program:

Program management	$ 9,000.00	
Clerical & professional services	620.00	
Telephone, telegraph & messenger	428.36	
Rent	787.92	
Storage	79.92	
Office expenses	3.79	$10,919.57

Fund Raising:

Campaign direction		$ 4,500.00
	Total disbursements	$51,481.18

The above disbursements, the auditor noted, formed the basis of the Committee's annual report to the New York State Board of Social Welfare. Whereas the Committee's breakdown showed $36,061.61 for Committee projects, $10,919.57 for managing and directing the organization, and $4,500 for raising contributions, the state's auditor commented: "Literature, stationery, printing, postage, etc., sent to prospective donors was entered as either public information, publications, etc. This is incorrect. The entries should have been allocated in both services rendered and fund raising costs in accordance with the function of the expenditure."

As an example, the auditor pointed to the last paragraph of a letter signed by Walter H. Judd on Committee letterhead, indicating an en-

closed postage-paid return envelope, which asked for financial support
from prospective contributors. This kind of literature, he suggested, currently allocated as services rendered, in fact should have been prorated
between fund raising and services rendered. There was also a question
involving the Committee's consent forms, which did not indicate that
the signer consented to have his name used for soliciting funds. The
auditor concluded his report with several comments and recommendations, among which were the following:

He thought the annual report should be amended so that fund-
raising expenses would be allocated properly. (An amended 1963 report, dated January 21, 1964, was filed by Secretary Liebman and
Treasurer Garside. Table 7.1 reveals that as a result of the amended
1963 report, the percentage of expenses to contributions climbed 15
percent to 43.6 percent and went even higher in all but one of the remaining years for which reports are available.)

The auditor recommended that New York's attorney general be informed "that the organization's fund raising and administrative costs are
very high." (The New York State Department of Social Welfare did in
fact refer the matter to the attorney general's office, but it is not known
what further action, if any, was taken.)

The auditor also recommended that the Committee's offices be visited in 60 days "to see if compliance in securing signatures on the
proper consent forms has been made." (A follow-up inspection was
made on February 5, 1964. On April 8, 1964, Marvin Leibman wrote
the New York State Board of Social Welfare that the Committee would
have acceptable written consents from all individuals listed on any material used to solicit funds in New York State.)

Tax Exemption and the AAUN

A non-public controversy that developed early in 1959 between the
Committee and the American Association for the United Nations
(AAUN) over annual budget comparisons led in 1960 to a public row
when the Committee attempted to change its non-tax exempt status with
the Internal Revenue Service (I.R.S.). Origin of the controversy was a

one-sentence remark in a steering committee memorandum entitled "Report on 1958," circulated early in 1969:

> . . . We have managed to carry on a historic program which is in the great tradition of American citizens banding together in the fight for our own security and the cause of freedom. All this was made possible through the contribution of some 6,000 individuals during 1958 totaling a little under $66,000. The [AAUN], *which supports the admission of Red China to the United Nations, has an annual budget of well over $300,000.*[18] (italics added)

The implication of the Committee's remark was that the AAUN's $300,000 was pitted against the Committee's $66,000, wrote Clark M. Eichelberger, the AAUN's executive director, to Liebman on February 19, 1959. "This, of course, is dishonest. A very small part of the budget of the AAUN is spent discussing the question of Chinese representation in the UN. Neither has the AAUN made an unqualified endorsement of the seating of Communist China delegates in the UN." Liebman replied that the budget comparison was not meant in any way to be dishonest but intended only to cite the effectiveness of similar type organizations in the area of foreign affairs public opinion and their budget disparities.[19] There the matter apparently rested until the Committee applied for, and was denied, tax exempt status from the I.R.S.[20]

Informed in a March 30, 1960, letter from the Treasury Department that the Committee failed to qualify, Marvin Liebman wrote Secretary of the Treasury Robert B. Anderson on May 26, 1960, pointing out, as he later would write to Dr. Judd, that the AAUN and the Institute of Pacific Relations, both "soft" in their policy toward Communist China, benefited from tax exempt status while the Committee did not.[21] Liebman sent copies of his letter to Anderson to William F. Buckley Jr., George E. Sokolsky, Frank Hannigan, and Roy W. Howard, attached to a memorandum explaining the problem and asking for some editorial help.[22] Almost the identical memorandum went to Congressman Francis E. Walter and Senator James O. Eastland: Walter, a steering committee member and then current chairman of the House Committee on Un-American Activities; Eastland, a signer of the original 1953 petition whose name ceased appearing on Committee materials after March 14, 1955, and since 1956 chairman of the Senate Committee on the Judiciary. Was there any chance, Liebman asked the legislators, that this matter could be explored? [23]

Thereafter, the Committee's tax status split into two issues: the substantive one with the I.R.S. and a fight between the Committee and the AAUN (actually, between Liebman and Eichelberger) over the implied challenge to the AAUN's tax exemption.

On the I.R.S. question, Liebman received a letter from I.R.S. Assistant Commissioner Harold L. Swartz in direct reply to his May 26 letter to Secretary Anderson. Swartz's explanation sought to assure the Committee that its status was determined "entirely on the facts involved and the statutory provisions which govern them." Swartz went into great detail, citing legal precedents and operative interpretations of the codes covering the four tests necessary for an organization to qualify for exemption. He promised that if the Committee submitted evidence in the future that it had changed its operational guidelines as specified in the applicable code, a careful consideration would be given to another request for exemption.[24]

On the Liebman vs. Eichelberger front, meanwhile, another dimension was added when steering committee member Paul H. Douglas asked Liebman about the problem. Liebman's answer reviewed the history back to the January 1959 remark in the Committee's "Report on 1958." [25] He told Douglas the Committee was not protesting the AAUN's tax exempt status but was asking for similar treatment. The Committee, he said, had never used the word "lobby" in referring to the AAUN or, for that matter, to itself. There followed a series of letters between Liebman and Douglas' administrative assistant, Frank W. McCulloch, the major outcome of which, Liebman later confided to Dr. Judd, was that Douglas had asked him to withdraw his past statements and make a public statement clearing the AAUN.[26] Liebman had a dilemma: If he did not bow to Douglas' wishes, the Committee might lose the highly prized Democratic senator; if he did accede to the request, however, he would not be acting according to what he believed was right. Liebman asked Judd's advice, making clear that if the solution meant retaining the Committee's bipartisan posture he would give in to Douglas. (No Judd reply was located.)

Liebman drafted a letter to Eichelberger which, edited, was sent to the AAUN's executive director, copies also going to Paul Douglas, Roy Howard, Walter Judd, Frank McCulloch, and George Sokolsky. It was not then or previously his intention, he said, to publicly injure the AAUN and jeopardize its tax exemption. Quoting at length from his own May 26 letter to Secretary Anderson, Liebman endeavored to show, in effect, that the AAUN and the Committee were similar in conducting educational and informational campaigns. Apparently, however, the answers failed to work. An August 31 letter to Liebman from McCulloch reviewed the previous correspondence, including Liebman's letter to Eichelberger, and pressed him further about retracting the erroneous information given to the Treasury Department and publicly released. On September 7, Liebman wrote McCulloch that he did not see what else he could do with Clark Eichelberger and thought it best to leave the matter alone. A week later, however, on September 14, Liebman wrote Secretary Anderson, with no copies indicated, stating: 1) it was not his intention to challenge the tax exemption of the AAUN; 2) contrary to his earlier understanding, the AAUN had never supported or advocated Communist China's entry in the United Nations, though its officers had supported discussion of the issue at the United Nations; 3) he was not aware of any AAUN legislative lobby on the question of China; and 4) the purpose of his original letter to Secretary Anderson was to suggest the Committee was entitled to tax exemption because a public stand on a controversial issue should not disqualify (and did not disqualify the AAUN) tax exempt status for organizations otherwise qualified.[27]

Later in the year, money matters still on his mind, Liebman wrote Charles Edison, enclosing a copy of a letter sent to 122 people who had contributed $100 or more to the organization but who had not given any money to the American-Asian Educational Exchange.[28] The AAEE, he told Edison, had been created to establish a group with identical overall aims as the Committee that could receive tax exempt contributions. Apparently, however, the successful battle for AAEE tax exemption had not worked out as anticipated: a majority of their contributors still gave to the Committee, but only a minority also gave to the AAEE. Part of Liebman's concern, he admitted, was that both the Committee and AAEE owed money to suppliers and to Marvin Liebman Associates.

The "China Lobby" vs. the "Red China Lobby"

About the same time as his letter to Edison, Liebman learned from an advertisement in the December 7 issue of *Publisher's Weekly* about the scheduled March 7, 1960, publication by Macmillan of Ross Y. Koen's *The China Lobby in American Politics*. As noted previously (chapter 1), Koen's book never was *legally* published by Macmillan despite the printing of more than 4,000 copies and the advance distribution of many to reviewers, bookstores, and libraries. After fourteen years of legal battles, it finally emerged in 1974, with only minor modifications, as a Harper and Row paperback.

The suppression of Koen's book offers an ironic backdrop to a literary project launched by the Committee which fared far better: *The Red China Lobby*. Indeed, as Liebman's records make clear, *The Red China Lobby*, published in 1963, was conceived by him as a direct counterattack on *The China Lobby in American Politics*, although he never intended it to be officially identified with the Committee.[29] Because the gradual decline of Koen's publishing venture coincides with the evolution of Liebman's, the two stories offer a fascinating confrontation between the "China Lobby" and the "Red China Lobby." The following juxtaposition is pieced together from documents in Liebman's files, from a 1969 article by Koen, from a 1970 study of the Koen incident by Paul A. Marsh, and from copies of Koen's correspondence with Macmillan (for which I am greatly indebted to Professor Marsh):[30]

Liebman's account of the Committee's involvement in the Koen incident is summarized in a March 1960 memorandum written to Priscilla Buckley, managing editor of *National Review* and sister of William F. Jr. and James L.[31] The Committee got wind of the impending book, Liebman wrote her on Committee letterhead, through a trade advertisement in an early December edition of *Publisher's Weekly,* and tried to get either a copy or a set of galleys. Told that neither the book nor the galleys was available, Liebman discovered that Committee member David N. Rowe, a Yale professor, had been sent a set of galleys by *Saturday Review,* which had asked him to write a review. Rowe was suspicious for several reasons, not the least of which was that the magazine must have known he would write an unfavorable review (Rowe said he understood the ploy of submitting galleys to a critical reviewer in order to provide an author with some ideas for revisions). Knowledge of the galleys prompted a telephone call from Liebman to Dr. Richard Carlton, a newly appointed senior editor for Macmillan's nonfiction department, who produced neither the galleys nor the book but instead bought Liebman lunch. Soon after, a Liebman staffer merely telephoned a Macmillan staffer who, unaware of the apparent secrecy, sent over a set of galleys. Informed of this simple and effective piece of espionage, Dr. Carlton told Liebman the book was set forward to a March 21 publication date. Galley's in hand, Liebman circulated them to friends in a search of libelous statements. But the person mentioned most often in the book, Alfred Kohlberg, thought it simply incompetent and not particularly libelous.

At this point, according to Professor Marsh's account, Liebman wrote Carlton enclosing a copy of a draft memorandum about the book written by Kohlberg, adding that he (Liebman) thought the work "a particularly shoddy reporting job and really not worthy of the Macmillan imprimature." Marsh claims this was the first criticism of Koen's book to Macmillan by "a prominent and quite active member of the China lobby . . ." Marsh continues:

> Unbeknownst to Koen, pressure was beginning to be exerted against Macmillan from other influential sources. It appears that the preface, or a complete galley proof of his work, found its way into the hands of Harry J. Anslinger, then U.S. Commissioner of Narcotics. Anslinger reacted to an allegation by Koen that some Chinese Nationalist officials had been engaged in smuggling narcotics into the United States with approval of the Nationalist Government. He wrote a letter on this matter to George C. K. Yeh, Nationalist China's Ambassador to the United States. Anslinger reassured Yeh that Koen's statements were "manufactured out of the whole cloth," and that, "This statement [of Koen's] is so fantastic that if

it is any measuring rod of the book I assume it can be similarly classified." A copy of Anslinger's letter was forwarded to Macmillan.[32]

Koen first learned of difficulties ahead with Macmillan on March 10, when telephoned by Macmillan's then president and told that their attorneys had some questions about Koen's language alleging Chinese diplomatic trafficking in narcotics.

Two days later (returning to Liebman's memo to Priscilla Buckley), at a March 12 dinner party Liebman attended at "the Galbraith's" (not further identified), the Committee's secretary chanced to meet the Macmillan employee who wrote the jacket blurb for *The China Lobby in American Politics*. She told Liebman the State Department had urged the publisher to withdraw the book from circulation because of the reference to narcotics smuggling by Chinese Nationalist officials. On March 21, Liebman got a postcard from Macmillan's publicity department saying the publication date had been postponed. But this was only temporary, Liebman learned from an editor at Macmillan. Liebman closed his memorandum to Miss Buckley by suggesting *National Review* do a story on the Koen matter, picking up additional details from Professor Rowe, who had submitted a critical review of the book to *Saturday Review,* and from Alfred Kohlberg.

Meanwhile, Macmillan began a frantic effort to recall all copies of the book. Koen learned that three outside specialist readers had been contacted, one of whom (not identified to him) wanted to delete or change the focus of the work's most important material. Thereafter, Koen and Macmillan gradually came to an impasse over the changes. Marsh concludes that "Koen and Macmillan were at a standstill, he refusing to perform a major revision of *The China Lobby* and Macmillan stalling and using its position to evade its contractual responsibilities." Talks between Koen and Macmillan lingered into 1961. Macmillan insisted on a major revision, but the real objection, says Marsh, "was the whole premise upon which the book was based: that there was a China lobby, and it had influenced United States foreign policy in Asia and towards China in particular, and that many of its activities, especially involving finances, were questionable at least." [33]

Back to Liebman and the birth of *The Red China Lobby*.

Shortly after hearing about the then-forthcoming Koen book, Marvin Liebman began writing a series of letters on Committee letterhead, attaching his own memorandum covering a proposed book about the "Red China Lobby." Liebman thought such a publication could have great impact. It could help counter lobbying efforts on behalf of Communist China during the upcoming 1960 presidential campaign. The book should be dignified and responsible in tone, he wrote Stanley K. Hornbeck, should state that "Red China Lobby" actually meant as little as "China Lobby," but that the reader should nonetheless be made to understand the "Red China Lobby" represented an "inherent danger" to the freedom of the world and U.S. national security.[34] Liebman noted that a similar study had been commissioned in January 1959 but had not materialized. Now, the manuscript was needed because a "massive campaign" was getting started to prepare the American people for concessions to Communist China. The opposition, without logic on its side, would resort to crying "China Lobby." As a matter of fact, Macmillan would publish on March 17 the opening salvo in this campaign—Ross Y. Koen's *The China Lobby in American Politics.*

Liebman wanted to counter the campaign with a psychological ploy—popularizing the phrase "Red China Lobby." This would take away a great deal from the historic "China Lobby" assault. Moreover, he wanted publication before the national political conventions in July, and he wanted the widest possible distribution. He listed suggested chapter headings and the persons he wanted to write them. March 1 was the tentative deadline for all manuscripts:

INTRODUCTION *by Joseph C. Grew*

THE RED CHINA LOBBY IN U.S. FOREIGN POLICY *by Walter S. Robertson*

THE RED CHINA LOBBY ON THE NATIONAL SCENE *by Walter H. Judd*

THE RED CHINA LOBBY IN THE DEPARTMENT OF STATE *by Stanley K. Hornbeck*

THE RED CHINA LOBBY IN THE ACADEMIC COMMUNITY *by Karl A. Wittfogel*

THE RED CHINA LOBBY IN RELIGION *by Daniel A. Poling*

THE RED CHINA LOBBY IN THE MASS MEDIA *by Victor Lasky*
THE RED CHINA LOBBY ABROAD *by Max Bishop*
THE RED CHINA LOBBY IN THE U.N. *by Christopher Emmet*
THE RED CHINA LOBBY AND GOVERNMENT ORGANIZATION
 INFILTRATION *by Alfred Kohlberg*

(As ultimately published in 1963, the book included neither the chapter titles nor the authors suggested in Liebman's January 1960 memorandum.)

In declining Liebman's invitation to write the chapter on the State Department, former Ambassador Hornbeck asked whether the title of the book was "well, fairly and advantageously apt?" He elaborated the next day in another letter:

> The people who coined the expression "China Lobby" propounded a falsehood, and those who have parroted and built upon that expression have engaged in a deliberately misleading propaganda. The implications of the word "Lobby" are deceptive and vulnerable. I cannot but wonder whether, in the effort to combat the falsehood thus purveyed it can be shown that there is in fact a Red China *Lobby*. Unless that can be done, is not the use of that expression highly vulnerable? [35]

Liebman answered Hornbeck that the word "lobby" *was* a misnomer. There was no "China Lobby." There was no "Red China Lobby." But there was a group working to change U.S. policy toward Communist China. And their pressures, everything considered, created a "lobby of sorts." [36]

The former Assistant Secretary of State for Far Eastern Affairs, Walter Robertson, declined with regrets. [37] He was not sure what the "Red China Lobby" was anymore than he was about the "China Lobby." True, proponents of the Chinese Reds had a strong influence in the past in molding China policy, but that was no longer true under John Foster Dulles. He believed the State Department supported Dulles' policy.

Liebman sent a letter offering the chapter declined by Hornbeck to J. G. Sourwine, chief counsel of the Senate Internal Security subcommittee of the Committee on the Judiciary. [38] A week later, however,

Liebman admitted to Forrest Davis, the future author (co-author, as events developed, Davis dying accidentally in a fire on May 4, 1962),[39] that the idea of getting various prominent people to draft chapters had not worked out.[40] Robertson, Hornbeck, Judd, Wittfogel, and Bishop said they lacked the time. Offering Davis the assignment, Liebman outlined what he had in mind, giving the names of Kohlberg, Hornbeck, Robertson, Wittfogel, and Judd as knowledgeable and excellent sources of information who would be willing to cooperate. Liebman foresaw a sale date of June 15, 1960.

Forrest Davis accepted the assignment and outlined his initial ideas for Liebman:[41] it should be an "attack" book, exposing the origin of the campaign to reverse China policy. Davis would recur to the old I.P.R. hearings by way of looking for the "Communist line" behind the new campaign.

Meanwhile, on March 22, Macmillan formally advised Ross Koen that his revised preface remarks about Chinese narcotics trafficking still were unacceptable to the publisher's attorneys.[42] Contained in this letter to Koen from Macmillan's trade department editor-in-chief was the full text of Commissioner Anslinger's letter to Chinese Ambassador Yeh ridiculing Koen's allegations.

Already, Liebman had turned to financing for *The Red China Lobby*. He wrote Alfred Kohlberg, saying he would try to get J. Howard Pew to underwrite the whole budget for the book (using Walter Judd as an intermediary). If Pew balked, he would try the William Volker Fund. Liebman wrote Pew on February 29, 1960, asking for $11,950 to cover the cost of publishing the book. Again, on March 29, he repeated the request. Pew replied he would not be interested in financing the entire cost, nor would he support the book until he had seen the manuscript.[43]

Liebman again contacted Kohlberg, updating him on the project, including the information that retired Admiral Arthur W. Radford had agreed to write the introduction. Financing had become a problem, he said, reminding Kohlberg of an earlier offer to put up $1,000. The time was right, Liebman wrote, to take advantage of the offer. Liebman's letter was dated April 4.[44] Alfred Kohlberg died on April 7 at the age of 73.[45]

Joint Planks: 1960

March 24, the day Marvin Liebman filled in Priscilla Buckley on the Ross Koen incident, he also sent separate letters to Senator Douglas and Charles Edison outlining the gist of a luncheon conversation in Washington the previous day with Walter Judd.[46] Dr. Judd felt, Liebman reported to both men, that the steering committee needed the bipartisan balance of another incumbent Republican senator, H. Alexander Smith having retired from the Senate in January 1959. The New Jersey lawyer would be kept as a member of the steering committee, but Senator Kenneth B. Keating (R, N.Y.) also was being invited to join (at the suggestion of Judd, Liebman told Edison but not Douglas). Ambassador Grew would be asked to become honorary co-chairman with Ambassador Austin. Liebman emphasized to both men the importance of keeping China policy bipartisan during the presidential campaign. He enclosed a Judd-revised draft of his own proposed *joint plank* for both party conventions. The plank would be submitted to all congressmen and senators for their endorsement—a tactic used in the 1956 campaign. Edison and Douglas were invited to comment on the draft.

On April 6, Liebman distributed a letter enclosing a pamphlet of a February 19, 1960, address by J. Graham Parsons, Robertson's successor as Assistant Secretary of State for Far Eastern Affairs.[47] The Committee's secretary explained that the speech, which attacked the Conlon Report recommendations without mentioning the study by name, was a major policy statement but had been given little publicity.[48]

A memorandum to "members" about the reorganization of the steering committee and the campaign for joint planks, dated April 19, explained how H. Alexander Smith's retirement had modified the original bipartisan structure of the steering committee and, accordingly, the Committee had invited Senator Keating to join the steering committee and Ambassador Grew to serve as honorary co-chairman along with Ambassador Austin. Regarding the campaign for the joint plank, the memorandum said the Committee would follow its 1956 course by submitting a joint plank draft to all incumbent congressmen and requesting their individual endorsement. The draft plank read:

We continue to oppose the seating of Communist China in the United Nations, thus upholding international morality and keeping faith with the thousands of American youths who gave their lives fighting Communist aggression in Korea. To seat a Communist China which defies, by word and deed, the principles of the U.N. Charter would be to betray the letter, violate the spirit and subvert the purposes of that charter. We further continue to oppose United States diplomatic recognition or any other steps which would build the power and prestige of the Chinese Communist regime to the detriment of our friends and allies in Asia and of our national security. Any such action would break faith with our dead and the unfortunate Americans still wrongfully imprisoned by Communist China and would dishearten our friends and allies in Asia whose continued will to resist Communist China's pressures and blandishments is so vital to our own security interests in that part of the world.[49]

By May 24, a month after the solicitation began, the Committee had received 134 endorsements from senators and representatives of both parties, Liebman wrote Douglas. The secretary said he was sympathetic to the senator's inability at that time to be associated with the joint-plank project as an initiator. He hoped, however, that Douglas would include his name in the list of endorsers since the absence of a founding member would look awkward.[50]

By June 8, the Committee had received 212 congressional endorsements (33 senators, 179 representatives, 100 Democrats, 112 Republicans), Liebman wrote the steering committee. Pre-convention plans included 1) preparing a press release for June 16 publication; 2) printing and mailing of advertising proof to all Committee contributors with a request for badly needed funds to publish the advertisement; and 3) arranging for Committee representatives to present the organization's plank before the platform committee hearings of both parties.[51]

Another Liebman letter on June 28 enclosed an advertising proof identifying 250 congressional endorsers and explained that 271 incumbent members of Congress, an additional 21, had since endorsed the plank.[52]

When the Democrats and the Republicans finished the business of nominating John F. Kennedy and Richard M. Nixon, Secretary Liebman notified "members and friends" about the party planks. The final count of congressional endorsers had reached 275 (127 Democratic representatives, 109 Republican; 17 Democratic senators, 22 Republican). As to the planks? "They were not as strong as many of us would have liked, but they were the best possible in view of the extreme pressure by a small minority in both Parties—pressure which would have either excluded planks altogether or would have weakened them considerably."

The memorandum said that Senator Thomas J. Dodd (D., Conn.) had represented the Committee before the party's platform committee. Dodd had told his fellow Democrats in part:

> We deeply regret that the policies and actions of the government of Communist China have interrupted the generations of friendship between the Chinese and American peoples. We reaffirm our pledge of determined opposition to the present admission of Communist China to the United Nations. Although normal diplomatic relations between our governments are impossible under present conditions, we shall welcome any evidence that the Chinese Communist Government is genuinely prepared to create a new relationship based on respect for international obligations, including the release of American prisoners. We will continue to make every effort to effect the release of American civilians and servicemen now unjustly imprisoned in Red China and elsewhere in the Communist empire.

Similarly, Senator Kenneth B. Keating, the new steering committee member, had represented the Committee before the Republican platform committee, saying, in part:

> Recognition of Communist China and its admission to the United Nations have been firmly opposed by the Republican Administration. We will continue in this opposition because of compelling evidence that to do otherwise would weaken the cause of freedom and endanger the future of the free peoples of Asia and the World. The brutal suppression of the human rights and the religious traditions of the Tibetan people is an unhappy evidence of the need to persist in our policy.[53]

On September 18, the Committee published a full-page advertisement in the International Edition of the *New York Times* in the form of an "Urgent Memorandum" from the American people to the fifteenth regular session of the General Assembly of the United Nations, scheduled to convene on September 20.[54] Subject of the 'memorandum' was

"Our Continued and Considered Opposition to the Admission of Communist China to the United Nations." The ad included a complete text of the Committee's original 1953 petition to the President, which was "just as valid today as it was seven years ago."

(Five days before the General Assembly vote on the China seating question, Marvin Liebman wrote to Ambassador Grew, in Manchester, Mass., that the Taiwan government, according to Ambassador T. F. Tsiang, wanted to honor him with one of their highest decorations. Ambassador Tsiang had asked Liebman to contact Grew informally about his willingness to accept the decoration. Ambassador Grew accepted.) [55]

The fifteenth General Assembly voted October 8 to postpone the China seating question for another year. The vote was 42 to 34 (22 abstentions) in favor of the U.S.-backed resolution, the smallest margin in the ten-year history of the question, prompting one U.S. delegate to the session, the late Senator Wayne Morse (D., Ore.), to remark that admission of Communist China was "inevitable." An unidentified spokesman for the Committee promptly called for the resignation or dismissal of Senator Morse from the U.S. delegation.[56]

With three-quarters of the year gone and but six weeks remaining before the Kennedy-Nixon showdown, Marvin Liebman decided to take stock. He sat down and composed a memorandum covering the activities of Marvin Liebman Associates, Inc., for the July through September quarter.[57] Aside from its lead-off summary of Committee projects (the firm, he said, acted on an estimated fifteen pieces of correspondence every day on behalf of the Committee), the document tells a great deal about the scope of Liebman's organizational virtuosity and the former Young Communist Leaguer's predilection for conservatively minded and anti-Communist causes:

> Under the firm's direction, and headed by columnist George E. Sokolsky, an Alfred Kohlberg Memorial Fund had raised $25,000 to that time. A final $75,000 to $100,000 was sought for a memorial project in Taiwan. The Republic of China had pledged to match all funds collected.[58]
>
> Young Americans for Freedom had been organized at a weekend conference at the Buckley family estate in Sharon, Connecticut, on September 10 and 11. Liebman downplayed his own role in the formation of this new

youth group, which he expected to encourage a renaissance of conservatism among youth across the country.[59] Instead, he reported only that his staff had worked on the project, that their offices were the headquarters for the YAF, that Douglas Caddy was the National Director, and that the firm would be working with YAF to organize and implement a national program.

The Historical Research Foundation, founded by Alfred Kohlberg, who bequested $175,000 for its work on how American foreign policy affected the lives of citizens, was headed by Charles Edison. On a volunteer basis, the Liebman firm had been working to get the Foundation tax exempt status. The firm also was helping to formulate projects; three were underway: a study of the meaning of Washington's "Farewell Address" for U.S. foreign policy; a study by Forrest Davis (co-author of *The Red China Lobby*) of U.S.–China relations since 1945; and a study of Alfred Kohlberg's files and correspondence by Dr. Medford Evans to determine the citizen's impact on his country's affairs.

Another client, the Committee for Public Affairs, associated with the McGraw-Edison Company (whose chairman until his retirement in 1961 was Charles Edison) was very active. Liebman's firm distributed a newsletter and bulletin to approximately 1,200 McGraw-Edison executives and sent out booklets and articles to this Committee's constituency. Among the distributed materials: Henry M. Wriston's "What Does It Take to be a Leader": Stanton Evans' "Soaking the Poor"; David Franke's "Revolt on the Campus"; and Ronald Reagan's "Business, Ballots, and Bureaus." Additionally, the firm helped initiate a quarterly forum on public affairs—the Thomas Edison Industries Forum—first addressed by William F. Buckley Jr. Douglas Caddy, executive director of the Committee for Public Affairs, attended a conference in Hershey, Pennsylvania conducted by the Effective Citizens Organization to coordinate the public affairs programs of important corporations.

The American-Asian Educational Exchange, Inc. had distributed 20,000 copies of the English edition of "The Unrelenting War"; prepared, in cooperation with *National Review,* a 40-page supplement on Sino-Soviet relations; sent out 25,000 reprints of "Report on Formosa" by Fr. Luigi d'Appolonia from *America* magazine; served as a clearinghouse for information on Asia and the United States; distributed "Free Front," a publication of the Asian People's Anti-Communist League, and "The New Colonialism" by the Assembly of Captive European Nations.

The firm was organizing a fifth anniversary dinner for *National Review* to be held on October 27 in New York City. Admiral Lewis L. Strauss, the Atomic Energy Commission's former chief, would be chairman for the affair which would give Conservatives the chance to herald one of the country's foremost Conservative journals.

To help raise Walter Judd's stature before the Republican convention, the firm had organized Americans for Walter Judd for Vice-President. Also, Douglas Caddy had worked for Youth for Goldwater for Vice-President. (This was not really a contradiction, Liebman explained, because these efforts brought both Judd and Goldwater to national attention.)

A group organized by the firm in 1959, the Committee for All Peoples, was revived. Originally it had protested the visit of Nikita Khrushchev to the United States. Now that the Russian leader was returning to attend the UN General Assembly session, the committee was placing advertisements and issuing press releases.

Among other activities, the firm was working to reorganize the American Jewish League Against Communism with George Sokolsky, optioning film rights to a novel by Constantine Fitzgibbon, "When The Kissing Had to Stop"; [60] initiating a Latin American committee to combat communism there; and circulating letters to editors across the country on activities of the "Communist menace," over the signatures of General Albert C. Wedemeyer, Admiral Charles M. Cooke, Governor Charles Edison, Dr. Karl A. Wittfogel, Professor David Nelson Rowe, and Liebman himself.

Since the organization's founding in January 1958, Liebman wound up his memo, the firm had established one of the leading reputations in the anti-Communist and conservative movement. He was proud of the firm's contribution. He believed it was a valid contribution for the country. The firm was privileged to be involved with distinguished Americans working together on the great issues of the day.

Adjusting to Democrats

In the fall of 1960 attention focused on the national television debates between presidential candidates Kennedy and Nixon. The UN vote postponing the China credentials problem came the day after Senator Kennedy's and Vice-President Nixon's second debate on October 7. That night Kennedy declared his strong belief in the defense of Formosa but felt the defense line should not be drawn around the Nationalist-held islands of Quemoy and Matsu as long as they were not essential to Formosa's defense. Nixon disagreed, saying the question was not the two tiny unimportant pieces of real estate but rather the principle—forcing the Nationalists off the islands and giving them up to the Communists would start a chain reaction because the Communists were after Formosa. On October 13, squaring off in the third debate, Nixon said the United States, were he President, would honor its 1955 treaty obligations and stand by the Nationalists if the Chinese Communists attacked Quemoy and Matsu as a prelude to an attack on Formosa. But he would not say exactly how the United States would respond, claiming this would be irresponsible in advance of the event. Kennedy stuck to his earlier position, maintaining that American treaty obligations covered Formosa and the Pescadores, not Quemoy and Matsu, adding that Eisenhower himself once had assured Senator Green of Rhode Island that the United States would not get involved in military hostilities merely in defense of Quemoy and Matsu.

The Committee was upset. It believed the Quemoy-Matsu issue involved U.S. national security interests and should have been kept out of partisan politics. Up to this point in the campaign the group had not *officially* backed candidates of either party, but the return to prominence of the offshore islands prompted a flurry of activity in the closing weeks. Action focused on a deliberately muted campaign to promote Dr. Judd for Secretary of State in the event of a Nixon victory. Aimed at Republican circles and organized under the chairmanship of both Charles Edison and retired Admiral Arthur W. Radford, a committee for Walter Judd for Secretary of State got more than 100 people, including prominent Committee supporters, to sign a letter urging Vice-President Nixon to consider Judd for the post. Liebman's firm raised $32,000 in three days—largely by getting Harlow Curtice, J. Howard Pew, Charles Edison, and Harry Bullis to sign a telegram to the various businessmen on Liebman's many lists—and the Republican National Committee provided the additional funds to put Dr. Judd on an NBC national television hook-up on election eve. The Judd effort died with Kennedy's election.

The above revelations stem from another Liebman staff memorandum written in January 1961 to summarize his firm's activities from October through December 1960.[1] To help remove the Quemoy-Matsu issue from the campaign, Liebman makes clear, the Committee also arranged for former military leaders to give out statements on the question. He identified four who cooperated: Generals Albert C. Wedemeyer and James A. Van Fleet and Admirals Radford and Ellis M. Zacharias. The memorandum claims the Committee played no "official" part on behalf of either party's candidates. Nonetheless, Liebman did report one example of Committee electioneering: several thousand copies of an article by Democratic Senator Douglas ("Should We Recognize Red China?") were reprinted and distributed in districts represented by congressmen who supported either a softer stand toward Communist China or outright recognition. Singled out in this context was Congressman Charles O. Porter (D., Ore.), who was "soundly" defeated by Dr. Edwin Durno, a member of the Committee, Liebman noted.[2] Others mentioned by Liebman—all first-term Democrats though not identified as such in the memorandum—were William Meyer of Vermont, John Foley of Maryland, Gerald Flynn of Wisconsin, and George Kasem of California. All lost.

Thus it may be speculated that in the aftermath of the campaign—when a key Kennedy foreign policy adviser, Congressman Chester Bowles (D., Conn.), advocated a "two Chinas" policy on British television while admitting that recognition of the People's Republic was "impossible"—the Committee's collective anxiety, so to speak, must have risen.[3] (After the election, Nixon has written, when he visited the President-elect in Florida, he raised the issues of China's recognition and UN admission.[4] Kennedy said he was opposed to recognition but had heard some strong arguments favoring the "two Chinas" approach to the UN problem. Nixon told Kennedy he opposed this policy. The real issue, he said, was not which side had the General Assembly vote or the veto power of the Security Council; at stake was the Charter provision limiting membership to "peace-loving nations." Admission of the Chinese Communists would make a mockery of this principle and would lend respectability to the Communist regime.)

The Committee's first public response to the incoming administration came after the appointment on December 12 of Dean Rusk as Secretary of State. Rushed into print and distributed as a pamphlet was a 1951 Rusk speech by the then Assistant Secretary of State for Far Eastern Affairs before the twenty-fifth anniversary dinner of the China Institute of America, an educational foundation registered in 1951 as a foreign agent of the Nationalist government.[5] An unsigned Introduction to the pamphlet referred to the continuity of China policy from Truman through Eisenhower, adding:

> There has been a good deal of speculation about the possibility of a major change in our China policy under the administration of President John Fitzgerald Kennedy. Particular attention has been given to President Kennedy's appointments to his foreign policy team: Dean Rusk as Secretary of State; Chester Bowles as Under-Secretary of State; Adlai E. Stevenson as Ambassador to the United Nations.
>
> The [Committee], in order to focus attention on the past sentiments expressed by Dean Rusk on the question of Communist China, takes pleasure in reprinting. . . .[6]

Liebman's concern over posssible changes in American China policy was expressed in a December letter to Senator Douglas which also may have been sent to other steering committee members.[7] Pressures would be extreme, he wrote, for a "new look" on China policy. Unless the

Committee counterattacked, those favoring Red China's admission to the United Nations, U.S. diplomatic recognition, a relaxation in trade relations, or a "two Chinas" policy might win out. Thus far the Committee had been successful because it had attracted top civic and political leaders on a bipartisan basis. People everywhere understood that the sentiments of the American people were genuinely represented by the Committee. This leadership on China policy, Liebman emphasized, should continue. The Committee's secretary then proposed a countering tactic to begin with the convening of the 87th Congress: resubmission of the 1960 "joint planks" statement, over the signatures of steering committee members, to legislators who had not previously signed. In hand, he said, were 246 congressional incumbents. Liebman wanted a majority of both Houses.

Senator Douglas' reply, by telegram late in December after a vacation, revealed an uneasiness about his association with the Committee which his memoirs would confirm a decade later.[8] He was still opposed to "admission and recognition," but Liebman's letter reflected indirectly on the intentions of the new Kennedy administration—something Liebman had not done with the Eisenhower administration. Douglas defended Kennedy, his former Senate Democratic colleague, at some length. He had great faith in the new President and the basic Americanism and soundness of his appointees. Although Douglas might differ with Governor Stevenson on some points, he questioned neither Stevenson's anti-Communism nor patriotism. He therefore would not sign the letter proposed by Liebman. He regretted, moreover, that the vast majority of the Committee's support seemed to come from those tinged with authoritarian sympathies who invariably lined up against measures designed to help the average citizen. Of course, there were exceptions. Perhaps the fault was with the "liberal mind" which placed excessive reliance on good will. But partly it was because the Committee's appeal was primarily pitched in negative terms. Douglas thought the Committee's argument should be based on preserving and extending freedom and thus made more appealing to Africans and Asians. Even the negative side of the Committee's case should be argued straightforwardly. Illustrating, the senator posed five questions: Would any good come from admission of the Peking regime to the United Nations or U.S. recognition? Was not the Soviet Union trying to wreck the United Nations? Would not the death of the United Nations be almost certain if mainland China were admitted? Were not the Chinese Communists resolved to overpower Formosa? Were they not ready for atomic war at the cost of half their citizenry?

Liebman, always sensitive to Douglas's feelings, replied immediately.[9] He had just heard from Dr. Judd about the proposed draft letter seeking additional endorsers. Douglas' and Judd's ideas seemed to be complementary. He also had spoken to Judd, who expressed the highest confidence in Dean Rusk's and John Kennedy's intentions in the field of foreign policy. Although the Committee had genuinely tried for a "positive" approach, the idea had not attracted too many liberals. Liebman was all for getting greater liberal support in order to enhance the Committee's key source of strength—*bipartisanship*.

Liebman wanted to maximize publicity for the "joint planks" statement after gathering more names. On February 2, 1961, in a memorandum to Senators Douglas and Keating and Representatives Judd and Walter, he reported that 326 congressional endorsers were listed on an enclosed advertising proof and three more had signed up since the printing. Did the men think it would be expedient, Liebman asked, to offer the statement as a bipartisan resolution for joint action by Congress? Unanimous approval would be very important. Otherwise, the Committee probably should publish the statement privately, listing the endorsers, maybe having it inserted in the *Congressional Record*. The advertisement ran in the *Washington Post* on February 20.[10] An AP story ran the same day in the *New York Times,* quoting the Committee as saying that 54 senators and 285 representatives had endorsed the statement—a majority of both Houses.

Congress Reacts

The Committee's statement, complete with endorsers, was placed in the *Congressional Record* on March 30 by Congressman Clement J. Zablocki (D., Wisc.), a frequent Committee supporter (and later a steering committee member) who replaced Dr. Judd in 1955 as chairman of the subcommittee on the Far East and the Pacific of the House Committee on Foreign Affairs.[11] Already, however, the first session of the 87th Congress had given attention to China policy. On January 17, for example, two days before the Senate Foreign Relations Committee approved the nomination of Chester Bowles as Under-Secretary of State, Senator Norris Cotton (R., N.H.), challenged the appointment. "Where does Chester Bowles stand with respect to Red China?" he asked. He noted that Bowles had recently expressed himself in opposition to diplomatic recognition, but he observed from earlier articles and speeches by the former governor and ambassador that Bowles actually supported a "two-Chinas" policy. "If his use of the words 'two Chinas' does mean what we know as the two-China policy, then he should not be confirmed." Senator Cotton, who endorsed the Committee's statement, introduced the initial Senate resolution (S. Res. 67) on January 26: "That it is the sense of the Senate that the Government of the United States should not recognize the Communist Chinese regime as the government of China and should oppose the seating of its representatives in the United Nations." [12]

No less than fourteen resolutions opposing the seating of the People's Republic in the United Nations, recognition of that government, or both, were introduced in the House.[13] Still, the Senate provided the leadership for the joint resolution which ultimately passed Congress. As reconstructed from the *Congressional Record,* the sequence of events went roughly as follows:

On April 13, Senator Jack Miller (R., Iowa), not a Committee "member" but an endorser of the February 20, 1961, statement, referred to an AP dispatch from London reporting that President Kennedy had told British Prime Minister Macmillan he needed twelve months to prepare the American people for P.R.C. membership in the United Nations and that the Kennedy administration had decided not to oppose a debate on the China credentials question at the next session of the General Assembly. Majority Leader Mike Mansfield (D., Mont.), a Committee "member" since April 12, 1955, immediately denied the report, referring Senator Miller to the President's press conference of the previous day; but Minority Leader Everett M. Dirksen (R., Ill.), also a Committee "member" since April 12, 1955 (as noted by the available letterheads), observed a "progressive weakening" in the opposition to admission in the General Assembly and acknowledged that debate on the question would constitute "a breach in the wall," adding:

> We undertook today to establish the position that the House and the Senate ought, by concurrent resolution, to reexamine the stand which the President uttered yesterday, and to flatly, firmly, and unequivocally assert ourselves that . . . the United States not recognize Red China and that we oppose her admission into the United Nations.[14]

The following day, April 14, Mansfield noted Dirksen's remarks and said that previous congressional resolutions on the matter, plus the policies of the previous President, had not prevented the growing sentiment in other nations favoring debate on the China question:

> This places the present President in a very difficult position as we approach the next meeting of that body [the General Assembly]. He inherits a policy which, despite its vigorous prosecution by President Eisenhower and past congressional expressions of opposition to seating Communist China, has not been able to check the trend.

Mansfield suggested that a joint bipartisan resolution be framed in "positive language" rather than the "apparently ineffective language which we have used in the past . . ." To wit:

> It is the sense of the Congress that it supports the President in his affirmation that the United States shall continue to meet its commitments to the people and government on Formosa and shall continue to support the Taiwan (Formosa) government in its membership in the United Nations.

But Senator Cotton thought the last phrase in the proposed language should read "continue to support the Taiwan Government *as the sole representative of the Chinese people* in the United Nations," in order, he said, to make the resolution "firm and reassuring" [15] (italics added). Mansfield said that raised the question of two Chinas; Cotton agreed, adding, "if we are not going to leave a loophole for the so-called two-China policy, what objection is there in saying so in plain, U.S. language?''

Several weeks later, however, in requesting his original resolution (S. Res. 67) be indefinitely postponed, Cotton acknowledged that ''various conferences have been held between the distinguished majority leader, the distinguished minority leader, myself, and many other Senators. A resolution worded to cover the situation has been agreed upon . . .'' Senator Dirksen got the floor: ''There have been a good many conferences, including those with high-level representatives of the State Department; and as a result there was prepared a concurrent resolution which I now submit for appropriate reference.''

There were ten ''Whereas'' clauses, but Dirksen read the resolving clause:

> *Resolved,* That it is the sense of the Congress that it supports the President in his affirmation that the United States shall continue to meet its commitments to the people and Government of the Republic of China and shall continue to support that Government as the representative of China in the United Nations.
>
> Further, the United States shall continue to oppose the seating of the Chinese Communist regime in the United Nations so long as that regime persists in defying the principles of the United Nations Charter. Further it is the sense of the Congress that the United States supports the President in not according diplomatic recognition to the Chinese Communist regime.[16]

The resolution next reached the Senate floor on July 25. Senator Thomas J. Dodd (D., Conn.), whose name began to appear on Committee materials in 1955 as a congressman, told his colleagues he was not satisfied with the statement of justification contained in the preamble of the concurrent resolution approved in the Senate Foreign Relations Committee that morning. ''I know that my colleagues are as opposed to Red China as I am. But I believe that it is a serious error not to spell out the justification of our action, in terms of specific charges that people in every country can understand.'' [17] In brief, these ''charges'' included Communist China's aggression in Korea, repression in Tibet, threats against its neighbors, dealing in narcotics, violations of the Korean armistice, failure to release American prisoners, use of germ warfare charges against the United States, general hostility towards the United States and the United Nations, and its open advocacy of the use of force to settle international disputes.

In the July 28 debate on Senate Concurrent Resolution 34 (the one finally reported out of the Foreign Relations Committee), Dodd submitted and won a "Whereas" amendment summing up his charges; Senator Dirksen inserted in the *Record* a Committee pamphlet plus names of congressional endorsers to the Committee's statement (as of June 1961); and the resolution passed, 76 to 0, 24 not voting.[18]

Later, during a House debate on the Mutual Security Act of 1961, Congressman John B. Williams (D., Miss), a Committee "member" since 1956, offered an amendment denying assistance to any nation which voted in the United Nations for seating the mainland Chinese. The first to rise in opposition to the amendment was Congressman Walter H. Judd: "I doubt that anyone here will think that I am in favor of the admission of Communist China to the United Nations. But surely this amendment is not the way to keep her out. In fact, I cannot think of many things that would do more to produce that very undesirable result than the passage of this amendment." After more debate the amendment was rejected, 102 ayes, 212 noes.[19]

Apparently Dr. Judd did not believe in "overkill."

Objection to Mrs. Roosevelt's Remarks

Although the earliest dated Committee-related materials furnished me by the John F. Kennedy Library include a form-type letter describing a Committee pamphlet,[20] Marvin Liebman had sent the new President an earlier and more sensitive communication. Indeed, the *only* Committee-related materials supplied by the State Department for the *entire* Kennedy administration concern a March 15, 1961, letter from Liebman to the President over remarks allegedly made by Mrs. Eleanor Roosevelt about the Republic of China.[21]

Liebman noted that Mrs. Roosevelt was a delegate to the General

Assembly then in session (the second part of the fifteenth General Assembly met from March 7 through April 21, 1961). He quoted newspaper reports as revealing that she had said in a Massachusetts speech "the fiction of Formosa representing the Chinese people will not be acceptable at the next session" of the General Assembly. Mrs. Roosevelt subsequently had clarified her remarks by saying "I said that the vote in the last session of the General Assembly pointed to the fact that we would not be able much longer to keep up the fiction that Nationalist China represents the whole of China." Liebman thought this was more reiteration than clarification. The Committee's secretary said many people might construe that Mrs. Roosevelt was speaking in the name of the administration. He thought the situation should be clarified, that the former First Lady should be asked to make sure that while she was a UN delegate her public pronouncements reflect government views. Either that, he said, or the government should announce she was a special situation, speaking only for herself and not subject to administration restrictions on her public statements. The reply to Liebman labored its way through the State Department and finally was signed by the Assistant Secretary of State for International Organization Affairs:

> Mrs. Roosevelt has informed us that her remarks about China were made during the question period that followed her speech, and that the press story did not, therefore, present them in their proper context. Consequently, they did not represent her views on this subject fully and accurately. Moreover, I know it would be of interest to you that Mrs. Roosevelt at the time was lecturing in a private capacity to fulfill an engagement she had made some time ago.[22]

New Projects and Old

In April Marvin Liebman wrote a memorandum describing some contemplated Committee projects and warning that the organization faced a tough battle ahead because of pressures from abroad and the tendency toward appeasement of Communist China at the top echelon of the American government.[23] He outlined six necessary projects:

1. A "film on Red China" to be produced by the Committee and narrated by Congressman Judd, Admiral Radford, Senator Douglas, and/or

General Van Fleet. The cost he estimated at $6,500.00 for the master print with additional prints at $50 each. The film could be put together by professionals in six weeks.

2. Wider distribution of "Who Will Volunteer? (The Quemoy Story in Pictures)," which Liebman thought a very effective piece of propaganda. He wanted a minimum 3,000 produced at $4,500.

3. A pamphlet by Dr. Stanley Hornbeck about the United States and Communist China for publication by the American-Asian Educational Exchange. Cost for 50,000—$4,000.

4. A new nationwide petition campaign but not as big as the original drive for one million signatures. Instead of the signed petitions being returned to the Committee, they would be mailed to the congressmen and senators in whose districts the petitions were signed. Approximate cost: $10,000.

5. A revival of the Forrest Davis Book on the "Red China Lobby," then three-quarters finished. Robert Hunter would edit and complete the manuscript for a soft cover pocket edition. A July release would receive publicity and be read in time for the next UN General Assembly session. Cost: $7,500.

6. Purchase of addressing and mailing equipment, $6,000.

Total cost for all projects, $38,500, was, Liebman said, above what the Committee could expect to raise from regular sources. He did not indicate where the money would come from.

So the Committee went back into the petition business. On April 25, Liebman wrote to Robert Morris, the former chief counsel of the Senate Internal Security subcommittee, enclosing copies of the new petition, and a memorandum of instructions on distribution.[24] He asked for help in circulating the petitions. A new wrinkle was added: as each petition was completed, it would be mailed directly to the appropriate representative or senator in Washington accompanied by a letter from the sender requesting the petition be forwarded to President Kennedy. The petition blank sent to Robert Morris in Dallas, Texas, was headed "A Petition To The President Of The United States: STAND FAST AGAINST APPEASEMENT OF RED CHINA." The 1960 "joint planks" statement also was printed on the petition.[25]

Another project mentioned in Liebman's memorandum was the completion of the "Red China Lobby" manuscript. On April 13, Liebman wrote Robert Hunter, enclosing a Liebman-revised outline for a book entitled "The United States and Communist China—Realities and Illusions," by Forrest Davis and Robert Hunter, with a foreword by Admiral Arthur W. Radford.[26] The admiral's introduction, the outline said, would put a national security cover on the China issue because any build up of Red China's power or prestige would seriously jeopardize U.S. security interests. Liebman's outline bears a reasonable resemblance to *The Red China Lobby* as ultimately published in 1963.[27] Moreover, his office apparently helped collect research materials. One letter to Liebman from the director of the Permanent Mission of China to the United Nations enclosed a chart ("Record of Votes taken by Member States at various regular sessions of the General Assembly on the Question of China's Representation in the United Nations"), sent in response to an April 21, 1961, letter from Liebman's secretary, "asking for information on the so-called question of Chinese representation in the United Nations for Mr. Hunter to be used in the preparation of a book relating to Communist China." [28]

The first screening of the film "Red China—Outlaw!" was held at 8:00 P.M. in the auditorium of the New Senate Office Building (Room G-308), on August 17, 1961.[29] The steering committee invitation said the film, 35 minutes in length, was narrated by Lowell Thomas and that Congressman Judd and Senators Dodd and Douglas were featured in the 16mm presentation. The film's narration, incidentally, had concerned Senator Douglas at one point. In a handwritten postscript on a letter to Liebman, Douglas strongly questioned the prospect of Walter Judd acting as narrator.[30] Although he personally liked Judd in many ways, Douglas knew him to be a "bitter partisan" who hated Democrats and would denigrate any national administration run by Democrats. Douglas speculated that the Kennedy administration would oppose recognition of the mainland but that the United Nations probably would admit her in the future. He thought this a mistake. But he also anticipated Judd's reaction—censuring the new administration. Douglas signed off, making it clear he did not want the film's narrator to be Walter Judd. The Committee's financial support, an issue of constant concern to the senator (as reaffirmed later by his brief section about the Committee in his memoirs),[31] provided Douglas's main theme in this same letter; here, as well, he expressed himself categorically.

To be sure, it is difficult to convey by paraphrase the senator's anxiety about this subject: He wanted explicit reassurances from Liebman that the Committee was not accepting funds from the Republic of China government on Formosa or from its leading families; he named the Kung's and the Soong's. The Committee could not allow its motives to be questioned, he said. The welfare of the country and the world was at stake. Those who made big money by devious means should not be supported under any conditions. Under no circumstances should the Committee be indebted to various Chinese.

Liebman replied promptly and unequivocably. The Committee had not, was not then, and would not in the future seek or accept any money from Chinese sources.[32] It even hesitated to take contributions from Americans of Chinese descent. Its purposes were entirely rooted in American interests, not in the Republic of China's. The Committee was not a "front." It was only coincidental that American and Republic of China interests were the same concerning Communist China. Liebman wanted Douglas to be "quite sure" about this, he continued, before emphasizing the need for keeping the Committee a bipartisan group.

The Ambassador Tsiang Correspondence

Senator Douglas's great concern about the sources of Committee funds would reoccur.

There is no evidence in the Committee's records that the China policy pressure group itself received any actual sums of money from Chinese government officials in the United States. But there is evidence that indirect financial support for various projects, including funds for social and travel amenities, was either solicited and/or collected by Marvin Liebman's firm on behalf of the American-Asian Education Exchange and the Committee. (It will be recalled that AAEE, which enjoyed tax exemption from the I.R.S. as an educational corporation, was perceived by the Committee's leadership as its "educational and informational" adjunct promoting identical China policy views; see pp. 166–67.) Some chronology is necessary:

Liebman had disclosed to his staff in January 1961 that Aid Refugee Chinese Intellectuals (ARCI), which he helped found in 1952, had terminated most of its activities by the end of 1960.[33] He had served as secretary from the beginning. Also, the American Emergency Committee for Tibetan Refugees (AECTR), which he served first as executive vice-chairman, then as director (Dr. Garside taking over the executive responsibilities) was in the process of winding up its activities. ARCI had spent some $2,459,150 during its lifetime; AECTR had raised approximately $707,503 in cash and supplies (medical needs and relief equipment), according to Liebman.[34] Unrelated to the above disclosures—but in order to keep these financial matters in a 1961 sequence—Marvin Liebman, as executive vice-chairman of American-Asian Educational Exchange, was sent a check for $1,700 made payable, per his instructions, to the Catawaba (*sic*) Corporation, by a Mrs. Helen Lin, writing on letterhead of the Permanent Mission of the Republic of China to the United Nations.[35] Mrs. Lin explained that Dr. Tsiang (Tingfu F.) had been extremely busy and had thus been delayed on this situation. Liebman returned the check to Dr. Tsiang several days later. The money made payable to the Catawba Corporation (a family-held corporation of the Buckley's) covering William Buckley's round trip fare to the Far East was being returned, he said, because business problems had forced Buckley to put off his trip.[36]

This February exchange between the Committee's secretary and the Republic of China's ambassador and chief delegate to the United Nations was the first of seven written communications between them during 1961 (as found in Liebman's Committee files). The second communication, in July, followed by one week a memorandum Liebman wrote to Walter Judd on his personal letterhead (at that time, Suite 909, 79 Madison Avenue, New York City) about the general subject of the financial problems associated with keeping the Peking regime out of the United Nations.[37] In this memo Liebman analyzed the seating question and made a strong appeal for additional funds. He told Judd he thought a showdown was imminent at the upcoming sixteenth General Assembly session convening in September. He thought the Kennedy administration's resistance to the admission of Communist China was weakening. Pressures from the British, some "neutralist" nations (unidentified), and well-known members of the administration (unnamed) were responsible. No question, Liebman said, that the vast majority of Americans still were against admitting the mainland. Extra efforts would have to be exerted by all interested citizens in order to stem the tide. Little time remained. Moreover, the funds were not available. Liebman traced the upcoming financial needs of the Committee and the AAEE, both of which, he made clear, were the key organizations involved in the fight.

All of the Committee's contributions since the first of the year ($40,193, according to an attached tentative statement) had been committed and spent for regular activities. Patient creditors were waiting. The Committee would need $24,000 minimum between then (July 14) and September or October. The money would be used to finish and distribute the 16mm documentary film on Red China narrated by Lowell Thomas, to complete plans for a September 21, 1961, Carnegie Hall rally, to continue the petition campaign, and to carry out the Committee's regular activities through October. The AAEE, which had raised $28,581 since the first of the year, would need $36,000 in the next four months to implement its proposed program: publication and distribution of a booklet by Stanley K. Hornbeck, "China and United States China Policy: A Brief Study of Some Facts and Not-Facts"; preparation by Forrest Davis of a definitive study of Sino-American relations and the workings of the Red China "lobby" in the U.S. (which may have been *The Red China Lobby* project then currently in progress); publication and distribution of "Communist China and Asia," a twice-monthly newsletter; publication of a planned full-page advertisement in the *New York Times* on September 19, the date scheduled for the opening of the General Assembly session; and implementation of the AAEE's regular activities for four months. Liebman closed his long memorandum with a question: From whom and in what way could the Committee and the AAEE obtain the money they needed?

Returning to Liebman's correspondence with Dr. Tsiang, the secretary wrote the Chinese scholar-diplomat on July 20, disclosing that two articles had been arranged for publication in September before the UN session got underway.[38] *This Week* magazine would publish an article on September 10 under Senator Barry Goldwater's byline (actually, he said, written by William Buckley) and *Reader's Digest* would publish an article by Admiral Arthur Radford. Both articles would argue that the United States should withdraw all political and monetary support from the world organization if Communist China gained entry. Two other articles, Liebman reported, were being arranged for *New Leader* and *National Review.*

On August 10, Liebman sent Dr. Tsiang a number of items, including: the July issue of *War/Peace Report,* which carried an article by "Mr. Z," whom Liebman identified as Urban Whitaker of San Francisco State College; [39] the August issue of the same publication carrying Liebman's reply to the Whitaker article; and other confidential (and not clearly identifiable) documents. Liebman thought Whitaker's conclusions might be well received by Ambassador Adlai Stevenson and the administration. He was not certain what action should be taken, but he would be pleased to go along with Ambassador Tsiang's recommendations. In a postscript, Liebman reminded the Ambassador of a conversation between them some time earlier about public relations difficulties of the Republic of China. He had been speaking to Gilbert Jonas, who worked with their old friend, Harold L. Oram, Inc. Jonas had sent along some public relations recommendations which Liebman thought had merit, so he was passing them along. Jonas was a sharp young fellow and, he believed, could accomplish things for the ambassador.

On August 23, Secretary Liebman sent Dr. Tsiang an advance copy of Admiral Radford's article for the October issue of *Reader's Digest.*[40] The Committee would be purchasing 50,000 reprints, he said, for distribution beginning September 20. He then referred to a telegram sent Dr. Tsiang concerning postponement of the showing of the Red China film—in order for revisions which, he thought, would make this picture first rate propaganda. He asked for the ambassador's comments on the film and closed by saying he wanted to talk to him about seeking his assistance in the film's distribution.

On September 11, Secretary Liebman sent a letter marked "confidential'' to Ambassador Tsiang, enclosing, he said, a proof of Senator Goldwater's article in *This Week,* to appear on September 17.[41]

On October 9, Secretary Liebman wrote Ambassador Tsiang about a Marvin Liebman and William F. Buckley Jr. trip to Taiwan, scheduled, Liebman said, for November.[42] At the ambassador's request, Liebman began, he was providing the name of the travel agent booking his and Buckley's trip. Checks for the ''passage'' should be made out to the travel agency but sent to him. He would arrange for them to be given the travel agent.

On November 13, Secretary Liebman wrote Ambassador Tsiang about the film ''Red China—Outlaw.'' [43] Fourteen requests had been received, he said, from overseas friends for prints of the film. The Committee would especially like the film distributed overseas because it was effective propaganda. The Committee would welcome the ambassador's cooperation if that could be arranged. Each print would cost $125. If the ambassador's budget could handle this matter, a check made out to Communications Distribution, Inc. for $1,750 should be sent to Liebman's office. (Communications Distribution, Inc. was the Liebman/Buckley publishing enterprise.) [44] A postscript to this final 1961 letter from Liebman to Ambassador Tsiang reported that the Committee's steering committee was trying to set up an interview with Ambassador Stevenson for November 17 on the Red China admission question—by then on the General Assembly's debate schedule for the very first time. Liebman would keep Dr. Tsiang posted on the interview and hoped-for press conference. Already lined up were Governor Edison, former Senator Smith, and Senator Keating. Word was awaited from Senators Dodd and Douglas. If events took place as anticipated, Liebman first would want to get the ambassador's ideas.

Taking On the Sixteenth General Assembly

Timed to coincide with the convening of the sixteenth regular session of the General Assembly was the Committee's big evening rally on September 21 at New York's Carnegie Hall—two days after the session began.

Liebman sent President Kennedy a letter in late August informing him the Committee would exert every effort in the weeks ahead to mobilize domestic and foreign opinion against China's admission.[45] Noting the President shared this view, the secretary thought it would be very pertinent if the President could restate his views on the seating question for repetition at the rally. That certainly would give added impact to the meeting, he said.

When the White House failed to reply by September 7, Liebman telegraphed the President, repeating, in brief, his earlier request. McGeorge Bundy, special assistant to the President for national security affairs, replied, thanking Liebman for his earlier letter, referring him to a one-sentence comment from the President's April 12, 1961 news conference and a two-sentence comment taken from an August 2, 1961 joint communique between the President and Chen Cheng, Vice-President of the Republic of China—both comments affirming U.S. opposition to the admission of Communist China.[46]

The rally was covered by the *New York Times* on page 2.[47] More than 3,000 people attended, cheered a "message" from Senator Barry Goldwater (R., Ariz.)—in sum: the United States should warn it would withdraw from the United Nations if the Chinese Communists were admitted—and listened to Senator Thomas J. Dodd (D., Conn.) and Congressman Francis E. Walter (D., Pa.). An adjacent column on the same page of the *Times* carried a report that the General Assembly's steering committee had endorsed a formal debate on the China credentials question by approving two proposals, one by New Zealand and another "more polemical" one by the Soviet Union. The United States supported the proposed debate: Deputy U.S. Representative Charles W. Yost emphasized the "singular importance" of the question. On September 25, the day President Kennedy spoke to the General Assembly, it voted the credentials issue on the agenda. The United States abstained. The "moratorium"[48] had ended.

The Committee of One Million and the rest of the world finally faced a debate on the seating question. The Committee reacted quickly, getting two publicity stories in the *New York Times* early in October: one demanded Mrs. Eleanor Roosevelt resign as a special adviser to the

U.S. delegation because of a remark made to a group in Charlotte, N.C., that no disarmament agreement could be effective while Communist China was out of the United Nations; the second article reported the Committee had obtained its one millionth signature for its 1961 petition drive.[49]

On November 8, Marvin Liebman proposed to the steering committee a publicity scheme he later postscripted to Ambassador Tsiang.[50] Basically, he wanted the Committee's leadership to come to New York and personally deliver to Ambassador Stevenson the approximately 75,000 signatures in hand—these, he indicated, over and above the "one million" names already sent to the White House. He also wanted these men to meet privately with Stevenson to discuss U.S. strategy, then to call a press conference with or without the Ambassador's participation. Liebman indicated his proposal was based on the following analysis:

The Republic of China had agreed *not* to veto Outer Mongolia under strong U.S. pressure. In exchange, Secretary of State Rusk had pledged to work assiduously to keep the Communist Chinese out and the Nationalists in. The United States would move to have the credentials question considered an "important question" under Article 18 of the Charter. This would make a two-thirds majority necessary. Both the United States and the Republic of China felt a two-thirds vote could be avoided for some time in the future. This solution satisfied the Republic of China.[51]

Liebman reported he had been told by good sources that Ambassador Stevenson tried to reverse this plan. He said Stevenson gave "legal problems" as the reason. The secretary believed, however, that Stevenson and other U.S. diplomats wanted the People's Republic. seated and were looking for some air between their wishes and Kennedy's instructions to hold the line against admission. Liebman thought Stevenson's move was made on his own, that the Chinese delegation protested and hinted they might take the matter directly to the President, and that Stevenson then capitulated and agreed to the Article 18 strategy. Even then, Liebman said, Stevenson still wanted the resolution to include a provision for a special committee of twelve nations which would examine the China question and present a report next year which might urge the General Assembly to accept a "two China" solution. Undoubtedly, Liebman concluded, the United States and/or the Chinese would have difficulty refusing the recommendations of a Special Committee they helped vote into being. That was why he wanted a meeting with Stevenson. Depending on how it came out, some Committee colleagues might even want to go right to Kennedy. Liebman closed by urging that everyone try hard to be in New York the following week.

Eight days later, Liebman dispatched two more communications on this subject: a telegram to Senator Douglas and a long letter to Ambassador Stevenson. Douglas was told that all other steering committee members had agreed to sign an open letter to Ambassador Stevenson and that Douglas' approval or comments were urgently needed.[52] The Stevenson letter, in Liebman's name only, transmitted the 75,000 petition signatures, summarized past presidential, congressional, and public hostility to the seating of mainland China (there could be no doubt, he said, where Americans stood), advised Stevenson of his responsibilities for articulating American public and official views, and recommended that the United States proceed on the "important question" strategy without proposing a special committee for future deliberations.[53]

Ambassador Stevenson answered even before the General Assembly's China debate began. Acknowledging receipt of the petitions, he said the U.S. government was continuing "to make every effort to preserve the seat of the Republic of China" and to prevent seating the People's Republic and agreed the petitions were "one illustration" of the sentiments of American citizens. U.S. policy, he continued, was also based on the "basic hostility which Communist China continues to show toward the United Nations and toward our country." Stevenson closed: "I note your suggestions as to the parliamentary means to be employed on this matter. This is the subject of continuous study and review within the Government, and I am glad to have your thoughts."[54]

On December 1, Stevenson addressed the General Assembly on the China question. His remarks—later printed in pamphlet form by the Committee[55]—provided an "exhaustive cataloguing," in the view of

Roger Hilsman, who interpreted one Stevenson argument (i.e., that Peking's admission "could seriously shake public confidence in the United Nations—I can assure you it would do so among the people of the United States") as a seeming reference to the activities of the Committee and its "allies" in Congress.[56]

Three resolutions reached a vote on December 15: 1) the General Assembly voted 61 to 34 with 7 abstentions to declare the China credentials question an "important question" requiring a two-thirds majority; 2) it voted 45 to 30 with 29 abstentions against admitting the mainland without expelling the Republic of China; 3) by a vote of 48 to 37 with 19 abstentions, the assembly rejected a Soviet Union proposal which called for admitting the People's Republic and expelling the Republic of China.[57] A clear-cut victory, said Liebman of the General Assembly's action in a year-end report to the steering committee.[58]

Eighteen months later, in a handwritten note to Liebman, Walter Judd pondered the upcoming 1963 General Assembly debate, detecting a big push to change China policy. Kennedy himself, he remarked, stopped admission in 1961. And it would be Kennedy and the Committee who would have to stop it again—if it could be stopped.[59]

Among the few Committee-related documents in the John F. Kennedy Library is a January 1962 letter to Marvin Liebman from Ralph A. Dungan, special assistant to the President: "The President has asked me to thank you for your letter, and to assure you that your word of commendation means a great deal to him." [60]

9

"To Keep Congress Firm"

During the second year of the Kennedy administration the Committee reached into different areas of China policy—despite the apparent misgivings of Dr. Judd. The 1960 "joint planks" statement was expanded to include new issues beyond the "recognition and admission" questions traditionally tied to the group's broadly based appeals. Opposition to any "two-China" solution in the UN, to any trade with the Chinese Communists, and support for the defense of Quemoy and Matsu islands were added to "A Declaration by Members of the United States of America in Opposition to Any Concessions to Red China." Every member of Congress, beginning in July 1962, received at least four solicitations except those who signed up after earlier invitations.[1]

Congressman Judd's apparent misgivings are deduced from a letter Liebman drafted in July.[2] It was a long and reflective letter, beginning with the news that Senators Douglas and Keating had endorsed the expanded statement and had approved its circulation to members of Congress. The secretary reminded the veteran lawmaker of his admiration for Judd's wisdom on foreign policy problems. He would continue to follow the congressman's advice. When Judd had requested a temporary halt to circulation of the statement, Liebman had concurred, he said, without opposition. Now, however, it was time to pursue the matter further. He began his reasoning by reflecting on the Committee's beginnings, about the need to strengthen Eisenhower's hand on China policy. This was accomplished, he said, by showing massive American support for an anti-Communist Chinese position. Those who objected were appeasers. Circulation of the original petition bolstered the administration's China policy and, presumably, was welcomed by Eisenhower and Dulles. Liebman agreed with Judd that the current Kennedy administration, including most people at the State Department, had dropped appeasement and accepted the Committee's approach. So he did not think that another large-scale congressional endorsement of the Committee's statement would be considered "pressure." Anyway, Liebman would rephrase the first paragraph to emphasize that pressure was not intended.

The statement's circulation, he added, was necessary "to keep Congress firm." It would show the legislators their constituents shared the Committee's views. In turn, the administration probably would welcome this public demonstration of congressional support on this issue.

Particularly in an election year, Liebman observed, legislators who detected a weakening on China policy among their constituents would change their positions. The new declaration could be used in the election. Circulating the statement among grass-roots people would act as a stimulus for action. It would give people something to do, allow them to seek out candidates, get their views on China policy, get them to discuss the statement and to commit themselves. Without this pressure, Liebman felt, those favoring concessions to the Chinese Communists could avoid taking a stand. He would, of course, go along if Judd still preferred, but he asked Judd to reconsider, saying the tactic would be to circulate the revised statement without publicizing it until a majority of Congress had endorsed it. That was July 18. On September 22, 1962, the *New York Times* ran a story reporting that 36 senators and 223 congressmen had joined in issuing the Committee's declaration calling for the defense of Quemoy and Matsu islands,[3] which once again had become newsworthy with reports that summer of military build-ups on the mainland opposite the two islands.

Also publicized during the summer was the plight of Chinese refugees in the Hong Kong area. President Kennedy had announced on May 23 the United States would admit several thousand previously cleared refugees under a special provision of the McCarran-Walter Act. An ad hoc group, the Emergency Committee for Chinese Refugees, was formed, consisting of Supreme Court Justice William O. Douglas, news commentator Lowell Thomas (narrator for "Red China-Outlaw!"), Senators Paul Douglas, John Tower (R., Tex.), and Congressman Judd. As a later Committee historical pamphlet commented: "In June, the Committee of One Million took the lead in organizing the ad hoc Emergency Committee for Chinese Refugees which was dedicated to focusing public attention on the tragic plight of tens of thousands of refugees who fled from starvation and enslavement in Red China to Hong Kong.'' [4] The addition of Justice Douglas, a man well known for his backing of philanthropic, environmental, humanitarian, and civil libertarian causes, obviously lent stature and national publicity value to the Emergency Committee for Chinese Refugees.

Yet another example of how Marvin Liebman, acting under the Committee's aegis, sought to achieve national publicity for a Far Eastern development carrying the potential of anti-Communist propaganda, had occurred in the late summer of 1961 before the sixteenth General Assembly session. Involved was the admission of Outer Mongolia to the United Nations, an action recommended by the General Assembly in April 1961 for later consideration by the Security Council. This move was seen by Under-Secretary of State Chester Bowles as an opportunity ''for taking an initiative that would have repercussions on the whole of our policy in Asia, including policy toward Communist China itself.'' [5] Later, Bowles credited the Committee with helping to ''disintegrate'' his initiative.[6] Twice, in fact, Marvin Liebman made the editorial page of the *New York Times* with long letters on the Mongolian issue.[7]

But one Liebman tactic failed. On August 3, he wrote Senator Eastland, saying the Committee had received many letters about Owen Lattimore's current visit to Outer Mongolia. Lattimore's presence in that country was creating special anxieties because of then current efforts toward U.S. recognition of that state. Liebman thought this was an appropriate matter for Eastland's Senate Internal Security subcommittee.[8] He suggested a number of questions about Professor Lattimore's passport, purposes, and intentions. An investigation at that time would be very helpful.

Responding, Senator Eastland said Lattimore's passport was in order, that travel to Outer Mongolia was not banned, that Lattimore, who had informed the State Department of his trip, was not representing the Department in any capacity.[9] The senator also had doubts that Lattimore was merely a tourist in Outer Mongolia, but he was uncertain whether it was appropriate or smart to investigate the journey. He would avoid engaging in a "fishing expedition," though if evidence were received by the Senate committee that Lattimore's activities involved internal security matters, then his panel might wish him to testify. If Liebman had any facts of interest, the senator signed off, his committee would be pleased to accept them.

Judd Defeated—Twice

Walter Judd lost his seat in Congress during the 1962 mid-term elections. He had served Minnesota's fifth district, which now comprises virtually all of the city of Minneapolis plus a couple of northern suburbs, continuously since 1943. He was defeated in a close election, after a tough campaign, by a 38-year-old Democrat, Donald M. Fraser, who had the aid of some fresh redistricting.[10] The Committee's prime mover on Capitol Hill since its inception in his own Far East and Pacific subcommittee in 1953, Judd was irreplaceable in Congress; likewise, he was irreplaceable as a Committee leader. (Contrary to Liebman's wishes, he would not take over as chairman of the group for several years. Evidently Paul Douglas was the stumbling block.)

Liebman waited until the end of the year, between Christmas and New Years, then sent the steering committee his thoughts on reorganization. (His memorandum was dated the same day as a condolence telegram to Mrs. Warren Austin in Vermont, whose husband had been listed either as honorary chairman or honorary co-chairman of the Committee since 1953 without ever having attended a meeting, according to available records.)[11] Liebman wanted Judd named chairman of the Committee.[12] He also proposed that Congressman Donald C. Bruce, a second-term Republican from Indiana, be named to the steering committee to fill Judd's slot as an incumbent Republican. Liebman apparently got approval for these changes from Ambassador Grew, Governor Edison, Senator Smith, and Dr. Garside. At least he wrote Senator Douglas as much on January 10, 1963, adding he would appreciate a fast response so that new letterheads could be prepared.

Several days later, however, on January 15, Liebman dispatched another letter to Douglas summarizing a telephone conversation the two had had, he indicated, earlier that day. Liebman was sure that others would acquiesce in balancing off a Chairman Judd with a Democratic liberal as co-chairman—in order to retain and enhance bipartisanship. The secretary even reminded Douglas what to tell the prospective candidate about his duties, including the information that all statements or other matters for issuance by the Committee first would be submitted for the candidate's approval. The Committee, Liebman said, had never sent out materials without having unanimous steering committee consent (neglecting to mention that it had, on occasion, issued various communications in the names of selected steering committee members only). Liebman added the steering committee would support anyone he recommended. Douglas had carte blanche in his choice.

But the next available Committee letterhead, dated February 25, 1963, reflected neither Liebman's proposals nor Douglas' apparent counterproposal.[13] Listed were: honorary chairman, Honorable Joseph C. Grew; and the steering committee: Senator Paul H. Douglas, Honorable Charles Edison, Honorable Walter H. Judd, Senator Kenneth B. Keating, Honorable H. Alexander Smith, Representative Francis E. Walter; treasurer, Dr. B. A. Garside; secretary, Mr. Marvin Liebman. This leadership carried on for several more months until Francis Walter died on May 31. On June 17, the Committee's letterhead lineup included only two incumbents, Senators Douglas and Keating, a situation rectified at month's end when Liebman told the remaining steering committee members that he had invited Democrat Thomas J. Dodd of Connecticut to join the group and that the first-term senator and former representative was willing (as were the other steering committee members).[14]

The Ambassador Tsiang Correspondence (Continued)

Early in 1962, after serving fifteen years as his country's chief delegate to the United Nations, Tingfu F. Tsiang became the Republic of China's ambassador to the United States. On February 7, 1962, Dr. Tsiang asked the Committee's secretary if he could get one of his friends to state the case against admission of mainland China in the *New York Times,* which, in a lead editorial on December 29, 1961, had argued that American diplomacy should adapt to the reality of two Chinas and implicitly had supported U.S. recognition of the People's Republic.[15] In response, Liebman communicated with Senator Douglas on February 12, enclosing a draft letter he had written for Douglas and advising that a considered reply from the Illinois senator to the *Times*'s new position would get the best possible attention. Douglas did not agree. He told a Liebman aide that while he was still opposed to recognition he would write his own statements and make them on his own time.[16]

On May 29, 1962, Ambassador Tsiang was mailed a letter by Harold L. Oram, president of the firm bearing his name and Liebman's former employer. Apparently enclosing a suggested public relations program for the Republic of China, Oram mentioned Liebman's efforts to organize an ad hoc group to aid Chinese refugees from Hong Kong. These improvised services were important to the main cause, but a more far reaching perspective was needed—such was the aim of the enclosed memorandum.[17] In July, commenting favorably on an article by Valentin Chu regarding the economic crisis on the mainland and requesting 200 copies (which Liebman apparently had had reprinted), Ambassador Tsiang asked Liebman if he had been able to get any accurate information about some highly classified report (not otherwise identified) by Walter W. Rostow, then State Department counselor and chairman of its Policy Planning Board. A story of the report was carried in the *Chicago Tribune* on June 16 and 17, the ambassador added.[18]

There is a break in the available Liebman/Tsiang correspondence until April 1963, when the ambassador, prompted by an April 16 letter published in the *New York Times,* sent Liebman a polemic. Was the letter in the *Times* the writer's own brain wave, Tsiang asked, or was it perhaps a "plot" inspired with or without the help of the mainland Chinese? [19] The ambassador said the letter reflected the view that the Chinese Communists were only modernizers, a notion which distorted and whitewashed Communist Chinese ideology and practice in an effort to sell Americans on Chinese Communism. Very clever, Tsiang admitted, this way of packaging the product. On May 2, in a letter written to the *Times* the day *before* the date appearing on Tsiang's letter to him, Liebman got his own rebuttal on the editorial page of the New York paper. "Chinese Communism is Communism and not anything else," Liebman wrote. "If aggressive Communism is a danger to the free world and to the United States, then Communist China is a danger." Liebman concluded: "Mr. Nash might well discuss 'futile obsessions with theories of Communism' with the North Koreans, the North Vietnamese, the Tibetans, the Indian border guards and the Chinese people themselves."

"Mr. Nash" was Ernest T. Nash, who signed himself in the *Times* as Co-Chairman, Committee for a Review of Our China Policy, a new organization, founded in San Francisco in March, which aimed to promote public debate on China policy. A near-lifetime resident of China but by then a U.S. citizen living in retirement in Woodland, Calif., Nash shared leadership in the group with former Oregon Congressman Charles O. Porter, one of the earliest congressional advocates of a change in China policy, the man defeated by a Committee member in 1960. In his letter to the *Times,* Nash had said that communism in China "exploded out of the decadent realities of Chinese life," that the predominant role of communism on the mainland was "to serve the Chinese revolution aimed at internal modernization; not to facilitate Chinese imperialism, nor to threaten the security of America, and certainly not just to please the Russians."

In addition to promoting China policy discussions in the United States, the Nash/Porter group hoped to encourage, in the words of a press release, "humanitarian use of U.S. surplus food, trade in nonstrategic goods and the exchange of visits by non-official citizens." [20] Toward these ends the new group, which functioned until March 1966, sought to state its case, appearing before various committees and associations and sending out an occasional press release from Porter's law offices in Eugene, Ore. (Once, appearing before the Senate Foreign Relations Committee in connection with the Foreign Assistance Act of 1963, Nash admitted his group's membership was small, charged no dues— and certainly had very different aims from those who claimed to represent One Million—but he nonetheless wanted the senators to "share our organization's sincerest conviction that, in depth, in quality, we represent at least a corner of the very heart and mind itself of the American people; a people unhappy about a foreign policy which has contributed [and I personally think we are as much if not more to blame than they are] to the estrangement of the greatest people in one hemisphere from the greatest people in another." The committee started with no money, he added, and worked entirely on a volunteer basis.)

Liebman went to Washington, D.C., several days after his rebuttal letter was published in the *Times,* where he learned from Tsiang about the ambassador's concern over reports of new agitation for trade with the mainland; on May 8, he reported this concern to Charles Edison and suggested the Committee act on the trade issue more or less as it had before.[21] His plan was to send 5,000 business leaders a letter appealing for signatures and contributions to be used in producing a full-page advertisement for the *Wall Street Journal.* In turn, the ad would be reproduced and distributed to members of Congress and other political leaders.

An Edison appeal for names and contributions began on May 21. A second appeal, enclosing a "Statement in Opposition to Trade with Red China," was dated June 17.[22] Liebman advised the steering committee on June 26 (in the same memorandum recommending the replacement of Francis Walter with Thomas Dodd) that close to 300 businessmen had endorsed the statement sent by Edison. But $12,927 was needed for a full page in the *Wall Street Journal,* and Liebman noted that that kind of money was not available. He attached a draft letter to be signed by all steering committee members to help solicit funds for the advertisement. Both Senators Douglas and Keating shied away—as they had once before—from attaching their names to the fund-raising letter.[23] On July 24, Liebman reported to Edison that 318 businessmen had endorsed the statement but had not contributed sufficient funds to print the statement as a full-page advertisement. On August 2, Liebman revealed that 329 businessmen had endorsed the statement on trade and contributed a total $5,076 toward an advertising campaign.[24] (That worked out to approximately $15.43 per businessman.) The ad was not published.

In June of 1963 a book highly critical of the Far Eastern policies of the Roosevelt and Truman administrations was published—*How The Far East Was Lost,* by Dr. Anthony Kubek, Professor of History, University of Dallas.[25] Dust jacket endorsements included David N. Rowe, the Yale professor, Robert Morris, former chief counsel to the Senate Internal Security subcommitee (both non-congressional endorsers of various Committee communications), and former Ambassador Patrick J. Hurley, whose jacket blurb said the book was "a scholarly, conscientious and well-documented history of that period during which the United States needlessly surrendered our ally, the Nationalist Government of the Republic of China, to the Communists."

Liebman read the book with great interest, he wrote to Ambassador Tsiang at the Chinese Nationalist Embassy in Washington. In particular, chapter 18, "Fall of the Mainland," was under consideration by the Committee for printing in pamphet form. Publishing something scholarly might help the Committee's "public posture," he added. Would the ambassador comment? Did he believe publication of chapter 18 could then be of assistance? In June, Liebman had heard from the Senate Internal Security subcommittee about the book. Benjamin Mandel, the subcommittee's longtime director of research, had asked Liebman if he could help line up favorable reviews for the Kubek volume. In the fall, the Committee published the chapter in pamphlet form as "The Lesson of China's Loss," with Walter Judd contributing an introduction. Dr. Kubek was grateful. He could not think of another organization, he wrote Liebman, which had done more to inform citizens about Communist China's record than the Committee. Communist China would have gained entry in the United Nations if it had not been for the Committee.[26]

On November 14, President Kennedy told a news conference:

> We are not planning on trade with Red China in view of the policy that Red China pursues. If the Red Chinese indicate a desire to live at peace with the United States, with other countries surrounding it, then quite obviously the United States would reappraise its policies. We are not wedded to a policy of hostility to Red China. . . .[27]

On November 20, an accountant working for the New York State Department of Social Welfare conducted a field audit at the offices of Marvin Liebman Associates, Inc. (see chapter 7).

On November 22, President Kennedy was assassinated.

The Hilsman Speech

Historically, of course, it is inaccurate to claim that Roger Hilsman's December 13 address on U.S. policy toward the People's Republic of China was an act of the Kennedy administration. Hilsman himself, however, has written that the speech was extensively prepared during the fall of 1963 and "clearly acknowledged that the policy of the Kennedy administration was based on a willingness to reach an accommodation with the Chinese Communist regime—provided only that the Chinese Communist regime was willing to modify its hostility in the same direction." [28] Delivered in San Francisco (the most favored city for important addresses on Far East policy), Hilsman's remarks attracted widespread attention and comment.[29] Hilsman later reflected on their significance:

> . . . The key difference between this speech . . . and Secretary Dulles' 1957 speech . . . lay in the basic assumptions on the question of Chinese Communist control. Dulles' speech assumed that the Chinese Communist regime was a 'passing and not a perpetual phase.' . . . This assumption, of course, was no longer valid, and although there had been no public statement announcing the fact, the United States had long ceased to base its policy on that assumption—a fact which had often been explained to our friends on Taiwan.[30]

The Committee delayed its response until the last day of the year (in order, Hilsman speculated, to coincide with the return of Congress). But Liebman had been busy preparing. Through Hilsman's courtesy he had received an advance copy. On December 23, Liebman wrote two almost identical letters to non-congressional members Christopher Emmet and Dr. Karl A. Wittfogel. With each letter he enclosed a rebuttal manuscript just received from David Rowe. Noting that Rowe had not referred to Hilsman directly until page 6 of the rebuttal, Liebman said he approved of this approach. He wanted to issue the Rowe statement on December 29 or 30 with a press release. And he wanted their advice on how to handle Senator Douglas on this situation.[31]

The Committee's statement, released December 31, dredged up an old 1949 quote from Congressman John F. Kennedy which had deplored America's postwar China policy. Then came a review of official and public objections since 1953 to any amelioration of hostility toward the mainland: "There is no other single issue of foreign or domestic policy which enjoys such overwhelming unanimity of opinion." Hilsman's name first appeared on page 3. He had, the statement said, publicly acknowledged the "two Chinas" policy, a formula both "contradictory and unworkable," for the first time. The speech represented "a substantial threat to our ally, the Republic of China, on Taiwan.

> It is a sign of political immaturity to evolve policies of deep concern to the Nation on hopeful assumptions and wishful thinking . . . We *know* what the Chinese Communists say they are and we have seen them in action. Why should we not accept these facts and act accordingly? Why must we try to create policies on what we hope they *might* become? The pursuit of policies based on illusion is not consistent with either the maintenance of the national security or American leadership of the Free World.[32]

In his book, Hilsman rebuts the Committee's rebuttal:

> . . . By a clever use of quotation marks around common expressions such as "live and let live," and "understanding" and "respect" for your enemies, the statement implied without saying so that these were the words of the speech—and so made it appear to advocate, not a policy of firmness combined with flexibility, but a policy of softness and cowardly accommodation.[33]

On December 31, the *New York Times* ran a little story about the Committee's statement on the bottom of page 22, reporting the group had charged Hilsman with having departed from official U.S. policy by promoting a "two Chinas solution."

The Johnson administration's dimly flickering signal through Hilsman, that "firmness combined with flexibility" could characterize American China policy if the Chinese government on the mainland mitigated its hostility toward the United States, came on the eve of another national election year. In fact, several days after the Committee released its rebuttal statement, Senator Barry Goldwater, a Committee endorser since 1955 who had urged U.S. withdrawal from the United Nations if the Red Chinese were admitted, formally announced his bid for the Republican presidential nomination. Late in January, France recognized the People's Republic, prompting the State Department to issue a statement that failed to reflect Hilsman's hopefulness: "an unfortunate step, particularly at a time when the Chinese Communists are actively promoting aggression and subversion in Southeast Asia and elsewhere." [34]

The Committee had tried to block French recognition. It published and circulated, in "cooperation with anti-Communist individuals and organizations in France," a statement entitled "An Appeal to the People of France, from Citizens of the United States, in the Name of Historic Friendship of your Peoples." The statement appeared as an advertisement in the European edition of the New York *Herald Tribune*. [35]

Several weeks after French recognition, Secretary of State Rusk dampened whatever optimism may have remained. "We have special and very grave concerns about Communist China," he said in Washington.

> And here let me clear away a myth. We do not ignore the Chinese Communist regime. We know it exists . . .
>
> Peiping continues to insist upon the surrender of Formosa as the *sine qua non* of any improvement whatever in relations with the United States. We are loyal to our commitments to the Government of the Republic of China, and we will not abandon the 12 million people of Free China on Taiwan to Communist tyranny. [36]

Still, one longtime Committee supporter decided on January 10, 1964, that his position on China policy required a slight change. "As things stand at this time," wrote the retired Republican senator from Vermont, Ralph Flanders, "I do not wish to remain irrevocably committed for the indefinite future to any policy relating to Communist

China, much though I dislike its rulers and everything connected with them.'' Flanders was responding—negatively as it turned out—to Marvin Liebman's annual request for a signed consent form required by New York State to allow the Committee to list him on its letterhead as a non-congressional endorser. Inaugurating the election-year campaign for congressional endorsers to the declaration, Liebman again faced some troublesome questions about the organization's financial practices and operational procedures. Not only Senator Douglas, but Republican Senator Kenneth Keating of New York, up for reelection, wanted formal assurances on four specific points before he would return his consent form.[37] Having discussed the matter with Douglas, Keating said the two of them were in full agreement about the need for formal assurances on each point: first, that no Committee employee nor the Committee itself would accept direct or indirect funds from Generalissimo Chiang Kai-shek; second, that neither Liebman nor any other Committee official would represent or accept funds and support from ''any other foreign group''; third, that the Committee's offices (still at Liebman's offices, 79 Madison Avenue, New York City) would not be maintained for the operations of ''any other political or foreign policy organization''; and finally, that all publicity releases issued by the Committee would be in Keating's office at least twenty-four hours before mailing or release to the press.

On February 5, Liebman answered Keating, agreeing on each point in language that closely paralleled Keating's own. Liebman also sent assurances to Senator Douglas. Replying, Douglas said he regretted the delays and inconveniences caused regarding materials to be issued by the Committee (a new arrangement had been worked out whereby Christopher Emmet would monitor Committee materials for the senator and report to Liebman on Douglas' behalf).[38] He said he was returning his signed ''consent card'' under separate cover along with a small contribution, as was his annual practice. Then he raised another sticky point: As both a senator and a member of the Committee's steering committee, he did not believe he should sign a letter pressuring other members of Congress to endorse the Committee's declaration. The proper degree of participation, Douglas felt, was the existence of his name as a steering committee member on the Committee's letterhead, but he did not want to press his Senate colleagues further by signing a solicitation letter. (Douglas would raise the same issue four months later, responding to Liebman's proposals for a full-page advertisement timed for the national political conventions and for a new letter to members of Congress who had not endorsed the declaration. Reminding Liebman of his earlier expressions on this point, Douglas declined to have his name included on a letter to fellow members of Congress.) [39]

The upcoming election campaign lent added significance to the Committee's annual declaration, for it could be used before the party conventions to demonstrate bipartisan congressional steadfastness on China questions and to pin down the commitments of candidates for public office during the campaign itself. Announcement of the 1964 declaration signers came on June 19, prior to both party conventions; 338 members of Congress (153 Democrats and 185 Republicans) endorsed the two-part declaration: 1) opposition to any "two-Chinas" formula in the United Nations and 2) to any easing of trade restrictions against the Chinese Communists. (In late September the Committee would prepare a press release raising the total endorsers to 345.) [40]

Early in the year Liebman began searching for a campaign year issue. Following a trip to Paris, he wrote to Secretary of State Rusk about reports he had heard that a high administration official was studying the feasibility of turning over the offshore islands of Quemoy and Matsu to the mainland's control. Negative, replied the officer in charge of the Department's Republic of China affairs several weeks later. There was "absolutely no truth" to the allegations.[41] Next, in April, Liebman tried to generate a congressional investigation of the Committee for a Review of Our China Policy, headed by former Congressman Porter and Ernest T. Nash. As in 1961, when Professor Owen T. Lattimore was his intended target, Liebman contacted Senator Eastland's Senate Judiciary Committee. Writing to Benjamin Mandel, longtime research director of the Judiciary Committee's Internal Security subcommittee, who had been around since the Institute of Pacific Relations hearings in 1951 and 1952, Liebman enclosed a pamphlet entitled "The Other Side" which he labeled as "straight Communist." [42] He also enclosed a membership list for the Porter/Nash group, saying he wanted Mandel to know what the former congressman was doing. A couple of weeks later Liebman followed up with another note on the same subject. Mandel asked him for a memorandum outlining what he thought the Senate Committee could best do. The Committee's secretary summarized his ideas in a confidential memorandum: he wanted the Internal Security subcommittee to conduct a preliminary and discrete investigation into Porter's source of funds and connections. Although the inquiry might simply confirm that the Oregonian was acting within his private rights in advocating "unpopular causes," it also might discover possible Porter connections with Communist China and/or Cuba. Liebman (himself in continuous contact with the Republic of China diplomats) did not recommend a public investigation until, he said, there was sufficient information to suggest that Porter was acting beyond his private rights. But he had no further information beyond what already had been sent to Mandel.[43] As far as is known, nothing further resulted from this exchange between Liebman and Mandel.

To be sure, Marvin Liebman was not singlemindedly preoccupied with the Committee's business in the pre-convention period. One writer has credited him with playing a key role in helping Goldwater get the Republican nomination.[44] He was active in the "Draft Goldwater Movement," helping to organize, and speaking at, a rally in Madison Square Garden on March 12.[45]

Liebman had wanted Senator Keating to make the Committee's presentation before the Republican Platform Committee in San Francisco in July. In making the request, he also raised a matter of "political delicacy." Although he was associated with many leaders of New York's Conservative Party, Liebman said he supported Keating for re-election and was disturbed about the possibility of a Conservative Party candidate. He offered to help. Keating replied that he would keep the offer in mind, that his plans for the convention were up in the air.[46] Senator Peter H. Dominick (R., Colo.), destined to play an ever larger role in the Committee's affairs, took the group's case before the platform committee.

Likewise, Liebman first had sought Senator Douglas for the counterpart role at the Democratic National Convention. When Douglas declined, former Ambassador Hornbeck was called on. Later, however, Senator Dodd, then a steering committee member who appeared on the Committee's behalf at the 1956 Democratic conclave, telephoned Liebman requesting the platform committee assignment. The Secretary wired Hornbeck, releasing him in favor of Dodd, who did the job.[47] The Democrats settled for a straightforward one-sentence plank ("We continue to oppose the admission of Red China to the United Nations"); the Republicans needed three sentences to cover China policy ("We are opposed to the recognition of Red China. We oppose its admission to the United Nations. We steadfastly support Free China.").

Public Attitudes: 1964

Buried by onrushing events in Vietnam and Indochina, Hilsman's faint signal of a potential China policy change flickered out in 1964, failing even to spark an issue in the Johnson/Goldwater campaign. So the election moved to its lopsided result with but one passing look at the People's Republic of China—in mid-October when the Chinese announced the successful testing of their first nuclear device. Did this neglect of China reflect public attitudes in 1964? Or was the country generally ahead of the administration in its willingness to accept new China policy approaches?

Growing American involvement in Vietnam, and the implications thereof for Sino-American relations, prompted the Survey Research Center (SRC) at the University of Michigan to probe American opinion in May and June on a variety of questions relating to China. The sample of 1,501 persons was comprised mostly of heads of households and wives of heads of households.[48]

The results must have startled many observers. For example, according to a summary of the SRC study prepared for the Council on Foreign Relations, more than one-fourth of the public was not even aware that mainland China was then ruled by a Communist government. Similarly, about one-fourth of the persons interviewed said they had not heard about the fighting in Vietnam. Of those who did know about

Communist China, a large majority believed the United States should be concerned about a Communist government in China. And most Americans who knew that mainland China was under Communist rule also realized that their own country had dealt more with the Soviet Union than with Communist China.

Interestingly, 39 percent of those who were asked if they had heard about another Chinese government besides the Communist one said they had not. "These data indicate," concluded the summary, "that the presence of the Nationalists as an alternative Chinese government is not a salient reality for most Americans." Of those who knew about the existence of two Chinese governments, a majority who expressed a direct opinion favored dealing with the Communists as well as the Nationalists, although a large minority favored dealing with the Nationalists only.

Overwhelmingly, the sample opposed the United States helping the Nationalists attack the Chinese Communists, fearing such action would involve America in war.

Regarding the United Nations, a clear majority said they would oppose a presidential suggestion to let Communist China join the world organization. But three out of four Americans favored the United States remaining in the UN even if Peking were admitted. Only 5 percent said they favored getting out if this occurred.

Was the American public willing to follow presidential initiatives designed to improve American relations with the People's Republic of China? (One may be forgiven for wondering how citizen Richard M. Nixon may have lingered over the responses here.) A large majority favored following a presidential suggestion for visits between Americans and mainland Chinese. Similarly, a large majority favored talking over Asian problems with the Communist Chinese government. Likewise, even 51 percent favored exchanging ambassadors with the Peking government.

Both those who favored and opposed increased contact with Communist China were equally opposed to United States withdrawal from Vietnam, favoring continued military aid to South Vietnam.

SRC's summary concluded with the following comments, which

the Committee's leadership later would consider in searching for ways to recruit the support of American "liberals."

> However, people who favor increased contact with Communist China are generally more likely than others to oppose the use of American forces in Viet Nam. Also, those people who favor contact with Communist China are generally more likely than others to be willing to make some compromise agreement with China on the issue of Viet Nam. These data indicate that a general willingness to deal with Communist China is usually accompanied by a preference for a non-military solution in Viet Nam.
>
> The general tendency of these attitudes to go together, however, is counter-balanced by the effect of education and age, both of which tend to produce a different pattern of attitudes. Better educated and younger people are somewhat more likely than others to favor increased contact with Communist China at the same time that they approve of a relatively militant policy in Viet Nam.

In sum, the Michigan pollsters discovered significant public ignorance about basic aspects of the situation in China and Asia, but they also uncovered an American mood more desirous of contact with the mainland than any administration to that time had been willing to permit. Fourteen years earlier, in January 1950, within four months of the official proclamation of the new Peking government, the Council on Foreign Relations had solicited the views of 720 "leading citizens" in twenty-three cities about American relations with China. "In the long run," concluded a summary of the majority opinions, "the United States would probably be in a better position to advance its interest in China if it maintained diplomatic relations with the Communist regime. While for the time being a policy of watchful waiting best suits the American interest, the eventual provision of acceptable guarantees would justify American recognition of the regime." [49]

10

Disappearing Bipartisanship

The 1964 election took a "heavy toll" of Committee congressional signers—75 in all, leaving 270 from the 345 reported in September. Liebman reported these numbers in a confidential memorandum to the steering committee in late November—a copy of which went to Ambassador Tsiang.[1] He would be in Washington the following week, Liebman wrote Tsiang, and wanted to set up an appointment to discuss the points outlined in the steering committee memorandum, among which were his suggestions for a revitalized steering committee. Senator Keating's loss to Robert F. Kennedy had removed the only Republican congressional incumbent from the steering committee, which then consisted of Keating, retired Republican Senator H. Alexander Smith, Democratic Senators Douglas and Dodd, and former Congressman Judd, in addition to Charles Edison, Treasurer Garside, and Secretary Liebman. Liebman wanted to return to the original concept of steering committee membership to reflect the Committee's "bi-partisan nature."[2] He proposed four fresh faces: Republican Senators John Sherman Cooper of Kentucky and Peter H. Dominick of Colorado, Republican Representative John M. Ashbrook of Ohio, and the Democratic Speaker of the House, John W. McCormack of Massachusetts, a member of the original steering committee of The Committee for One Million. Keating and Smith would be carried as "members" but dropped from the steering committee; former Ambassador Grew would continue as honorary chairman.

Liebman's canvass of the steering committee brought a quick response. Both B. A. Garside and Governor Edison replied the next day, Garside indicating approval of Liebman's reorganization plans, Edison proposing Senator Roman H. Hruska (R. Nebr.) instead of Senator Coo-

per, and also recommending that H. Alexander Smith be made honorary
co-chairman together with Ambassador Grew. Liebman got out an immediate addendum, reporting the Hruska-for-Cooper substitution (in
order to maintain the "liberal-conservative" balance) and the suggestion
that Smith be invited to become honorary co-chairman. Senator Douglas
resisted the Hruska move. He thought that Senators Cooper and Dominick would offer balance on the Republican side but that Hruska and
Dominick would not.[3] Douglas agreed with the H. Alexander Smith appointment. (Parenthetically, Douglas admonished Liebman for sending
out a mailing he had not personally received which inferred that the
Democratic election victory would be interpreted as a mandate for concessions to the Communists. Despite Liebman's explicit assertions that
such would be an incorrect interpretation, Douglas felt the implications
were strong.)

Whether Douglas alone was responsible for stopping the Hruska invitation is unclear. By December 28, however, the Committee had
received acceptances for steering committee membership from three
prominent conservative Republicans: Senators Bourke B. Hickenlooper
of Iowa and Dominick of Colorado, and Representative Ashbrook. Additionally, as Liebman wrote Dominick, the Committee had high hopes
that Democratic Representative Thomas E. Morgan of Pennsylvania, a
congressman since 1945 and, since 1959, chairman of the then House
Committee on Foreign Affairs, would "complete the roster." [4] Morgan
obliged on January 4, 1965.[5] By January 15, Liebman reported on
"current developments" using a newly designed and printed letterhead
listing the reorganized steering committee: Honorary Co-Chairmen
Grew and Smith; Democratic Senators Douglas and Dodd; Republican
Senators Dominick and Hickenlooper; Democratic Congressman
Morgan; Republican Congressman Ashbrook, plus Judd, Edison, Garside, and Liebman.[6]

Curiously, before the month was out two more senators joined the
steering committee: Democrat William Proxmire of Wisconsin and Republican Hugh Scott of Pennsylvania. Judging from copies of their acceptance letters to Senator Dodd, the Connecticut Democrat had recruited both of his colleagues. The addition of Proxmire and Scott,

Liebman exulted, would lend "added stature" and bolster the group's claim of bipartisan support and leadership.[7]

In his November 25 confidential memorandum discussing reorganization, Liebman also recommended a handful of projects for the coming year. The annual congressional declaration depleted by 75 names, he wanted to attract new congressional endorsers with a version covering the traditional Committee positions—i.e., admission to the United Nations, diplomatic recognition, trade relations—while adding two more: 1) opposition to "permitting" the Chinese Communists, directly or through their agents, to gain any additional territory in Asia by force or threat of force; and 2) opposition to *any* treaty obligations with them.[8] Liebman had in mind launching another nationwide petition drive (it would be the third since the 1953–54 and 1962 efforts) using the declaration to stimulate grass-roots organizational support at the local level. Also, he recommended another documentary film to replace the outdated but still circulated "Red China—Outlaw," produced in 1961. Script and film footage would be planned for showing abroad with local languages dubbed in. Other contemplated projects: reprints of a *Reader's Digest* article by Walter Judd, "Keep Red China Out!" an article by journalist Guy Searls explaining Communist China's legal problems in the United Nations, a rebuttal article by Clare Booth Luce to counter a recent piece by former Ambassador George Kennan in the *New York Times Magazine*,[9] reprints of a December 1, 1964 *Look* article reporting on Communist Chinese activity in Africa, and translation of *Ambassades pour Subversions* by Madame Suzanne Labin, a pamphlet said to cover the activities of PRC embassies worldwide. Additionally, Secretary Liebman recommended that three full-page advertisements be published in New York during the next General Assembly debate on the admission question. (There was no debate during the 1969 election year.) Lastly, Liebman observed that various unidentified cooperative ventures were being worked out with John Fisher, president of the American Security Council, whose new radio editorial series was edited by steering committee members Dodd and Judd.

Liebman had requested an appointment with Ambassador Tsiang for early in December on his outlined proposals. On December 20, the

New York Times ran a UPI story, datelined St. Louis, reporting on a *St. Louis Post Dispatch* story by Richard Dudman which announced the formation in Washington of a new conservative group, the American Conservative Union (ACU), put together by early backers of Senator Goldwater. A key organizer was said to be Marvin Liebman, who had played a "major early role" in getting the nomination for Goldwater.[10] Two days later, the *Times* printed a follow-up UPI account that named members of the ACU's new seventeen-member board, including Representative Donald C. Bruce (R., Ind.), as chairman, Representative John M. Ashbrook as vice-chairman, and Robert E. Bauman as secretary.[11] Other board members were indentified as William F. Buckley Jr., John Chamberlain, Brent Bozell, John Davenport (all writers), and Representative Katherine St. George (R., N.Y.)—all but Davenport long associated with the Committee.

Soon Liebman would find something for the ACU to do on the Committee's behalf: circulation of the new petition in support of the 1965 declaration. By January 15, 1965, work was underway on Liebman's projects. Liebman wrote the steering committee that Dr. Judd had assumed responsibility for raising funds for the new film, budgeted at $14,225, but had collected only $4,100 so far, meaning the film would have to be abandoned unless the balance were raised in ten days.[12] Two legislators had asked that their names be removed as congressional endorsers—Republican Ogden R. Reid, New York (since turned Democrat) and Democratic Senator Edward V. Long of Missouri. The possibility of getting Elmo Roper and Associates to conduct a private survey was being considered because the Council on Foreign Relations had published a survey by the University of Michigan's Survey Research Center (see chapter 9) which some steering committee members and others felt was inaccurate and misleading. Regarding finances, Liebman said the Committee was in "relatively good shape," with $5,900 in the bank—not enough, however, to finance the documentary film. (That summer, the Committee would indicate in its annual report to the New York State Department of Social Welfare that for the fiscal year ending March 31, 1964, it had collected $62,027 in contributions, with $23,782 going toward Committee projects, $16,957 toward managing and directing the organization's affairs, $15,891 toward raising contributions [fund-raising expenses], leaving a balance of $5,396.) [13]

A Liebman memorandum which spelled out the Committee's new technique for enlisting congressional endorsers in 1965 was directed to the four steering committee members whose names would be used in the solicitation: Senators Dodd and Dominick, Representatives Ashbrook and Morgan.[14] Dodd and Dominick would sign a letter to potential senatorial endorsers, with a return envelope and signature form addressed to Dodd for the Democratic senators and to Dominick for the Republicans. Similarly, Representatives Ashbrook and Morgan would solicit their colleagues, the former receiving the Republican replies, the latter the Democratic. On March 15, Liebman wrote Dr. Judd that 51 senators and 265 representatives—a majority in both Houses—had endorsed the declaration.[15] The petition campaign could begin.

About 100,000 petitions would be distributed. Judd was asked to sign the letter of transmittal to accompany the petitions, a draft of which Liebman enclosed for his consideration. Moderating the language somewhat, Judd returned the draft several days later. The modifications, he explained, were intended to attract the unconvinced or the fence sitters. Stronger language would only produce cheers from people already on their side.[16] Judd added that he had sent a commendatory telegram to President Johnson in support of the President's foreign policy in Vietnam. The greatest danger was not in meeting aggression firmly, he had told Johnson, but in the appearance of weakness and divisiveness at home. Johnson had replied, telling Judd he understood the point and had been encouraged ''by the increasing evidence of real unity and conviction among our people in support of our determination to carry out our commitments in Vietnam.''

On April 20, the New York Times ran an AP dispatch reporting that 321 legislators—51 senators and 270 representatives (5 more than on March 15)—had joined in a declaration opposing concessions to Communist China on four points: no representation in the United Nations; no U.S. diplomatic recognition; no U.S. trade relations; and no U.S. acquiescence in, or approval of, ''Communist China's aggression, direct or indirect, against her neighbors.'' Senator Dominick had released the declaration which, the story added, would be circulated in petition form throughout the country.

Although the Committee again had gotten majority endorsements in both Houses (however slim the Senate margin), a sampling of letters received from non-endorsers hinted at what would be a recurring new problem to contend with: the burgeoning call for a flexible American position vis-à-vis the Far East. A freshman Democratic congressman from Iowa's second district, John C. Culver (now a senator), answered the invitation to endorse the declaration by noting he had been appointed a member of the House Foreign Affairs Committee and wanted to try and develop a flexible and objective outlook on foreign policy. "Without detracting in any manner from this distinguished membership," he said about the Committee (one of whose steering committee members, of course, was Representative Morgan, chairman of the House Foreign Affairs Committee), "I must, at the present time, decline this invitation to participate in an organization advocating a particular foreign policy." Likewise, Representative Teno Roncalio (D., Wyo.), wrote Liebman that as a freshman congressman trying to represent a district "not uniform on this issue," he had to decline the offer. "I do recognize you," he added, "as a very valid special interest group and I will be happy to consider your views when this matter becomes a thing of immediate concern to me." Freshman Republican Congressman Barber B. Conable Jr., N.Y., answered that while he had not signed the declaration he wanted to record his vigorous opposition to any concessions to the People's Republic. Nonetheless, he felt the United States ought to "maintain a probing, flexible policy whose constant goal is improvement of international relations and lessening the possibility of war." The United States ought to "avoid a rigid and inflexible attitude which will prevent us from progressing beyond today's total absence of communications." Vermont's Republican Senator George D. Aiken answered in more personal terms: "[S]ince I came to the United States Senate 24 years ago I made it a policy not to allow my name to be used—no matter how worthy the organization. It has proved a good policy and I feel I can be a better Senator because of it." [17]

To circulate the Committee's new declaration/petition Liebman rallied numerous individuals and organizations: Among them: Robert Welch of the John Birch Society; Dean Clarence E. Manion, legal counsel to the Citizens Foreign Aid Committee; John Roussolet, then a former congressman from California and an official of the John Birch Society; Dr. Carl Thomas McIntire; J. Daniel Mahoney, state chairman of the New York Conservative Party; and Donald C. Bruce, chairman of the newly organized American Conservative Union, to whom Liebman wrote that the Committee's petition would help ACU members register their antipathy to appeasement and thus would be important at the grassroots level even though Vietnam was not directly mentioned in the declaration.[18] Also, the Young Americans for Freedom (YAF), which Liebman helped organize, was asked to help. Liebman detailed to David Jones how the YAF could cooperate: Although the petition was directed at Red China, its successful circulation would emphasize that a forceful stand against Communist aggression in Vietnam had the American public's support.[19] But by the end of August, the petition campaign had fallen far short of Liebman's expectations. Only slightly more than 100,000 signatures were in hand.[20]

Signs of Change

Senator Paul Douglas was sufficiently concerned about Marvin Liebman's close association with conservative and militantly conservative groups and causes to write him about it. In a long letter accompanying his annual $25 contribution in 1965, Douglas raised what Liebman must have regarded as nettlesome points. Naturally, the Committee's secretary had every right to carry on public relations work for so-called "right wing" groups, Douglas said, just as he had the same right to belong to ADA. But the senator wanted Liebman to make clear that the Committee was not connected with his other PR activities. Specifically, he wanted no sharing of offices. (At that time, and from the inception of Marvin Liebman Associates, many of Liebman's organizational interests were *headquartered* at his physical offices—in 1965, at Suite 905, 79 Madison Avenue, New York City. Thus *headquarters* was the letterhead address of the organization, though other organizational activities might very well be carried on elsewhere.) On a touchier matter, Douglas asked that Liebman neither initiate nor encourage any personal attacks on people who differed with them on China policy. He preferred to see issues debated on their merits and was sick at heart about all the smearing. Though opposed to granting the People's Republic recognition or admission to the United Nations—an issue on which he believed liberals and conservatives could still unite—he felt the Committee had become increasingly dependent on and tied to individuals and organizations of the extreme right. The appointments of Senators Proxmire and Scott to the steering committee partially corrected this problem, but he wanted his views known. Then he reiterated his concern that no money, either directly or indirectly, be accepted by the Committee from Chiang Kai-shek's people. Once before Liebman had reassured him on this point, but Douglas made it plain that constant vigilance was necessary. Liebman replied, avoiding Douglas' specific points. Instead, he explained that of all the groups he worked on, either professionally or as a volunteer, the Committee was unique. Its achievements and continuing value were based on bipartisan support. The Committee was a rare bridge between the numerous contesting viewpoints in the country's political system; Liebman would do nothing to jeopardize the organization or extend its prestige beyond its immediate concerns.[21]

The Committee's new documentary film, "Appeasement—Ally of Red China," was produced in April. On March 1, a tentative shooting script had been sent to a number of people for their suggestions and changes: William F. Buckley Jr., William A. Rusher, James Burnham, and William F. Rickenbacker (all editors of the *National Review*), plus David Martin, Walter Judd, B. A. Garside, H. L. Cheng, Gene Loh, and Republic of China Ambassador T. F. Tsiang.[22] Liebman was considering promotional ideas for selling film prints. He drafted a memorandum on letterhead of Communications Distribution, Inc., Room 330, 150 East 35th Street, New York City, the identical street address of the *National Review*. In fact, Liebman and William F. Buckley Jr. jointly ran Communications Distribution, Inc. (CDI).[23] Liebman sent film promotion ideas to James P. McFadden, assistant publisher of *National Review*.[24] Included was a concept for a brochure built around a reprint of an advertisement in the *National Review,* which ran on May 4, 1965. A subhead in the ad asked, "What will we give away after Vietnam?" Pressures were mounting to negotiate. "This stirring film will give you all the facts you need to help arouse the American people to give a resounding 'No!' to appeasement—of Red China or any other oppressor." Prints were offered at $125 each for the 28-minute sound documentary. Checks should be made payable to Communications Distribution, Inc.

By August Liebman thought he detected a possible threat to the Committee's cohesion: lagging public interest. The problem was twofold, he wrote the steering committee: first, the UN admission question had been stalled by the world body's virtual inactivity; second, escalation of the war in Vietnam had quieted demands in the United States for diplomatic recognition or even trade with the Chinese Communists.[25] But the Committee had had its share of successes in 1965: A majority in both houses of Congress for the congressional declaration had been enrolled in only three months—a unique achievement, he felt, for a nongovernmental, private group. And 100 prints of "Appeasement—Ally of Red China" were then in circulation. On the debit side, the petition campaign had not been as successful as anticipated, and the Committee had a deficit of $8,064, having collected only $38,151 in contributions over the first eight months of the year. The secretary proposed reactivating the petition campaign in cooperation with other organizations. He named the American Conservative Union, the American Legion, and Young Americans for Freedom. Also, he announced that the Committee would be represented with "observer units" at the upcoming Asian People's Anti-Communist League meeting in Manila. Congressman John M. Ashbrook, Marguerite Atterbury, and political consultant F. Clifton White would represent the Committee; Dr. Judd, Professor David N. Rowe, and six young students would represent the American Afro-Asian Educational Exchange. Contemplating another pro-trade movement, Liebman wanted to revive the once-used "no trade with the enemy" statement. He thought the 1965 declaration ought to be published in both the *New York Times* and the *Washington Post* during the next UN go-around. He saw Red China again becoming an "issue" and estimated that $35,000 would be needed to complete the program for the balance of the year.

Anticipating the "issue," Liebman drafted a letter for the steering committee's signature for delivery to Secretary of State Dean Rusk. The gist was that the United States would have to stress the strength of its opposition to the seating of mainland China at the upcoming General Assembly session because this year looked like a more difficult battle than ever before. American steadfastness, the best weapon in this fight, needed forceful reaffirmation by Rusk and President Johnson. Liebman thought Senator Dominick should take the lead in circulating the letter among steering committee members. On September 23, Senator Dodd suggested several word changes but accepted the sense of the original draft. As finally posted, however, the letter was signed only by Dodd and requested a meeting to present Rusk a letter signed by all congressional members of the steering committee.[26] Their hope was, Dodd wrote the secretary, that the display of broad bipartisan support evidenced by the delegation's visit to him would strengthen the administration's posture at the United Nations and perhaps even influence wavering delegations. The State Department finds no record of a Rusk reply to Dodd, and there is no evidence in Marvin Liebman's Committee files that the proposed encounter ever took place. Yet the Committee's 1966 report to the New York State Department of Social Welfare includes, under a statement of services rendered for the fiscal year ending March 31, 1966, the notation that "Various press conferences were organized including a meeting between the Committee's Steering Committee and Secretary of State Dean Rusk." [27]

The Committee published its pre-vote, full-page advertisement a week before the General Assembly session, listing 331 members of the 89th Congress as signers of the declaration.[28] Among them was an irked Senator John O. Pastore (D., R.I.), who was so "intensely displeased" by the ad that he withdrew from the Committee. What bothered him the most, he wrote, was that the copy constituted a subtle threat that put the Committee in the position of lobbying the United Nations over the heads of U.S. constitutional authorities. Amazed at this liberty and unwilling to be associated with any future indiscretion, Pastore wanted his name removed. This did not alter his consistent opposition to Red China, he added, a record compiled within the proper framework of representative government. Pastore chided the group further: the President of the United States had the authority and responsibility in foreign affairs; he had chosen the able and dedicated Ambassador Arthur Goldberg to represent him at the United Nations. Rightly, the ambassador spoke for the American people at the United Nations. Although the objective of the Committee coincided with the government's present policy, Pastore dreaded to think about the harm to national security if the reverse were true and the same encroachment were committed. Troubled times in the world called for "sanity—not vanity." [29] As far as can be determined from available evidence, this was the first such protest to a Committee advertisement by a member of Congress since the group's inception in 1953.

Liebman replied after the UN vote, admitting that one Committee function was "lobbying," which annually took the form of publishing the group's statement in the *New York Times* and sending various publications to UN delegates. [30] Their motive, he said, was to remind these delegates of the strongly felt American sentiments on this issue. The *Times* was used because it was read by all UN delegates.

The 1965 vote was the closest ever, as Liebman had anticipated: by a 47 to 47 tie, with 20 abstentions, the General Assembly defeated a resolution expelling the Nationalist Chinese delegation and awarding China's seat to the People's Republic of China. An earlier vote on an American-sponsored resolution once again had defined the seating issue as an "important question" requiring a two-thirds majority for adoption (or 63 votes in 1965). The U.S. resolution carried 65 to 49 with 11 abstentions. Although the tie vote thus was not as close as it appeared, still this was the first time Nationalist China had been denied a plurality since the question first arose in 1950. [31]

Marvin Liebman may have relaxed somewhat in the closing days of 1965. Now there were 184,300 American troops in Vietnam compared to 23,300 at the end of 1964. [32] The likelihood of greater pressure for some measure of conciliation with the mainland Chinese may have seemed more remote with this growing military involvement in Southeast Asia. Liebman could not then have foreseen that the anti-war movement would focus attention on Far Eastern policy and force changes in the Committee as well. Nor could he have realized that a mistake he made early in December would cost him part of his independent authority on the Committee.

The *Yale Daily News* Letter

Several weeks after the General Assembly vote a sizable group of Yale students and faculty members published a full-page advertisement in the *New York Times* calling for a "nationwide reappraisal" of American policy in the Far East. "Are we prepared to live in the same world with China?" the copy asked. The United States and China were on a collision course. Four national administrations had followed a policy of hostility toward the mainland Chinese. At least as a first step, the statement argued, the People's Republic ought to be admitted to the United Nations. More than 1,000 students and several hundred faculty members were said to have signed the full statement, many of their names appearing in the ad. Actually, the sponsoring group, Americans for Reappraisal of Far Eastern Policy, had been launched on the Yale campus in the fall of 1965 before the UN vote. So the *Times* reported in the same issue which featured the advertisement.[33] On October 21, the group had sponsored seminars on more than twenty campuses, linked together by a telephone hookup which allowed speeches to be heard nationwide.

Marvin Liebman reacted to the December 10 advertisement angrily and, he soon would realize, foolishly. His response, written on Committee letterhead, was a memorandum sent to the *Yale Daily News* and addressed to the Yale faculty members who had signed the statement. As written, the Liebman memorandum was published in the *Yale Daily News* on Tuesday, December 14. "We can understand, albeit deplore, young students lending their names to a statement on a matter of international and national concern of which they are obviously ignorant," he wrote in the first paragraph. "This ignorance may be caused by either inadequate mental processes or the quality of the instruction they receive from their teachers on international affairs. But, for presumably adult faculty members to lend their names to such an unrealistic bit of political hokum as is represented in the text of the statement is discouraging indeed." Thereafter, Liebman escorted the Yale faculty through a "look at the facts," which started with the admonition that "it might have been wise for the originators of the statement to consult with their principal" (Red China). The letter went on—*and on*—in this vein, ending with the cry, "Mao Tse-tung is under no illusion about his ultimate objective. Why should members of the faculty of Yale?"

On the Committee's letterhead as a steering committee member, of course, was the name of Thomas J. Dodd, then in the first year of his second term as the senior and fervently anti-Communist senator from Connecticut. Dodd withheld his fire until after the holiday season, then unloaded on Liebman, sending copies of his letter to other members of the steering committee.[34] As a member of the Senate Foreign Relations Committee, Dodd was "most unhappy" about the wording of Liebman's letter. Indeed, had it not been for his "very strong personal belief in the fundamental position of the Committee of One Million and in its potential utility, your letter would have caused me to submit my resignation." The senator had received a number of letters complaining about Liebman's harsh language. "As matters stand, I must warn you in all candor that I shall be obliged to consider submitting my resignation unless we can have an ironclad understanding that no future statements or Letters to the Editor will be issued without the approval of the Steering Committee."

Dodd acknowledged that Liebman's letter on the whole, "was an accurate restatement of the position the Committee of One Million has time and again taken on the subject of Red China." Most unfortunately, however, was the wording of Liebman's opening paragraph. Dodd continued: "Such gratuitous abuse may only have the consequence of hardening the attitude of those we seek to persuade and of winning them the sympathy of those who may yet be undecided." Future Committee statements, Dodd said, should not only be approved in advance by the steering committee, but "it would be best if we could agree that in future such letters be sent out not over your signature but over the signature of one of the officers of the Committee, acting on behalf of the Steering Committee and with their approval."

Chastised, Liebman let the matter cool for ten days, then wrote an apology to Dodd and a memorandum to the steering committee.[35] Both communications ignored Dodd's second suggestion about not sending out his own letters to newspaper editors. Instead, Liebman offered a procedure for clearing statements. Time was always important, he noted, since most responses were rebuttal statements and had to be issued as soon as possible. In the future he would mark these statements "most urgent" and send them special delivery or by telegraph (depending on length), hoping for quick approval and/or changes. The secretary agreed with Dodd, after re-reading his letter to the Yale paper, that the language was "intemperate" and had negated the valid points in the message. He regretted and apologized for the "incorrect interpretation" his intemperance may have reflected on the Committee's sound positions and steering committee members.

The 1966 Congressional Hearings

Senate and House hearings that focused on U.S. policy toward Asia and Communist China preoccupied the Committee during the first few months of 1966. The first hearings took Liebman by surprise. Indeed, they were announced by Chairman Clement J. Zablocki (D., Wisc.) of the House subcommittee on the Far East and the Pacific—an original signer of the 1953 petition and a rather consistent endorser of Committee positions ever since. Again, Liebman reacted quickly—and again, not without repercussions. On the day the Zablocki hearings opened, January 25, the Committee's secretary responded with three messages: an "urgent memorandum" to the steering committee, a letter to Congressman Zablocki, and a letter to new Republic of China Ambassador to the United States Chow Shu-kai. To the steering committee he pointed out that "nearly all" of those named to testify on Zablocki's press release supported a "soft" approach to Communist China.[36] If the hearings should attract major publicity, he said, a preponderantly one-sided show would be most unfortunate, particularly for its effects on America's friends and allies in the Far East. Liebman urged steering committee members to contact Zablocki so the Committee's position would receive as much publicity "as the other point of view." Specifically, he wanted the hearings broadened to include testimony from a list of experts identified in his letter to Zablocki, copies of which he routed to steering committee members. Liebman listed twelve individuals: Walter S. Robertson, former Assistant Secretary of State for Far Eastern Affairs; Professor David N. Rowe, Department of International Relations, Yale University; Dr. Walter H. Judd; Dr. Stanley K. Hornbeck; Professor Franz Michael, Institute of Sino-Soviet Studies, George Washington University; Professor Frank Trager, Department of International Affairs, New York University; Dr. Robert Strausz-Hupe, University of Pennsylvania Foreign Policy Research Institute; Dr. Stefan Possony, Director, International Political Studies Program, Hoover Institute, Stanford University; General Albert C. Wedemeyer; Admiral Arthur W. Radford; Admiral Arleigh Burke; and Professor Paul M. Linebarger, School of Advanced International Studies, Johns Hopkins University.[37]

Liebman's letter to Zablocki regretted that the Committee had not been given advance notice of the hearings. Those scheduled to testify, he said, represented contrary viewpoints to the Committee and to the majority of Americans, including Congress. While the minority viewpoint should of course be heard, so should the majority. These remarks prompted steering committee members Douglas and Dominick to notify Liebman immediately that his sentences prejudging the testimony of witnesses should be struck from the letter to Zablocki. But the letter already had been sent. No matter. Zablocki's reply, dated February 3, thanked Liebman for his January 25 letter and said the staff of the Foreign Affairs Committee had been instructed to ascertain whether each of Liebman's recommended witnesses would be willing and able to testify.[38] Five were—and did—Possony, Rowe, Hornbeck, Robertson, and Michael.[39] (The last to testify, Professor Michael, wrote Liebman and Zablocki that he was "very perturbed" by Liebman's attempt to categorize proposed witnesses as "soft" and so forth; he had not had advance knowledge of Liebman's letter to Zablocki and felt that academic testimony should be given on a personal basis and not organized into opposing camps.) [40]

The third Liebman letter of January 25 went to the new Chinese

ambassador to the United States, Chow Shu-kai.[41] Liebman enclosed a
copy of his "urgent memorandum" to the steering committee, discussed
a couple of pamphlets then in progress (advising that drafts of both
would be sent to the ambassador when ready), said he would like to get
together soon and closed with a postscript that Congressman Melvin
Laird (R., Wisc.), Republican Whip in the House (and later the Secretary of Defense in the first Nixon administration), would be "taking a
hand" in the subcommittee's hearings and would no doubt make sure
that "our" viewpoint was heard. Ambassador Chow replied that he was
deeply appreciative of Liebman's initiative in urging Congressman Zablocki to seek testimony from people associated with the Committee.[42]

  After eight of the Zablocki subcommittee's twelve public hearings
on U.S. policy in Asia, Chairman J. W. Fulbright's Senate Foreign
Relations Committee inaugurated the first public session in a new
series of hearings on "U.S. policy with respect to Mainland China." [43]
The first witness, Columbia University Professor A. Doak Barnett, got
front-page coverage in the *New York Times* with his recommendation for
"basic changes" in America's China policy (essentially: abandonment
of "containment and isolation" in favor of a policy of containment
without isolation); the last three paragraphs of the story, on the jump
page, quoted from Walter S. Robertson's testimony given the same day
at the start of the final three days of the House hearings (Recognition of
the P.R.C. "would bring prestige and power to a regime that threatens
every principle to which America gives allegiance"). Next day the
Times carried a front-page report that President Johnson had quietly authorized a major relaxation in travel regulations to Communist China by
allowing scholars and writers who could arrange for entry to travel
there. China policy was back on the front page the following day as well
with Professor John K. Fairbank's testimony before the Senate Foreign
Relations Committee (high administration officials were overreacting to
"Peking's vast blueprints" for exporting the Chinese Communist revolution). A couple of days later on a network television show, Vice-
President Hubert H. Humphrey picked up Doak Barnett's "containment
without isolation" proposal, indicating an attempt would be made to
approach China much as the Soviet Union had been approached in the

late 1950s and praising the Fulbright hearings as "among the most fruitful procedures under way in this Government." Humphrey's remarks also made page 1 of the *Times*. [44]

By March 21, when the China policy review once again got back on page 1—198 academic "experts" in Asian affairs signed a document urging the United States to drop opposition to seating the People's Republic in the United Nations and to open negotiations toward the establishment of formal diplomatic relations—[45] the Committee was impelled to act. None of its spokesmen as yet had faced the Foreign Relations Committee microphones (though Dr. Judd and Professor Rowe both would testify on March 28, the next to last day of the hearings). As he may have been contemplating how to counteract the mounting publicity supporting China policy changes, Liebman got hit with another blow that Monday afternoon: the telegraphed resignation of Senator William Proxmire from the steering committee. The Wisconsin Democrat wanted his name deleted by the time the Committee released a public statement re the Senate's hearings.

Liebman replied immediately by letter, regretting that a brief press release carrying Proxmire's name as a steering committee member already had been mailed, adding that no public statement directed at Senator Fulbright would bear his name. [46] He asked Proxmire if it would be possible to postpone public disclosure of his resignation until the steering committee had had a chance to meet. Such a meeting, he stressed in a memorandum that day to the steering committee, was "vitally important" because of Proxmire's resignation and the intensification of efforts to change China policy. Because other "urgent business" would take him out of the country for a week, he proposed a steering committee meeting in Washington early in April. [47] One was arranged for April 6 in the Senate office of Paul Douglas. Before it even convened, the *Times* editorialized that the country was far ahead of the administration in its willingness to try new approaches to China policy. [48] Nonetheless, the newspaper also gave front-page coverage to the testimony of Dr. Judd, Professor Rowe, and Professor George E. Taylor of the University of Washington, all of whom defended current China policy and vigorously opposed the proposals of the other witnesses at the Senate hearings. [49]

Minutes of the April 6 steering committee policy meeting record that Dr. Judd served as chairman (Judd later made a point of writing Liebman that Senator Douglas, at Judd's insistence, chaired the meeting although he had sat at the head of the table in Douglas' office).[50] Besides Judd, Douglas, and Liebman, five others attended the Capitol Hill conference that spring afternoon: Senator Dominick, Dr. B. A. Garside, and three legislative aides of steering committee members—David Martin representing Senator Dodd, Richard Murphy representing Senator Hugh Scott, and Howard Shuman, Senator Douglas' legislative assistant. The Committee's basic problems in the context of recent developments, according to Liebman's minutes, were complacency on the part of those who agreed with their views (a majority, said the minutes) and a lack of funds. Because the conservative community was committed to the Committee's positions, the major thrust for changes in China policy was coming from the liberal community. Accordingly, they should aim toward mobilizing "liberal anti-Communist support" without taking conservative support for granted. Fearing the loss of additional legislators to the policy reappraisal fever, the Committee would seek to hold its present congressional membership without trying to add new endorsers.

Several other proposals were accepted: first, Senator Dodd's aide, David Martin, would make arrangements for the Library of Congress' facilities to be employed for the preparation of studies on subversive Chinese Communist activities in Africa, Latin America, and Asia which could then be published and distributed either by the Senate Judiciary Committee's Internal Security subcommittee and/or The Committee Of One Million; [51] second, Dr. Judd would ask former Secretary of State Dean Acheson, his old China policy adversary from the Truman administration, with whom he had been in correspondence and who had taken a strong stand against concessions to the mainland, to draft an article for *Foreign Affairs* and/or Committee distribution; [52] third, Senator Douglas agreed to help enlist support in the liberal community, while Liebman was asked to contact Professor Frank Trager of New York University about the drafting and circulation of a statement among a list of liberal Americans; [53] fourth, Senator Douglas would host a briefing session for leading syndicated columnists based in Washington to consolidate their support for present U.S. policy; fifth, the Committee would try to publish the edited testimony of Dr. Judd and Professors Rowe and Taylor given at the Fulbright hearings. Finally, to rectify Senator Douglas' persistent bugaboo, raised again at this meeting, the Committee would take steps to move its headquarters address and telephone to avoid confusion with other organizations located at Liebman's Madison Avenue offices. Possibly because the Democratic senator's assistance was essential to the success of any campaign directed at the liberal community, Liebman acted swiftly on this revived request. By April 15, 1966, he had made arrangements to move the Committee's headquarters to Room 709, 1790 Broadway, New York City—the offices of Committee Treasurer B. A. Garside.[54] April 15 also was the day Liebman and Garside signed the group's annual report to the N.Y. State Department of Social Welfare, listing contributions for the fiscal year as $66,343. The Committee's address was given as 79 Madison Avenue, which remained the organization's official address on the 1967 and 1968 New York reports—before the Liebman era ended and the organization moved to Washington.

As Liebman began coordinating the projects agreed to at the meeting in Washington, he also started corresponding with the man destined to take over the Committee's promotional activities three years hence. Lee Edwards had written Liebman several days before the steering committee meeting soliciting work for his Washington D.C. public and political relations firm.[55] Apparently Liebman invited the former assistant press secretary to Senator Barry Goldwater to submit some ideas. Edwards, later the author of a highly flattering political biography of California Governor Ronald Reagan, replied in April with an outline of five different projects spread out over a five-month period.[56] For a fee of $4,000 per month, Edwards proposed: 1) supervising the preparation and writing of a series of speeches for selected congressmen and senators on various aspects of China policy and publicizing the speeches after delivery in Congress; 2) arranging for articles to be written for national magazines under the by-lines of congressmen and senators; 3) surveying radio and television production companies and stations to find those interested in presenting the Committee's positions; 4) contacting people on Capitol Hill and acting in a liaison capacity; and 5) preparing and distributing a "Fact Book" for the fall elections that would encompass the complete record of America's China relations and would be designed to make a major issue of the China question in the 1966 congressional elections. Although Edwards and Liebman soon would begin working together on some of these projects, Liebman's next message to Edwards concerned organizational plans for another emerging Liebman-promoted group—the World Youth Crusade for Freedom, which Professor David Rowe and Tom Charles Huston, then chairman of Young Americans for Freedom, were helping to get underway.[57]

The "Liberal Campaign"

In late May Liebman wrote Senator Douglas a confidential letter about the "Liberal Campaign," advising that he had employed a young public relations man identified with liberal groups, Gilbert Jonas, who happened to agree with the Committee's China policy positions.[58] Jonas had recommended that Professor Trager be asked to draft and submit a statement to a handful of liberal academics, who, in turn, would allow their names to be used in the solicitation of several thousand other scholars—thus counteracting the publicity given the 198 "experts" named in the March 21 story in the *Times*. But Liebman considered the Trager statement as drafted too long to be effective, offering too many points of disagreement. He and Jonas had decided to shorten the statement, make it appeal to every type of American liberal (not just academics), and to circulate it on an independent basis and *not* (Liebman's emphasis) as a Committee project. That's where Senator Douglas came in. Liebman asked him to edit the redrafted statement in order to attract the maximum number of liberal anti-Communists, then mail it with a covering letter on his own letterhead to several "liberal leaders": Leo Cherne, Research Institute of America; Professor Trager, the original drafter; George Meany, President of the AFL-CIO; Professor John Roche of Brandeis University; and Dean Acheson. After Douglas had received a sufficient number of acceptances, the statement would be circulated on a special letterhead, without the Committee's name or address, to a list of 3,000 prominent liberals put together by Jonas. Either a press conference or an advertisement would be chosen as the final publicity vehicle. Ideally, Liebman wanted the statement released in time for the China debate at the United Nations in the fall.

As envisioned by the Committee's secretary, the "liberal campaign" worked out approximately (but not entirely) as planned. Senator Douglas invited nine people to be sponsors: Trager, Meany, Cherne, Roche (but not Acheson from Liebman's original suggestions); Professor Wesley R. Fishel, Michigan State; Professor Sidney Hook, Rockefeller Foundation; author Edgar Ansel Mowrer; Professor Bertram D. Wolfe, then on leave of absence; and publisher Sol Stein of Stein and Day.[59] The senator's solicitation letter acknowledged that healthy differences of opinion existed in the nation on the question but doubted that liberals as a whole opposed administration China policies despite the recent statements, conferences, and resolutions which gave that impression. By August 4, according to Liebman, Professors Fishel and Trager and Leo Cherne had accepted Douglas' invitation.[60] An estimated budget of $14,362 was proposed to implement the plan, consisting of a mailing, a couple of advertisements and some advertising reprints.

On the last day of October, one month before the General Assembly voted on the China question, the *New York Times* ran a story on page 8 headlined "114 LIBERALS URGE UN TO BAR PEKING." Eight prominent signers of a statement (not excerpted or reproduced) were named, including Senator Douglas and three of those solicited by him—George Meany and Professors Fishel and Wolfe. The story's last four paragraphs reported that similar opposition to the recognition and seating of the Chinese Communists was being expressed in an advertisement by The Committee of One Million elsewhere in the same edition of the newspaper (page 12). The advertisement, the story continued, contained the names of 334 members of the 89th Congress (51 senators and 283 representatives) who had signed a declaration expressing similar opposition to Communist China. Liebman's original plan for the "Liberal Campaign" had envisioned no public association between the group of liberals and the Committee. Clearly, however, he had chosen to publish the Committee's 1966 declaration statement on the same day as the "Liberal Campaign" story, and the *Times* had decided to link the two statements in its coverage.

Actually, the "Liberal Campaign" was one among several contemplated Committee-related projects for the latter half of 1966. In response to the formation in June of the new National Committee on United States-China Relations, which cited its intention to sponsor public discussion of U.S. China policy and to seek ways of lessening tensions between the two countries,[61] Liebman drafted a long "Most Confidential Memorandum" for "All Concerned." [62] Pro-appeasement forces were making progress toward changing public opinion and U.S. China policy, he said. Their effort had momentum and it was effective. For these reasons, it had to be totally counteracted. Liebman ticked off assets of both sides in the struggle: on the Committee's side, two—grass-roots support from the American people plus Chinese Communist intransigence; for the opposition, five—the "establishment," national religious organizations, second and third level State Department employees, and a handful of headline-commanding legislators (specifically mentioned: Senators Fulbright, Morse, and Kennedy, whether Edward M. or Robert F. not indicated). In the past, Liebman added, the Committee's basic task had been to solidify the group's support in Congress, to keep the pressure on Capitol Hill, to maintain bipartisan support. Within the past year, however, attrition had occurred in the Committee's position. Now more than ever before, he said, the Committee must concentrate on maintaining bipartisanship. Liebman's memo reads like a fiery manifesto, urgent and combative, a hortatory warning that bold new ventures were needed to mobilize a counterattack against his worst fears—American appeasement of the Peking regime. Above all, bipartisanship was the Committee's key contribution in the battle to prevent appeasement of Communist China.

But another momentous event (far more consequential than the partisan political makeup of an American anti-Communist organization) soon would affect international attitudes toward the People's Republic of China. Unforeseen by Marvin Liebman or anyone else in the Western world in the summer of 1966 were the worldwide repercussions of a June 1 announcement in *People's Daily* proclaiming the beginning of the Great Proletarian Cultural Revolution. A period of unprecedented turmoil in the brief history of the People's Republic, this three-year siege of domestic divisiveness reinforced ballyhooed myths and stereotypes about a raging, despotic, aggressive, paranoid, and dogmatic Communist society led by a madman, fostering a new and sinister image of a "China in ferment." [63] Soon the Western press would tell of young Red Guards rampaging the streets, of gigantic purges in the Chinese Communist Party, of rampant violence and near anarchy, of a frenzied China paralyzed by a "crisis of authority." Early in 1967 author Theodore White would write a television documentary for Wolper Productions called "China: Roots of Madness," which depicted the Cultural Revolution as an hysterical development in China's continuing saga of communism. Metromedia and other independent television stations began airing the film in February. By spring the Peking regime had recalled all but one of its ambassadors abroad. In August of that year Red Guards burned the British consulate in Peking, beating the charge d'affaires.

Writing his June 1966 memorandum, of course, Liebman could not then know that his Committee's cause would be bolstered by such startling developments. At the time, he proposed an extensive ten-month campaign to begin in September. He wanted a budget of $170,000, more money than ever before available through the Committee's traditional contributors. He described plans for the then upcoming "Liberal Campaign," reported on a new ad hoc clergyman's group (American Clergymen's Committee on China), mentioned proposed academic conferences, then turned to what he called right-wing support. Because the Committee's position was fully supported by the "American right," conservative organizations should be given specific assignments. Right-wing groups could be put to work distributing a proposed paperback edition of *The Red China Lobby*. He identified *Human Events,* Young Americans for Freedom, Constructive Action and, potentially, the John

Birch Society. YAF leaders already had agreed to provide people for "activist agitation." Facts about pro-appeasement organizations which could not be publicized by the Committee because of "various internal problems" could and would be made known through *National Review, Human Events,* and other conservative publications. Even the Senate Internal Security subcommittee of the Judiciary Committee and the House Committee on Un-American Activities would be solicited to start investigations of opposition groups. Here the idea was to attack the credibility of organizations and individuals who promoted the pro-appeasement line. Liebman was convinced the anti-P.R.C. position could be maintained at least through 1967 if sufficient funds were raised to activate all his plans, but he was not too optimistic about how much of the $170,000 could be raised through appeals to the general public. The opposition, he lamented, did not seem to be as inhibited by a lack of funds.

As with the "Liberal Campaign," Liebman organized the new groups so that others would be perceived as providing the initiative. Favoring a behind-the-scenes role for himself, he wrote a series of memoranda and letters in July and August which demonstrated his capacity for coordinating and maximizing the use of available resources. On July 13, for example, he contacted his old friend on the staff of the Senate Internal Security subcommittee, Benjamin Mandel, questioning the relationship between author Felix Greene and a New York philanthropic foundation and suggesting a follow-up might lead to learning how the "Red China Lobby" was being financed.[64] One week later, on the floor of the U.S. Senate, Senator Milward L. Simpson (R., Wyo.), delivered a speech entitled "Felix Greene: Red China's Man in America," charging that Greene was an "emotional" foreign agent of the Chinese Communists even if not a legal one.[65] This would be among the speeches reprinted by the Committee for use in a "Candidate's Kit" during the upcoming congressional elections.

The "Candidate's Kit" project, originally proposed by Lee Edwards in April, got a Liebman go-ahead on July 14.[66] Whether Senator Simpson's speech was among those prepared by an Edwards-hired writer is unknown, although Liebman later acknowledged that Edwards had been assigned the task of getting speeches delivered in Congress.[67] On June 28, 1966, Congressman Ashbrook, a Committee steering committee member, was recognized for thirty minutes on the House floor for an address entitled "The Red China Lobby," which identified and disparaged numerous individuals, groups, and publications that Ashbrook said were lobbying for Communist China. On September 12, Representative John Buchanan (R., Ala.) also received thirty minutes for a speech entitled "Red China: A Realistic Appraisal." [68] Later reprinted by the Committee, this address expressed concern over recent changes in emphasis on China policy. (In the summer of 1967, Lee Edwards would remind Liebman that his Washington office had succeeded in 1966 in placing key addresses in Congress on topics like the Red China lobby.) [69]

Political consultant F. Clifton White received a memorandum from Marvin Liebman on July 28 elaborating steps and procedures for setting up a "dummy organization" called the "Businessman's Committee Against Trade with Red China." [70] The Committee's secretary enclosed a drafted statement and a transmittal letter, advising White to find a well-known businessman who would allow his personal or business letterhead to be used for all correspondence. Liebman suggested that a vice-president of the National Association of Manufacturers might cooperate in locating and organizing the right mailing lists. The "dummy organization" would be set up with White and others as officers.

Several days after sending the memorandum to White, Liebman wrote a detailed memorandum to Dr. Daniel A. Poling specifying the necessary organizational and financial requirements for a "Clergymen's Emergency Committee on China." [71] Overall plans called for a six-month expenditure of $130,000, which Liebman admitted was relatively large, especially when compared to the Committee's, but which he said was probably less than 20 percent of "opposition" expenditures. Dr. Poling would serve as chairman, the Reverend David C. Head as executive secretary. Included in this prospectus were time schedules and detailed budgets for advertising, mailings, fact kits, speakers bureaus— everything one would want to know to launch and implement a political action group.

Still another proposal was dispatched on August 11, this one for an American Student Committee for a Free China (ASCFC).[72] Liebman had discussed this idea in Washington with David Jones, then executive director of the American Conservative Union, and Tom Charles Huston. Because the already functioning World Youth Crusade for Freedom (WYCF), which Liebman seemed to regard as the YAF's foreign policy "front" (his quotes) had established liaison with Asian students, Liebman proposed the new group be openly affiliated with the WYCF to avoid duplication of work. In fact, he wanted David Keene, then the chief of WYCF's American secretariat, named as ASCFC's national chairman. Though a formal organization would not be established, national headquarters would be in New York City. The entire operation would be the responsibility of Don Pemberton, subject to consultation with David Keene, David Jones, and Tom Charles Huston. Liebman's detailed outline of projects included plans for a national student conference on China in Washington, D.C. to be aimed at important campus leaders. Tom Charles Huston should run this event, using, if necessary, Lee Edward's professional assistance. Huston replied to this idea on YAF letterhead listing him as national chairman representing the Indiana University School of Law. He said the conference could not be organized unless $100 "scholarships" were offered to each participant ($200 for those living west of the Mississippi) as an inducement to attract student newspaper editors and student body presidents. If the money was not forthcoming, forget it, he said in effect. Several days later, Huston drafted a letter about the conference to Patrick Buchanan at the New York law office of former Vice-President Richard M. Nixon.[73] He would like Mr. Nixon as one of the principal speakers sometime in October and would schedule the event to suit Nixon's commitments.

Apparently this conference failed to materialize—at least there was no mention of one in a mid-October Liebman memorandum otherwise concerned with the Student Committee for a Free China.[74] Making clear that his own role in the student group was confined to advising, counseling, and raising and handling the money, Liebman pinpointed a list of procedures and techniques for mobilizing student representatives on the nation's campuses. A national headquarters was being established at

521 Madison Avenue, New York City, to conduct administrative chores for ASCFC, WYCF, and YAF's New York State chapter. But the major job, he emphasized, was up to Keene, Pemberton, Solovioff, and Huston. The day this memorandum was written, the Committee also mailed more than 900 "Candidate's Kits" to aspirants for federal and gubernatorial office, using a list obtained from the Republican National Committee.[75]

As the UN debate approached, Liebman picked up "scuttlebutt" that U.S. Ambassador to the United Nations Arthur Goldberg was urging the Johnson administration to let him offer a "two-Chinas" solution to the seating question, making use of a recently released report of the United Nations Association (UNA).[76] Liebman concocted a plan for rebutting the UNA report in the press and passed it along to Walter Judd.[77] But events overtook the situation. Before Liebman had time to act, the *New York Times* published a strong editorial on November 12 not only supporting some type of "two-Chinas" solution but also ridiculing the Committee's own October 31 "declaration" advertisement as an example of how the seating question had been "confused by emotions, guesswork, and some old-fashioned thinking." The editorial buttressed its arguments with the UNA's conclusions favoring seats for both 'Chinas.' No one could be certain how the average American felt about the issue, said the *Times*, but a majority of those who had given any "serious thought" to the seating question would accept a "two Chinas" solution. Taking on the Committee by name, the *Times* invited a rejoinder, which ran over Liebman's signature on the day of the General Assembly vote.[78] But the day after the *Times* editorial, Max Frankel noted in the paper that a year of upheavals in China had "changed its reputation from that of a formidable challenger of the United States throughout Asia and of the Soviet Union inside the Communist world to that of a hobbled giant riddled by dissent and thus incapable of sustained growth and self-assertion." The debate in China, he wrote in a separate article, concerned the war in Vietnam, Sino-Soviet relations, and general problems of national defense, but "the overriding pressures and preoccupations are domestic, related above all to the problem of governing China and, if anything, divert attention and energy from foreign affairs."

The seating issue in 1966 was resolved by a much wider margin than the 1965 tie vote. With seventeen nations abstaining, an Albanian-sponsored resolution to expel the Nationalists and seat the Communists was rejected 46 (for) to 57 (against) in the 121-nation General Assembly. An Italian resolution supported by the United States and calling for a study of Chinese representation fared even worse, losing 34 to 62 with 25 abstentions. Earlier, the "important question" tactic had passed, 66 to 48 with 7 abstentions, a gain of 10 favorable votes over the 1965 vote. Clearly, in the minds of many observers, the Cultural Revolution and its excesses had frightened a number of Afro-Asian nations.

Liebman was ebullient. He cabled President Chiang Kai-shek "heartiest congratulations," attributing the victory to the Generalissimo's leadership and to exceptional diplomacy by the Chinese diplomats in America with whom he had the honor to cooperate, naming Ambassadors Chow Shu-kai, Liu Chieh, and I-Cheng Loh of the Chinese News Service.[79] Walter Judd complimented Liebman by congratulating the Committee, which, he said, meant mainly Liebman and the "Free Chinese." Liebman was flattered, replying that the real credit was due B. A. Garside, Governor Edison, and Judd himself. Together, he added, they were "quite a team!" [80]

Exeunt Ribicoff, Javits, Douglas

Some members of the team, around this time, decided not to play any longer. In response, he said, to Committee advertisements placed without notifying individual members, Senator Abraham Ribicoff (D., Conn.) submitted his resignation on November 11 before the UN vote.[81] Then, on December 14, began what came to be known as the "Javits caper." [82]

Ostensibly, the senior Republican senator from New York simply withdrew his membership from the Committee in a letter to Marvin Liebman.[83] Unfortunately for the Committee, however, the senator also "went public" with the letter, releasing it to the press, to 49 other Senate colleagues and 248 congressmen—all Committee members—and even to the White House, all of which was intended to generate national publicity, which it did, right on the heels of the Committee's victory in the United Nations.[84]

Complicating this unwanted attention, from the Committee's perspective, the *New York Times* correctly reported in the same story about the Javits resignation that Marvin Liebman also had sent a memorandum on December 14 to congressional endorsers which disclosed that the Committee's annual declaration, having served its purpose well, would be discontinued effective immediately and names of congressional endorsers removed from letterheads and other Committee publications.[85] The story left the impression that Liebman's memorandum was hastily contrived to counteract Javits' action. Liebman could not be reached for comment, the story added, "but his memorandum suggested that members of Congress had begun to have doubts about continuing to endorse the committee's policy." This remark tended to support the senator's contention, quoted in the story, that the Committee's position was inflexible and "forecloses even the hope of negotiation" with the People's Republic. The article was careful to note that Javits had begun his letter of resignation as follows: "It is most heartening to me that you have been reevaluating the position of those with responsibilities like mine who have been members of the Committee but can no longer continue."

Later, on December 28, Liebman explained in a memorandum to the steering committee that the reevaluation referred to by Javits actually had taken place before the senator's withdrawal (though the secretary would acknowledge in January that the declaration had been withdrawn largely to avoid further loss of signers because of the Javits resignation).[86] Javits, Liebman revealed on December 28, had withdrawn from the Committee on four different occasions since his first association in 1954. (Actually, Javits was among the original 210 signers of the 1953 petition to Eisenhower.) His association had been renewed after each resignation, Liebman recalled, in time for the next election, allowing him to pacify one set of constituents during a campaign and another in the off years. This was the first time Javits had resigned publicly, but then this was the senator's first venture into vice-presidential politics, Liebman added.

Liebman went on to disclose how his December 14 memorandum had been accepted by "available" members of the steering committee and placed in the mail about an hour after he received a telephone call from Javits' then administrative assistant, Richard R. Aurelio. The gist of the call, said Liebman, was that Javits was withdrawing as a congressional endorser to maintain his "flexibility" but did not want any publicity over the matter. Liebman thanked Aurelio for his courtesy, told him of the Committee's decision to discontinue use of the declaration, and said the memorandum was going in the mail "within the hour." This, Aurelio seemed to agree, would solve the withdrawal problem for Senator Javits. The next day, according to Liebman's account, they were startled to see Javits' resignation, although they subsequently learned the senator's office had taken steps to guarantee widespread publicity. Despite the incident, Liebman concluded, congressional support for the Committee's position had not been substantially weakened; on the contrary, he thought it would be strengthened in the 90th Congress, whose members, he fully expected, would be called on to support "another" Committee statement in 1967.

Whether Liebman had in hand Paul Douglas' December 22 resignation from the steering committee when he wrote the above is unknown. Douglas said he was taking on several new jobs, wanted to lighten his load, and (without mentioning Javits) wished to be excused quietly and without publicity.[87] He still was opposed to recognizing the Peking regime, still favored American policies in Vietnam. He wanted his name removed from the masthead, but he enclosed a check for $25. Despite their differences on domestic policy, he signed off, Douglas had found the Committee secretary "considerate" and "personally fair" and wished him well. Left unmentioned was any comment about the senator's defeat in November to Republican Charles H. Percy.

Paul Douglas' loss was great, Liebman soon would acknowledge, because his membership on the steering committee prevented the opposition from calling the Committee an "extremist right-wing group."[88]

A Different Approach?

Liebman fully understood the potential for fast changes in China policy. In a 1966 year-end report he quoted at length from an article in the *New York Times* by Drew Middleton which said that many UN delegates felt American public opinion was changing rapidly. To Liebman that meant 1967 probably would witness a redoubling of efforts by what he liked to call the "pro-appeasement forces." [89]

Coming off what he described as the Committee's most active year programmatically and financially, the anti-Communist organization now faced difficult decisions: 1) should the group maintain grass-roots educational activities while continuing to maximize congressional support? 2) should it forsake Congress and concentrate on the grass roots? 3) should the Committee revise its leadership structure to enlist other national groups and individuals? The secretary opted for a revised and broadened steering committee as 1967 got underway. [90]

Dr. Judd, he suggested, should be named chairman, heading a proposed steering committee of four incumbent senators, four incumbent congressmen, two governors, two professors, and former Assistant Secretary of State for Far Eastern Affairs Walter S. Robertson. Senators Dodd, Dominick, and Hickenlooper should remain, but Republican Senator Scott should be dropped in favor of Democrat Frank J. Lausche of Ohio. Congressmen Ashbrook and Morgan should remain, with Representatives Frances P. Bolton (R., Ohio) and Clement J. Zablocki (D., Wisc.) added. Additionally, Governors John Connally of Texas and Tim Babcock of Montana should join the steering committee as should Professors David Rowe and Frank Trager. Governor Edison should become treasurer, Dr. Garside assistant treasurer; Liebman should remain secretary. (Six of the eight proposed legislators were members of their respective foreign policy committees in Congress.) In this same January memorandum the secretary offered other observations and suggestions:

First, on the logistics of dealing with a large steering committee for the release of public statements, he was uncertain how to proceed, posing the old problem of the need for rapid action; perhaps an executive committee of two or three members could be given authority for approving statements in advance.

Second, now that four new groups had been organized—clergymen, businessmen, students, and liberals—Liebman felt they could perform valuable grass roots chores. Additionally, the academic community could be worked by the American Afro-Asian Education Exchange (AAEE), also run from Liebman's office. This group, whose leadership overlapped the Committee's to a large extent, enjoyed I.R.S. tax exemption as an educational and informational nonprofit organization. (Indeed, AAEE, as noted in note 95 below, was set up specifically to channel contributions otherwise unavailable to the non-tax exempt Committee.)

Third, Liebman recommended another national petition campaign for the first six months of the year. To get the drive started, there were several possibilities. One was to redraft in a more "positive" form the Committee's five-year-old declaration, withdrawn from public circulation, he admitted here, to avoid further loss of signers after the Javits resignation. A congressional majority probably would be unobtainable at first. Governors would be solicited. When a good number of governors and congressmen were signed on, the statement would be printed on the petition forms and distributed through the grass roots organizations.

In this connection, Liebman said he was giving thought to starting yet another organization in order to bring back into the fold some of the Committee's old friends (Mrs. Luce was one). Such a group would emphasize a "positive program" in support of "Free China" and its accomplishments. By its very name this new group would reaffirm American dedication to a totally free China. Perhaps former Presidents Truman and Eisenhower would serve as honorary co-chairmen. Even Dean Acheson might get involved. New leadership—something the Committee had failed to enlist—was badly needed. The "tired old-China hands"—himself, the Walter Judds, the Charles Edisons, the David Rowes, the B. A. Garsides—needed replacement by fresh faces and energies—in short, a broader-based constituency. Maybe the proposed new group, Americans for a Free China, could recruit new leadership. (Several months later Liebman would expand on this theme: The days of the Committee and the AAEE were numbered, he would write Dr. Judd; it was time to try another approach.) [91]

To discuss the above ideas, an informal meeting of the steering committee was called for January 18 in the Senate office of the only incumbent legislator to attend, Senator Dominick (others present: Judd, Rowe, Liebman, and Richard Murphy representing Senator Hugh Scott).[92] The main topic was the make-up of the new steering committee. Liebman's earlier recommendations were slightly modified. Dr. Judd consented to serve as chairman pro tem of the steering committee until someone else could be found. Three senators and one representative would be invited to join: Senators John Sherman Cooper (R., Ky.), Frank J. Lausche (D., Ohio), and John J. Sparkman (D., Ala.— one of the six original sponsors of The Committee for One Million back in 1953), and Representative Clement J. Zablocki (D., Wisc.), chairman of the Far East and Pacific subcommittee of the House Committee on Foreign Affairs, who had cooperated with the Commmittee during his 1966 hearings on U.S. policy toward Asia.

Zablocki was the only invitee among the four to join the steering committee. His acceptance letter asked for a financial statement. Because, he said, he had not always agreed totally with the Committee's positions, the congressman presumed that all public statements would be released only after consultation with the steering committee, a response which prompted Liebman to write Judd that Zablocki seemed to prefer a "softer" line than the Committee's. Maybe his presence would be inhibiting; Judd should decide whether to let him aboard.[93]

Using Marvin Liebman letterhead, the Committee's secretary wrote to Ambassador Chow Shu-kai at the Washington embassy detailing decisions taken both at the January 18 steering committee meeting and a January 20 meeting of the AAEE.[94] A copy of the letter was indicated to Gene Loh (I-Cheng Loh). Liebman reported on the steering committee changes: the decision to go ahead with a petition campaign but hold off temporarily the circulation of a new statement to members of Congress; the current activities of the students, clergymen, and businessmen groups; and his discussions about an American Committee for a Free China. Here, he said, both B. A. Garside and Leslie Severinghaus, Henry Luce's brother-in-law, were enthusiastic, and Severinghaus would talk to the Luces. Liebman enclosed drafts of the proposed new

Committee statement plus other enclosures covering current projects. He solicited the ambassador's comments.

By coincidence, a New York City resident wrote the Committee at this time of his recent $25 contribution, wondering whether the group was associated with any organization that could accept tax deductible contributions. Liebman replied that the Committee did not enjoy tax exemption but worked closely with the AAEE, which did.[95] This close association was not publicized, of course, but any tax deductible contribution to the Exchange sent to him at the above address (1790 Broadway) would be entirely put to work on the Committee's current program. (Senator Douglas now gone, moreover, the Committee shortly would move back to Liebman's own offices at 79 Madison Avenue.)

In March, Liebman exchanged letters with Representative John H. Buchanan (R., Ala.), a former pastor serving his second term in Congress, who some months later would join the Committee's steering committee. Delighted to hear of Buchanan's recent appointment to the Far East and Pacific subcommittee of the House Committee on Foreign Affairs, Liebman said that Lee Edwards thought the congressman might be interested in occasionally getting in touch with different experts in the Asian field—especially China. With strong recommendations, he passed along the names and addresses of Professors David Rowe, Karl Wittfogel, Stefan Possony, and Richard Walker, plus writer Eugene Lyons and retired Admiral Arthur Radford. Buchanan thanked Liebman for his thoughtfulness, adding that Dr. Judd was one of the greatest men Congress had ever seen.[96]

Political unrest on the Chinese mainland had dulled the Committee's opposition during the first few months of 1967, Liebman wrote Judd in early April; thus, except for supporting the Student Committee For a Free China, the Committee had been relatively inactive.[97] But there were rumors afoot this inactivity might quickly change. The Committee should be prepared. He thought the "positive" redrafted statement approved at the January steering committee meeting but temporarily withheld from congressional circulation should be quietly circulated to all members of Congress. (Instead, however, the statement project was dropped.)

Liebman remained preoccupied with the idea of a fresh organization fighting for "Free China." Nothing much had come of the idea, he wrote B. A. Garside in April, enclosing an outline of preliminary thoughts for an American Friends of a Free China and a prospectus of the proposed group. He wanted these items circulated for comment, thinking that an upcoming dinner for Republic of China Vice-President C. K. Yen might be the springboard for launching the new effort. Moreover, he felt the "liberal" attitude toward China possibly was changing somewhat in their direction. Garside responded at length, saying he admired Liebman's practical approach for trying to rebuild ties between Chinese and Americans. Still, he was skeptical because of the formidable obstacles: How could you get people for years lined up on different sides of the issue to work together? Where would you find leaders not already committed who would be willing to work hard. Realizing that 90 percent of the organizational and promotional work had to be accomplished by an executive with Liebman's qualifications—and who else could do the job?—would the new people cooperate with "Mr. Committee of One Million?" Finally, how would the group make clear its friendship toward the many millions of non-Communist mainland Chinese as well as the Chinese on Taiwan? Liebman may have felt encouraged by Garside's reply, despite the probing questions. It was then he sent Walter Judd the comment about the Committee's days being numbered.[98] Did Judd think the time was right for a new group. Could one attract leadership and support? He enclosed his outline and prospectus, adding that he hated to pile more reading on Judd but this was important. The time could be right for a different approach. Apparently the time was not right. Nor would it be until four years later, months after the dramatic reversal at the United Nations in 1971. Too late.

More Speeches

One of Lee Edwards' original proposals to Marvin Liebman, it will be recalled, was the idea for getting speeches researched, written, and placed with selected legislators. In the summer of 1967, at Liebman's request, according to Edwards, the Washington-based public relations man renewed the proposal, suggesting eight different topics and a fee schedule which took into account their 1966 speech-project experience: cooperative senators were more difficult to find than cooperative congressmen. Edwards proposed fees of $400 for writing a senator's speech, with an additional $300 added for actual delivery; and $300 for writing a representative's speech, with an additional $200 added for actual delivery. Two weeks should be allowed for the writing, another two for placing the speeches. Several weeks later Edwards was delighted to learn the speech-writing assignment would go forward.[99] He suggested four speeches, two for unnamed senators, two for unnamed representatives. One of the speeches, for a senator, would cover Red China's military threat to the Free World; another, for a congressman, would examine the objectivity of the tax-exempt National Committee on U.S.-China Relations; the third, for a congressman, would investigate the Red Guards on the Chinese mainland; and the last, for a senator, would analyze the irrationality of trading with Red China. Already, two of the speeches were underway, Edwards said, adding they would be in the *Congressional Record* by early August if everything went according to plan.

On August 3, Liebman wrote to Gene Loh (I-Cheng Loh) at the Chinese Information Office in New York, copying Ambassador Chow Shu-kai and enclosing drafts (unavailable) of what he said were the initial two speeches to come out of Lee Edwards's office.[100] The Committee's secretary wanted the speeches polished up as soon as possible for placement and delivery in the Senate and invited comments on the drafts. Located in the same box of documents in the Marvin Liebman Collection as the above letter is an unsigned, unattributed, typewritten memorandum dated August 10, 1967, entitled "Points for Discussion with Gene Loh." Seven points are listed: the first, concerning the speeches and Lee Edwards, is a reminder to get comments on the drafts, mention that Edwards had a writer in mind for another speech on the Red Guards, ask whether they should go ahead, say that Karl Hess was preparing a paper on the 1966 Fulbright hearings, and note that a balance of $700 remained for the writers of the initial two speeches. Mostly, the other discussion points covered miscellaneous items relating to travel plans, expenses, and various printing projects for the American-Asian Educational Exchange, the World Anti-Communist League, and the Student Committee for a Free China. Item number 5, headed simply "Rusher," told of September travel plans to Taipei, hotel arrangements, and noted that AAEE had paid $1,112 for air fare to "WAR." Point number 6 itemized the printing bill for an "Anti-Semitic pamphlet" (total: $3,242); most of the pamphlets were sent to the Student Committee for a Free China. Finally, item number 7 of the memorandum noted that the AAEE had sent out 7,000 copies of "Mao's China: The Decline of a Dynasty."

On August 11, Liebman sent comments to Edwards on drafts of the speeches urging him to return the final drafts and hold off any further activity on this project until two addresses had been given in the House and/or the Senate.[101]

Of the four topics suggested in July by Edwards as subject matter for speeches, one, scheduled for a senator—attacking the logic of trading with Communist China—was the subject of an address at Rider College in New Jersey by Senator Strom Thurmond (R., S.C.), "Trade Agenda with Red China." This address was not delivered on the Senate floor. Rather, it was inserted in the *Congressional Record* on December 5, 1967, by Senator Peter Dominick, who identified himself as a steering committee member of The Committee of One Million by way of introducing his colleague's "cogent and lucid analysis of the fallacies of trade with Red China." (Earlier, another steering committee member, Representative Ashbrook, commenting that in 1966 he had on several occasions contributed some remarks on the "Red China Lobby," included in the *Record* an article by William F. Buckley Jr. entitled "Red China Lobby Tried New Tack.") [102]

An attempt by Edwards to place a speech with Texas Republican Senator John Tower failed in the summer of 1968. Edwards sent Liebman a blind copy of his letter to Tower, which said the "attached" speech on U.S.-Communist China relations was first-rate and would attract press attention. In fact, The Committee of One Million (one of his clients, Edwards told Tower) thought so much of the speech it would pay for reprinting 100,000 to 200,000 copies if the senator would allow his frank to be used in the mailing. Senator Tower's reply returned the speech with the comment that he did not make major addresses on the Senate floor during election years and when platform-writing time was at hand.[103] Moreover, he had learned by experience that getting outside organizations involved in mass franking of materials, especially during a heated election year, was not a good office policy.

Another senator more willing to cooperate before the 1968 election was Ernest F. Hollings (D., S.C.). In September, Liebman sent a 24-page statement on China policy (prepared for the Committee by one of its "top China experts") to David Martin, in care of the office of Senator Dodd, asking him to see if Senator Hollings would deliver the speech on the Senate floor, adding the Committee would supply substantial *Congressional Record* reprints.[104] On September 20, observing that the General Assembly soon would convene to consider the question of UN membership for Communist China, Senator Hollings delivered an address on the Senate floor entitled "Shall We Appease Communist China?" [105] The South Carolina lawyer concluded his speech by saying he was personally proud to be associated with The Committee of One Million as a member of its "congressional steering committee."

Actually, Hollings' name was not among those recommended for steering committee membership at a February 1968 steering committee meeting held in the office of Senator Dominick. Liebman had prepared for that meeting (probably the only time that year, he wrote Judd, the boys would be able to get together) by outlining his ideas for 1968.[106] It was the Committee's task, in this election year, to counter the efforts of those individuals, organizations, and publications that would intensify efforts to change China policy. Although the strength behind American policy had been the widely based bipartisan support the Committee had helped mobilize, the present balance of the steering committee was not sufficiently representative, with three Republican senators (Dominick, Hickenlooper, Scott) and only one Democrat (Dodd, censured by the Senate in 1967, a point Liebman ignored in the memorandum); [107] two Republican congressmen (Ashbrook and Buchanan) and two Democrats (Morgan and Zablocki). Either the Committee should enlist two additional Democratic senators or reduce the steering committee membership from eight to four—a senator and congressman from each party. Liebman recommended a reduction, proposing seven new names. In addition to Senator Dominick and Representative Morgan, who should remain on the steering committee, he suggested Senators Harry F. Byrd (D., Va.), Robert C. Byrd (D., W. Va.), Spessard L. Holland (D., Fla.), or George A. Smathers (D., Fla.); and Representatives Frances P. Bolton (R., Ohio), E. Ross Adair (R., Ind.), or William S. Mailliard (R., Calif.), all of whom had endorsed the Committee's last previous declaration. These recommendations were suggested for "letterhead" purposes. He did not wish to reflect on the most valuable support and leadership of the present members over the years.

Three of the Committee's then eight incumbent legislators attended the steering committee meeting on February 6—Senators Dominick and Hickenlooper and Representative Buchanan. They were joined by Chairman Judd, Secretary Liebman, and David Martin.[108] Liebman's idea for reducing the steering committee's size was rejected. Although the Committee agreed to maintain an eight-member steering committee (of congressional participants), three resignations were handed in that day by Senators Hickenlooper and Dodd and Representative Buchanan, which left Senators Dominick and Scott plus Representatives Ashbrook, Morgan, and Zablocki. It was decided that two Democratic senators, in the following order of preference, would be invited to join: Gale W. McGee (Wyo.), Henry M. Jackson (Wash.), Edmund Muskie (Maine), Robert C. Byrd (W. Va.), Frank J. Lausche (Ohio), and Birch Bayh (Ind.). Also, Congressman E. Ross Adair (R., Ind.) would be asked to fill the Republican representative vacancy left by Buchanan's resignation, and former Senator Paul Douglas would be sounded out to see if he would serve with Dr. Judd as co-chairman. Only Republican Representative E. Ross Adair from the suggested list of recruits joined The Committee of One Million's steering committee. Until September of 1968, moreover, when Senators Hollings and E. L. Bartlett (D., Alaska), joined the group,[109] the Committee's letterhead appeared without any congressional incumbents, listing only Chairman Judd, Treasurer Edison, Assistant Treasurer Garside, and Secretary Liebman—the original stalwarts.

The Committee's longtime banner of respectability—bipartisan-ship—had been frayed by the winds of time. Still, there were several years of life left, the ironic legacy, to some immeasurable degree, of China's tumultuous Cultural Revolution.

11

Nixon's the Key

By June 1968 the Committee's congressional endorsers had dwindled to 42 Democrats and 54 Republicans in the House, including the Honorable Gerald R. Ford of Michigan.[1] By this time there was no Senate count. The congressional majorities were gone. Either their position was deteriorating, Liebman wrote to Walter S. Robertson, and/or the politicians up for reelection probably thought the issue was too "controversial" that year.[2]

Also in June Liebman wrote Judd that it was vitally important for former Vice-President Nixon whom, he knew, stood with them on China, to make a major statement on China policy.[3] He hoped this could be done before Vice-President Humphrey took the totally pro-appeasement line on Communist China which Liebman had information he would do. Liebman urged Judd to meet with Nixon. The letter gives no indication that its author had read Nixon's October 1967 article in *Foreign Affairs,* which had argued that America's post-Vietnam policy in the Far East "must come urgently to grips with the reality of China." Although Nixon had not meant "rushing off to grant recognition to Peking, to admit it to the United Nations and ply it with offers of trade," still, he had proffered the need for a "positive policy of pressure and persuasion" aimed at inducing change and persuading China that its own national interests required "turning away from foreign adventuring toward solutions of domestic problems." In such fashion Nixon skillfully had blended hints of potential conciliation with more traditional American slogans about Chinese aggressiveness and expansionism.

A blind copy of Liebman's letter to Judd was sent to Tom Charles Huston, then an army captain in Virginia, along with an accompanying letter telling Huston that their position on Red China had deteriorated rapidly. Richard Nixon was now the key. He had to come out forcefully against appeasing Peking. This would be both in the national interest and Richard Nixon's political interest. Anything Huston could do would be appreciated.

Huston replied several days later.[4] He thought it would be possible to enlist Nixon's support for a firm position against unilateral concessions to the Chinese Communists . . . *at that time,* he underlined. Nixon was especially concerned about their nuclear power potential and its impact on the rest of free Asia. Huston had heard Nixon say that China would be the most serious problem the next President would deal with. Although members of Nixon's foreign policy staff were nearly in agreement toward a hard line approach, Huston felt sure Nixon was concerned with the long-term problem, which might preclude emphasizing hard line rhetoric during the campaign. Huston felt Walter Judd should clear anything written for submission to Nixon. It would help for Judd to talk to Nixon, although the major work, Huston emphasized, came at the staff level where the key decisions about what Nixon would *see* were made. (Later, of course, Huston himself would join the White House staff as a speechwriter, where he would be remembered not for any speech but for a special report to the President recommending the Interagency Group on Domestic Intelligence and Internal Security—the "Huston Plan.") [5]

Exit Liebman

Before election day dawned, an incident marred the long-time relationship between Marvin Liebman and Walter Judd. Judging from Judd's strongly worded letter of rebuke—it would be a hard letter for him to compose and Liebman to read, he said—the secretary had mailed a Committee-related letter to eighteen newspapers over Judd's signature without obtaining Judd's authorization.[6] Worse, the language of the Liebman letter, Judd said, constituted a personal attack on U.S. Ambassador to the United Nations Arthur Goldberg. In eleven lifetime political campaigns, Judd chided, he never once attacked the opposition candidate as an individual; he always attacked positions, never persons. He opposed unsound views. But the public would determine whether those views reflected on an opponent. Liebman knew, he said, how strongly the Committee's chairman felt about use of his name. Why was the letter so important that it could not first be cleared? He had assured members of the steering committee that releases or policy statements would not be issued without their participation. Liebman had a right, Judd continued, to sign the letter himself, but apparently did not do so because he felt Judd's name would mean more. If that was the case, the major reason was that Judd was extremely careful about the use of his name. Judd said he wanted the names of the eighteen newspapers in case he decided to advise them he had not written, read, or signed the letter (nor would he have done so after reading it). Liebman had "great talents" and "extraordinary loyalty and industry," qualities which did not, however, justify unauthorized use of another man's name. Finally, Judd said there was no need for a reply. The act was done. They would continue their work.

Stunned, Liebman wrote the only handwritten letter found in the Committee's files—a brief, deeply apologetic note expressing regrets for his overenthusiasm and imprudence, pleading for forgiveness, promising no reoccurrence.[7]

Thereafter, Liebman's Committee activities apparently stalled. In October, Lee Edwards exchanged letters with Fulton Lewis III of Fulton Lewis Productions and Newscope, indicating an agreement had been reached for the Committee to solicit funds from some of their mailing lists in order to purchase prints of a film, "Red China—Barred" (a credit line would be added to the film: "Produced for the Committee of One Million by Newscope").[8] Judd wrote Liebman about the film in December, asking that a print and bill be sent to "General Wego Chiang" (actually, Chiang Wei-kuo, second son of Chiang Kai-shek), a task Liebman expedited by having Lee Edwards arrange to tell Fulton Lewis to send the film to the General via the Chinese embassy diplomatic pouch in order to save time.[9]

Several days after Richard Nixon was inaugurated President in January 1969, Marvin Liebman wrote to William F. Buckley and Walter Judd about two upcoming conferences on China. To Buckley he said it was no accident that a conference on China at the Center for the Study of Democratic Institutions in Santa Barbara that coming weekend was being held within a week of the inauguration.[10] The Hutchins conference was aimed directly at Nixon.[11] Liebman foresaw dozens of similar meetings down the road which he admitted could not be matched in prestige, publicity, or funds.

To Judd he wrote that a planned conference in March on U.S.–China relations was the opening gun of a gigantic campaign.[12] He was terribly concerned. Worse, he had failed to come up with any constructive ideas for counteracting the campaign. Many people who shared their beliefs, he added prophetically, might be too confident about Nixon's dedication to existing China policy and to the likelihood that Communist China would save them either by diplomatic blunder or an act of aggression.

Abruptly, Marvin Liebman Associates, Inc., closed its doors several weeks later. On February 4, Liebman wrote the acquisitions librarian at the University of Oregon, saying that for personal and business reasons he was thinking of changing careers and discontinuing his present firm. Would the library "still" be interested in his papers? [13]

The very next day Liebman wrote a similar letter to Dr. Stefan T. Possony at the Hoover Institution for War, Revolution, and Peace at Stanford University. He listed twenty-six groups that he had represented since he started his business in 1958. He was consulting his accountant and attorney, he said, regarding the possible tax benefits of donating his files and materials as a personal gift from his corporation. Would the Hoover Institution be interested?

The papers were shipped on March 4, 1969.[14] They arrived at Stanford University on March 22 and were opened for research later in the year—111 manuscript boxes, a cornucopia of America's post-World War II "anti-Communist impulse."

Marvin Liebman, a bachelor, moved to London in 1969, where he is reported to have established residence in an impressive Georgian-Victorian villa in the fashionable W.2 section and to have become a theatrical producer.[15]

The Committee moved to Washington.

China Report, a new Committee newsletter, made its debut in April 1969. Altogether, fourteen issues were published in the two and a half years between the first number and the late October 1971 General Assembly vote which robbed the Committee of its raison d'être. They were produced by the Committee's new secretary, Lee Edwards, at his Washington offices, which also became the Committee's headquarters address.[16] These fourteen newsletters close the pages, literally and figuratively, on the country's self-appointed "watchdog" of China policy. Seen in the context of the dramatic developments of the first Nixon administration, they reveal the public face of the Committee's fading fortunes.

The Nixon administration opened its doors early in 1969 as Marvin Liebman was closing his. On January 27, the President told his first presidential news conference: "The policy of this country and this Administration at this time will be to continue to oppose Communist China's admission to the United Nations." Several days later, however, Henry A. Kissinger, then heading the National Security Council, found a Nixon memo on his desk. "I think we should give every encouragement to the attitude that this Administration is exploring possibilities of rapprochement with the Chinese. This, of course, should be done privately and should under no circumstances get into the public print from this direction." [17]

Thus, privately, the new China game already had begun; publicly, however, the administration's first China gambit was quickly thwarted when the People's Republic abruptly canceled the scheduled resumption of ambassadorial contacts in Warsaw, which the Chinese themselves had proposed several months earlier. In suspension since January 1968, the talks would have been the 135th meeting between the two countries over a fourteen-year period. As Nixon went off to Europe in March to tell French President Charles de Gaulle, according to the Kalbs' account, that he was "determined to open a dialogue with Peking," the Chinese themselves clashed with the Russians on an uninhabited island in the middle of the Ussuri River, touching off another historic Sino-Soviet border dispute which most China watchers later would call the basic reason for China's interest in rapprochement with Washington.

China Report's premiere issue in April played the Sino-Soviet dispute as its lead story, topping Nixon's January news conference comment about continued American opposition to a UN seat for the People's Republic (in an article which failed to take note of Nixon's words "at this time"). A short historical analysis of the border problem concluded that while friction at the frontiers and competition for leadership of the Communist world would continue between the two Communist giants, this did not mean that Moscow and Peking could not work together against the Free World—witness Vietnam. The first issue of the newsletter also observed that Peking had heaped "an unprecedented barrage of vitriolic propaganda" at President Nixon since his inauguration. These attacks, it pointed out, showed that Communist China continued to isolate itself from the international community. Thus cancellation of the Warsaw talks "should have come as no surprise."

Four issues of *China Report* were published in 1969, three in 1970, and seven in 1971. Before the advent of "ping-pong diplomacy" in the spring of 1971 signaled almost a rush toward reconciliation, *China Report* concentrated on ritualistic propaganda attacks against the mainland's internal and external problems, also keeping a wary eye on each small sign of movement in American China policy. As a result, its pages reflect the Committee's increasing frustration about the gradual softening of relations between the two countries which had never formally recognized each other's existence.

In July 1969, for example, when the State Department announced relaxation of travel and tourist regulations to the Chinese mainland, Chairman Judd described the action as "illogical and ill-timed"; Peking, he added, "has done nothing to justify this unilateral act of goodwill by the United States." Similarly, freshman Democratic Senator Alan Cranston's introduction of a "sense of the Senate" resolution that U.S. diplomatic recognition did not of itself "indicate approval of the form, ideology, or policy of that foreign government" (a move interpreted in the press as paving the way for possible recognition of the People's Republic) was dismissed by *China Report* as meaningless.[18] In the September 1969 issue, Secretary of State William Rogers' remarks during an Asian tour about American willingness to get a "dialogue" going with the Chinese Communists brought this angry reaction from the Committee's newsletter: "Clearly, the United States has gone the extra mile and then some in this latest diplomatic maneuver to persuade Peking to be more responsible.' Any further initiative on our part would be counter-productive—and humiliating."

In the several months that preceded the next issue of *China Report* (January/February 1970), the United States exercised its first major initiative toward the People's Republic of China since the Korean War. Acting independently and unilaterally without demanding a quid pro quo, the State Department announced in mid-December a three-phase relaxation in trade regulations. Understandably, the American move intensified speculation about possible further relaxations in Sino-American relations at a time when Sino-Soviet talks over border problems reportedly were not going well.[19] The newsletter reacted cautiously to the American action:

> The Committee of One Million is certain that these diplomatic moves were made in good faith and believes that they should not be interpreted as an abandonment of our position against the recognition of Communist China or opposition to its admission to the United Nations.
>
> Nevertheless, the Committee is firmly convinced that the *certain* disadvantages of these initiatives far outweigh the *possible* advantages.
>
> Psychologically, such unilateral actions by us will only encourage the truculence and intransigence of Communist China. . . .

Also in this issue, and the next one (March/April) as well, was a story about a Committee challenge to CBS News which illustrates the group's ebbing status as the "watchdog" over U.S. China policy. Briefly, CBS-TV had produced and aired a news special, "Triangle of Conflict," on November 18, 1969 (before the American trade initiatives), analyzing relations between China, Russia, and the United States.

After the broadcast, Dr. Judd fired off a telegram to CBS President Frank Stanton requesting equal time for a reply under the Federal Communications Commission's "Fairness Doctrine" rule. Judd claimed the network had failed to include "a single one of the many acknowledged China experts in this country who disagree with the conclusion attributed to anonymous 'Washington officials' that 'U.S. policy towards China was clearly out of date . . . , that fundamental change was needed.' " An assistant general counsel of CBS rejected the request.

Answering, Dr. Judd spelled out the Committee's basic disagreement with the broadcast, i.e., reporter Marvin Kalb's concluding statement: "The summertime possibility of a Sino-Soviet war shocked many Washington officials into acknowledging, perhaps for the first time, that U.S. policy towards China was clearly out of date, that fundamental change was needed." At least one of those officials, Judd insisted, should be named.

China Report urged its readers to write CBS President Stanton, pointing to editorial support from the *Chicago Tribune,* the *Indianapolis News,* and the *Arizona Republic.* But the network turned down the "equal time" request once again, according to the newsletter's March/April issue, which excerpted from the FCC's judgment: "It would not appear on the basis of information presently before the Commission that CBS has failed on an overall basis to afford reasonable opportunities for the presentation of conflicting views regarding the issues discussed in its program." *China Report* said the Committee would proceed with production of its own half-hour documentary film on Communist China. Foreseeing a large audience for the "documentary that CBS banned," Lee Edwards expected the film to be ready in August.

Another indication of the Committee's depressed publicity value occurred in April when the *New York Times* published a long Sunday background piece on the "once powerful China Lobby" which failed to mention the Committee's still current hassle with CBS.[20] In the months ahead, "once powerful" would reappear in the nations's press as a descriptive for the "China Lobby." [21]

Six months elapsed before *China Report* reappeared as an October/November number. During that timespan, Sino-American diplomatic exchanges fell into limbo, the victim, many observers felt, of the U.S. "incursion" into Cambodia in the spring. (Later, it was reported that Americans and Chinese held two "very good sessions" in Warsaw in January and February, 1970, during which substantive discussions on outstanding issues may have begun.) [22]

Reproducing without comment portions of a *Wall Street Journal* article about the lack of Chinese response to the ten-month old U.S. trade initiatives, the newsletter also excerpted from an article by Professor Stefan Possony, "The Chinese Communist Cauldron" (originally published in *Orbis*, Fall 1969), which cautioned that "the United States will be tempted to pursue an opportunistic policy toward China along the line of least immediate resistance" and concluded with a reminder from Confucius: "Do not seek quick results, nor look for small gains. Seek quick results, and you will not achieve success; look for small gains, and you will not accomplish big projects."

Eight days before the General Assembly voted on the seating question in 1970, the Committee published its annual advertisement in the *New York Times*. A large photo of Mao Tse-tung accompanied the headline "Recognize him?" Those who had recognized Red China, the copy said, had come to regret it. The ad listed Dr. Judd as chairman, Lee Edwards as secretary, and Dr. William H. Roberts as treasurer of the Committee.

China Report was none too sanguine in its analysis of the UN vote: "UN Rejects Peking Again; Outlook for '71 is Questionmark" said the January/February 1971 issue. The story reported that for the first time in history a majority of nations (51 to 49, 25 abstentions) had voted in favor of the resolution admitting the Chinese Communists and expelling the Chinese Nationalists. Once again, the "important question" ploy (approved 66 to 52 with 7 abstentions) had subjected the issue to a two-thirds majority. Although the People's Republic still remained 16 votes short of the necessary two-thirds, the newsletter reported that four factors had accounted for the shift in votes from the 1969 results (56 to 48 *against* admission) to the slender majority *for* admission in 1970:

1. The recognition of Peking by Canada only four weeks before the U.N. vote.

2. The weak speech by the United States in the annual debate which was limited to a defense of the Republic of China rather than the usual listing of Peking's many offenses against the civilized world, including the United Nations.

3. The superficial appearance of greater stability and quiet on mainland China, following the horrifying excesses of the Cultural Revolution.

4. The unceasing propaganda barrage, led by the *New York Times,* that the time has come to be "realistic" and admit Red China with its 750 million oppressed subjects into the U.N.

The UN outcome in 1971, the story speculated, would depend on two things:

1. The internal and external conduct of Red China.
2. The willingness of the U.S. to continue its strong leadership in support of the U.N. and its principles, which require exclusion of the present outlaw in Peking.

Clearly, however, neither *China Report* nor any other publication could have foreseen the effect on international diplomacy of a handful of American table-tennis players. The newsletter was not published in March. And the next issue, dated April 15, undoubtedly went to press both before Premier Chou En-lai's highly publicized reception for the ping-pong team (with his remark that he had never seen North America) and the White House's April 14 follow-up announcement of further relaxations of trade restrictions against the People's Republic. Still, the April issue kicked off a "Stop Red China" campaign, Dr. Judd insisting that P.R.C. admission in 1971 was not inevitable although the situation was "serious."

In May, the *New York Times* reported that President Nixon's steps toward closer relations with the People's Republic had received calm approval on Capitol Hill and that Walter Judd, "once a spokesman for the Nationalist Government's cause, has faded from the scene." [23] *China Report* and Dr. Judd counterattacked. A cartoon on the cover of the May issue, published two days after the death of former steering committee member Thomas Dodd, depicted Mao playing ping-pong with one hand while holding a knife behind his back with the other. In a by-lined article, Dr. Judd lectured his readers in anti-Communist cliches: Power politics was "a dangerous and risky business, particularly when a free country like the U.S. is pitted against two Communist countries. . . . We must remember that the Soviet Union and Red China are both Communist, both avowedly dedicated to world communization. Their essential disagreement with each other is not whether but *how* they can communize the world." The newsletter implored its readers to write President Nixon and members of Congress urging a strong stand on the UN question and reprinted an interview with Judd in which a reporter had written that Nixon's "soft" diplomacy toward Communist China would put the President "on a collision course with many of his strongest supporters."

In the ensuing weeks, a spate of newspaper stories written from the Chinese mainland deluged readers of *Newsday, Wall Street Journal,* and the *New York Times* among other publications. The newsletter responded, in an issue dated June 28, with a front-page assault, claiming mounting congressional opposition on the seating question. While it deplored the "thaw" in Chinese-American relations, *China Report* avoided a frontal attack on the President. Instead, he was urged to take a strong stand on the "important question" vote at the UN to prevent the abandonment of the two-thirds majority vote. The Committee's publication then quoted columnist Holmes Alexander: "The politics on the matter are that the China policy has alienated many old friends of Richard Nixon and not made any new ones who will stick when the going gets rough."

The startling events of mid-July, however, showed that Nixon believed he could successfully outflank his own conservative supporters on China policy. Suddenly, amid the horrid national controversy over the struggle in Vietnam, the President triumphantly told the nation on July 15 that he would be the first American President to visit China—"the People's Republic of China" at that. Henry Kissinger, nursing a feigned "stomach upset" in Pakistan, had flown secretly to Peking to negotiate the symbolic climax to the end of America's long isolation of the mainland.

China Report, out July 28, tried to dampen the "euphoria" in the news media and the country, as Senator Peter H. Dominick put it, and published a front-page letter "To Mr. Nixon from The Committee of One Million." The President was urged to ask Premier Chou En-lai seven questions in Peking: about the release of American servicemen; the status of the mainland Chinese as an "aggressor" in the Korean War; genocide in Tibet; responsibility for the deaths of American soldiers in Vietnam through the supply of arms and ammunition to the

Vietcong; the harsh descriptions of Nixon in the Peking press; the abandonment of Mao Tse-tung's power-grows-out-of-the-barrel-of-a-gun
philosophy; and descriptions of the United States as an "imperialist
aggressor" surrounded by "running dogs." Further needling Nixon, the
newsletter quoted from candidate Nixon's 1968 campaign pronouncements and reprinted an article about the Committee which said that an
upcoming "open letter" to the President (eventually published as a full-
page advertisement in the *Washington Post*) would be an "unmistakable
warning" and "virtual ultimatum" that he should block admission of
Communist China to the United Nations "or lose the support of your
conservative followers."

Underscoring these declarations, *China Report* included in this
issue the results of a Committee-commissioned six-state telephone survey taken in mid-June by Opinion Research Corporation of Princeton,
N.J. "Highlights" of the survey, based on 1,980 telephone interviews,
said the newsletter, included the following results to the question, "Do
you favor or oppose the admission of Communist China to the United
Nations?"

	Favor	Oppose	No Opinion
Six-State Total	40%	42%	18%
California	44	37	19
Florida	38	43	19
Illinois	40	43	17
New Jersey	50	41	9
Ohio	37	41	22
Texas	30	48	22

Said Secretary Lee Edwards: "It is obvious that not only are there no
legal or moral reasons for admitting Red China to the United Nations
but there are some sound political reasons for Mr. Nixon to see to it that
Red China is not admitted. The six states surveyed are key electoral
vote states—states that Mr. Nixon *must* win if he expects to be reelected
in 1972" (italics in original).

Yet the momentum of events proved irrepressible. America's ven-
erable policy of denying UN membership to the mainland Chinese,

steadfast through five national administrations including Nixon's, finally collapsed. On August 2, Secretary of State Rogers told a news conference the United States probably would vote to seat the People's Republic of China in the world body that fall but would oppose attempts to expel the Nationalist government—in other words, the long-resisted "two-Chinas" solution to the UN dilemma.[24] Commented columnist Joseph Kraft: "The China lobby has been shown to be one of the all-time world-historical paper tigers. There is almost no resistance to the not very gentle letting-down of Chiang Kai-shek."[25] Added James Reston, writing from Peking:

> Mr. Nixon has made the bold and historic move to establish communications with China. He has not been the prisoner of his own past politics, prejudices and propaganda. . . .
> Fortunately, Mr. Nixon is dealing here in Peking with a wise and experienced professional, who understands the ambiguity of life. . . .
> In short, Chou En-lai draws a distinction between propaganda and policy. Let Washington say what it likes, he says, and Peking will disagree, even in violent terms, but after both sides sound off, let's keep to the main point and have Nixon come here for serious conversations.[26]

Seemingly undaunted, the August 24 *China Report* declared on page 1 that despite the administration's turnaround position on seating the Communist Chinese, "such action is not inevitable." In desperation, the newsletter attempted to bolster this contention by citing legal arguments drawn from UN Charter provisions. An adjacent article reproduced AFL-CIO President George Meany's quip that Nixon's trip to China represented "the No. 1 stunt of the No. 1 stunt man of our time." A dozen prominent conservatives, said the publication, had announced "suspension of support" for the Nixon administration. (Among them: *National Review* editor William F. Buckley Jr., who later would suspend his "suspension of support" long enough to join the presidential press party to the Chinese mainland.)

Finally, the Committee faced its last hurrah in its seventh and last issue of *China Report,* a September/October number. Screamed the banner headlines: "BATTLE CAN BE WON! Dr. Judd Kicks Off Last-Ditch

Battle To Keep Communist China Out of the UN.'' A smilingly reflective photograph of editor Buckley adorned page 1. Its caption an-
nounced the world premier of a 60-minute, 16mm, color documentary
film on ''life as it *is* inside Communist China.'' The film, narrated by
Buckley, was entitled ''U.S.-China Policy: Danger at the Crossroads.''
The lead article on the page sought to demonstrate how the ''two-
Chinas'' solution, historically hated by the Committee, could at the last
minute ''be used to win the battle.'' Chairman Judd argued that if the
Nationalist Chinese could be kept in the United Nations, Communist
China would stay out, for its leaders had expressed no change in their
oft-repeated unwillingness to share the Chinese seat with the Republic
of China. ''So if we can convince President Nixon he must stand firm
on a plan which will guarantee Taiwan its membership in the UN then
Peking stays out. There is no question in my mind that *if* the full weight
of U.S. political power can be committed to save Free China's rightful
place in the UN we'll have won again.''

It was a very big ''if,'' as Judd knew too well, and he offered no
reassurances. Instead, he fought the ''last ditch battle'' on legal terrain,
posing, then answering questions about the UN Charter, citing chapters,
articles, and sections to prove, for the final time to his own constituency, the case against expulsion of the Nationalists and admission of the
Communists to the United Nations.

Evidently the ''last ditch battle'' was the most lavishly funded in
the Committee's entire history. For the fiscal year ending March 31,
1971, according to its final (and unofficial) report to the N.Y. State
Department of Social Welfare, the Committee listed public contributions
of $310,860.[27] The figure was three times the largest amount ever
before reported and almost eight times as large as the $46,515 reported
for the last fiscal year of Liebman's reign as Committee secretary,
which ended March 31, 1969. (Parenthetically, the 1969 report was
signed for the Committee in November by Secretary Lee Edwards and
Assistant Treasurer B. A. Garside. Treasurer Charles Edison had died
on July 31, 1969, the sixteenth anniversary of Dr. Nicholas de Rochefort's originative testimony before Dr. Judd's Far East and Pacific subcommittee in 1953.)

Where did the huge increase in contributions come from? There are no clues. How was it spent? In part, according to information pieced together from *China Report,* on more than 1 million mailing pieces, 25,000 petitions, 1,000 candidate's Information Kits, 5,000 copies of Professor Kubek's *Introduction to the Amerasia Papers,* 3,000 copies of a Committee booklet, *Twenty Years of Tyranny,* and, presumably, on "an exciting new eyewitness documentary film on life as it *is* inside Communist China," narrated by William F. Buckley Jr.

On September 16, the *New York Times* quoted "authoritative administration officials" as saying the United States had decided in principle to work actively for the assignment of China's permanent seat in the Security Council to the People's Republic. The United States would co-sponsor a resolution calling for the "dual representation" plan; if successful, Nationalist China simply would remain one of the General Assembly's member nations. A text of the U.S. resolution would not be released until adequate co-sponsorship had been arranged. Failing this, the *Times* speculated, the United States might drop the Security Council seat provision and concentrate on retaining membership for "Taiwan."

The *Times'* story concluded with a quote from Dr. Judd on behalf of the Committee—the last such Committee mention in the newspaper before the October 25 turnaround vote: "If Communist China is admitted with the assistance of the United States, we will inescapably be strengthening that common enemy of all the world's freedom-loving peoples." (Unspoken—and unneeded—was the name of Judd's lifelong anathema.) This latest signal that the Nixon administration would negotiate for "Taiwan's" retention in the General Assembly by supporting Peking's right to China's permanent seat in the Security Council cornered the Committee. Already outflanked and compromised on the one-China issue, the eighteen-year-old "voice-of-the-people" (as Judd once remarked) was forced to back the hated two-Chinas solution, then hope that Peking would reject this ploy and refuse UN admission.

But the denouement was different.

An American resolution skirted the membership issue, insisting only on Nationalist China's "continued right of representation," but it never came to a vote. On the evening of October 25 in the great hall of the General Assembly, after a month of debate that included "rougher pressure tactics'' by the U.S. delegation on its allies ''than any of them could recall,'' the Albanians pressed for a vote on their resolution to expel the Chinese Nationalists and seat the Chinese Communists.[28] American Ambassador George C. Bush (later to become the second American envoy to Peking, then director of the CIA) won the right to have the ''important question'' vote on the Albanian resolution decided first. At 9:47 P.M., the answer flashed across the tally board: 59 to 55 against the two-thirds rule, with 15 abstentions.[29] A huge cheer erupted. The Chinese Nationalist delegates quickly left the hall. Ninety minutes later, an anticlimactic vote on the substance of the Albanian resolution settled the historic matter, 76 to 35 in favor, with 17 abstentions—not one NATO nation supporting the American position.

Commented Hugh Scott of Pennsylvania, Senate minority leader and longtime Committee stalwart, ''a good many nations we have helped generously with foreign aid over many years have shown a classic lack of appreciation.'' [30] Buried in the *Times'* massive coverage of the event was a small story with a Washington dateline. What was left of the ''China Lobby,'' the story began, said it would fight on: ''The Committee of One Million, the leading pro-Nationalist group in this country, went to court today to try to get its $75,000 movie attacking Communist China on television after all three major networks had refused to sell the organization time. Last Friday, the Federal Communications Commission ruled 4 to 1, with two members not participating, that the networks' decision did not violate the 'fairness doctrine' of the 1934 Communications Act.'' The Committee had 40,000 dues-paying members, the article said, and a $300,000 budget that year, its largest since 1953. A Committee statement said the United Nations ''must be prepared for an outcry from the American people for a reduction and even the elimination of United States support for the world organization.'' The statement had been issued by the group's chairman, former Representative Walter H. Judd.

Postscript: The Committee for a Free China

Virtually on the eve of President Nixon's departure for Peking, 73-year-old Walter Judd began anew. At a news conference in Washington on February 15, 1972, he announced formation of the Committee for a Free China (CFFC).[31] Five years had elapsed since Marvin Liebman's proposal for a revitalized China policy group—American Friends of a Free China.

Judd's other founders included remnants of the diehard pro-Nationalist forces in Congress—Senators Strom Thurmond and Barry Goldwater plus seven representatives whose names failed to make the announcement story in the *Los Angeles Times*. Later CFFC literature identified three of them: Congressmen Clement Zablocki (D., Wisc.), John Buchanan (R., Ala.), and Daniel Flood (D., Fla.), all longtime Committee supporters. Chairman of the new group was the indefatigable Dr. Judd. Lee Edwards was secretary.

In June of 1972—forever enshrined in American politics as the month of the Watergate break-in of Democratic National Committee headquarters—*China Report* reappeared with a new masthead: against a grey and brown background, a huge black mainland China and a tiny speck of white representing the island of Taiwan. The first edition ignored any comment on the historic February 27 "Shanghai Communiqué" stating Washington and Peking positions on Asian policy questions.

China Report remained under wraps for the balance of the 1972 election year. Four issues were published in 1973 and sporadically thereafter into 1976. Although the lead-off issue of 1973 reported on a meeting attended by twenty-one officers and members of a National Advisory Board, none was named. Later issues identified a handful of officers as Reverend Raymond de Jaegher, Professor Anthony Kubek, General Thomas A. Lane, Ret., Dr. Charles Moser, and Senator Carl Curtis (R., Nebr.). A budget of $100,000, up from 1972's $80,000, the newsletter said, was established. Various projects, contingent on available funds, were approved: a Capitol Hill reception/briefing in March for new representatives and senators in Congress; a fall seminar for college newspaper editors in cooperation with the Student Committee for a Free China; a revised and updated version of the hour-long documentary produced for The Committee of One Million; and continuation of the refugee assistance campaign. "The euphoria which followed the

President's trip to mainland China," said Dr. Judd, "is already being replaced by a more realistic understanding of the true nature of that communist regime."

The May/June 1973 issue of *China Report* said that fifty-one congressmen, under the leadership of Representative Trent Lott (R., Miss.), had signed their names to a May 9 Special Order on the floor of the House calling on Congress and the President to stand fast in United States support for the Republic of China. The newsletter published photographs taken at a May 22 CFFC Senate reception on Capitol Hill. Hosts for the occasion were Senators James L. Buckley of New York and Goldwater, General Albert C. Wedemeyer, Ret., and Admiral Arleigh Burke, Ret. Five senators attended: Buckley, Thurmond, Curtis, Jesse Helms (R., N.C.), and William Scott (R. Va.).

The 87-year-old Chiang Kai-shek died on Taiwan on April 5, 1975. Among members of the American funeral delegation designated to pay this country's respects to its durable Nationalist ally were Mrs. Anna Chennault, Senator Barry Goldwater and, fittingly, Dr. Walter Henry Judd.

12

An Appraisal

Studies of issue-oriented interest groups run a risk of inflating the group's measure of influence on the issue in question. I will try to avoid that tendency in evaluating the Committee's role in the evolution of post-Korean War China policy. To be sure, were it not for a handful of factors, it might be tempting to dismiss the political behavior of The Committee of One Million as merely the routine labors of a typical American pressure group—in this instance, laboring to *prevent* changes in China policy. But consider the handful:

First is the suppression of Ross Y. Koen's *The China Lobby in American Politics*—a factor unrelated to the Committee's direct behavior, as far as is known, if not to its immediate purposes; second is the Committee's formation; third, its leadership; fourth, Marvin Liebman's communications with Chinese diplomats; finally, the Committee's co-optation of Congress on China policy.

Undeniably, this present study has moved forward from inception with the fate of its predecessor in mind. An appraisal of the Committee must begin with the unsettling knowledge that the first major analysis of the "China Lobby" was printed, circulated in advance of official publication, withdrawn from circulation, ultimately revised to avoid a threatened lawsuit, then found wanting in other particulars and left legally unpublished for fourteen years—from 1960 to 1974. There is, of course, no evidence the Committee itself exercised direct influence over Macmillan's decision to withdraw the book from circulation (although Marvin Liebman, by his own account to Priscilla Buckley, met early on with a Macmillan senior editor to learn what he could about the matter). The most that fairly can be said about the Committee's contribution to this incident is that its zealous promotion of hate-China themes helped perpetuate an hysteria which made possible the intimidation of a major American publisher. However insufficient a conclusion for evaluating the Committee's potency, still, a book about *The China Lobby in American Politics* went unpublished while *The Red China Lobby,* conceived by Liebman as the Committee's counterattack book, was published in 1963.

Formation of The Committee for One Million remains cloaked in governmental secrecy—actually, double-cloaked: the CIA refuses to reveal whether the late Nicholas de Rochefort, who concocted the scheme and originally contacted the White House, was an Agency employee at any time before, during, or after the Committee's formation; and the former House Committee on Foreign Affairs (now, International Relations) refuses to release Dr. de Rochefort's executive session testimony of July 31, 1953, before Dr. Judd's Far East and Pacific subcommittee. Hence questions remain about the very emergence of the Committee. Was de Rochefort, then a French citizen living in the United States, acting on his own initiative in soliciting White House support for an anti-Chinese Communist American organization in the immediate aftermath of the Korean War armistice? Or was this "expert on psychological warfare" (in the words of his obituary in the *New York Times*) acting in association with current or former employees of the CIA? (Dr. Judd's November 9, 1953, letter to Charles Edison crediting his own subcommittee with developing the original idea for the Committee failed to mention de Rochefort and his testimony.) As farfetched as this line of inquiry may once have appeared about an organization which attracted the allegiance of so many distinguished citizens, revelations about the covert domestic activities of the CIA have legitimized these questions. No longer is it farfetched to hypothesize that the Committee may have been conceived as a small, covert, domestic propaganda operation designed to stiffen American resistance to any conciliatory diplomatic moves toward the Peoples Republic of China. Nor is it farfetched to hypothesize further that only a few of the organization's key leaders—perhaps fewer than few—may have been privy to the group's clandestine origins. That Dr. de Rochefort's association with the Committee was very brief is apparent from the minutes of the December 30, 1953, steering committee meeting which acknowledged his severance from the group and thanked him for his "splendid work." Lacking more information about de Rochefort's governmental associations at this time, or about his congressional testimony, the Committee's formation must remain an open, albeit obscure, question in the chronicle of America's post-Korean War China policy. Congress, of course, could help by making public de Rochefort's testimony before Dr. Judd's subcommittee. Congressman Morgan, a member of the steering committee of The Committee of One Million from 1965 at least through 1969, remains chairman of the House committee with jurisdiction over the testimony.

Empirical questions aside for the moment, the origins of the Committee raise several important questions about political values in a democratic society: Should members of Congress be permitted to use executive committee sessions to organize and provide leadership for political interest groups? Should committees of Congress be permitted to listen in secrecy, then withhold from public scrutiny, testimony and resulting decisions affecting the creation of such groups? Should members of Congress assigned to foreign policy committees be permitted to take active roles in the leadership of foreign policy interest groups? With these questions in mind, let us move on to the third factor distinguishing the Committee's political behavior—its operational leadership.

Seemingly awkward as a decision-making structure, the steering committee actually was well suited to the group's major purposes. Although it functioned without a formal chairman until late in the day, which may have impeded policy decisions to some extent, relatively few occasions arose in the Committee's eighteen-year history requiring a steering committee meeting. In part, this condition resulted from the organization's necessarily defensive posture: its publicly unstated goals, after all, were to "strengthen Eisenhower's hand" or "keep Congress firm"—i.e., to maintain the government's rigidity on all China policy questions. Defending the status quo, as an operational exercise, meant grinding out quantities of anti-Peking propaganda while attacking signs of potential change in attitudes or policies. Day-to-day decisions on the wording of various publicity releases or other materials were, for the most part, handled by Secretary Liebman, sometimes in consultation with the full steering committee or individual members, sometimes not. Because the Committee functioned like a political tale of two cities— from New York, the letterhead address at Liebman's offices near Manhattan's mass communications centers and the United Nations, and from Washington D.C. (Capitol Hill to be more exact)—most matters were handled by correspondence or telephone. The twin-city arrangement had advantages: New York gave the group a dateline for propaganda *away* from Capitol Hill, deemphasizing Committee leadership roles played in Washington by key lawmakers; Capitol Hill, on the other hand, gave the group its legitimacy and clout, including the perquisites of office available to the steering committee's incumbent senators and congressmen.

One consequence of this arrangment was Liebman's substantial independence of action, enhanced in 1958, several months after his return from the Far East, with the advent of Marvin Liebman Associates, Inc. Chastised on several occasions for outbursts of unrestrained militancy and forced to explain his behavior to Senator Douglas from time to time, Liebman nonetheless acted with genuine authority on behalf of the Committee. He initiated and executed the vast majority of Committee projects. His wide range of national and international contacts among anti-Communist activists in and out of government added both to his stature as a specialist in the harsh rhetoric of anti-communism and to his client list. Liebman collected anti-Communists for use on the Committee's and other letterheads. Since they were repeatedly used for fundraising purposes, the myriad lists comprised an important resource without which the Committee would have been financially handicapped. Thus Liebman's leadership role was twofold: as secretary he initiated and disseminated the group's propaganda; as fund raiser he solicited the funds that not only paid for the propaganda—but also for the fund-raising and public relations services of Marvin Liebman Associates, Inc. To raise this point is not to doubt his zealous anti-communism nor his belief in the righteousness of the Committee's cause. On the contrary, the one-time Communist Party member clearly was committed to his political conversion. Rather it is simply to suggest, in the vernacular of the present day, that he had "a good thing goin'."

The leadership arrangement also underplayed the role of Dr. Judd, with whom Liebman enjoyed a close working relationship (at least until the fall of 1968 when he signed Judd's name to a publicity release without the latter's permission). Judd's jehad against Chinese Communism was total. From the Committee's opaque inception until its last-ditch stand, it remained his personal "crusade." Yet the former medical missionary played a subtle, regnant role until forced to take official command as chairman in the group's declining years. The one steering committee member who never missed a meeting, according to available minutes, Judd resisted too much public spotlight, especially in the earlier years, preferring to work behind the scenes on China policy on the strength of his strategic committee position in Congress and his personal relationship with President Eisenhower. This, of course, followed his seminal role in the formation and organization of The Committee for One Million. Irrespective for the moment whether de Rochefort's idea had other forebears, Judd heard it in executive session of his subcommittee (if not before), liked it, recruited key activists, arranged the petition-bearing ceremony at the White House, toured the Far East as leader of a six-week, congressional study mission, and returned to report to the newly formed steering committee (before submitting his official report to Congress) that the Committee's work was greatly important and should be carried on for the moral support it provided America's friends in the Far East. Judd's initiatives, moreover, take on added significance in the light of Eisenhower's apparent desire to retain some flexibility for future relations with the Chinese mainland.

Inclined toward sententious rhetoric and known as a tough Republican partisan (Paul Douglas said he hated Democrats), Judd understood what kept the Committee's congressional coalition credible. Thus his contacts with Liebman increased when questions critical to the Committee's survival were at stake: fund-raising ventures and, most importantly, the composition of the steering committee. Here, Judd and Liebman shared an intense protectiveness toward their "bipartisan" letterhead, sensing when to compromise in order to retain it. Usually, the issue centered around Senator Paul Douglas.

Indeed, bipartisanship during the Eisenhower and Kennedy phases of The Committee of One Million meant, for all practical purposes, the name of the Illinois Democrat. No other Democrat on the steering committee approached his prestige within the Democratic Party. No other name counted as much when the Committee sought to attract liberal support. And no other Committee leader raised as many sticky questions about funds, financing, and the group's tirelessly repeated polemics. The retention of Paul Douglas on the steering committee until the end of his Senate career made plausible the Committee's oft-repeated claim to bipartisanship. His last major Committee role was his part in the seven-month campaign in 1966 to take advantage of what Liebman perceived as a split in liberal ranks over the Vietnam War and China policy (i.e., a majority opposing both, with a strong minority perhaps willing to take a public position against Peking's recognition or UN membership). Shortly after 114 "liberals and intellectuals" publicly endorsed these positions, Douglas lost his Senate seat and resigned from the steering committee.

If Douglas was irreplaceable for the purpose of justifying the group's claim as a bipartisan-led organization, his resignation marked the end of effective bipartisanship. No Democrat of his stature replaced him. Within six weeks the Committee had lost Ribicoff and Javits (never activists but nonetheless important as publicizable members) then Douglas. Thereafter, its recruitment problems magnified. After a brief attempt to retain some sense of bipartisanship, Dr. Judd officially surfaced as chairman, spelling a final phase of leadership dominated by conservative bitter-enders and, early in 1969, a new secretary.

Never in the Committee's history, of course, had there been a public outcry for a radical reversal in U.S. China policy. Through the balance of the Johnson administration, growing American involvement in the Vietnamese War diminished the likelihood of any substantial change in Sino-American relations. Indeed, the containment of Chinese Communism frequently was proffered as the basic rationale for America's military role in Indochina. Talk of rapprochement reached its nadir. Still, Liebman's organization raised over $66,000 in 1966 and approximately $110,000 in 1967. Then, in 1968, Liebman's last full year as secretary, the Committee's donations fell to an all-time low—not quite $23,000.

The Committee's unique leadership, finally, sprang from the group's ingenious name, which never did conform to organizational reality. Among the million or more people who signed the first petition, perhaps 20,000 to 40,000 remained intermittent financial contributors and thus were designated "members" of the Committee. Another several hundred sympathizers of some prominence signed consent cards allowing their names to be used in fund-raising solicitations and as "members" on myriad letterheads. Next were the numerous congressmen and senators who either allowed themselves to be listed as "members" or endorsed the group's annual statements on China policy positions. Then, of course, there was the steering committee, which met infrequently, and rarely in full attendance: Honorary Chairman Warren Austin, who never attended a meeting; former Ambassador Joseph C. Grew, who attended few; a score of incumbent legislators over the years but never more than eight at one time; plus Charles Edison, Frederick C. McKee, B. A. Garside, and Marvin Liebman. Practically speaking, then, leadership consisted of Judd, Liebman, Edison (from time to time) with assistance from McKee and Garside, the other enduring pro-Nationalist diehards. In sum, the Committee's leadership consisted mainly of Walter Judd's "crusade" and Marvin Liebman's business.

The fourth distinguishing factor in appraising the Committee's role in post-Korean War China policy concerns evidence of Marvin Liebman's harmonious associations with Republic of China diplomats in the United States. That there was considerable contact is undeniable. Moreover, that Liebman exchanged ideas and advice on matters involving Committee policies, projects, and propaganda techniques is equally undeniable from Liebman's own files. Liebman sent Chinese diplomats copies of steering committee reports and various other memoranda. He consulted both in person and by correspondence on a variety of subjects. The 1963 anti-trade Committee campaign got underway immediately after Ambassador Tingfu F. Tsiang told Liebman in Washington that he was concerned about reports of new agitation for trade relations with the Chinese Communists. In 1967 Liebman sent Ambassador Chow Shu-kai a detailed letter spelling out the work of the reorganized Committee (Dr. Judd having taken over the chairmanship) and the American Afro-Asian

Educational Exchange, both groups regarded as coterminous. Similarly, there are scattered references to Liebman's cooperative ventures with I-Cheng Loh of the Chinese Information Service.

Although there is no evidence that Republic of China funds found their way *directly* into the Committee's coffers, there is evidence in the Committee's files that minor amenities (travel arrangements, air fare, dinners) and perhaps even purchases of Committee film prints may have been paid for by Chinese sources. If so, the money was paid to Committee suppliers (not directly to the Committee), including Communications Distribution, Inc., in which Liebman and William F. Buckley Jr. shared an interest.

Not much else can be said with assurance about Marvin Liebman's association with Chinese diplomats. Regardless, the Committee's secretary often expressed himself publicly (and even privately) as if those Americans working to change U.S. China policies were engaged in clandestine and conspiratorial lobbying—perhaps even at the behest of Peking—while guardians of the status quo like themselves were simply loyal supporters of U.S. government policy. There is evidence enough in his own files to conclude that Liebman's position on this matter was, at the very least, duplicitous.

Chapter 2 of this study ended with Ross Koen's judgment that the Truman administration's loss of initiative on China policy, especially after war broke out in Korea, strengthened "China Lobby" sentiment in the country, facilitating congressional dictation of policies toward China. Conception of the The Committee for One Million in Judd's sub-committee (even if only part of the conceptual process) does no harm to Koen's thesis. Indeed, the Committee's governmental birthplace may be seen as but the beginning of its co-optation of Congress on China policy.

Over the long political life of the Committee, moreover, many congressional resources were employed to further the organization's objectives. Basically, this condition was facilitated by Liebman's ability to design promotional schemes that utilized the overlapping roles of legislative "members" and by the steering committee's approval of them. Although available evidence shows the steering committee met infrequently (rarely in full attendance), it invariably met on Capitol Hill in the offices of one "member" or another. Sometimes, aides of missing senators attended and acted on behalf of their bosses. The first screening of the Committee's "Red China—Outlaw!" was held in the auditorium of the New Senate Office Building in August 1961. Committee speeches, advertisements, statements, and broadsides frequently appeared in the *Congressional Record*. Individually, these amenities (most, of course, the legitimate perquisites of office enjoyed by all legislators) do not appear significant. Taken as a whole, however, and added to the knowledge that the steering committee's incumbent congressional majority represented the group's major claim to "official" authority, the Committee's co-optation of Congress on China policy becomes more credible.

In essence, Dr. Judd and his 1953 followers formalized the so-called "China bloc" in Congress. Whether by accident or design, they created a lobbying group one of whose major purposes was the lobbying of their own colleagues on China policy. The *firming* of Congress, moreover, did not require enormous financial resources because the Committee's key resource—its incumbent steering committee members—remained available to perform the necessary chores. The Committee maintained congressional approval by framing statements in narrowly doctrinaire and emotional rhetoric which many campaign-conscious congressmen felt could be ignored only at their own electoral peril. Additionally, the Committee's existence became the fundamental congressional reality on the China issue with which Presidents Eisenhower, Kennedy, and Johnson had to deal. Annual expressions of support for carefully phrased anti-Peking positions did not help increase presidential options. To be sure, the Committee was born, raised, and reorganized in an era of intense national bitterness toward the mainland Chinese. Frozen assumptions and postures were not confined to Congress. On all matters touching the nation's anti-Communist impulse, strident appeals fared better than reasoned debates.

Still, the longevity of the Committee may be seen as an instance of congressional initiative on post-Korean War China policy. Paradoxically, in recent years—especially through the Vietnamese light-years—

Congress has been criticized for failing to venture into territories of presidential power. In the case of China policy, however, missionary certainty doggedly prevailed. "Perpetual missionaries, these Americans."

As to the normative questions posed earlier: Should members of Congress be permitted to use executive sessions to organize and provide leadership for political interest groups; to listen in secrecy, then withhold from public scrutiny testimony and decisions affecting the creation of such groups; and, in the case of lawmakers assigned to foreign policy committees, take active roles in the leadership of such groups?

Secrecy, which inspired pro-Nationalist sympathizers to rhetorical tantrums over suppression of the Yalta Agreements, the Wedemeyer Report, and documents deleted from the 1949 White Paper, helped conceive The Committee for One Million.

Suppressing information—whether international agreements (Yalta), fact-finding reports (Wedemeyer), books (*The China Lobby in American Politics*), presidential justifications for congressional resolutions (Tonkin Gulf), inter-party spying (Watergate), or the organization of pressure groups (The Committee for One Million)—is rarely a necessary condition, and never a sufficient one, for the defense of liberty. Government officials who distort the difference between politically embarrassing information and genuine national security secrets also distort and diminish the democratic process.

The Marvin Liebman Collection (abbreviated MLC in the Notes) at the Hoover Institution on War, Revolution, and Peace at Stanford University consists of 111 manuscript boxes, 30 of which comprise Liebman's files on The Committee of One Million. These 30 boxes contain well over 100 separate files plus assorted loose materials (pamphlets, scripts, brochures, publicity releases, etc.) covering his tenure as secretary of the organization from its inception to early in 1969.

Liebman's files arrived at Stanford in March 1969 and were opened for research later that year. I first examined them in August 1972, again in April 1974. The other 81 manuscript boxes in this collection contain the files of numerous political organizations and campaigns Liebman either helped organize and/or provided services. Most of these groups are listed on p. 61 in the text.

A word about the abbreviations used in citing the *Congressional Record:* the matter is a simple one of which Congress and session. Thus 81C2 stands for 81st Congress, second session, followed by year, volume, part, and page number.

1. Origins of the "China Lobby"

1   The original publication often is cited because a number of review and library copies, though recalled by the publisher, remained in circulation as collector's items: Ross Y. Koen, *The China Lobby in American Politics* (New York: Macmillan, 1960). Here, the recent paperback will be cited unless the original book is indicated: Ross Y. Koen, *The China Lobby in American Politics* (New York: Harper & Row, 1974). The original manuscript was based on Koen's 1957 doctoral dissertation at the University of Florida: "The China Lobby and Formulation of American Far Eastern Policy: 1945–1952."

2   The memorandum was inserted in the *Congressional Record* on April 13, 1950, by California Republican Senator William F. Knowland. See *Congressional Record,* 81C2 (1950), 96(4):5157.

3   Professor Lattimore's opening statement at the hearing was given on April 6, 1950. Defending himself against Senator McCarthy's charges and deploring the senator's publicity techniques, he said it was possible that those who opposed aid to the Nationalist government were not necessarily pro-Communist nor disloyal to the United States and that those who were engaging in "violent propaganda for all-out aid [to the

Nationalists] do not have a monopoly of opposition to communism.'' He and the senator obviously differed on these points, Lattimore said, adding: "Judging from his unquestioning acceptance and extensive use of propaganda of the so-called China Lobby, he is at least its willing tool.'' See U.S. Senate, Committee on Foreign Relations, Subcommittee Pursuant to S. Res. 231, *Hearings on the State Department Employee Loyalty Investigation,* 81C2 (1950), pt. 1, p. 419.

4 *Congressional Record,* 81C2 (1950), 96(4):5157.

5 *Congressional Record,* 81C2 (1950), 96(5):6773.

6 See "The China Lobby: A Case Study,'' *Congressional Quarterly Weekly Report* (Special Supplement) 9, No. 25-A (June 29, 1951):939–58; Charles Wertenbaker, "The China Lobby,'' *The Reporter,* April 15, 1952, pp. 2–24; and Philip Horton, "The China Lobby—Part II,'' *The Reporter,* April 29, 1952, pp. 5–24.

7 See U.S. Senate, Committee on Armed Services and Committee on Foreign Relations, *Hearings on the Military Situation in the Far East,* 82C1 (1951), pts. 1–5.

8 This sentence appears on page 31 of the original Macmillan version of *The China Lobby in American Politics* but is excluded in the 1974 Harper & Row paperback.

9 Among the many special studies in the historiography of Sino-American relations (not otherwise cited here), cf.: Kenneth S. Latourette, *The History of Early Relations between the United States and China 1784–1844* (New Haven: Yale University Press, 1917); Paul A. Cohen, *China and Christianity: The Missionary Movement and the Growth of Chinese Antiforeignism 1860–1870* (Cambridge: Harvard University Press, 1963); Paul A. Varg, *The Making of a Myth: The United States and China 1897–1912* (East Lansing: Michigan State University Press, 1968); Thomas J. McCormick, *China Market: America's Quest for Informal Empire 1893–1901* (Chicago: Quadrangle Books, 1967); John W. Masland, "Missionary Influence Upon American Far Eastern Policy,'' in *The Pacific Historical Review* 10, No. 3 (September 1941): 279–96; John Carter Vincent, *The Extraterritorial System in China: Final Phase* (Cambridge: Harvard University Press Monograph 30 published by East Asian Research Center, 1970); and, for an overall perspective, Warren I. Cohen, *America's Response to China* (New York: Wiley 1971).

10 Marilyn B. Young, *The Rhetoric of Empire: American China Policy, 1895–1901* (Cambridge: Harvard University Press, 1968), p. 12.

11 Charles S. Campbell Jr., *Special Business Interests and the Open Door Policy* (New Haven: Yale University Press, 1951), p. 31. All references to this organization are from this study.

12 *Ibid.,* pp. 21–22. For a study of ACDC, see William R. Braisted, "The United States and the American China Development Company,'' *The Far Eastern Quarterly* 9, No. 2 (February 1952): 147–65.

13 George F. Kennan, *American Diplomacy 1900–1950* (New York: Mentor Books, 1962), originally published by the University of Chicago Press in 1952. Wrote U.S. Navy Captain Alfred T. Mahan in 1900: "It is permissible, nay, incumbent . . . to insist, in the general interest, by force if need be, that China remain open to action by

European and American processes of life and thought. She may not—cannot—be forced to drink, but she must at least allow the water to be brought to her people's doors." See Alfred T. Mahan, *The Problem of Asia* (Boston: Little, Brown, 1900), p. 174.

14 See B. A. Garside, *One Increasing Purpose: The Life of Henry Winters Luce* (New York: Revell, 1948). According to *Who's Who in America 1954–55*, vol. 28., Dr. Garside's honorific results from an L.H.D. degree awarded by the College of the Ozarks in 1935.

15 See C. F. Remer, *Foreign Investments in China* (New York: Macmillan, 1933), ch. 15, esp. pp. 250–60.

16 A. Whitney Griswold, *The Far Eastern Policy of the United States* (New Haven: Yale University Press, 1938, 1966), p. 61. Griswold estimates between 1,000 and 1,500 missionaries in China in 1899.

17 Robert McClellan, *The Heathen Chinee: A Study of American Attitudes Toward China, 1890–1905* (Columbus: Ohio State University Press, 1971), p. 65.

18 John B. Gardner, *The Image of the Chinese in the United States, 1885–1915* (Ann Arbor, Mich.: University Microfilms, Inc.), Ph.D. dissertation, University of Pennsylvania, 1961, p. 186. Paradoxically, a decrease in anti-Chinese sentiment and increase in sympathetic feelings is attributed to the effectiveness of the exclusion laws.

19 McClellan, *Heathen Chinee*, p. 17.

20 Joseph Keeley, *The China Lobby Man* (New Rochelle, N.Y.: Arlington House, 1969). Also, see John N. Thomas, *The Institute of Pacific Relations: Asian Scholars and American Politics* (Seattle: University of Washington Press, 1974), pp. 36–64; and Horton, "The China Lobby—Part II," pp. 19–22.

21 See Floyd Russel Goodno, "Walter H. Judd: Spokesman For China in the United States House of Representatives," Ed.D. dissertation, Oklahoma State University, 1970, pp. 3–4. Also, see *Congressional Directory,* 87C1 (Washington D.C.: G.P.O., 1961), p. 77; and *Congressional Quarterly Fact Sheet,* July 15, 1960.

22 *Congressional Record,* 78C1 (1943), 89(1):1342. The date was February 25, 1943.

23 Stanley K. Hornbeck, *Contemporary Politics in the Far East* (New York: Appleton, 1916), p. 4. For a brief summary of Dr. Hornbeck's State Department career, see *Register of the Department of State* (Washington D.C.: 1939), p. 121. Also, see Richard Dean Burns, "Stanley K. Hornbeck: The Diplomacy of the Open Door," in Richard Dean Burns and Edward M. Bennett, eds., *Diplomats in Crisis* (Santa Barbara, Calif.: ABC-CLIO, 1974), pp. 91–117.

24 The "non-recognition doctrine" is briefly reviewed in *The China White Paper August 1949* (Stanford: Stanford University Press, 1967), pp. 13–15. The White Paper originally was issued as *United States Relations With China: With Special Reference to the Period 1944–1949* (Washington D.C.: G.P.O., 1949).

25 Henry L. Stimson and McGeorge Bundy, *On Active Service In Peace and War* (New York: Harper, 1947), p. 243.

26 See Russell D. Buhite, *Patrick J. Hurley and American Foreign Policy* (Ithaca, N.Y.: Cornell University Press, 1973), pp. 47–61; and Don Lohbeck, *Patrick J. Hurley* (Chicago: Henry Regnery, 1956), pp. 102–18.

27 Dorothy Borg, *The United States and the Far Eastern Crisis of 1933–1938* (Cambridge: Harvard University Press, 1964), p. 569, n.101.

28 A. T. Steele, *The American People and China* (New York: McGraw-Hill, published for the Council on Foreign Relations, 1966), pp. 21–22. As late as September 1940, writes Steele, only 28 percent of Americans were willing to risk war with Japan to prevent the Japanese from controlling China.

29 James C. Thomson Jr., *While China Faced West: American Reformers in Nationalist China, 1928–1937* (Cambridge: Harvard University Press, 1969). "To an increasing number of articulate mission leaders," Thomson writes on p. 41, "as they tried to gain perspective on their revolutionary surroundings, communism began to appear less simply as a threat and more fundamentally as a challenge: a challenge to put Christ's teachings to work in China among the poor, the sick, and the oppressed; a challenge to transform the social order or risk final expulsion by the tide of a stronger faith that promised to do much of what Christians had left undone."

30 For more on the American Committee for Non-Participation in Japanese Aggression, see John W. Masland, "Missionary Influence," *Pacific Historical Review*.

31 See "The China Lobby: A Case Study," *Congressional Quarterly Weekly Report,* pp. 954, 956; and *Who's Who in America 1954–55,* vol. 28.

32 W. A. Swanberg, *Luce and His Empire* (New York: Scribner's, 1972), pp. 183–84, 214.

33 *Life,* June 30, 1941, pp. 82–96. Luce's grand plan for "Christianizing and Americanizing China" is found in Swanberg, *Luce,* p. 189, and *passim.*

34 Thomson, *While China Faced West,* p. 9.

35 Swanberg, *Luce,* p. 214 (italics in original). The Luce holdings in pretelevision 1944 are listed on this page by Swanberg:

Medium	*Circulation*
Time	1.16 million U.S. weekly (special editions for classroom, Canada; Pony editions for military; Air Express editions for Mexico, South America; V-Mail editions for U.S. Navy; special editions for other foreign countries printed in Sweden, Australia, Persia (Iran), Egypt and India)
Life	4 million U.S. weekly, 317,000 abroad
Fortune	170,000 monthly
Architectural Forum	40,000 monthly
Radio March of Time	Heard weekly by estimated 18 million in U.S.
Time Views the News	Heard daily on radio (figures unavailable)
Movie March of Time	New edition every four weeks in 10,000 U.S. and foreign theatres

36 Cf., for example, Edgar Snow, *Red Star Over China* (New York: Random House, 1938); Agnes Smedley, *Battle Hymn of China* (New York: Knopf, 1943); Guenther Stein, *The Challenge of Red China* (New York: McGraw-Hill, 1945); Harrison Forman, *Report from Red China* (New York: Holt, 1945); Theodore White and Annalee Jacoby, *Thunder Out of China* (New York: William Sloane Associates, 1946); Israel Epstein, *Unfinished Revolution in China* (Boston: Little, Brown, 1947); and Lawrence K. Rosinger, *China's Crisis* (New York: Knopf, 1945). Most of these books, it will be noted, were published during World War II. The best informed American magazine on the Chinese Communist movement, according to Kenneth E. Shewmaker, *Americans and Chinese Communists,1927–1945: A Persuading Encounter* (Ithaca: Cornell University Press, 1971), p. 284, was *Amerasia*, published from March 1937 to July 1947, with a circulation of under 2,000. Professor Shewmaker's excellent analysis of "The Conspiracy Thesis" hypothesis (pp. 269–96) includes numerous references to prewar writings about the Communist movement in China, many of them from the pages of *Amerasia*, whose purpose, says Shewmaker (p. 285), "was to promote the development of an informed public opinion regarding United States relations with the Pacific countries. Ostensibly, its editors eschewed a dogmatic editorial line and did not intend the journal to be a 'propaganda organ' for any particular doctrine, policy, institution, or nation. Yet . . . *Amerasia* championed the cause of Chinese communism. It also provided its readers with much factual material on the Far East."

Critical views of Chiang Kai-shek and the Kuomintang also were published in at least one popular national magazine of the period, the *Saturday Evening Post:* cf., for example, Edgar Snow, "Sixty Million Lost Allies," June 10, 1944, pp. 12–13; Darrell Berrigan, "Uncle Joe Pays Off," June 17, 1944, pp. 20–21; and, after General Stilwell was recalled from China in October 1944, Mark Gayn and Edgar Snow, "Must China Go Red?" May 12, 1945, pp. 9–10.

37 Charles F. Romanus and Riley Sunderland, *Stilwell's Mission to China* (Washington D.C.: Department of the Army, Office of the Chief of Military History, 1953), p. 23.

38 *Foreign Relations of the United States: Diplomatic Papers, 1942, China* (Washington D.C.: G.P.O., 1956), p. 14; telegram dated February 10, 1942.

39 *Ibid.*, p. 19 for Hamilton memorandum dated February 16, 1942; p. 20 for Hornbeck memorandum dated February 16, 1942.

40 Tang Tsou, *America's Failure in China 1941–50* (Chicago: University of Chicago Press, 1963), p. 92.

41 A vivid account of his experiences in China set against a background of that country's relations with the major powers is found in John Paton Davies Jr., *Dragon by the Tail* (New York: Norton, 1972).

42 A biographical sketch of Dr. Rowe is found in U.S. House of Representatives, Committee on Foreign Affairs, Subcommittee on the Far East and the Pacific, Report: *United States Policy Toward Asia*, 89C2 (1966), House Doc. No. 488, pp. 227–30.

43 Accounts of the "ABMAC Affair" are offered in Keeley, *China Lobby Man*, pp. 54–71; Thomas, *Institute of Pacific Relations*, pp. 38–39; and Koen, *China Lobby*,

pp. 134–35. For Alfred Kohlberg's own account, see U.S. Senate, Committee on the Judiciary, Subcommittee on Internal Security, *Institute of Pacific Relations: Hearings,* 82C2 (1952), pt. 14, pp. 4936–37. The "Kohlberg Affidavit" so-called, given on April 16, 1952, is exhibit no. 1321-C, pp. 4934–44.

44   Biographical material on Edison is found in his obituary in the *New York Times,* August 1, 1969, p. 33, which reports that his poems were published years later as "Flotsom and Jetsom" with 1,000 copies sent to friends.

45   "Kohlberg Affidavit," p. 4937.

46   Keeley, *China Lobby Man,* devotes a chapter to "The Amazing Dr. William," pp. 72–78, reported to have been a charter member of the Socialist Party in 1900. The book, privately printed in 1921 and titled *The Social Interpretation of History: A Refutation of the Marxian Economic Interpretation of History* was said to have been read by Dr. Sun Yat-sen, who found William's concept of socialism agreeable to his own innate tendencies.

47   Part of this letter is reproduced in the "Kohlberg Affidavit," p. 4937. Kohlberg's "study," according to Thomas, *Institute of Pacific Relations,* p. 41, was "a rambling, confusing, eighty-eight page document consisting largely of quotations from *Far Eastern Survey, Pacific Affairs,* and various Communist publications." But Kohlberg publicized his charges well, sending copies to IPR members and trustees, and mailing thousands of letters to journalists, government officials, and influential citizens.

48   A recent study of the Stilwell period claims the War Department wanted to prevent the general's recall from becoming an election issue on which Republicans might have attacked Democrats; the use of Chinese Communist troops was, of course, one point of dispute in the events leading to the recall. See Chin-tung Liang, *General Stilwell in China, 1942–1944: The Full Story* (New York: St. John's University Press, 1972), p. 274. Varying accounts of Stilwell's recall are found in *The Stilwell Papers,* arranged and edited by Theodore H. White (New York: William Sloane Associates, 1948), pp. 345–54; Herbert Feis, *The China Tangle* (Princeton: Princeton University Press, 1953), pp. 185–201; Barbara W. Tuchman, *Stilwell and the American Experience in China, 1911–45* (New York: Macmillan, 1970), pp. 483–509; Davies, *Dragon by the Tail,* pp. 333–41; Anthony Kubek, *How The Far East Was Lost* (Chicago: Regnery, 1963), pp. 218–20; and Tang Tsou, *America's Failure in China,* pp. 90–124.

49   John King Fairbank, *The United States and China,* 3d ed. (Cambridge: Harvard University Press, 1971), pp. 306–10.

50   Tang Tsou, *America's Failure in China,* pp. 98, 108, 109, 116. Also, see Romanus and Sunderland, *Stilwell's Mission to China,* p. 275.

51   Feis, *China Tangle,* p. 170.

52   Hurley did not yet know Kohlberg, according to Buhite, *Hurley,* p. 266, and did not meet him until 1947, when they struck up a friendship, but Hurley never formally joined the ACPA; p. 286. In later testimony before the Senate panel investigating the dismissal of General Douglas MacArthur, Hurley said the leaks could only have come from the State Department. See *Military Situation in the Far East,* pt. 4, pp. 2936–37.

53 See Buhite, *Hurley*, pp. 147–49. Additional details of Hurley's appointment are found in Feis, *China Tangle*, pp. 178–79; and Lohbeck, *Hurley*, pp. 278–80.

54 Hurley's brief written instructions plus his later understanding of his mission are summarized in *The China White Paper August 1949*, p. 71. Lohbeck, *Hurley*, p. 280, emphasizes Roosevelt's oral instructions, saying the President told Hurley there would be no compromise on the American government's support for Chiang Kai-shek's leadership. Whether this was or was not American policy became a matter of dispute. See Feis, *China Tangle*, p. 179; and Buhite, *Hurley*, pp. 149–50, 160.

55 *Foreign Relations of the United States: Diplomatic Papers, 1944, China* (Washington D.C.: G.P.O., 1967), pp. 659, 687–88. On the immediately succeeding pages in *Foreign Relations* are letters written the same day by Mao Tse-tung to Roosevelt and by Hurley to Mao, the latter expressing Hurley's gratitude "for the splendid cooperation and leadership that you have shown in bringing your party to the offer of agreement . . . I have appreciated those qualities of mind and of heart that you have brought to bear on a solution of a most difficult problem. Your work is a contribution to the welfare of a United China and to the victory of the United Nations."

56 Buhite, *Hurley*, p. 171.

57 See *ibid.*, pp. 179–80; and Lohbeck, *Hurley*, pp. 336–38. For a firsthand account of official contact between the American military and the Chinese Communist leadership during this period, see David D. Barrett, *Dixie Mission: The United States Army Observer Group in Yenan, 1944* (Berkeley: Center for Chinese Studies Research Monograph Number 6, University of California, 1970).

58 Buhite, *Hurley*, p. 180. Buhite believes this period probably marked a turning point in Hurley's attitude toward the Communists. Thereafter, Hurley was "much more alert to the true aims of the CCP and much less flexible about the matter of unification under Chiang Kai-shek" (p. 181).

59 *Ibid.*, p. 187. Hurley's role as a mediator in China is further discussed and evaluated in *ibid.*, pp. 315–23; *The China White Paper August 1949*, pp. 73–112; Feis, *China Tangle*, pp. 208–25, 255–303; Lohbeck, *Hurley*, pp. 307–52; and Tang Tsou, *America's Failure in China*, pp. 288–345. A critical and insightful appraisal by one of the Foreign Service officers later maligned by Hurley, Senator Joseph McCarthy, and others is found in John S. Service, *The Amerasia Papers: Some Problems in the History of US-China Relations* (Berkeley: Center for Chinese Studies Research Monograph Number 7, University of California, 1970), pp. 75–135. The documentary history of Hurley's negotiations is scattered through the 1944 and 1945 volumes of *Foreign Relations of the United States: Diplomatic Papers*.

60 See the Chargé in China to the Secretary of State, February 28, 1945, *Foreign Relations of the United States: Diplomatic Papers, 1945, China* (Washington D.C.: G.P.O., 1969), pp. 242–46.

61 Buhite, *Hurley*, pp. 192–93. For more on Hurley's problems with government officials, see Feis, *China Tangle*, pp. 255–60; and Lohbeck, *Hurley*, esp. pp. 197–98, 229, 239, and 278.

62 Buhite, *Hurley*, pp. 182–83.

63 *Ibid.*, pp. 181, 210–38.

64 "Oral Statement by President Truman to Dr. T. V. Soong Concerning Assistance to China, September 14, 1945," *The China White Paper August 1949*, p. 939. See p. 107 for Hurley quote.

65 An equally provocative domestic question, in the context of later partisan recriminations over China policy, was the extent to which American backing of Chiang Kai-shek and the Nationalists was based on Democratic fears of a Republican attack on foreign policy. This question, among others in a similar as well as policy vein, are raised by Robert Dallek, "The Truman Era," in Ernest R. May and James C. Thompson Jr., eds., *American–East Asian Relations: A Survey* (Cambridge: Harvard University Press, 1972), pp. 356–76. Some additional questions: Did Roosevelt's recall of Stilwell constitute abandonment of support for Chiang Kai-shek? Did the United States actually desire a CCP-KMT military and political coalition in order to coordinate the war effort against Japan? Was the American government willing to supply arms and ammunition to the CCP? Did the United States follow a clear policy line in China? Did fear of a future Chinese Communist government dictate wartime policy judgments? What was the role of the military in setting policy? Of the OSS?

66 Ambassador Hurley's November 26, 1945, letter of resignation is found in *The China White Paper August 1949*, pp. 581–84. In December, shortly after Hurley's resignation, the Senate Foreign Relations Committee conducted executive session hearings on the Far Eastern situation. Hurley was the major witness. The hearings were not made public by the committee until 1971, but part of Hurley's testimony was used by Professor Anthony Kubek in *How the Far East Was Lost*, pp. 288–313, to make the point that "If a thorough investigation of Hurley's charges had been carried out—the supposed purpose of the hearings—*the loss of China to the Reds* might have been prevented. Unfortunately, the hearings ended in a complete whitewash." See p. 288 (italics added). Professor Kubek cites these hearings as U.S. Senate, Committee on Foreign Relations, *Investigation of United States Far Eastern Policy*, December 1945. The hearings were released as U.S. Senate, Committee on Foreign Relations, *United States–China Relations*, 92C1 (Washington D.C.: G.P.O., 1971).

2. The "China Lobby" and the "Loss of China"

1 Herbert Feis, *The China Tangle: The American Effort in China from Pearl Harbor to the Marshall Mission* (Princeton: Princeton University Press, 1953); Tang Tsou, *America's Failure in China, 1941–50* (Chicago: University of Chicago Press, 1963); and Anthony Kubek, *How the Far East Was Lost: American Policy and the Creation of Communist China, 1941–1949* (Chicago: Regnery, 1963).

2 H. Bradford Westerfield, *Foreign Policy and Party Politics: Pearl Harbor to Korea* (New Haven: Yale University Press, 1955); Felix Greene, *A Curtain of Ignorance: How the American Public Has Been Misinformed about China* (Garden City, N.Y.: Doubleday, 1964); A. T. Steele, *The American People and China* (New York: McGraw-Hill, published for the Council on Foreign Relations, 1966); Robert P. New-

man, *Recognition of Communist China?: A Study in Argument* (New York: Macmillan, 1961); Earl Latham, *The Communist Controversy in Washington: From the New Deal to McCarthy* (Cambridge: Harvard University Press, 1966); Joseph Keeley, *The China Lobby Man: The Story of Alfred Kohlberg* (New Rochelle, N.Y.: Arlington House, 1969); Kenneth E. Shewmaker, *Americans and Chinese Communists, 1927–1945: A Persuading Encounter* (Ithaca, N.Y.: Cornell University Press, 1971); Ronald J. Caridi, *The Korean War and American Politics: The Republican Party as a Case Study* (Philadelphia: University of Pennsylvania Press, 1968); Barbara W. Tuchman, *Stilwell and the American Experience in China, 1911–45* (New York: Macmillan, 1970); Ross Terrill, "John Carter Vincent and the American 'Loss' of China," in Bruce Douglass and Ross Terrill, eds., *China and Ourselves* (Boston: Beacon Press, 1971); and James Peck, "The Roots of Rhetoric: The Professional Ideology of America's China Watchers," in Edward Friedman and Mark Selden, eds., *America's Asia: Dissenting Essays on Asian-American Relations* (New York: Vintage Books, 1971).

3 Cf. Foster Rhea Dulles, *American Policy Toward Communist China, 1949–1969* (New York: Crowell, 1972); John Paton Davies Jr., *Dragon by the Tail* (New York: Norton, 1972); John King Fairbank, *The United States and China*, 3rd. ed. (1948; Cambridge: Harvard University Press, 1971); U.S., Senate, Committee on Foreign Relations, *United States-China Relations*, 92nd Cong., 1st sess. (Washington D.C.: G.P.O., 1971); Ernest R. May and James C. Thomson Jr., eds., *American-East Asian Relations: A Survey* (Cambridge: Harvard University Press, 1972); John N. Thomas, *The Institute of Pacific Relations: Asian Scholars and American Politics* (Seattle: University of Washington Press, 1974); O. Edmund Clubb, *The Witness and I* (New York: Columbia University Press, 1974); Gary Arthur May, *The China Service of John Carter Vincent, 1924–1953* (Ph.D. dissertation, University of California, Los Angeles, 1974); Robert P. Newman, "Lethal Rhetoric: The Selling of the China Myths," in *Quarterly Journal of Speech,* April 1975, 61(2); Norman A. Graebner, "The Republican Commitment to Chiang: The Truman Years," paper delivered at the Duquesne History Forum, October 30, 1974, Pittsburgh, Pennsylvania; and E. J. Kahn Jr., *The China Hands: America's Foreign Service Officers and What Befell Them* (New York: Viking Press, 1975).

4 Very briefly, the so-called *Amerasia* Affair began stormily in the summer of 1945 with the arrest of six suspects charged with a conspiracy to violate the Espionage Act. Involved in the alleged leakage of government information to the magazine *Amerasia* were two of the publication's editors, two State Department employees, a naval officer, and a reporter. Presented to a grand jury by the Department of Justice, the case produced three indictments out of the six persons originally charged. One case later was dropped; the remaining two defendants pleaded guilty and "no defense" to lesser charges. The highly controversial case became the subject of congressional investigations and executive branch hearings. Cf., Latham, *The Communist Controversy in Washington,* pp. 203–16; Shewmaker, *Americans and Chinese Communists, 1927–1945,* pp. 284–94; and, for an exhaustive account by one of the six accused individuals who was cleared of complicity by a unanimous vote of the grand jury, John S.

Service, *The Amerasia Papers: Some Problems in the History of US-China Relations* (Berkeley: Center for Chinese Studies Research Monograph Number 7, University of California, 1970), pp. 17–52.

5   Shewmaker, *Americans and Chinese Communists,* pp. 270–72. In this chapter, "The Conspiracy Thesis," the author finds the "devil theory" totally inadequate for analyzing the works of most writers who reported about their experiences with the Chinese Communists. "Although the possibility remains that one or two of those accused were in fact conspiring with Communist organizations to subvert the government of Chiang Kai-shek or to indoctrinate the American public," he writes on p. 296, "the 'devil theory' is just too simple."

6   See Edward M. Bennett, "Joseph C. Grew: The Diplomacy of Pacification," in Richard Dean Burns and Edward M. Bennett, eds., *Diplomats in Crisis: United States-Chinese-Japanese Relations, 1919–1941* (Santa Barbara, Calif.: ABC-CLIO, 1974), p. 87.

7   See Richard Dudman, "Entrepreneurs of the Right," in Robert H. Salisbury, ed., *Interest Group Politics in America* (New York: Harper & Row, 1970), p. 120.

8   Russell D. Buhite, *Patrick J. Hurley and American Foreign Policy* (Ithaca, N.Y.: Cornell University Press, 1973), p. 277.

9   See Keeley, *China Lobby Man,* pp. 233–35. Kohlberg's first person account of how ACPA got started may be seen in appendix K, pp. 366–86, *ibid.,* his 1952 affidavit before the Senate Internal Security subcommittee investigation of the IPR.

10   See Ross Y. Koen, *The China Lobby in American Politics* (New York: Harper & Row, 1974), pp. 57–58; and Keeley, *China Lobby Man,* p. 236. Between these two accounts there is a discrepancy over exactly when the "Manchurian Manifesto" was released.

11   Keeley, *China Lobby Man,* pp. 236–37.

12   See *ibid.,* pp. 196–201, for the origins of *Plain Talk.* Benjamin Mandel's past association with the Communist Party is identified in Thomas, *Institute of Pacific Relations,* p. 79.

13   Koen, *China Lobby,* p. 59.

14   See Albert C. Wedemeyer, *Wedemeyer Reports!* (New York: Holt, 1959), pp. 382, 388.

15   Tang Tsou, *America's Failure in China,* pp. 460–61, italics added.

16   *Life,* October 13, 1947, p. 35.

17   See "The China Lobby: A Case Study," *Congressional Quarterly Weekly Report* (Special Supplement), June 29, 1951, 9(25-A):939–58.

18   Cf. Freda Utley, *The China Story* (Chicago: Regnery, 1951); John T. Flynn, *While You Slept: Our Tragedy in Asia and Who Made It* (New York: Devin-Adair, 1951); and Joseph R. McCarthy, *America's Retreat from Victory: The Story of George Catlett Marshall* (New York: Devin-Adair, 1954). Anthony Kubek's scholarly approach to this general thesis, *How the Far East Was Lost,* was published in 1963.

19 Shewmaker, *Americans and Chinese Communists,* p. 275.

20 *Ibid.,* p. 291.

21 Westerfield, *Foreign Policy and Party Politics,* p. 266.

22 The speech was given on January 11, 1947. See Arthur H. Vandenberg Jr., ed., *The Private Papers of Senator Vandenberg* (Boston: Houghton Mifflin, 1952), p. 522–23.

23 Tang Tsou, *America's Failure in China* p. 452.

24 *The China White Paper August 1949* (Stanford: Stanford University Press, 1967), 1:252. Originally issued as *United States Relations With China: With Special Reference to the Period 1944*–1949 (Washington D.C.: G.P.O., 1949).

25 Tang Tsou, *America's Failure in China* p. 586.

26 As quoted in *ibid.,* p. 466.

27 Westerfield, *Foreign Policy and Party Politics,* pp. 263–64. Also, see Koen, *China Lobby,* p. 93.

28 Westerfield, *Foreign Policy and Party Politics,* p. 268. In Tang Tsou's judgment, ". . . the China Aid Act represented a compromise between two conflicting views which reflected the inconsistent elements of the traditional policy. Marshall came to be the embodiment of the traditional view that American interests in China were not worth a war, while his Republican critics held to their conception of America's traditional purposes in China. Marshall relied on the principle of non-intervention while his Republican critics appealed to the principle of upholding China's integrity against the encroachment of other powers." See *America's Failure in China,* p. 475.

29 Dulles, *American Policy Toward Communist China,* pp. 73–74.

30 Koen, *China Lobby,* p. 79.

31 This account of Kohlberg's activities surrounding the 1948 election is found in Keeley, *China Lobby Man,* pp. 217–22.

32 See the *New York Times,* June 25, 1949, pp. 1, 5. The Republicans: Baldwin (Conn.), Brewster (Maine), Bricker (Ohio), Bridges (N.H.), Butler (Neb.), Cain (Wash.), Cordon (Ore.), Ferguson (Mich.), Knowland (Calif.), Martin (Pa.), Morse (Ore.), Mundt (S.D.), Reed (Kan.), Taft (Ohio), Thye (Minn.), and Young (N.D.). The Democrats: Downey (Calif.), Holland (Fla.), Magnuson (Wash.), McCarran (Nev.), and Russell (Ga.). Senator Vandenberg was not asked to sign.

33 For the complete text of Hurley's August 7, 1949 release, titled "A Few Comments About One Thousand Pages of White Paper," see *Congressional Record,* 81C1 (1949), 95(8):10941–42. Acheson waited twenty years before venting his feelings about attacks on the White Paper: "The conclusion of the summary," he wrote in part, "was unpalatable to believers in American omnipotence, to whom every goal unattained is explicable only by incompetence or treason." See Dean Acheson, *Present at the Creation* (New York: Norton, 1969), p. 303.

34 See Don Lohbeck, *Patrick J. Hurley* (Chicago: Regnery, 1956), p. 427.

35   *The China White Paper August 1949,* 1:xvi.

36   *New York Times,* August 22, 1949, pp. 1, 6.

37   *Congressional Record,* 81C1 (1949), 95(9):11881–82.

38   As quoted in Keeley, *China Lobby Man,* p. 239.

39   *Ibid.,* pp. 154–55. Also, see *Department of State Bulletin* 21, no. 531 (September 5, 1949):350–52, 359.

40   As reported in Francis Valeo, *The China White Paper* (Washington D.C.: Library of Congress Legislative Reference Service, 1949), p. 56.

41   See *Far Eastern Survey,* September 7, 1949, 18(18):208, 209–10. Fairbank posed another good question: "Believing as we did in the right of private association, why did not our policy support more vigorously those elements in Chinese society which really represented our principles?"

42   *Ibid.,* p. 212 (italics in original).

43   Richard H. Rovere, *Senator Joe McCarthy* (New York: Harcourt, Brace & World, 1959), pp. 141–42. Also, see Robert Griffith, *The Politics of Fear: Joseph R. McCarthy and the Senate* (New York: Hayden, 1970); Allen J. Matusow, ed., *Joseph R. McCarthy* (Englewood Cliffs, N.J.: Prentice-Hall, 1970); Latham, *Communist Controversy in Washington;* Charles E. Potter, *Days of Shame* (New York: Coward-McCann, 1965); and, for a defense of the senator, William F. Buckley Jr. and L. Brent Bozell, *McCarthy and His Enemies* (Chicago: Regnery, 1954). America's compulsive anti-Communism is analyzed in Michael Parenti, *The Anti-Communist Impulse* (New York: Random House, 1969), which includes two chapters, 9 and 10, on American reactions to China's turn toward Communism.

44   See McCarthy, *America's Retreat from Victory,* p. 147.

45   For an account of Kohlberg's relationship with McCarthy which includes the circumstances of their first meeting, see Keeley, *China Lobby Man,* ch. 8, "His Good Friend Joe," pp. 95–112.

46   For McCarthy's testimony before the Tydings hearings, see U.S. Senate, Committee on Foreign Relations, Subcommittee Pursuant to S. Res. 231, *Hearings on the State Department Employee Loyalty Investigation,* 81C2 (1950), pp. 1–175, 277–92. McCarthy's March 30, 1950 accusations on the Senate floor, including the extended debate, are found in *Congressional Record,* 81C2 (1950), 96(4):4372–4408. For a comparison of McCarthy's and Kohlberg's charges against the IPR and others, see Koen, *China Lobby,* Appendix B, pp. 221–29.

47   Latham, *Communist Controversy,* pp. 271–73; see chs. 10 and 11 for an analysis of McCarthy's tactics and charges. Also, on the Tydings hearings, see Thomas, *Institute of Pacific Relations,* pp. 65–76.

48   On MacArthur's dismissal, see U.S. Senate, Committee on Armed Services and Committee on Foreign Relations, *Hearings on the Military Situation in the Far East,* 82C1 (1951); on the IPR, see U.S. Senate, Committee on the Judiciary, Subcommittee to Investigate the Administration of the Internal Security Act and Other Internal

Security Laws, *Hearings on the Institute of Pacific Relations*, 82C1 and 2 (1951–1952); on the Jessup nomination, see U.S. Senate, Subcommittee of the Committee on Foreign Relations, *Hearings on the Nomination of Philip C. Jessup to Be United States Representative to the Sixth General Assembly of the United Nations*, 82C1 (1951); and, for the hearings on foundations, see U.S. House of Representatives, Select Committee to Investigate Tax-Exempt Foundations and Comparable Organizations, *Hearings on Tax-Exempt Foundations*, 82C2 (1954).

49   Rovere, *Senator Joe McCarthy*, p. 136.

50   The dates were October 12, 1949, and January 10, 1950. Transcripts of these executive sessions were made public in June 1974 by the Senate Committee on Foreign Relations as part of its Historical Series. See U.S. Senate, Committee on Foreign Relations, *Hearings Held in Executive Session on the World Situation, 1949–1950*, 81C1 and 2 (1949–1950), pp. 71–103 for the October 12, 1949 session, and pp. 105–71 for the January 10, 1950 session.

51   See Committee Print, "The United States and Communist China in 1949 and 1950: The Question of Rapprochement and Recognition," a staff study prepared for the Senate Committee on Foreign Relations, 93C1 (1973), p. 15.

52   Koen, *China Lobby*, pp. 98–99.

53   See *Hearings Held in Executive Session on the World Situation, 1949–1950*, September 11, 1950, pp. 339–66. Acheson's concern about Chinese involvement in the war is found on p. 354.

54   *New York Times*, October 31, 1950, p. 22.

55   Caridi, *The Korean War and American Politics*, p. 107.

56   See *Hearings on the Military Situation in the Far East*, pt. 3, p. 2116.

57   Charles Wertenbaker, "The China Lobby," *The Reporter*, April 15, 1952, pp. 2–24; and Philip Horton, "The China Lobby—Part 2," *The Reporter*, April 29, 1952, pp. 5–24. Wertenbaker was a former *Time* correspondent. Part I contains a year-by-year chronology of pertinent events from 1937 through March 1952.

58   Koen, *China Lobby*, p. 202.

3.   The Formation and Organization of The Committee for One Million

1   *New York Times*, June 7, 1964, p. 87. All references to Dr. de Rochefort are taken from this obituary unless otherwise indicated.

2   "Si l'armistice est conclu en Corée, la question de l'admission du Gouvernement Communiste Chinois sera posée à l'UN."

3   "Il s'agirait donc de provoquer un vaste mouvement de caractère international, s'opposant à l'entree de la Chine Rouge à l'UN, quelque peu analogue à la 'Pétition pour la paix' de Stockholm, machinee par les Soviets. Dirigée par un organe International avec des sections dans chaque pays, une telle campagne de petitions et de re-

unions de protestations pourrait dans une certaine mesure influencer les Gouvernements respectifs. Elle aurait en tout cas pour effet de demontrer que, loin de se trouver isolés, les Etats-Unis ont, dans leur résistance, l'appui de l'opinion publique dans le monde entier ce que renforceait leur prestige international." Letter, N. de Rochefort to C. D. Jackson, June 17, 1953, Official File 85-DD, White House Central Files, Eisenhower Library. I am indebted to my friend Laurence Vittes for the translation.

4   Letter, Jackson to de Rochefort, June 22, 1953, Official File 85-DD, White House Central Files, Eisenhower Library.

5   Letter, de Rochefort to Jackson, August 11, 1953, *ibid.*

6   Memorandum, C. D. Jackson to Walter Bedell Smith, September 2, 1953, *ibid.*

7   Four congressmen were unable to provide a copy of the testimony for review. Originally, in March 1972, the office of Representative Alphonzo Bell (R., Calif.) verified existence of the testimony. The current chairman of the House Committee on International Relations (formerly the House Committee on Foreign Affairs), Representative Thomas E. Morgan (D., Pa.), was a member of the steering committee of The Committee of One Million from 1965 at least through 1969. In reply to my request, Chairman Morgan wrote in part: "Although Committee regulations do not permit making executive session transcripts available, I have explored the possibility of making an exception in your case. Unfortunately, this presents problems which I have not been able to solve." Letter, Thomas E. Morgan to author, April 18, 1972. The Clerk of the House of Representatives, W. Pat Jennings, wrote Congressman Thomas M. Rees (D., Calif.), in response to the author's request, that "the Clerk is not authorized to release Committee executive session transcripts that are not over fifty years old." Letter, W. Pat Jennings to Thomas M. Rees, September 8, 1972, original included with letter from Rees to me, September 11, 1972. A final unsuccessful attempt to read the transcripts in 1974 was through the office of Congressman Donald M. Fraser (D., Minn.), who won his seat in 1962, defeating Dr. Judd.

8   "Minutes of a Meeting of the Steering Committee of the Committee for One Million (Against the Admission of Communist China to the United Nations) held in Washington D.C., at 11:00 A.M., on Wednesday, December 30, 1953," Box 21, MLC.

9   To put these momentous events in some chronological perspective, on July 16, 1973, the existence of the White House taping system was publicly revealed; on October 10, 1973, Vice President Spiro T. Agnew resigned; on July 24, 1974, the Supreme Court ruled 8 to 0 that President Nixon had to turn over 64 tapes to the Watergate special prosecutor; and on August 9, 1974, the President resigned. The two books which illuminated techniques and practices of the CIA are Victor Marchetti and John D. Marks, *The CIA and the Cult of Intelligence* (New York: Knopf, 1974), and Philip Agee, *Inside the Company* (New York: Bantam Books, 1975). The articles in the *Times*, written by Seymour M. Hersh, began on December 22, 1974, and reported that dozens of secret illegal activities, including break-ins, wiretapping, and inspections of mail by CIA members, had taken place inside the United States since the 1950s. The immediate effect of the disclosures was the resignation of at least four top CIA officials of the agency's counterintelligence division, which allegedly had conducted the domestic spying operations.

In January 1975, President Ford's special commission to investigate the allegations, headed by Vice President Nelson Rockefeller, got underway behind closed doors; CIA Director William E. Colby publicly admitted for the first time that the agency had spied on American political dissenters, opened the mail of private citizens, *planted informers inside domestic protest groups,* and assembled secret files on more than 10,000 Americans (see *Los Angeles Times,* January 16, 1975, p. 1); and the Senate voted to create a select committee to study government intelligence operations. Senator Frank Church (D., Idaho) was named chairman and Senator John G. Tower (R., Tex.) vice chairman. A House select committee on the same subject, under the chairmanship of Representative Otis Pike (D., N.Y.), began deliberations some months later. Meanwhile, in June 1975, the Rockefeller commission concluded its five-month inquiry with acknowledgement that the CIA had violated the law but with the further observation that "the great majority of the CIA's domestic activities comply with its statutory authority" (see *Los Angeles Times,* June 11, 1975, p. 1).

The first congressional report to emerge from the intelligence probes, following months of new allegations, disclosures, and CIA admissions, was the Senate Select Committee's interim report of November 1975 on *Alleged Assassination Plots Involving Foreign Leaders,* 94C1 (1975). In December 1975, both the congressional select committees completed public hearings, but the CIA regained the front pages later in the month when Richard S. Welch, an admitted agent, was murdered in Athens, Greece. At the end of January 1976, the House committee ended its investigation with the full House voting not to release the committee's report. But leaks of the findings were reported in the press, notably, a 24-page supplement in New York's *Village Voice* on February 16, 1976, said to be identical to the committee's report. The most interesting section of the supplement from the standpoint of this book is a brief section (on page 89 of the *Village Voice*) entitled "CIA Presence in the Executive Branch," which discusses the role of CIA "detailees"—agency employees surreptitiously assigned to other government departments and agencies. (For an elaboration of the threat represented by "detailees," see I. F. Stone, "The Schorr Case: The Real Dangers," *New York Review of Books,* April 1, 1976, p. 8.) Finally, at the end of April, the Senate Select Committee, calling for a new law to curb covert action as an implement to foreign policy, released its final reports. See Senate Select Committee to Study Governmental Operations with Respect to Intelligence Activities, *Foreign and Military Intelligence, Book I,* and *Intelligence Activities and the Rights of Americans, Book II, 94C2 (1976).*

10   Letter, John F. Blake to me, June 5, 1975. Section (b)1 of the Freedom of Information Act (5 U.S.C. 552) as amended states that provisions of the legislation do not apply to matters that are "specifically authorized under criteria established by an Executive order to be kept secret in the interest of national defense or foreign policy and (B) are in fact properly classified pursuant to such Executive order." Similarly, section (b)3 states that provisions of the act are inapplicable to matters "specifically exempted from disclosure by statute." In an earlier letter to me declining comment on de Rochefort (April 14, 1975), the Agency had justified its refusal, under FOIA's section (b)3, by citing section 6 of the CIA Act of 1949, as amended, which exempts from disclosure requirements "the organization, functions, names, official titles, salaries, or numbers of personnel employed by the Agency."

11   See *Foreign and Military Intelligence, Book 1*, p. 115. The section covering the Allen W. Dulles era begins on p. 109 and includes, on p. 110, the following:

> Washington policymakers regarded the Central Intelligence Agency as a primary means of defense against Communism. By 1953, the Agency was an established element of government. Its contributions in the areas of political action and paramilitary warfare were recognized and respected. It alone could perform many of the kinds of activities seemingly required to meet the Soviet threat. For senior officials, covert operations had become a vital element in the pursuit of United States foreign policy objectives. . . .
>
> A crucial factor in securing the Agency's place within the government during this period was the fact that the Secretary of State, John Foster Dulles, and the DCI [Director, Central Intelligence Agency] were brothers. Whatever the formal relationships among the State Department, the NSC, and the Agency, they were superseded by the personal and working association between the brothers. Most importantly, both had the absolute confidence of President Eisenhower. In the day-to-day formulation of policy, these relationships were crucial to the Executive's support for the Agency, and more specifically, for Allen Dulles personally in the definition of his own role and that of the Agency.

12   For confirmation of Congressman Morgan's acceptance of steering committee membership, see letter, Thomas E. Morgan to Marvin Liebman, January 4, 1965, Box 8, MLC.

13   Letter, Marvin Liebman to Jo Duvall, October 12, 1953, Box 21, MLC. This is the earliest dated letter signed by Secretary Liebman covering the Committee's organizational phase. It was written ten days before presentation of the initial petition to President Eisenhower at the White House and before The Committee for One Million was officially organized.

14   "The President's Appointments Thursday, October 22, 1953," White House Central Files, Eisenhower Library. This document is not further identified by file number for reasons to be explained in note 15.

15   Letter, Dwight D. Eisenhower to Walter H. Judd, October 24, 1953, White House Central Files, Eisenhower Library. One of a series of documents relating to presentation of the petition to the President, this letter was not among the materials concerning the Committee originally supplied to me by the Eisenhower Library. In October 1971, the Library said it was unable to locate the signed petition presented to Eisenhower on October 22, 1953, or a copy of the President's reply to the petition. In March 1972, in response to another inquiry about Committee-related materials, the Library said it had been "re-reviewing our closed and security classified materials and have degraded the petition presented to President Eisenhower on October 22, 1953. We also located some additional correspondence between President Eisenhower and Congressman Walter Judd concerning this petition." The "degraded" materials are not clearly marked as to their whereabouts in the Library.

Regarding the added italics in the Eisenhower letter to Judd, the President's reference to a conversation with Secretary of State Dulles about the petition is interesting. Although Dulles apparently was already "in possession of a copy of the same document," the State Department, in response to several requests from me, has turned up nothing dated before June 18, 1954, relating to the Committee. Portions of the John Foster Dulles Papers are located at the Eisenhower Library, but they remain closed to research. My repeated efforts to obtain access to the collection through John W. Hanes Jr., chairman of the reviewing committee, an investment banker and, from 1953 to 1957, a special assistant to Secretary Dulles, have failed. Curiously, in the Townsend Hoopes biography of Dulles, *The Devil and John Foster Dulles* (Boston and Toronto: Little, Brown, 1973), there is no reference to the 29 linear feet of Dulles' Papers listed in the Eisenhower Library's 1974 catalog. Hoopes incorrectly leaves the impression (see p. 539) that all of Dulles' Papers are deposited at Princeton University.

16 Letter, Walter H. Judd to Dwight D. Eisenhower, October 22, 1953, White House Central Files, Eisenhower Library.

17 Letter, Charles Edison to Walter H. Judd, October 27, 1953, Box 21, MLC. The President's receipt of the petition made page eight of the *New York Times*. The article, which said the petition was presented by former Governor Edison, former Ambassador Joseph C. Grew, and Congressman Judd, quoted Edison as saying that the movement would be expanded into The Committee for One Million. See the October 23, 1953 edition, p. 8.

18 Letter, Walter H. Judd to Charles Edison, November 9, 1953, Box 21, MLC. The letter bears the notation "(Dictated but signed in Congressman Judd's absence)."

19 Letter, Marvin Liebman to Stefan T. Possony, February 5, 1969, Hoover Institution Archives (as shown to me).

20 Richard Dudman, "Entrepreneurs of the Right," Robert H. Salisbury, ed., *Interest Group Politics in America* (New York: Harper & Row, 1970), pp. 120–26; originally printed in *Men of the Far Right* (New York: Pyramid Books, 1962), pp. 144–50.

21 Sponsor's names are in apparent alphabetical order (though the last two names are misplaced) without titles as follows: Charles Edison, Joseph C. Grew, Herbert Hoover, Walter H. Judd, John W. McCormack, John Sparkman, and H. Alexander Smith. Among the sponsors, only Edison and Judd apparently were active in the group's organizational efforts. Along with Frederick C. McKee, Dr. B. A. Garside, and Marvin Liebman, they helped recruit the petition's original 210 signers. For the petition itself, see "A Petition to President Dwight D. Eisenhower," October 22, 1953, White House Central Files, Eisenhower Library.

22 *Ibid.*, Judd to Eisenhower, October 22, 1953. That Eisenhower was skeptical about "prolonged nonrecognition" of China first was noted, without documentation, in Robert J. Donovan, *Eisenhower: The Inside Story* (New York: Harper, 1956). "The President was not convinced," writes Donovan on p. 132, "that the vital interests of the United States were best served by prolonged nonrecognition of China. He had serious doubts as to whether Russia and China were natural allies."

23 Copy of letter from Alfred Kohlberg to Warren R. Austin, November 27, 1953, Box 21, MLC. Here, the petition referred to was the printed one then being circulated for a million signatures, not the one originally presented to Eisenhower. The language of both was identical in substance with several minor style changes. The paragraph in the *Times*'s editorial which Kohlberg found objectionable read: "This is not an attempt to make a permanent policy for the United States. It is conceivable—although not as of now probable—that a situation might arise, including a change in the character and behavior of the Peiping regime, that might make its membership in the United Nations desirable. That situation does not exist now nor is it in any immediate prospect. The petition deals with conditions as they are." See *New York Times,* November 27, 1953, p. 26.

24 Dated November 5, 1953, this appeal for funds intended for mailing to signers of the original petition to the President provides the earliest available document on Committee letterhead in the Marvin Liebman Collection. See Box 21.

25 Letter, Walter H. Judd to Warren R. Austin, November 9, 1953, Box 21, MLC. "Honorary" was added to Austin's title by January 1954. Although Austin's name remained on consecutive Committee letterheads until his death in 1962, never once was he listed as having attended a steering committee meeting. There is no evidence that Austin took any active role in the organization.

26 Present at this meeting, according to the minutes, were Judd, Grew, Liebman and, by proxy and by telephone, Edison. Also, Dr. B. A. Garside and Harold L. Oram attended on a "consultative" basis.

27 Judd and Edison were the others. White House documents and Committee materials suggest that only Judd, Edison, and Grew actually were received by the President although others may have intended to participate. The night of the petition ceremony, Ambassador Grew made a brief statement over radio station WMAL in Washington. He said that Americans should not let important issues of principle go by default and that the admission of Communist China to the United Nations would "wreck" the organization, encourage subversive totalitarian movements, and vastly increase the dangers of a new war. See his statement for WMAL, October 22, 1953, attached to a letter from Grew to Edison, October 23, 1953, Box 21, MLC.

28 John Dos Passos once declined an offer to write a Committee fund-raising letter but said he would send a check "as soon as I can coax a little fresh money into my bank account." See letter, John Dos Passos to Marvin Liebman, May 10, 1962, Box 4, MLC.

29 Reverend Poling would later head the Committee's National Protestant Clergyman's Committee.

30 Ray Brock, H. L. Chesser, Henry Dormann, Paul F. Douglas, Edward R. Easton, Hollis P. Gale, Marx Lewis, H. B. Lundberg, Harry T. Madison, J. E. Masters, Milton Nevins, Irving M. Olds, and Boris Shub.

31 The speech, on February 2, 1953, called attention to the Truman order of June 1950 which, Eisenhower said, had ordered the seventh Fleet "both to prevent attack upon Formosa and also to insure that Formosa should not be used as a base of operations

against the Chinese Communist mainland." This had meant, in effect, he added, that the United States was serving as a defensive arm of the Communist Chinese. He therefore issued instructions "that the Seventh Fleet no longer be employed to shield Communist China . . . This order implies no aggressive intent on our part. But we certainly have no obligation to protect a nation fighting us in Korea." See *Department of State Bulletin* 27, no. 711 (February 9, 1953):209.

32 Donovan, *Eisenhower,* p. 231.

33 *Congressional Record,* 83C1 (1953), 99(4), 5115–17. Knowland's resolutions were S. Res. 112 and S. Con. Res. 29, the latter intended for House concurrence.

34 *Ibid.,* 94(5):5971–73.

35 See Donovan, *Eisenhower,* pp. 132–37. This account tells of presidential efforts to eliminate uncompromising language from the proposals. For example, Senator William E. Jenner (R., Ind.) wanted to guarantee that the United States would neither recognize the People's Republic nor consent to its entry in the United Nations "under any circumstance"; and Senator Everett M. Dirksen (R., Ill.) sought a rider which would have automatically terminated American contributions to the world body if China were admitted. Donovan says Eisenhower met with GOP leaders on June 2 and argued that passage of the Dirksen rider would "seriously impede him in the conduct of foreign affairs."

36 *Congressional Record,* 83C1 (1953); see 99(5):6760, for introduction of H. Con. Res. 114 and 99(11):A3765–A3766 for the text.

37 *Ibid.,* pt. 6, p. 7402.

38 *Ibid.,* pp. 7983–84. Chairman Chiperfield's H. Con. Res. 126 closely followed the version passed by the Senate on June 3, but his H. Con. Res. 129, which the House ultimately acted upon, was a modification of Representative Battle's H. Con. Res. 128 and Representative Church's H. Con. Res. 127.

39 *Ibid.,* pt. 7, p. 9405.

40 *Ibid.,* pt. 8, p. 10579. He made the remark on July 30, several days before the session ended on August 3, 1953.

41 Other subcommittee members who did not sign the Committee's petition were Chester E. Merrow (R., N.H.), A. S. J. Carnahan (D., Mo.), and Henderson Lanham (D., Ga.).

42 *Special Study Mission to Southeast Asia and the Pacific, Report,* Committee Print, House Committee on Foreign Affairs, 83C2, January 29, 1954 (Washington: G.P.O., 1954), p. vii.

43 Letter, Walter H. Judd to Dwight D. Eisenhower, November 9, 1953, Official File 106, White House Central Files, Eisenhower Library. Judd wrote that he was leaving that day on his mission and thanked the President for helping with the use of an airplane.

44 *Newsweek,* July 30, 1962, p. 22. For more on the Oram firm's activities, see Douglass Cater and Walter Pincus, "The Foreign Legion of U.S. Public Relations," *The Reporter,* December 22, 1960, p. 16.

45 "Minutes of a meeting of the Steering Committee . . . December 30, 1953." The author of the minutes is not identified.

46 The report concluded that "a free Asia is vital to the security of the free world and, therefore, to the security of the United States." It declared that the United States "must steadfastly refuse to recognize the Communist regime in China and must resist its admission to the United Nations." Admission, it added, would make a mockery of the UN Charter, would be a smashing victory for world communism and smashing defeat for freedom, and would be an abandonment to Communist enslavement of 450 million people. See *Special Study Mission to Southeast Asia and the Pacific*, pp. 99–101.

47 "Minutes of a Meeting of the Steering Committee . . . December 30, 1953."

48 Letter, steering committee to Charles Edison, November 5, 1953, Box 21, MLC. Presumably Edison, as a member of the steering committee, was automatically put on the mailing list. The letter indicates that the Committee intended to return to the White House after it had collected one million names.

49 See, for example, John D. Venable to Ward Harris, December 9, 1953, Box 21, MLC, in which the author writes of the Committee's campaign to "reinforce official opinion." This box contains a thick file of similar letters under the heading "General Miscellaneous Correspondence."

50 See, for example, Charles Edison to the Most Reverend Fulton J. Sheen, January 7, 1954, Box 21, MLC.

51 Letter, Charles Edison to Robert R. McCormick, January 22, 1954. (The *Chicago Tribune* ran a story on January 25, 1954, on p. 10 of pt. 1 in the Three Star Final edition, according to the paper's Book Copy Service, but only the Four Star Final edition is available on microfilm.)

52 Letter, Jack R. Howard to Charles Edison, January 27, 1954, Box 21, MLC.

53 Letter, Mrs. Ralph de Toledano to Jack Howard, February 2, 1954, Box 21, MLC. In the same file is a letter from Edison to George Sokolsky dated January 25, 1954, thanking the latter for "last night's broadcast."

54 Letter, Nora de Toledano to William Randolph Hearst Jr., February 11, 1954, Box 21, MLC.

55 Letter, W. R. Hearst Jr. to Charles A. Edison, June 24, 1954, Box 21, MLC. An attached editorial from the *New York Journal American* of June 27 was entitled "Sign Now!" and began: "We hope President Eisenhower impresses on Prime Minister Churchill and Foreign Secretary Eden this weekend that one thing the American people will not stand for is acceptance of Red China into the civilized community of nations." Under the editorial was a coupon marked for sending to the "Committee for One Million."

56 Draft of letter to Warren Austin for Governor Edison's signature, Box 21, MLC.

57   Memo, Nora de Toledano to Edison, January 26, 1954, attached to draft of letter. Whether the article was written is unknown. Huss later co-authored, with George Carpozi Jr., *Red Spies in the U.N.* (New York: Coward-McCann, 1965).

58   *Newsweek,* March 29, 1954, p. 14.

59   Letter, Charles Edison to Herbert Hoover, March 29, 1954, Box 21, MLC. A check of every issue of *Newsweek* for the subsequent six-month period failed to find a Hoover reply.

60   Letter, Sherman Adams to Charles Edison, July 6, 1954, Box 21, MLC. Thanking Edison on behalf of the President, Adams added: "Other friendly Governments have been informed on every pertinent occasion of the firm opposition of this Government and the American people [to admission]. Our allies are also aware that the United States does not intend to recognize the Chinese Communist regime. You may be sure that the President and Secretary Dulles will reiterate this Government's attitude on both matters whenever required."

61   The telegram from Edison and Judd began: "Reinforcing your statement of yesterday, The Committee for One Million at 3:56 PM, July 6 received its one millionth individual signature to its petition. . . . Our nation must continue to take the moral leadership on this issue. The . . . success of the Committee's efforts convincingly upholds your own view that 95 per cent of the American people will support all measures taken to prevent appeasement of communism by rewarding its aggression." See telegram, Charles Edison and Walter H. Judd for The Committee for One Million to Dwight D. Eisenhower, July 8, 1954, Records Services Division, Department of State. The President, at his July 7 news conference, had answered an "admission question" by saying he was "completely and unalterably opposed under the present situation to the admission of Red China into the United Nations. I personally think that 95 per cent of the population of the United States would take the same stand." Eisenhower said that if the mainland Chinese got into the United Nations the question of American participation in the organization would have to be decided at that point. See the *New York Times,* July 8, 1954, p. 12.

62   See "A Brief History of an Authentic and Effective People's Movement," undated Committee pamphlet covering the years 1953 through 1965, p. 4. The Public Affairs Service of the U.C.L.A. Research Library has a copy.

4.   "Watchdog" Over the Geneva Conference

1   "United States Objectives and Courses of Action With Respect to Southeast Asia," *New York Times,* July 5, 1971, p. 9. This document from the Pentagon Papers first was revealed publicly on this date as part of the ninth and last in the newspaper's series of articles on the Pentagon's secret study of U.S. participation in the Vietnam War.

2   *New York Times,* July 5, 1971, p. 13, as quoted from the Pentagon Papers study.

3 "Excerpts from memorandum for the record, Jan. 30, 1954, by Brig. Gen. Charles H. Bonesteel 3d on meeting of President's Special Committee on Indochina," *ibid.*, p. 9.

4 *Department of State Bulletin* 30, no. 761 (January 25, 1954):108.

5 *Ibid.*, no. 759 (January 11, 1954):pp. 39–42. The article was based on a speech given December 7, 1953 before the Richmond Public Forum, Richmond, Virginia.

6 *Ibid.*, 763 (February 8, 1954):181.

7 Memorandum, Charles Edison and John W. McCormack to "Initial Signers," February 22, 1954, Box 21, MLC, italics added.

8 Letter, Stanley K. Hornbeck to Edison and McCormack, February 23, 1954, Box 121, Stanley K. Hornbeck Collection, Hoover Institution Archives.

9 "Confidential Memorandum," Marvin Liebman to "Initial Signers and Friends of the Committee for One Million," March 5, 1954, Box 21, MLC.

10 Draft and signed versions of minutes of a meeting of the steering committee held on Friday, February 26, 1954, at 11:30 A.M. on Capitol Hill, Box 21, MLC. Excepting Warren Austin, the full steering committee was present: Governor Edison, Ambassador Grew, Representatives Judd and McCormack, and Senators Sparkman and Smith. "Consultative" attendees included Liebman, Oram, Nora (Mrs. Ralph) de Toledano, and John Venable. Governor Edison presided. The file containing both versions of the minutes includes a letter from Liebman to Edison, dated March 2, 1954, which acknowledges enclosure of the minutes but fails to indicate which version.

11 "Confidential Memorandum," Marvin Liebman to "Initial Signers and Friends of the Committee for One Million," March 5, 1954.

12 *Congressional Record*, 83C2 (1954), 100(2):2108–9. Both Flanders and Malone suspected the State Department was "at work."

13 *Ibid.*, p. 2545, as inserted in the *Record* by Smith.

14 *Ibid.*, p. 2598. A couple of weeks after the steering committee's meeting on Geneva, Judd wrote to Eisenhower's chief of staff, Sherman Adams, asking him to become a sponsor of a new campaign called "The Free China Fund," a joint effort of two older China support groups—Aid Refugee Chinese Intellectuals, which Judd had helped father in 1952, and the American Bureau for Medical Aid to China, founded in 1938. On the advice of the State Department, however, Governor Adams replied that he could not become a sponsor, though he was sympathetic to the aims of medical and refugee aid. Judd answered that he understood perfectly but had extended the invitation so that Adams would know about efforts to turn around some of the damage of earlier years when the purpose of U.S. foreign policy, as he put it, was to build up the Communist enemy to the detriment of America's loyal Asian friends. For this exchange of correspondence, see Official File 116-G, White House Central Files, Eisenhower Library.

15 Two "initial signers" who submitted resolutions were Representatives Radwan (H. Con. Res. 222 and H. Con. Res. 223) and Bentley (H. Res. 627). Other resolutions were offered by Representatives Hosmer (H.J. Res. 557), Utt (H.J. Res. 558),

Burdick (H. Con. Res. 231), Lane (H. Res. 452 and H.J. Res. 562), and O'Neill (H. Con. Res. 255), and Senator McCarran (S.J. Res. 171). See *Congressional Record Index,* 83C2 (1954), 100(13):92–93 for full identification of the resolutions.

16 For the Lane introduction, see *Congressional Record,* 83C2 (1954), 100(2):2318. This was H. Res. 452 submitted February 25, 1954. Mansfield's speech is found in pt. 3, pp. 3611–13.

17 *Department of State Bulletin* 30, no. 767, Robertson (March 8, 1954):348–52; no. 768, Robertson, (March 15, 1954):398–400 (this address originally was given on February 26 at Charleston, South Carolina, on the occasion of the transfer of two U.S. naval destroyers to the Republic of China), and McConaughy, pp. 402–06; no. 772, Dulles (April 12, 1954):539–42 and Martin, pp. 543–46; no. 774, Jenkins (April 26, 1954):624–27; no. 776, Lodge (May 10, 1954):721–25; no. 777, Dulles (May 17, 1954):739–44 (this comprised the text of the Secretary's radio-television report to the nation on May 7); no. 780, Jenkins (June 7, 1954):859–62; no. 783, Dulles, June 28, 1954, pp. 971–73; and 31, no. 791, Robertson (August 23, 1954):259–63.

18 This speech originally was delivered on April 2, 1954 before the American Academy of Political and Social Science in Philadelphia.

19 Italics added. Jenkins was referring to the paragraph in the Berlin communiqué that the Geneva Conference did not imply diplomatic recognition where recognition otherwise did not exist.

20 Cablegram, Charles Edison to John Foster Dulles, April 26, 1954, Box 21, MLC.

21 Letter, Donald J. Simon, Chief, Records Services Division, State Department, to me, March 13, 1972.

22 Letter, W. Reginald (Rex) Wheeler to John Foster Dulles, June 16, 1954, Records Services Division, State Department.

23 Letter, John Foster Dulles to W. Reginald (Rex) Wheeler, June 28, 1954, Records Services Division, State Department (italics added).

24 *Congressional Record,* 83C2 (1954), 100(7):9426, 9469–70. McCarran did not sign the original petition. He died on September 28, 1954.

25 *Ibid.,* pp. 9584–85, 9587, 9588.

26 *Ibid.,* pt. 8, pp. 9996–97. In the course of this speech, Gillette remarked that the Senate news ticker had announced the information about the Committee's receiving its millionth signature.

27 *Ibid.,* pp. 10141–42.

28 *Ibid.,* See pp. 10636–49 for the debate and the roll call vote.

29 *Ibid.,* pt. 9, pp. 11944–45, 12520.

30 Memorandum, Marvin Liebman to "Steering Committee and Friends," May 19, 1954, Box 11, MLC. Files and other Committee materials were stored in offices of the Free China Fund, Room 705, 1790 Broadway, New York City, the address of Dr.

B. A. Garside. Liebman did not start his own firm until 1958; until that time he worked for the Oram firm. This fact may account for the absence of certain materials from the Marvin Liebman Collection covering the Committee's first five years. The Committee's first offices were located, as noted, at 36 West 44th Street; the Oram firm at 8 West 40th Street; Governor Edison operated from his New York apartment, Suite 38A of the Waldorf Towers in Manhattan.

31   Letter, Marvin Liebman to Walter Judd, June 14, 1954, Box 21, MLC.

32   "Excerpts from Part II of the Special Committee's Report on Southeast Asia, April 5, 1954," "Cablegram from Secretary Dulles to Ambassador Dillon in Paris, April 5, 1954," "Cablegram from Secretary of State Dulles to Under Secretary Walter Bedell Smith, May 12, 1954," *New York Times,* July 5, 1971, pp. 9, 10.

33   "Excerpts from memorandum from Admiral Arthur W. Radford, Chairman of the Joint Chiefs of Staff, to Secretary of Defense Charles E. Wilson, May 26, 1954," *ibid.,* p. 10. (Italics in original.)

34   Memorandum, Walter H. Judd to the President, June 26, 1954, White House Official File 168-C-3, Eisenhower Library.

35   Letter, Thomas E. Stephens to Walter H. Judd, July 1, 1954, Official File 181-C-3, White House Central Files, Eisenhower Library.

36   "Copy" of letter, John W. McCormack to Charles Edison, August 3, 1954, Box 21, MLC.

37   "A Brief History of an Authentic and Effective People's Movement," undated Committee pamphlet covering the years 1953 through 1965, p. 4.

38   Letter, Marvin Liebman to Dwight D. Eisenhower, September 16, 1954, Official File 168, White House Central Files, Eisenhower Library.

39   The participating organizations were listed as follows: Aid Refugee Chinese Intellectuals, American Bureau for Medical Aid to China, American China Policy Association, American Jewish League Against Communism, Ass'n of Former Polish Political Prisoners, China Institute in America, China Society, Committee Against Trade with the Soviet Bloc, [the Committee], Council Against Communist Aggression, Sino-American Amity Association, and Sun Yat Sen Group.

40   The law firm of Nordlinger, Riegelman, Benetar, and Charney was registered in 1965 with the Justice Department, under terms of the Foreign Agents Registration Act of 1938, as an agent of the Republic of China. See *China and U.S. Far East Policy 1945–1967* (Washington D.C.: Congressional Quarterly Service, 1967), p. 26. In a 1960 magazine article, attorney Harold Riegelman was named as a registered foreign agent of Nationalist China who often sent letters to the editor of the *New York Times* in support of Nationalist Chinese causes but failed to identify his role as agent. See Douglass Cater and Walter Pincus, "The Foreign Legion of U.S. Public Relations," *The Reporter,* December 22, 1960, p. 17. The matter was considered in 1963 hearings before the Senate Foreign Relations Committee. Included in the Senate committee's report are letters between the Department of Justice and Riegelman's attorneys arguing the point, *viz.,* should he have identified himself in letters to the *Times* as a foreign

agent? Yes, the Justice Department concluded. See U.S. Senate, Committee on Foreign Relations, *Hearings on Activities of Non-diplomatic Representatives of Foreign Principals in the United States,* 88C1 (1963), pt. 1, pp. 137–45.

41   Letter, Dwight D. Eisenhower to Marvin Liebman, September 22, 1954, Official File 168, White House Central Files, Eisenhower Library.

42   Letter, Dwight D. Eisenhower to Messrs. T. H. Chang, K. C. Chao, C. C. Kao, Y. C. Chien, and A. K. Hu, September 21, 1954, Official File 168, White House Central Files, Eisenhower Library.

43   For Ambassador Lodge's September 21 statement at the opening session of the Ninth General Assembly revealing U.S. strategy for refusing to discuss the substance of the admission question, see *Department of State Bulletin* 31, no. 797 (October 4, 1954): 507.

5.   Emerging from "Hibernation"

1   Of the twenty-eight senators who signed the Committee's first petition to the President, only four voted against censure (Knowland, Martin, Welker, and Young); nineteen supported the action (Bennett, Daniel, Douglas, Eastland, Ferguson, Flanders, Gillette, Humphrey, Ives, Kilgore, Magnuson, Monroney, Neely, Payne, Potter, Robertson, Smith of Maine, Watkins, and Williams); the two Committee senatorial sponsors, Smith of New Jersey and Sparkman, also supported censure—"condemned" became the operative word in the amended S. Res. 301. Three Committee signers had died by this time (Hoey, Hunt, and Maybank), and two (Bricker and Wiley) were not present for the roll call vote, which ended 67 yeas, 22 nays. See *Congressional Record,* 83C2 (1954), 100(1)16392.

2   McCarthy's attack on the President came on December 7. See *China and U.S. Far East Policy 1945–1967* (Washington D.C.: Congressional Quarterly Service, 1967), p. 71.

3   The State Department on November 23 issued the strongest possible protest in condemning the sentencing for "alleged espionage." See *Department of State Bulletin* 31, no. 806 (December 6, 1954):856–57. Fecteau was released by the Chinese in December 1971. On January 31, 1973, President Richard M. Nixon conceded that Downey was a CIA agent. See *New York Times,* February 1, 1973, p. 20.

4   Called "defensive in character," the treaty was directed "against threats to the security of the treaty area from armed attack and provides for continuing consultation regarding any such threat or attack." See *Department of State Bulletin* 31, no. 807 (December 13, 1954):895. Dulles thought the treaty changed the status quo for the United States in the Pacific area, he told a news conference, because it put "Formosa and the Pescadores in precisely the same category . . . as the Republic of Korea, Japan, the Philippines, Australia, and New Zealand." For these and other comments, plus the treaty text, see *ibid.,* pp. 896–99.

5   Letter, Henry R. Luce to the President, January 22, 1955, Official File 168-C, White House Central Files, Eisenhower Library.

6   Telegram, Walter H. Judd to President Eisenhower, January 22, 1955, Official File 168-B-1, White House Central Files, Eisenhower Library. For an account of the role played by Dag Hammarskjöld, UN Secretary-General, in trying to negotiate the release of the Americans, see Brian Urquhart, *Hammarskjöld* (New York: Knopf, 1972), pp. 94–131.

7   Letter, Dwight D. Eisenhower to William F. Knowland, January 31, 1955, Official File 99-V. White House Central Files, Eisenhower Library.

8   Letter, Sherman Adams to Walter H. Judd, February 1, 1955, *ibid.*

9   Both the agenda and the memorandum are located in Box 11, MLC. Other agenda items included discussion of presenting the stored petitions to the President; a report by the secretary of The Committee for One Million; and consideration of actions to implement the decisions of the meeting.

10   Various Committee documents differ as to the total number of signatures collected. The most prevailing figures are 1,037,000 and 1,032,017.

11   The declaration of the fifth session of the American Assembly, which met at Arden House, Harriman, N.Y., did not specifically advocate Peking's entry in the United Nations "on the basis of facts as they now exist," but did, instead, note and deplore "a tendency to adopt a rigid policy of permanent opposition under all circumstances to the seating of this regime." See *New York Times,* August 3, 1954, pp. 1–2. Approximately sixty participants attended this conclave on international affairs, the idea for which had originated with General Eisenhower when he was president of Columbia University.

12   The National Planning Association's Committee on International Policy issued a statement in December 1954 calling for a truly bipartisan foreign policy and advocating a fresh approach to the problem of two Chinas. The United States was urged "to strive for a realistic understanding with Communist China without sacrificing prestige or national interest." Though twenty-seven people signed the statement, two later said their signatures were not authorized. See *New York Times,* December 10, 1954, p. 1.

13   Specifically mentioned was a purported study released by the Democratic National Committee which, according to the memo, attacked the treaty with Nationalist China and apparently favored the neutralization of Formosa under the United Nations. There is, however, no evidence of such a study in the party's publication, *Democratic Digest,* or in the *New York Times* or the *Congressional Record.*

14   One Committee document contains a draft statement to President Eisenhower for signature by steering committee members. January is crossed out and February 1955 is written across the document, which says: "Acting on behalf of 1,032,017 American citizens from the forty-eight States, the territories of Alaska, Hawaii, and Puerto Rico, and from other parts of the world, we respectfully submit the attached petition to which they have affixed their signatures expressing their opposition to the admission of Communist China to the United Nations." See Box 11, MLC. Additionally, the new steering committee wrote to some of the initial petition signers asking them to join The Committee of One Million. A sentence in this letter reads: "We wish to present to the President,

within the shortest possible time, our signed petition with the 1,032, 017 signatures of Americans already received." See letter, Paul H. Douglas, Charles Edison, Joseph C. Grew, Walter H. Judd, H. Alexander Smith, and Francis E. Walter to Dan Thornton, March 4, 1955, Official File 143-F, White House Central Files, Eisenhower Library.

15   Representative John W. McCormack favored winding up The Committee For One Million. See chapter 4 note 36. McCormack became Majority Leader of the House in the 84th Congress and was replaced on the steering committee by Representative Francis E. Walter (D., Pa.). Senator Sparkman was replaced by Illinois Democrat Paul H. Douglas.

16   Copy of letter, Charles Edison to Walter H. Judd, March 11, 1955, Box 21, MLC.

17   Memorandum, Marvin Liebman to "Friends of The Committee For One Million," March 14, 1955, Official File 143-F, White House Central Files, Eisenhower Library. The memorandum was sent to the White House by then ex-governor of Colorado Dan Thornton, who had received the Committee's March 4 appeal and had written to Sherman Adams seeking advice about the Committee and other unrelated matters. Adams replied that Thornton's endorsement of the Committee's position on the seating of Communist China in the United Nations was a personal decision "but I can assure you it would be fully consistent with the Administration attitude." *Ibid.*

18   The advertisement appeared on page 19 of both newspapers on April 12, 1955. The Committee later claimed that seventeen other newspapers reprinted the advertisement "as a public service"; see "A Brief History of an Authentic and Effective People's Movement," undated Committee pamphlet covering the years 1953 through 1965, p. 4.

19   Press release, "The Committee of One Million," for release April 12, 1955, Box 11, MLC.

20   *New York Times,* April 12, 1955, p. 10. The lead read: "A reorganized bipartisan group announced yesterday plans to carry the case against the admission of Communist China to the United Nations to President Eisenhower and to Allied nations in West Europe."

21   See *Congressional Record,* 83C2 (1954), 100(2):2108.

22   The follow-up appeal stated that affirmative responses had been received by more than half of those who received the March 4 letter, adding: "Because of the crucial situation, and our plans to present the Petition to President Eisenhower and publish the Statement in *New York Times* as soon as possible, we have set Monday, March 21st, as the deadline for all responses."

23   Letter, William F. Knowland to the President, March 11, 1955, Official File 168-C, White House Central Files, Eisenhower Library. The senator's letter was acknowledged the following day by a presidential aide.

24   The deceased senators were Clyde R. Hoey (D., N.C.); Lester C. Hunt (D., Wyo.); and Burnet R. Maybank (D., S.C.).

25   April 12, 1955 press release.

26   Copy of letter and enclosure, Alfred Kohlberg to Dwight D. Eisenhower, February 25, 1955, in my possession. I am indeed grateful to H. Arthur Steiner, Emeritus Professor of Political Science, U.C.L.A., for giving me his collection of Alfred Kohlberg letters, pamphlets, broadsides, etc. Professor Steiner remained on Kohlberg's mailing list from early in 1953 to the spring of 1960, when Kohlberg died. For a biography of Kohlberg, see Joseph Keeley, *The China Lobby Man* (New Rochelle, N.Y.: Arlington House, 1969).

27   "Information Bulletin," undated mimeograph, "The Committee Of One Million," p. 6, Box 11, MLC. Christopher Emmet was listed as editor.

28   See Kenneth T. Young, *Negotiating With the Chinese Communists: The United States Experience, 1953–1967* (New York: McGraw-Hill, published for the Council on Foreign Relations, 1968), pp. 44–5.

29   See *Department of State Bulletin* 31, no. 827 (May 2, 1955):738. Secretary Dulles acknowledged on April 26 that he had neither seen nor approved the Department's statement. Asked if he would be willing to negotiate directly with the Chinese Communists if they agreed to participation by the Republic of China, or whether he preferred talks under the auspices of the United Nations, Dulles answered: "We believe it to be preferable that negotiations should be held under the auspices of the United Nations, and I do not give up hope that they might be held under those auspices." For the complete transcript of the news conference, see *ibid.*, no. 828 (May 9, 1955):755–59.

30   See "Memorandum," Marvin Liebman to steering committee, April 29, 1955, Box 11, MLC. Instead, Liebman's memorandum discussed how the Committee managed to get several paragraphs hostile to Communist China in a speech by George Meany, president of the AFL, before the American Society of Newspaper Editors in Washington D.C. Liebman also announced that a statement by religious leaders of all faiths was being prepared for independent release, said that response to the April 12 advertisements was encouraging, outlined plans for publicity (including the official presentation of the petition to the President), proposed the publication of an information bulletin to some 3,500 "supporting members," and reported that, to date, approximately $22,000 had been received from 3,500 people who had accepted Committee membership.

31   Letter, Walter H. Judd to the President, May 3, 1955, Official File 116-V, White House Central Files, Eisenhower Library.

32   Letter, Dwight D. Eisenhower to Walter H. Judd, May 6, 1955, *ibid.*

33   See *New York Times,* May 18, 1955, p. 6, under the headline, **"Unit Here Warns on Peiping Parley**——Committee of One Million Asks Reds Prove Good Faith Before New Talks." White House and State Department records indicate that Liebman's letter to the President along with the Committee's "Statement on Discussions with Communist China" were answered by Assistant Secretary of State Walter S. Robertson, but this letter is unavailable. Part of Robertson's response was printed in the Committee's undated "Information Bulletin," on p. 1: "The points to which the Statement calls attention are valid and timely. Our relationship with our staunch and loyal

free Chinese allies must not, and I believe will not, be sacrificed in any discussions which may eventuate between us and the Chinese Communists.''

34   *Idem.* (italics in original).

35   Undated "Information Bulletin,'' p. 2. Although a later Committee pamphlet said this letter was formally presented to the President, there is no evidence in the Eisenhower Library or the *New York Times* to confirm this point.

36   The seven: Reverend Dennis J. Comey, S.J.; Reverend Frederick A. McGuire, C.M.; His Eminence (Archbishop) Michael; Reverend Daniel A. Poling; Reverend Charles Ernest Scott; Most Reverend Theodotus S. DeWitow; and Bishop Herbert Welch.

37   See the *New York Times,* June 23, 1955, p. 4.

38   *Congressional Record,* 84C1, (1955), 101(17):A4990–91. For an account of U Nu's role earlier in 1955 to achieve a peacekeeping mission between the U.S. and the P.R.C., see Kenneth T. Young, *Negotiating with the Chinese Communists,* pp. 43–44.

39   Letter, Bryce N. Harlow to Walter H. Judd, July 11, 1955, Official File 116-V, White House Central Files, Eisenhower Library, The *Congressional Record* fails to reveal any *Newsweek* inclusion by Dr. Judd during this period.

40   Letter, Walter H. Judd to the President, July 14, 1955, Official File 116-V, White House Central Files, Eisenhower Library.

41   Letter, Dwight D. Eisenhower to Walter H. Judd, July 14, 1955, *ibid.*

42   Letter, Walter H. Judd to the President, August 9, 1955, and letter, Dwight D. Eisenhower to Walter H. Judd, August 10, 1955, *ibid.*

43   The announcement on July 25 that talks would begin August 1 was released one week before Congress adjourned. See *Department of State Bulletin* 33, no. 841 (August 8, 1955):219–20.

44   The complete text of the advertisement was inserted in the *Congressional Record* the following day by Senator Alexander Wiley (R., Wisc.), an original signer of the 1953 petition whose name did not appear on either the April 12 or the August 1, 1955 advertisement. See *Congressional Record,* 84C1 (1955), 101(10):12832–33. The *Times'* story on p. 3 carefully (and correctly) attributed the charges of Peking's involvement in narcotics to U.S. Commissioner of Narcotics Harry J. Anslinger, also reporting the Committee was using the charges as an argument against admission of mainland China to the United Nations.

45   *Ibid.,* pt. 1, p. 345.

46   *Ibid.,* pp. 348–49. The article relied on extensive quotations from Commissioner Anslinger and made these assertions: That the Chinese Communists were engaged ''in the massive and profitable export of narcotics to southeast Asia, Japan, and the United States''; that Anslinger had provided ''abundant proof that this flood of dope comes from Red China''; that the foreign sale of narcotics was supervised ''by the National Trading Co. of Peking, a state agency''; that by 1949 the Bureau of Narcotics had

realized that "the Communist smuggling operation had reached these shores"; that "the first big United States case involving Communist heroin came in January 1952"; and that "As long as the Chinese Communists keep dumping huge quantities of drugs on the underworld markets, no police effort is going to keep the stuff entirely out of the United States."

47 Undated "Information Bulletin," p. 1. The reprinted article, "Dope from Red China," by Rodney Gilbert, was taken from the magazine's September 1954 issue, pp. 16–17, 50–53. Showing a picture of Anslinger standing over a narcotics haul, the article made liberal use of Anslinger's previous statements.

48 Included were *all* senators and representatives listed in the April 12, 1955, advertisement, plus twelve additional representatives (but no senators) as follows: ten Republicans (E. Ross Adair, Ind.; Bruce Alger, Tex.; H. Carl Anderson, Minn.; Page Belcher, Okla.; Asher L. Burdick, N.D.; E. P. Farrington, Hawaii; Gerald R. Ford Jr., Mich.; Charles W. Gubser, Calif.; Carroll D. Kearns, Pa.; and Jack Westland, Wash.) and two Democrats (Robert T. Ashmore, S.C., and H. B. McDowell, Jr., Del.).

49 Alfred W. McCoy, with Cathleen B. Read and Leonard P. Adams II, *The Politics of Heroin in Southeast Asia* (New York: Harper & Row, 1972), pp. 145–48.

50 *Ibid.*, p. 148 (italics added).

51 Young, *Negotiating With the Chinese Communists*, p. 49. The first session of the 84th Congress adjourned on August 2, 1955.

52 *Congressional Record*, 84C1 (1955), 101(9):11485.

53 *Ibid.*, p. 11523.

54 *Ibid.*, p. 11763.

55 *Ibid.*, p. 11798. McCarthy did not request immediate consideration of S. Res. 141, only that it be referred to the Foreign Relations Committee. For a debate between him and the committee's chairman, Senator Walter F. George (D., Ga.), a supporter of the ambassadorial talks, see *ibid.*, pp. 11799–800.

56 *Ibid.*, pt. 10, p. 12585.

57 *Ibid.*, p. 12586.

58 *Ibid.*, p. 12692. Twelve years later, in 1967, Representative Zablocki would join the steering committee of The Committee of One Million.

6. "Strengthening Eisenhower's Hand"

1 Accompanied by a letter signed by steering committee members dated February 7, 1956, a copy of this newsletter was sent to Under-Secretary of State Herbert Hoover Jr. The newsletter was among the few Committee-related materials furnished me by the Records Services Division of the State Department.

2 H. Con. Res. 265 was brought to the House floor on July 18 by Congresswoman Edna F. Kelly (D., N.Y.), who signed the Committee's 1953 petition and a later advertisement. It was attached to a House report listing all previous congressional

expressions on the subject back to 1948. Expressing continued objection to any Chinese Communist participation in the world body, the resolution passed, 391 to 0, 41 not voting. See *Congressional Record,* 84C2 (1956), 102(10):13376–78. First in the Senate to speak on its behalf was Minority Leader Knowland, who emphasized the resolution's bipartisan support. The Senate vote was 86 to 0, ten not voting; see *ibid.,* pp. 13939–43. The following day, July 24, Dr. Judd extended his remarks to include in the Appendix a July 24 article from the *Washington Daily News* which reported the Committee's drive for identical planks in the party platforms and said the campaign was stimulated by apprehension that a "squeeze play" might seat the People's Republic in the United Nations after the November elections. See *ibid.,* Pt. 20, p. A5839.

3 Included in the advertisement was the Committee's proposed plank for the party platforms: "We oppose the seating of Communist China in the United Nations, thus upholding international morality and keeping faith with the thousands of American youths who gave their lives fighting Communist aggression in Korea. To seat a Communist China which defies, by word and deed, the principles of the United Nations Charter would be to betray the letter, violate the spirit, and subvert the purposes of that Charter. It would break faith with our dead and the unfortunate Americans wrongfully imprisoned by Communist China. It would betray our friend and ally, the Republic of China." Printed below the statement was a list of 180 "Congressional Sponsors" of the proposed plank (104 Republicans, 76 Democrats). See advertisement, "An Appeal to the Democratic and Republican Conventions: Keep Red China Out of the U.N.," Box 11, MLC.

The Republican platform came closest to the Committee's proposed plank, using two complete sentences and part of a third (in italics) as follows: "We continue to oppose the seating of Communist China in the United Nations, *thus upholding international morality. To seat a Communist China which defies, by word and deed, the principles of the United Nations Charter would be to betray the letter, violate the spirit and subvert the purposes of that Charter. It would betray our friend and ally, the Republic of China.* We will continue our determined efforts to free the remaining Americans held prisoner by Communist China."

The Democratic platform used none of the Committee's phrasing: "We pledge determined opposition to the admission of the Communist Chinese into the United Nations. They have proven their complete hostility to the purpose of this organization. We pledge continued support to Nationalist China. We urge a continuing effort to effect the release of all Americans detained by Communist China." See Kirk H. Porter and Donald Bruce Johnson, *National Party Platforms 1840–1960* (Urbana: University of Illinois Press, 1961), p. 525 (Democratic) and p. 557 (Republican).

4 See letter, Marvin Liebman to Stanley K. Hornbeck, August 22, 1956, and "draft statement for Dr. Hornbeck to present to the Democratic Platform Committee," undated, Box 121, Stanley K. Hornbeck Collection, Hoover Institution Archives.

5 Joseph C. Grew, *Invasion Alert* (Baltimore: Maran, 1956), p. vi. The back cover invites readers to write the Committee for additional copies. The cover is subtitled "Red China Drives on the UN."

6   The story in the *Times,* on page 3, said the book was published under the auspices of the Committee, while the *Daily News* editorial, later reprinted on Committee letterhead as a broadside, carried an inset photograph of Ambassador Grew.

7   For this exchange of correspondence, see General File 105-Q-Con "L," White House Central Files, Eisenhower Library. On March 9, 1972, Mr. Lockett replied to a query of mine that his ghost job on *Invasion Alert* was the only writing assignment ever undertaken for the Committee, which reported that the book had been translated, in whole or in part, into eighteen languages.

8   The others were former Ambassadors Stanley K. Hornbeck and Warren Austin; Senators Paul H. Douglas, H. Alexander Smith, Mike Mansfield, Ralph E. Flanders, and Karl Mundt; and Representatives Walter H. Judd, Francis E. Walter, and Joseph W. Martin Jr. More than 500 independent radio stations were said to have cooperated. See "A Brief History of an Authentic and Effective People's Movement," undated Committee pamphlet covering the years 1953 through 1965, p. 5.

9   *Congressional Record,* 84C2 (1956), 102(4):4688–89.

10   *Ibid.,* p. 4688.

11   Letter, Paul H. Douglas, Charles Edison, Joseph C. Grew, Walter H. Judd, H. Alexander Smith, and Francis E. Walter to "Dear Friend," June 1, 1956, General File 119 "C," White House Central Files, Eisenhower Library. An account of the decision to postpone the eleventh regular session of the General Assembly is found in *United Nations Review,* June 1956, 2(12):1–2. Briefly, a postponement proposal was offered by Chile, Cuba, and Ecuador on March 26, 1956. Secretary-General Dag Hammarskjöld then requested his office be notified of the member nations' wishes by April 30, at which time 54 nations had replied: 51 concurred, one objected, and two were willing to postpone the session but preferred opening at the usual time.

12   *Congressional Record,* 84C2 (1956), 102(8):11325–26. The letter's purpose, said the senator, was to ask the Secretary of State to disclose the identity of officials issuing stories about U.S. inability to exclude the People's Republic from the next session of the General Assembly.

13   Letter, Marvin Liebman to "Steering Committee and Members," November, 1956, Box 11, MLC.

14   The Committee's fifth newsletter printed a "correction" of this statement: "We have been informed that this statement is erroneous. The National Director of Americans For Democratic Action has stated that 'ADA has taken no action whatever to bring about recognition of Communist China or its admission to the UN.' We deeply regret our incorrect interpretation of the ADA's stand. We are happy to be informed that this nationwide liberal movement does *not* favor the admission of Communist China to the UN or the recognition of the Peiping regime by our Government" (italics in original).

15   The Chamber's president, John S. Coleman, said that trade should be on the same basis as the nonstrategic trade with the Soviet Union and her European satellites.

See *New York Times,* November 19, 1956, p. 25. For coverage of Liebman's reply, see *New York Times,* November 23, 1956, p. 9.

16   The exact date of this mailing is unclear. Later, the Committee claimed a circulation of 35,000 for its newsletter.

17   See *Department of State Bulletin* 36, no. 922 (February 25, 1957):301–2. Dulles' answer, in effect, was that the People's Republic was holding imprisoned Americans illegally as a means of pressure by which to get handchosen reporters to visit the Chinese mainland.

18   See *China and U.S Far East Policy 1945–1967* (Washington D.C.: Congressional Quarterly Service, 1967), p. 79. Dulles was asked to comment on Senator Green's remarks at a February 19 news conference. He said that it was premature to be talking about recognition, that we should not forget too fast that the Communists fought the United States and the United Nations in Korea, that America suffered 150,000 casualties, and that the Communists prevented a political settlement, seized Tibet, fomented war in Indochina, threatened war against Taiwan, and held people in prison. See *Department of State Bulletin* 36, no. 924 (March 11, 1957):404–5.

19   *Congressional Record Appendix,* 85C1 (1957), 103(16):A1278–80.

20   *Department of State Bulletin* 36, no. 927 (April 1, 1957):531–32.

21   *Congressional Record,* 85C1 (1957), 103(3):3625. Senator Bridges yielded to Senator Knowland, who referred him to Dulles' China policy statement from Canberra. Similarly, Senator H. Alexander Smith pointed to Dulles' "corrective announcement" from, he erred, the Philippines; *idem.*

22   *Department of State Bulletin* 36, no. 953 (May 13, 1957):772–73. Earlier, on April 4, Secretary of Commerce Sinclair Weeks hinted of possible change in the administration's policy, saying he found "some merit" in the desire of other allied countries for relaxation of the ban. See *China and U.S. Far East Policy 1945–1967,* p. 80.

23   Letter, Paul H. Douglas, Charles Edison, Walter H. Judd, H. Alexander Smith, and Francis E. Walter to "Dear Friend," May 13, 1957, General File 105-Q Con "C," White House Central Files, Eisenhower Library.

24   See "A Brief History of an Authentic and Effective People's Movement," p. 6, which reports that "Relations Between the United States and Communist China" was published in March, 1957, indicating the memorandum may have been updated and revised for the May mailing.

25   Letter, Stanley K. Hornbeck to Marvin Liebman, May 14, 1957, Box 121, Stanley K. Hornbeck Collection, Hoover Institution Archives.

26   Initially published by Columbia University's Graduate School of Business in December 1956, *The United States and the Far East* consisted of background papers prepared for the meeting. The "Final Report" (pp. 221–26) said that recognition of Peking "would not be appropriate or timely," but that nonrecognition "must be continuously reappraised." Liberalization of trade was advocated. One of the 58 participants, incidentally, was Committee supporter Hornbeck.

27 *Department of State Bulletin* 36, no. 938 (June 17, 1957):967–68. The statement made clear the United States would continue a total embargo on trade against mainland China.

28 Memorandum and advertising page proof, steering committee, June 6, 1957, General File 105-Q Con "C," White House Central Files, Eisenhower Library.

29 The Committee's congressional supporters were active on the Hill as well. On May 31, Senator Knowland deplored the British decision to lift the embargo on certain materials many of which, he said, should be considered strategic "by any rule of reason." See *Congressional Record*, 85C1 (1957), 103(6):8127–28. Senator Edward J. Thye (R., Minn.) included among the Committee's June 9 advertisement's "members," inserted in the June 19 *Record* a speech in which he had argued for maintenance of the trade embargo against the People's Republic until all American prisoners there were released. See *ibid.*, pt. 7, pp. 9754–55. The House debated the trade issue on June 28. Congressman Robert C. Byrd (D., W. Va.), a Committee supporter, said the developing pressure for trade with the Chinese Communists was one further step into the "quicksands of appeasement," but Dr. Judd, agreeing with Byrd, said few people actually wanted reconsideration of the present policy. See *ibid.*, pt. 8, pp. 10576–88. On July 12, Judd put in the *Record* a *Saturday Evening Post* editorial, "Trading With Red China Isn't Necessarily Realistic," which quoted the Committee as a source for the assertion that 25 million people were enslaved on the mainland. See *Congressional Record Appendix*, 85C1 (1957), 103(20):A5619.

30 *New York Times*, June 11, 1957, p. 4. The statement was addressed "to all free men," the story said, and was aimed at the nations planning to drop trade restrictions.

31 Letter and enclosures, Marvin Liebman to Howard P. Jones, June 13, 1957, Records Services Division, State Department. According to "A Brief History of an Authentic and Effective People's Movement," pp. 6–7, the Committee launched a postcard campaign, aimed especially at Committee Chairman Warren Magnuson (D., Wash.), and President Eisenhower, to protest any U.S. trade with Communist China. No evidence of any hearings on this subject by the Senate Committee on Interstate and Foreign Commerce during the 85th Congress was found.

32 Letter, Marvin Liebman to Dwight D. Eisenhower, July 11, 1957, and Statement to President Eisenhower (for release to the press July 16, 1957), General File 122 China-Communist, White House Central Files, Eisenhower Library. Of the 176 names, only 7, including steering committee members Charles Edison and Frederick C. McKee, were included among the names appearing in the Committee's June 9 advertisement in the International Edition of the *New York Times*.

33 Memorandum, Fisher Howe to A. J. Goodpaster, with "Suggested Reply" attached, July 30, 1957, Records Services Division, State Department and letter, Sherman Adams to Marvin Liebman, July 31, 1957, General File 122 China-Communist, White House Central Files, Eisenhower Library.

34 "Confidential Report," Marvin Liebman to steering committee, undated 1957 document, p. 1. This document is the sole source of information about the secretary's travels.

35 I am indebted to the Bureau of Charitable and Proprietary Organizations, New York State Board of Social Welfare, for its cooperation and assistance.

36 Letter and advertising page proof from International Edition of the *New York Times,* Marvin Liebman to Walter S. Robertson, September 30, 1957, Records Services Division, State Department. *Western World* was a bilingual transatlantic magazine published in Brussels, Belgium, from 1957 through 1959, which featured articles by politicians and political commentators about events affecting NATO countries.

37 Letter, Walter S. Robertson to Marvin Liebman, October 4, 1957, Records Services Division, State Department.

38 Kenneth T. Young, *Negotiating with the Chinese Communists: The United States Experience, 1953–1967* (New York: McGraw-Hill, published for The Council on Foreign Relations, 1968). See chs. 4, 5, and 6 for a discussion of the first 73 meetings and pp. 130–34 for a discussion of the proposals for an exchange of newsmen.

39 See *Department of State Bulletin* 35, no. 895 (August 20, 1956):313–14. Newsmen continued to needle Dulles on this issue, observing that since the Secretary of State controlled the issuing of passports the American press was placed in the position of covering foreign news at the sufferance of the Secretary of State. Three U.S. newsmen later defied the passport ban and traveled to the Chinese mainland.

40 For the texts, see *Department of State Bulletin* 33, no. 847 (September 19, 1955):456–57.

41 See *ibid.* 37, no. 942 (July 15, 1957):91–95.

42 Asked at a July 2 news conference whether he meant international communism or communism in China was in a "passing and not a perpetual phase," Dulles replied, in part: "I meant primarily the type of communism that is now reflected by what we call international communism. I do not think that it is by any means safe to predict that in every country in the world there may not be some form of socialism, because Communist regimes practice what they call socialism, really. . . ." See *ibid.,* no. 943 (July 22, 1957):139–45, for this and other answers to questions about the speech.

43 Letter and enclosures, Marvin Liebman to Dwight D. Eisenhower, May 16, 1958, Records Services Division, State Department; and letter and enclosures, Marvin Liebman to Sherman Adams, May 16, 1958, General File 142-F-1, White House Central Files, Eisenhower Library.

44 See *Congressional Record,* 85C2 (1958), 104(3):3004–7; pt. 5, pp. 6218–19; pt. 20, pp. A3172–73. The date of Representative Walter's extension of remarks was April 2, 1958. The advertisement was headlined: "Building Communism's Military Machine—with the hands of Non-Communists . . . An Appeal to Sanity."

45 *Ibid.,* pt. 5, pp. 6351–52. The editorial, "Trading With Red China," drew a parallel between the Chinese action in calling off further negotiations on trade and the then suspended Sino-American ambassadorial talks. Until the Americans provided a negotiator with ambassadorial rank (to replace the transferred U. Alexis Johnson), the Chinese would not resume the talks. The object, here as with the Japanese, the editorial said, was "face," not negotiations.

46   Letter, Douglas Dillon to Marvin Liebman, May 23, 1958, Records Services Division, State Department.

47   Letter, Sherman Adams to Marvin Liebman, May 19, 1958, General File 142-F-1, White House Central Files, Eisenhower Library.

48   Edison's support was acknowledged by Liebman in a 1961 memorandum to his associates. See memorandum, Marvin Liebman to "Staff and Associates," January 1961, Box 16, MLC.

49   News release, "Committee Calls Chinese Withdrawal from Korea Phoney . . . ," Box 10, MLC. The Chinese were withdrawing from North Korea because of unrest in Communist China, the release stated.

50   *New York Times,* May 19, 1958, p. 19.

51   *Ibid.,* July 15, 1958, p. 7. The story was positioned under another article which claimed the People's Republic was pressing the United States for an immediate reply on resumption of the Geneva talks.

52   Paul H. Douglas, "Should We Recognize Red China?" *The New Leader,* July 21–28, 1958, pp. 7–8. Douglas said that to recognize Red China and admit the country to the United Nations "would be to invite disaster." The Committee later reported that 30,000 reprints of this article were distributed in the United States and abroad. (Two years earlier, Senator Douglas had published a similar article in *The New Leader,* "Why the United States Should Bar Red China."

53   *Department of State Bulletin* 39, no. 1002 (September 8, 1958):385–90.

54   See Edward Hunter, *The Black Book on Red China* (New York: A Free Enterprise Publication distributed by The Bookmailer, Inc., 1958). The inside front cover says the book was prepared by Mr. Hunter for the Committee in cooperation with International Research on Communist Techniques, Inc.

55   Letter and enclosure of Grew article, Marvin Liebman to John Foster Dulles, May 16, 1958, Records Services Division, Department of State. Liebman added that the article had been distributed by the North American Newspaper Alliance on September 14.

56   Draft letter, September 29, 1958, Box 11, MLC.

57   "A Brief History of an Authentic and Effective People's Movement," p. 8.

58   *New York Times,* January 19, 1959, p. 22. This article was inserted in the *Congressional Record* on January 27 by Senator Styles H. Bridges (R., N.H.). See *Congressional Record Appendix,* 86C1 (1959), 105(18):A542.

59   Letter and enclosures, Paul H. Douglas, Charles Edison, Joseph C. Grew, Walter H. Judd, H. Alexander Smith, and Francis E. Walter to "Dear Friend," February 17, 1959, Records Services Division, Department of State.

60   "A Brief History of an Authentic and Effective People's Movement," p. 9.

61   "Memorandum of Conversation Three Telephone Conversations," Ernest H. Fisk and Marvin Liebman, April 1, 2, 3, 1959, Records Services Division, Department of State. Various notations on this two-page document indicate that it may have been

declassified on December 20, 1971, after my December 3, 1971 inquiry to the Department.

62 "A Brief History of an Authentic and Effective People's Movement," p. 9.

63 *Congressional Record Appendix,* 86C1 (1959), 105(21):A3957.

64 Letter, Marvin Liebman to "Dear Friend," June 3, 1959, Box 6, MLC. Ultimately the decision was reversed.

65 See chapter 4, note 40.

66 Letter, Paul H. Douglas, Charles Edison, Joseph C. Grew, Walter H. Judd, Francis E. Walter to Henry Cabot Lodge, October 20, 1959, Records Services Division, Department of State. A "P.S." explained that former Senator Smith, an active member of the steering committee, was working as a special advisor to the Department of State and felt he should not sign the letter. Smith was named chairman, with the rank of ambassador, to the eleventh meeting of the Columbo Plan nations in Indonesia. The appointment was announced on October 26, 1959, but Smith remained on the steering committee. See *Department of State Bulletin* 41, no. 1064 (November 16, 1959):51 (1064):733.

67 Letter, Henry Cabot Lodge to Paul H. Douglas, October 27, 1959, Records Services Division, Department of State.

68 Letter, Marvin Liebman to Walter H. Judd, July 18, 1962, Box 4, MLC.

7. Stirrings in Congress and Elsewhere

1 *Congressional Record,* 86C1 (1959), 105(1):1291.

2 On the controversy over the newsmen's passports, cf., beginning in 1957, in *ibid.,* 85C1, 103 (1957): Senator A. S. Mike Monroney (D., Okla.), pp. 1841–42; Senator Hubert H. Humphrey (D., Minn.), pp. 1847–51 and pp. 15736–37; Senator Thomas C. Hennings Jr. (D. Mo.), pp. 3440–41; Senator J. William Fulbright (D. Ark.), p. 15264; Representative George S. McGovern (D., S.D.), p. 15959; and Representative Robert W. Hemphill (D., S.C.). On the trade issue in the same session, see Representative Thomas M. Pelly (R., Wash.), p. 9049 and Representative Charles O. Porter (D., Ore.), p. 15083. Other China policy questions were raised during this session by Representative Stewart L. Udall, (D., Ariz.), pp. A1885–86 and p. A4318 and Senator Wayne Morse (D., Ore), p. A5375. In 1958, cf. in *ibid.,* 85C2 (1958), 104: Senator J. William Fulbright (D., Ark.), pp. 8295–96 and A6904–06 and Representative Charles O. Porter (D., Ore.), p. 17675. Also, prior to Senator Wiley's initiative, see the remarks and inclusions of Senator Frank Church (D., Ida.), *ibid.,* 86C1 (1959), 105(1):1094–96, and his speech March 20, 1959, pp. 4734–36.

3 For an early example, see *ibid.,* 85C1 (1957), 103(11):15245–46.

4 *Ibid.,* 86C1 (1959), 105(7):8760–67.

5 *Ibid.,* pp. 8762–69. The other senators were Joseph S. Clark (D. Pa.), Albert Gore (D., Tenn.), Russell B. Long (D., La.), William Proxmire (D., Wisc.), and Wayne Morse (D., Ore.).

6   *Ibid.*, pp. 9363–65.

7   Ibid., pp. 9913–20, and pt. 8, pp. 10131–37.

8   *Ibid.*, pt. 12, pp. 16083–94.

9   *Department of State Bulletin* 41, no. 1057 (September 28, 1959); 460. Also confirmed as delegates were Ambassador Lodge, Walter S. Robertson, and George Meany. Alternates included Charles W. Anderson Jr., Virgil M. Hancher, Erle Cocke Jr., Mrs. Oswald B. Lord, and Harold Riegelman.

10   "Tensions in Communist China," S. Doc. 66, 86C1, (Washington: G.P.O., 1960). On September 11, 1959, S. Res. 186, calling for 1,000 additional copies of the study for use by the Senate Foreign Relations Committee, passed the Senate without debate. See *Congressional Record*, 86C1 (1959), 105(15):19101. Senator Wiley discussed the report on several occasions during the next congressional session. See *ibid.*, 86C2 (1960), 106 (1, 3, 17):744–45, 3174–76, and A947.

11   "United States Foreign Policy in Asia," Study No. 5, *United States Foreign Policy: Compilation of Studies*, 87C1, S. Doc. 24 (Washington: G.P.O., 1961), pp. 391–551. Thirteen studies, prepared by outside organizations for the Senate Foreign Relations Committee, are included. Richard P. Conlon, president, Conlon Associates, Ltd., reports in his letter of transmittal (p. 395) that the Asian study was conducted by himself, Mr. Leon Sloss, and three University of California professors: Richard L. Park, Guy J. Pauker, and Robert A. Scalapino.

12   Press release, "The Committee of One Million," November 4, 1959, Box 22, MLC.

13   Letter, Marvin Liebman to "Dear Friend," November 9, 1959, Box 121, Stanley K. Hornbeck Collection, Hoover Institution Archives.

14   Letter, Marvin Liebman to Richard J. Shepard, August 7, 1962, Box 16, MLC.

15   Only the examination reports for these five years were located. See Boxes 11, 22, 23, MLC.

16   See Registration Statement, "The Committee Of One Million," received August 14, 1959, New York State Department of Social Welfare.

17   See Field Audit Report of Charitable Organizations, The Committee of One Million Against the Admission of Communist China to the United Nations (Reg. No. 7351), November 20, 1963 (date of audit), New York State Board of Social Welfare, pp. 1–6. The discussion in the text, including Table 7.1, is based on official records of this agency.

18   "Report on 1958," steering committee to "Members and Friends," undated, Records Services Division, State Department.

19   Letter, Marvin Liebman to Clark M. Eichelberger, February 24, 1959, MLC.

20   Following is a partial reconstruction based on a series of documents located in Box 8, MLC. In part, this discussion refers to unavailable documents. (For example, although Liebman's copy of his May 26, 1960, letter to Secretary of the Treasury Ander-

son was not located, Liebman himself quoted extensively from it in a subsequent letter to Eichelberger.)

21   Letter, Marvin Liebman to Walter H. Judd, August 11, 1960, Box 8, MLC. As to Liebman's comment about IPR's tax-exempt status, I am indebted to W. L. Holland, editor of *Pacific Affairs,* for the following facts: In the aftermath of the 1951–1952 McCarran Internal Security Subcommittee hearings and report about IPR activities, the organization lost its tax exempt status in 1955 and sued in 1957 for recovery of 1955 taxes. On March 31, 1960 (two months before Liebman's letter to Secretary Anderson), a U.S. District Court ruled, in effect, that the IPR was an educational organization entitled to tax exemption under the law. Later, both the International IPR and the American IPR were dissolved, some of the former's assets, including *Pacific Affairs,* moving to the University of British Columbia, some of the latter's, including *Far Eastern Survey* (now *Asian Survey*) moving to the University of California.

22   Identical memoranda, Marvin Liebman to William F. Buckley Jr., George E. Sokolsky, Frank Hannigan, and Roy W. Howard, May 26, 1960, Box 8, MLC. Liebman's letter to Secretary Anderson got some attention in the *National Review Bulletin,* June 11, 1960, pp. 4–5. "Why is the [Committee] denied tax-exemption privileges for supporting U.S. Government policies in the Far East," the item said, "while the American Association for the United Nations and the Institute of Pacific Relations enjoy the privileges of tax-exemption while publicly campaigning for a change in such policy?" In this same Box 8 file is another clipping of a news story from an unidentified newspaper which summarizes Liebman's charges and quotes him as denying the Committee had engaged in lobbying to influence legislation—the reason most often cited by the I.R.S. for denying tax-exemption.

23   Identical letters, Marvin Liebman to Francis E. Walter and James O. Eastland, May 26, 1960, Box 8, MLC.

24   Letter, Harold L. Swartz to Committee, attention Marvin Liebman, August 22, 1960, Box 8, MLC. The applicable code: section 501(c) (3) 1954 Code. As cited by Swartz, the four tests included: "1. It [the organization] must be organized exclusively for one or more of the purposes specified in the section ["educational" was one]; 2. Its net income must not inure in whole or in part to the benefit of private shareholders or individuals; 3. It must not by any substantial part of its activities attempt to influence legislation by propaganda or otherwise; and 4. It must not participate, or intervene, in any political campaign on behalf of any candidate for public office." Swartz added that "an organization is not educational if its principal function is the mere presentation of unsupported opinion."

25   Letter, Marvin Liebman to Paul H. Douglas, July 5, 1960, Box 8, MLC.

26   Letter, Marvin Liebman to Walter H. Judd, August 11, 1960, Box 8, MLC.

27   Draft and edited letters, Marvin Liebman to Clark M. Eichelberger, August 29, 1960; letter, Frank W. McCulloch to Marvin Liebman, August 31, 1960; letter, Marvin Liebman to Frank W. McCulloch, September 7, 1960; and letter, Marvin Liebman to Robert B. Anderson, September 14, 1960, Box 8, MLC.

28   Letter, Marvin Liebman to Charles Edison, December 9, 1960, MLC. Some years later Liebman responded to an inquiry by a New York resident on this subject. See chapter 10, note 95.

29   Forrest Davis and Robert Hunter, *The Red China Lobby* (New York: Fleet, 1963). The Committee is not identified either in the preliminary pages or the text as being associated with the book's preparation or publication.

30   See Ross Koen, "Two Postscripts to the McCarran Hearings," in *Bulletin of Concerned Asian Scholars,* May 1969, 1(4):27–31; and Paul A. Marsh, "The Macmillan Company and Ross Koen's 'The China Lobby in American Politics,' " *Canadian Far Eastern Newsletter,* April 1970, 22(218):4–6.

31   Memorandum, Marvin Liebman to Priscilla Buckley, March 24, 1960, Box 11, MLC.

32   Paul A. Marsh, "Macmillan Company and Ross Koen's 'China Lobby,' " p. 5. In the 1974 paperback edition of Koen's book, the reference remains, slightly amended as follows: "There is, for example, evidence that some Chinese have engaged in the illegal smuggling of narcotics into the United States with the full knowledge and connivance of members of the Chinese Nationalist Government." See Ross Y. Koen, *The China Lobby in American Politics,* edited and with an introduction by Richard C. Kagan (New York: Harper & Row, 1974), p. xxi. In the original manuscript printed by Macmillan, "a number of" replaced the word "some" in the above sentence.

33   Paul A. Marsh, "Macmillan Company and Ross Koen's 'China Lobby,' " p. 6.

34   Letter, Marvin Liebman to Stanley K. Hornbeck, January 29, 1960, Box 121, Stanley K. Hornbeck Collection, Hoover Institution Archives. Also, in *ibid.,* see memorandum, "A Study of the Red China Lobby." By coincidence, Liebman's letter to Hornbeck was written within a week of a story about the Committee in the *Nation* entitled "Lobby of a Million Ghosts" by John O'Kearney, in which the secretary was quoted as saying, "If there is a China Lobby, we are it." See the *Nation,* January 23, 1960, p. 76.

35   Letters, Stanley K. Hornbeck to Marvin Liebman, February 1 and 2, 1960, Box 11, MLC.

36   Letter, Marvin Liebman to Stanley K. Hornbeck, February 10, 1960, Box 121, Stanley K. Hornbeck Collection, Hoover Institution Archives.

37   Letter, Walter S. Robertson to Marvin Liebman, February 5, 1960, Box 11, MLC.

38   Letter, Marvin Liebman to J. G. Sourwine, February 9, 1960, Box 11, MLC.

39   *New York Times,* May 5, 1962, p. 18. Davis was a columnist and editorial writer for the *Cincinnati Enquirer* while he worked on *The Red China Lobby.*

40   Letter, Marvin Liebman to Forrest Davis, February 16, 1960, Box 11, MLC.

41   Memorandum, Forrest Davis to Marvin Liebman, undated, Box 11, MLC.

42 See copy of letter, A. L. Hart Jr., to Ross Y. Koen, March 22, 1960, furnished to me by Professor Paul A. Marsh, Evergreen State College, Olympia, Washington.

43 Letter, Marvin Liebman to Alfred Kohlberg, February 26, 1960, Box 11, MLC. The Pew family was associated with the Sun Oil Company. J. Howard Pew joined the company in 1901, served as president from 1912 to 1947, then became a director. Letters, Marvin Liebman to J. Howard Pew, February 29, 1960, and March 29, 1960; and letter, J. Howard Pew to Marvin Liebman, April 1, 1960, Box 11, MLC.

44 Letter, Marvin Liebman to Alfred Kohlberg, April 4, 1960, Box 11, MLC. The ups and downs of getting the book published are suggested by other materials in Box 11. Apparently Liebman failed to get sufficient financing in 1960 and lost interest until 1961. See, for example, his letter to Davis, October 20, 1960, *ibid.*

45 Joseph Keeley, *The China Lobby Man* (New Rochelle, N.Y.: Arlington House, 1969), p. 148. A month before he died, according to this account, Kohlberg had written a lengthy critique of Ross Koen's book. At a testimonial dinner in Kohlberg's honor on July 26, 1960, which Marvin Liebman would help organize as part of a campaign to raise money for an Alfred Kohlberg Memorial Fund, author William F. Buckley Jr., concluded his remarks: "Mr. Kohlberg's efforts will be unceasing. That *is* inevitable. We shall not hear the end of him. I count that among the certitudes that govern my existence. If any of us ever strays, to find himself in the shadow of hell, we will find a letter pinned on the gates, addressed to us by name, copy to the *New York Times.* 'Before you go any further,' Alfred Kohlberg will have written, 'are you aware that Satan has belonged to 23 Communist fronts?' " See *ibid.,* p. xx (italics in original). Indeed, it *will* be some time before mere mortals hear the end of Alfred Kohlberg. His papers were acquired by the Hoover Institution in 1961 but will not be available for research until after May 1, 1991.

46 Letters, Marvin Liebman to Paul H. Douglas, March 24, 1960, and Marvin Liebman to Charles Edison, March 24, 1960, MLC.

47 Letter and enclosed pamphlet, Marvin Liebman to "Dear Friend," April 6, 1960, Box 22, MLC. "The American Role in Pacific Asian Affairs," originally delivered as a speech before the Wisconsin Bar Association, was published in *Department of State Bulletin* 42, no. 1081 (March 14, 1960):404–10.

48 In the speech, Parsons had offered a point-by-point refutation of what he termed "a variant of an often-proposed solution known as the 'two Chinas' policy." But he also said he shared the conclusion of the recently released Rockefeller Brothers Fund statement on mainland China, which had said that short-run policy alternatives were "lacking in creative possibilities." Still, the Rockefeller report had called for "candid recognition" of the realities of Peking's position and had acknowledged an urgent need for first hand information about the Communist revolution. For the full statement, see *New York Times,* December 8, 1959, pp. 1, 24.

49 Memorandum, Marvin Liebman to "members," April 19, 1960, MLC. The letterhead would read: Honorary Co-Chairmen, Warren R. Austin, Joseph C. Grew; Steering Committee: Paul H. Douglas, Charles Edison, Walter H. Judd, Kenneth B.

Keating, H. Alexander Smith, Francis E. Walter; Treasurer, Frederick C. McKee; Assistant Treasurer, B. A. Garside; Secretary, Marvin Liebman.

50 Letter, Marvin Liebman to Paul H. Douglas, May 24, 1960, MLC. Douglas' name did appear on the proof of an advertisement containing the proposed plank and the names of 250 congressional endorsers.

51 Memorandum, Marvin Liebman to steering committee, June 8, 1960, Box 4, MLC. Liebman's correspondence includes the first page only of a longer letter, on Committee letterhead, dated June 16, 1960, to Senator Douglas, which indicates the writer was displeased in general with the manner in which arrangements for the Democratic Party's platform committee hearings were being conducted.

52 Letter and attached advertising proof, Marvin Liebman to "Dear Friend," June 28, 1960, General File 109-A-9, White House Central Files, Eisenhower Library.

53 Memorandum, Marvin Liebman to "Members and Friends," August 5, 1960, MLC. In 1956, during its pre-convention drive for joint planks, the Committee received 180 congressional endorsements.

54 Committee advertisement, September 18, 1960, International Edition, *New York Times,* General File 105-Con"C," White House Central Files, Eisenhower Library.

55 Letters, Marvin Liebman to Joseph C. Grew, October 3, 1960, and Joseph C. Grew to Marvin Liebman, October 5, 1960, MLC.

56 *New York Times,* October 10, 1960, p. 3.

57 Memorandum, Marvin Liebman to "Staff and Associates," October 1, 1960, Box 16, MLC.

58 Letterhead of the fund, *ibid.,* lists the honorary chairman as Herbert Hoover. George E. Sokolsky was chairman, George E. Armstrong and Karl A. Wittfogel, vice-chairmen; Frederick G. Reinicke, treasurer; and B. A. Garside, secretary.

59 See Charles Lam Markmann, *The Buckleys* (New York: Morrow, 1973), pp. 168–72. According to this account, Liebman helped formulate the principles (known as "The Sharon Statement") under which the YAF was organized.

60 Liebman offered the book to several Hollywood producers, including Samuel Goldwyn. See letter, Marvin Liebman to Samuel Goldwyn, September 20, 1960, Box 12, MLC.

8. Adjusting to Democrats

1 Memorandum, Marvin Liebman to "Staff and Associates," January 1961, Box 16, MLC. Admiral Radford was chairman of the Joint Chiefs of Staff from 1953 to his retirement in 1957. His name began appearing on Committee letterheads as a "member" in 1959.

2 The actual vote was Durno (97,614), Porter (92,563), a 51.3 percent majority. Mr. Porter is unaware of any special work the Committee may have done in his district

during this campaign, reporting only that his opponent capitalized on "my 'wanting to get in bed with Mao Tse-tung.' " Letter, Charles O. Porter to me, September 30, 1974.

3 *China and U.S. Far East Policy 1945–1967* (Washington D.C.: Congressional Quarterly Service, 1967), p. 100.

4 Richard M. Nixon, *Six Crises* (New York: Doubleday, 1962), pp. 408–9.

5 In 1951, Henry R. Luce headed the board of directors of the China Institute of America. For this and other facts relating to the Institute's status, see *Congressional Quarterly Weekly Report, Special Supplement* 9, no. 25-A (June 29, 1951):946–47. For the Committee pamphlet, "The United States and China," see Box 22, MLC. A Committee contributor from Pennsylvania took objection to the pamphlet, writing that Rusk's later statements and published remarks about China should have been included. Liebman replied the pamphlet was a "tactical move," that there was little reason to believe Rusk supported a firm anti-Red China policy, but the Committee hoped to be able to force him to confirm his former stand during the Senate's confirmation hearings.

6 Rusk's 1951 speech, delivered while Americans fought Chinese in Korea, was implacably hostile to the People's Republic: "We do not recognize the authorities in Peiping for what they pretend to be. . . . It is not the Government of China. It does not pass the first test. It is not Chinese."

7 Letter, Marvin Liebman to Paul H. Douglas, December 14, 1960, Box 4, MLC.

8 Telegram, Paul H. Douglas to Marvin Liebman, December 27, 1960, MLC. In his memoirs, Paul H. Douglas, *In the Fullness of Time* (New York: Harcourt Brace Jovanovich, 1971), p. 493, the senator offers only one brief glimpse of the Committee: "While the members . . . were chiefly domestic conservatives, I saw no harm in co-operating with them as long as they were loyal Americans. I insisted, though, that they accept no money from Chiang Kai-shek or his agents. We were mutually uneasy in this alliance, but they treated me decently. Perhaps my contribution was to impart a saner view about the motives of most of those who differed with us on China."

9 Letter, Marvin Liebman to Paul H. Douglas, December 27, 1960, Box 4, MLC.

10 Committee advertisement, *Washington Post,* February 20, 1961, p. A12. The statement was an exact duplicate of the 1960 "joint planks" statement.

11 The list of endorsers included one less name, for a total of 338, than the February 20 advertisement (Congressman Harold D. Cooley [D., N.C.] was missing). Congressman Zablocki said the statement had been circulated by the Committee. See *Congressional Record,* 87C1 (1961), 107(4):5372–74.

12 *Ibid.,* pt. 1, pp. 930, 1267.

13 See House Concurrent Resolutions 222, 233, 288, 291, 292, 293, 294, 302, 303, 349; and House Resolutions 260, 272, 273, and 298, in *Congressional Record Index,* 87C1 (1961), 107(17):157.

14 *Congressional Record,* 87C1 (1961), 107(5):5731–32.

15   *Ibid.,* pp. 5917, 5918.

16   *Ibid.,* pt. 6, p. 7049. The date was May 3, 1961. Dirksen said he was honored to submit the resolution on behalf of himself and Senator Mansfield. On May 9, Senator Styles Bridges (R., N.H.) placed in the *Record* the complete congressional history of resolutions passed on the question between 1951 and 1959. See *ibid.,* pp. 7598–99.

17   *Ibid.,* pt. 10, p. 13364.

18   *Ibid.,* pp. 13942–62. The House took up S. Con. Res. 34 on August 31, 1961, debating, then passing the resolution, 395 to 0; *ibid.,* pt. 13, pp. 17768–78.

19   *Ibid.,* pt. 12, pp. 16302, 16306.

20   Letter, Marvin Liebman to "Honorable Sir," enclosing pamphlet describing the Committee's history from 1953 to 1961, March 31, 1961, White House General File, John F. Kennedy Library. (The Kennedy Library materials are not otherwise coded for citation.)

21   Letter, Marvin Liebman to John F. Kennedy, March 15, 1961, Records Services Division, Department of State. Copies of the letter are indicated as having been sent to Secretary of State Rusk, Ambassador Stevenson, and Mrs. Roosevelt.

22   Letter, Harland Cleveland to Marvin Liebman, April 4, 1961, Records Services Division, Department of State.

23   "Confidential Memorandum," Marvin Liebman, April 5, 1961, Box 1, MLC. (No recipients were listed.)

24   Letter and enclosures, Marvin Liebman to Robert Morris, April 25, 1961, MLC.

25   The earliest dated congressional forwarding letter attached to petitions sent to the White House came from Representative Bruce Alger (R., Tex.), a Committee "member" representing (coincidentally) Dallas County. See forwarding memorandum, Bruce Alger to "The President," May 22, 1961, White House General File, John F. Kennedy Library. Most of the materials provided by the Kennedy Library relate to these petitions. From May 22, 1961, to April 17, 1962, there are petitions from Alger, Representatives John J. Rhodes (R., Ariz.), John P. Saylor (R., Pa.), Charles McC. Mathias Jr. (R., Md.), Charles S. Gubser (R., Calif.), and Senators Henry M. Jackson (D., Wash.) and John G. Tower (R., Tex.). Many petitions were acknowledged by White House assistants. Box 7, MLC, contains numerous letters from legislators indicating cooperation with the Committee's new petition campaign.

26   Letter and book outline, Marvin Liebman to Robert Hunter, April 13, 1961, MLC.

27   Forrest Davis and Robert Hunter, *The Red China Lobby* (New York: Fleet, 1963). On page 115, the authors summed up the first twenty-one months of the Kennedy administration's China policy, saying that American prestige in the Far East was at an all-time low, that a "two-Chinas" solution was the administration's aim, and that a policy best described as "strategic appeasement" was being followed.

28   Letter and chart, H. R. Wei to Marvin Liebman, April 24, 1961, MLC.

29   Invitation from Committee steering committee, Box 121, Stanley K. Hornbeck Collection, Hoover Institution Archives. A later Liebman memorandum added that U.S. Narcotics Commissioner Harry J. Anslinger was in the film and that 270 film prints had been circulated. See memorandum, Marvin Liebman to steering committee, January 3, 1962, MLC. An even later Committee pamphlet claimed 300 prints in distribution.

30   Letter, Paul H. Douglas to Marvin Liebman, May 16, 1961, MLC.

31   Douglas, *Fullness of Time,* p. 493.

32   Letter, Marvin Liebman to Paul H. Douglas, May 19, 1961, MLC.

33   Memorandum, Marvin Liebman to "Staff and Associates," January 1961, Box 16, MLC, p. 7. The memo said that ARCI had aided 23,910 refugees, 11,750 of whom had resettled in Taiwan.

34   The leadership of AECTR included Lowell Thomas, the noted commentator, and Dr. Judd, Justice William O. Douglas, and Dr. Magnus I. Gregerson.

35   Letter and enclosure, Helen Lin to Marvin Liebman, February 21, 1961, Box 20, MLC.

36   Letter and enclosure, Marvin Liebman to T. F. Tsiang, February 24, 1961, Box 20, MLC. For more on the Catawba Corporation, see Charles Lam Markmann, *The Buckleys* (New York: Morrow, 1973), pp. 28, 31, 36–39, 41.

37   Confidential memorandum, Marvin Liebman to Walter H. Judd, July 14, 1961, Box 18, MLC.

38   Letter, Marvin Liebman to T. F. Tsiang, July 20, 1961, Box 20, MLC.

39   Letter and enclosures, Marvin Liebman to T. F. Tsiang, August 10, 1961, Box 20, MLC.

40   Letter, Marvin Liebman to T. F. Tsiang, August 23, 1961, Box 20, MLC.

41   Letter, Marvin Liebman to T. F. Tsiang, September 11, 1961, Box 20, MLC.

42   Letter, Marvin Liebman to T. F. Tsiang, October 9, 1961, Box 20, MLC.

43   Letter, Marvin Liebman to T. F. Tsiang, November 13, 1961, Box 20, MLC.

44   See Markmann, *The Buckleys,* p. 325.

45   Letter, Marvin Liebman to John F. Kennedy, August 29, 1961, White House Central Files, John F. Kennedy Library.

46   Letter, McGeorge Bundy to Marvin Liebman, September 18, 1961, White House Central Files, John F. Kennedy Library. Accompanying materials indicate the letter was drafted at the State Department.

47   See the September 22, 1961 edition. The rally also was addressed by Dr. Judd, William F. Buckley Jr., and theologians Dr. Daniel A. Poling and Bishop John W. Comber. A special tape recording by Madame Chiang Kai-shek was played. In Congress on September 22, five days before adjournment, Representative Judd included in the *Record* the rally speech by Senator Dodd, while Representative Walter also included his own speech. See *Congressional Record,* 87C1 (1961), 107(16):20880–82. The day before adjournment, articles by Admiral Radford and Sena-

tor Goldwater on the same subject were inserted in the *Record*. See *ibid.*, pp. 21319–20, 21829–30. Also, see an address by Representative Walter the same day, *ibid.*, pp. 21453–54.

48 "Moratorium" was the name frequently used in diplomatic circles to describe the strategy of postponing the China question each year. Secretary of State Rusk acknowledged at a news conference that he helped invent the "moratorium" idea during his earlier service in the State Department. See *Department of State Bulletin* 45, no. 1151 (July 17, 1961):110.

49 *New York Times*, October 1, 1961, p. 40. *Ibid.*, October 5, 1961, p. 2.

50 "Confidential Memorandum," Marvin Liebman to Senators Dodd, Douglas, and Keating; Representatives Judd and Walter; Charles Edison; H. Alexander Smith; November 8, 1961, Box 23, MLC.

51 According to Roger Hilsman, who served the Kennedy administration first as director of the Bureau of Intelligence and Research in the State Department and then as Assistant Secretary of State for Far Eastern Affairs, President Chiang Kai-shek agreed to abstain on Outer Mongolia's admission because he was finally persuaded that a veto would have provoked African states into voting against the Republic of China on the China credentials question. See his *To Move a Nation* (Garden City, N.Y.: Doubleday, 1967), pp. 309–10.

52 Telegram, Marvin Liebman to Paul H. Douglas, November 16, 1961, Box 4, MLC.

53 Letter, Marvin Liebman to Adlai E. Stevenson, November 16, 1961, Box 7, MLC. Although Liebman said the Committee was planning to release the letter to the press on November 20, 1961, the *New York Times*, for one, failed to print such a story.

54 Letter, Adlai E. Stevenson to Marvin Liebman, November 28, 1961, Box 7, MLC.

55 See "Red China and the United Nations," by Adlai E. Stevenson, with an introduction by Walter H. Judd, Box 23, MLC. Judd's introduction included this comment: "Administrations may change, but facts do not. And the facts with respect to Red China's lack of qualifications for membership in the U.N. remain the same under President Kennedy as they had been under Presidents Truman and Eisenhower."

56 See Roger Hilsman, *To Move a Nation*, p. 310.

57 *New York Times*, December 16, 1961, pp. 1, 4.

58 Memorandum, Marvin Liebman to steering committee, January 3, 1962, MLC. Liebman remarked that the fight was certainly not over, pointing out that the *New York Times*, on December 29, 1961, had come out in an editorial for the "two China" policy. See page 22 for the editorial, "A Policy For China," which observed that the People's Republic probably would reject this concept.

59 Letter, Walter H. Judd to Marvin Liebman, July 11, 1963, MLC.

60 Letter, Ralph A. Dungan to Marvin Leibman, January 26, 1962, White House Central Files, John F. Kennedy Library. The letter evoking this response failed to show up either in Liebman's files or the President's.

9. "To Keep Congress Firm"

1 See letter, Marvin Liebman to H. Alexander Smith, October 8, 1962, MLC.

2 Letter, Marvin Liebman to Walter H. Judd, July 18, 1962, Box 4, MLC.

3 *New York Times,* September 22, 1962, p. 11. The article added that the declaration also opposed a "two-China" policy but said nothing about a third added position in opposition to any trade concessions.

4 "A Brief History of an Authentic and Effective People's Movement," undated Committee pamphlet covering the years 1953 through 1965, p. 13.

5 Roger Hilsman, *To Move a Nation* (Garden City, N.Y.: Doubleday, 1967), p. 305. At the time the director of the State Department's Bureau of Intelligence, Hilsman provides an account of the short-lived effort within the Department to generate a more flexible Asian policy, telling how the Committee, referred to here as the "China Lobby," resisted the effort. "In Congress, the stalwarts of the China Lobby," he writes on p. 307, "including members of both parties, mustered their forces and quietly let it be known that they intended to destroy Kennedy's foreign aid program with crippling amendments unless the administration abandoned its plan to recognize Mongolia." Shortly thereafter, he adds, the effort ended.

6 Chester Bowles, *Promises To Keep* (New York: Harper & Row, 1971), pp. 398–99. Bowles makes clear throughout his discussions of China policy that his own views, often expressed during the 1950s, were that American policy should be based on Asian realities. He suggests that John F. Kennedy often agreed with him before becoming President; but he was distressed, if not surprised, "when the President asked me, during my confirmation hearings before the Senate Foreign Relations Committee in late January 1961, to play down the differences between my ideas about China and the generally accepted wisdom generated by the partisans of Chiang Kai-shek." See pp. 396–98. Regarding The Committee of One Million, Bowles says, on p. 393, that its "effective lobbying made any reappraisal of our relationships with Chiang Kai-shek and the mainland a matter so controversial that only a few foolhardy souls within the government, like myself, dared even to discuss it."

7 Liebman argued in both letters that Outer Mongolia was not an independent state. On May 2, 1961 (p. 36), he responded to an April 21 article speculating that the United States was considering recognition. On July 22 (p. 20), he answered a July 13 editorial in the *Times* supporting both U.S. recognition and UN entry for Outer Mongolia. (The United States did not recognize Outer Mongolia. Late in October 1961, the country became a member of the United Nations.)

8 Letter, Marvin Liebman to James O. Eastland, August 3, 1961, MLC. Lattimore, of course, had been a key figure in the subcommittee's 1951–1952 investigation of the IPR.

9 Letter, James O. Eastland to Marvin Liebman, August 17, 1961, MLC. Also, see Hilsman, *To Move a Nation,* p. 307, for accounts of other attempts to exploit the Lattimore trip.

10   Fraser received 87,002 votes, Judd 80,865. Minnesota lost one congressional seat as a result of the 1960 census. A special session of the Minnesota legislature approved a compromise redistricting plan late in 1961 which added approximately 172,000 people, all residents of Minneapolis, to the 5th C.D. See *Congressional Quarterly Weekly Service,* September 28, 1962, pp. 1647–49.

11   Telegram, Marvin Liebman to Mrs. Warren R. Austin, December 26, 1962, Box 2, MLC.

12   Memorandum, Marvin Liebman to steering committee, December 26, 1962, Box 23, MLC.

13   See letter, Marvin Liebman to "Dear Friend," February 25, 1963, Box 23, MLC. Enclosed was an essay by Admiral Arthur W. Radford, Ret., "The Recognitionists," later used as the foreword to *The Red China Lobby* by Forrest Davis and Robert Hunter. Some of those listed as "non-congressional members" on this particular letterhead: Robert S. Allen, John Dos Passos, Max Eastman, James T. Farrell, Bob Feller, Sidney Hook, H. V. Kaltenborn, Mrs. Alfred Kohlberg, Victor Lasky, Eli Lilly, William Loeb, Henry R. Luce, Adolph Menjou, Robert Morris, Norman Vincent Peale, Katherine Anne Porter, Albert C. Wedemeyer, and Karl A. Wittfogel.

14   Memorandum, Marvin Liebman to Paul Douglas, Charles Edison, Walter H. Judd, Kenneth B. Keating, H. Alexander Smith, June 26, 1963, MLC. See Box 4 for Liebman's June 4, 1963 letter inviting Senator Dodd to join.

15   Letter, Tingfu F. Tsiang to Marvin Liebman, February 7, 1962, Box 20, MLC.

16   Letter and draft of letter to the *New York Times,* Marvin Liebman to Paul H. Douglas, February 12, 1962, Box 4, MLC. See memorandum, Muriel Rubens to Marvin Liebman, attached to *ibid.*

17   Copy of letter, Harold L. Oram to H. E. Dr. P. (*sic*) F. Tsiang, May 29, 1962, Box 20, MLC.

18   Letter, Tingfu F. Tsiang to Marvin Liebman, July 5, 1962, Box 20, MLC. The reports had been picked up in Asia and had caused much alarm, Tsiang added. A two-part story by Willard Edwards appeared in the *Chicago Sunday Tribune,* June 17, 1962, pp. 1–2, and the *Chicago Daily Tribune,* June 18, 1962, p. 4. The writer said that Walt W. Rostow was the leading sponsor of a "master plan for historic changes in United States foreign policy." Such a plan included the expansion of contacts with the Red Chinese, who "can be encouraged to 'evolution' into a peaceful state by showing them we have no aggressive intentions."

19   Letter, Tingfu F. Tsiang to Marvin Liebman, April 24, 1963, MLC. The letter was addressed to Liebman in care of the American Afro-Asian Educational Exchange. The letter to the *Times* had appeared on April 16, 1963, p. 34.

20   Press release for release Friday, March 22, 1963, "Committee for a Review of Our China Policy." I wish to thank Mr. Nash and Mr. Porter for providing documents and materials about the formation and organization of this group.

21   Memorandum, Marvin Liebman to Charles Edison, May 8, 1963, Box 9, MLC.

22   Letters, Charles Edison to (various), May 21, 1963, and June 17, 1963, Box 23, MLC.

23   See Keating's letter, July 2, 1963, and Douglas', July 11, 1963, both in Box 9, MLC. In April 1962, Douglas had wired Liebman that after a talk with Senator Keating, he, too, believed that members of Congress should not solicit funds to place their congressional colleagues on the spot over any particular issue. See telegram, Paul H. Douglas to Marvin Liebman, April 23, 1962, Box 4, MLC.

24   Memorandum, Marvin Liebman to Charles Edison, July 24, 1963, Box 9, and "Informational Memorandum," Marvin Liebman to "Members and Congressional Endorsers," August 2, 1963, MLC.

25   Anthony Kubek, *How the Far East Was Lost* (Chicago: Regnery, 1963).

26   Letter, Marvin Liebman to T. F. Tsiang, August 7, 1963. (Similar letters soliciting views about reprinting a chapter were sent to others.) Letter, Ben Mandel to Marvin Liebman, June 27, 1963, and letter, Anthony Kubek to Marvin Liebman, September 27, 1963, Box 6, MLC.

27   See *China and U.S. Far East Policy 1945–1967* (Washington, D.C.: Congressional Quarterly Service, 1967), p. 130. Several weeks earlier the U.N. General Assembly had barred the People's Republic for the fourteenth consecutive year.

28   Roger Hilsman, *To Move a Nation,* p. 352. For the original speech, see *Department of State Bulletin* 50, no. 1280 (January 6, 1964):11–17.

29   The *New York Times* story by Max Frankel said the speech represented the first major statement from either the Kennedy or Johnson administrations on a new policy toward mainland China. Frankel's separate analysis of the talk said it was the work of China specialists Kennedy had assembled "and whom he had urged to take a new and realistic view of the problem." The President "was always afraid of a needlessly bitter domestic furor over China because he did not believe that Peking's conduct could yet be affected by mere words from Washington."

30   Roger Hilsman, *To Move a Nation,* p. 351.

31   Letter, Marvin Liebman to Christopher Emmet, December 23, 1963, Box 6, MLC. The file includes a draft entitled "A Two-China Policy For the Far East" by Professor David N. Rowe.

32   "Statement Commenting on American China Policy With Reference to Address Made By Assistant Secretary of State Roger Hilsman in San Francisco on December 13, 1963," Box 6, MLC (italics in original).

33   Roger Hilsman, *To Move a Nation,* p. 356. On the drafting of the speech, Hilsman says, on p. 352, that it was carefully phrased "to avoid providing labels and slogans to those who would oppose it."

34   *China and U.S. Far East Policy 1945–1967,* p. 133.

35 See "A Brief History of an Authentic and Effective People's Movement," p. 15. An article about the advertisement appeared in the *New York Times,* January 24, 1964, p. 2, explaining why the same ad was refused for its international edition. The Committee had failed to certify that it had the consent of the 72 persons named as sponsors of the statement, which, the article noted, had appealed to the French people to oppose President de Gaulle's decision to recognize Peking. Also, the *Times* reported that *Le Monde,* the French daily, had refused to run the advertisement.

36 *Department of State Bulletin* 100, no. 1290 (March 16, 1964):395.

37 Letter, Kenneth B. Keating to Marvin Liebman, January 28, 1964, Box 5, MLC.

38 Letter, Paul H. Douglas to Marvin Liebman, January 31, 1964, Box 4, MLC.

39 Letter, Paul H. Douglas to Marvin Liebman, May 15, 1964, Box 4, MLC.

40 *New York Times,* June 19, 1964, p. 5. For the press release, see item #381, Box 24, MLC.

41 Letter, Marvin Liebman to Dean Rusk, February 6, 1964, and letter, Paul M. Popple to Marvin Liebman, February 5, 1964, Box 8, MLC.

42 Letter, Marvin Liebman to Benjamin Mandel, April 28, 1964, Box 5, MLC.

43 Letter, Marvin Liebman to Benjamin Mandel, May 14, 1964, and letter, Benjamin Mandel to Marvin Liebman, May 27, 1964, Box 5, MLC. "Confidential Memorandum," Marvin Liebman to Benjamin Mandel, May 28, 1964, Box 5, MLC. Included here was speculation that Porter was making the mailing list of the "Committee For A Review of Our China Policy" available to overseas sources which "presumably" included Communist Chinese agencies.

44 See Richard Dudman's UPI story, with St. Louis, Mo. dateline, in the *New York Times,* December 20, 1964, p. 68.

45 See *New York Times,* May 15, 1964, for a story about an advertisement in the *Washington Evening Star* which also reports on Liebman's activities on behalf of Senator Goldwater. Boxes 33, 34, and 35 in the Marvin Liebman Collection cover the Goldwater campaign.

46 Letters, Marvin Liebman to Kenneth B. Keating, May 26, 1964, and Kenneth B. Keating to Marvin Liebman, June 2, 1964, Box 5, MLC.

47 For all correspondence relating to the 1964 Democratic National Convention, see Box 4, MLC.

48 The entire report of the findings, as prepared for the Council on Foreign Relations, is found in A. T. Steele, *The American People and China* (New York: McGraw-Hill published for the Council on Foreign Relations, 1966), pp. 251–313.

49 Joseph Barber, ed., *American Policy Toward China: A Report of the Views of Leading Citizens in Twenty-Three Cities* (New York: Council on Foreign Relations, 1950), p. 8. The 720 respondents, all male members of informal discussion groups known as Committees on Foreign Relations, were mostly well-educated businessmen,

professionals, educators, editors, etc., who were shown twenty-nine declarative statements on aspects of Sino-American relations and asked to underline the word (agree, uncertain, disagree) which most nearly approached their views.

10. Disappearing Bipartisanship

1 "Confidential Memorandum" and letter enclosing same, Marvin Liebman to T. F. Tsiang, both dated November 25, 1964, Box 8, MLC.

2 Memorandum, Marvin Liebman to steering committee, November 17, 1964, Box 8, MLC.

3 Reply memoranda, Charles Edison to Marvin Liebman and B. A. Garside to Marvin Liebman, both dated November 18, 1964, Box 8, MLC; "Confidential Memorandum," Marvin Liebman to steering committee, November 19, 1964, Box 8, MLC; and letter, Paul H. Douglas to Marvin Liebman, December 2, 1964, Box 4, MLC.

4 Letter, Marvin Liebman to Peter H. Dominick, December 28, 1964, Box 4, MLC.

5 Letter, Thomas E. Morgan to Marvin Liebman, January 4, 1965, Box 8, MLC. Representative Morgan, it will be recalled from chapter 3, note 7, was among the congressmen unable to provide me with a copy of the executive session transcript of the July 31, 1953, testimony of Nicholas de Rochefort before the Far East and Pacific Subcommittee of the House Committee on Foreign Affairs.

6 "Report Memorandum," Marvin Liebman to steering committee, January 15, 1965, Box 8, MLC. The Committee's address remained 79 Madison Avenue, New York City, Suite 905, the offices of Marvin Liebman Associates, Inc.

7 See letters, William Proxmire to Thomas J. Dodd, January 26, 1965, and Hugh Scott to Thomas J. Dodd, January 28, 1965. Both names would appear on Committee letterheads in March. Also, see Memorandum, Marvin Liebman to steering committee, January 29, 1965, Box 8, MLC.

8 "Confidential Memorandum," Marvin Liebman to steering committee, November 25, 1964, Box 8, MLC. Proposed opposition to P.R.C. territorial gains in Asia referred to the escalation of fighting in Vietnam and Indochina, another issue with which Liebman had become involved. In May 1964, he was reported to have helped prepare an advertisement listing the names of 127 Americans killed in hostile action in Vietnam which urged action against North Vietnam. The advertisement appeared in the *Washington Evening Star* on May 12, 1964. Liebman's participation in the project was reported in the *New York Times,* May 15, 1964, p. 12.

9 George F. Kennan, "A Fresh Look at China Policy," *New York Times Magazine,* November 22, 1964, pp. 27, 140–47.

10 An unsigned, undated memorandum on Marvin Liebman Associates, Inc. letterhead argues for the creation of a nationwide conservative organization entitled, for convenience only according to its author, "Americans for Conservative Action." The document clearly was written sometime after the 1960 national election, which the first

three pages analyze. Major conclusion: a Republican President could have been elected in 1960 if the conservative vote could have been mobilized behind someone commanding conservative allegiance. See Box 11, MLC. Later, Liebman would list among his clients the American Conservative Union and the Conservative Party.

11 *New York Times,* December 22, 1964, p. 17.

12 "Report Memorandum," Marvin Liebman to steering committee, January 15, 1965, Box 8, MLC.

13 The report was signed on June 11, 1964 by Marvin Liebman and B. A. Garside. See annual report, "The Committee of One Million," received June 15, 1964, New York State Department of Social Welfare.

14 Memorandum, Marvin Liebman to John M. Ashbrook, Thomas J. Dodd, Peter H. Dominick, and Thomas E. Morgan, February 10, 1965, Box 8, MLC. Senators Douglas and Proxmire both rejected solicitation of their colleagues. See telegram, Paul H. Douglas to Marvin Liebman, February 2, 1965, and letter, William Proxmire to Marvin Liebman, February 8, 1965, Box 8, MLC.

15 Letter, Marvin Liebman to Walter H. Judd, March 15, 1965, Box 8, MLC.

16 Letter, Walter H. Judd to Marvin Liebman, March 22, 1965, Box 8, MLC.

17 Letters, John C. Culver to Marvin Liebman, February 7, 1965; Teno Roncalio to Marvin Liebman, February 8, 1965; Barber B. Conable, Jr. to Marvin Liebman, May 4, 1965; and George D. Aiken to Marvin Liebman, January 22, 1965, Box 2, MLC.

18 These letters, all dated April 27, 1965 with one exception (letter to Dean Manion dated the 28th), are from Box 7, MLC.

19 Letter, Marvin Liebman to David Jones, April 7, 1965, Box 20, MLC.

20 Memorandum, Marvin Liebman to steering committee, August 31, 1965, Box 8, MLC.

21 Letters, Paul H. Douglas to Marvin Liebman, March 10, 1965, and Marvin Liebman to Paul H. Douglas, March 12, 1965, Box 4, MLC.

22 See memorandum and tentative shooting script, "Appeasement—Ally of Red China," item #409, Box 25, MLC.

23 Liebman confirmed this CDI association with Buckley in a postscript to his letter to David Jones, April 7, 1965, Box 20, MLC. CDI also published the *National Review*'s semi-monthly newsletter *Combat,* which lasted from 1968 to 1972, according to Charles Lam Markmann, *The Buckleys* (New York: Morrow, 1973), p. 325.

24 Memorandum, Marvin Liebman to James McFadden, April 30, 1965, Box 2, MLC.

25 Memorandum, Marvin Liebman to steering committee, August 31, 1965, Box 8, MLC.

26 Copy of letter, Thomas J. Dodd to Dean Rusk, October 1, 1965, Box 4, MLC. For the original draft, see letter, Marvin Liebman to Frank Lee, September 3, 1965, MLC.

27 See attachment to p. 4, Annual Report, "The Committee of One Million," received May 18, 1966, New York State Department of Social Welfare. On October 15, 1965, the Committee issued a press release calling on Rusk to issue a strong statement against the admission of the Chinese Communists to the United Nations. See item #482, Box 26, MLC.

28 *New York Times,* November 8, 1965, p. 12.

29 Letter, John O. Pastore to Committee of One Million, November 16, 1965, MLC.

30 Letter, Marvin Liebman to John O. Pastore, November 24, 1965, MLC.

31 Eight countries which formerly had backed the Nationalists abstained; six switched to outright support of Peking from the last previous vote in 1963. See *China and U.S. Far East Policy 1945–1967* (Washington, D.C.: Congressional Quarterly Service, 1967), p. 167.

32 *Ibid.,* pp. 169–70.

33 *New York Times,* December 10, 1965, pp. 53, 21. Among others the national committee included Dr. John C. Bennett, president of Union Theological Seminary; Professors John K. Fairbank, David Reisman, Robert A. Dahl, F. S. C. Northrup, C. Vann Woodward, Mary C. Wright; plus Norman Thomas of the Socialist Party and former Representative Charles O. Porter.

34 Letter, Thomas J. Dodd to Marvin Liebman, January 6, 1966, item #517, Box 26, MLC.

35 Letter, Marvin Liebman to Thomas J. Dodd, January 17, 1966, and memorandum, Marvin Liebman to steering committee, January 17, 1966, Box 4, MLC.

36 "Urgent Memorandum," Marvin Liebman to steering committee, January 25, 1966, Box 9, MLC.

37 Letter, Marvin Liebman to Clement J. Zablocki, January 25, 1966, Box 9, MLC.

38 See letter, Peter H. Dominick to Marvin Liebman, February 1, 1966, and telegram, Paul H. Douglas to Marvin Liebman, February 2, 1966. Also see letter, Clement J. Zablocki to Marvin Liebman, February 3, 1966, Box 9, MLC.

39 Professors Possony and Rowe testified on February 15, former Ambassador Hornbeck and Assistant Secretary of State Robertson on March 8, and Professor Michael on March 9. See U.S. House of Representatives, Committee on Foreign Affairs, Subcommittee on the Far East and Pacific, Report: *United States Policy Toward Asia,* 89C2 (1966), H.D. No. 488. At the request of Representative William T. Murphy (D., Ill.), a member of the subcommittee, a number of Committee materials, including its annual declaration and a list of congressional endorsees as of January 1966, were included in the record. See *ibid.,* pp. 431–45.

40 Letter, Franz Michael to Marvin Liebman, February 2, 1966, and copy of letter, Franz Michael to Clement J. Zablocki, February 2, 1966, Box 9, MLC.

41   Letter, Marvin Liebman to Chow Shu-kai, January 25, 1966, Box 9, MLC. Ambassador Chow had replaced Ambassador T. F. Tsiang, whose resignation prompted Liebman to solicit publishers Henry Luce and DeWitt Wallace about a possible testimonial dinner in Washington D.C. for Dr. Tsiang. Luce responded with a pledge of $2,000, Wallace with $500, but the plans were called off two weeks later when it was learned that George Meany also was planning an AFL-CIO testimonial dinner for Tsiang in Washington. A smaller dinner in New York, hosted by Luce, Senator Dodd, and Dr. Judd, was held on June 23, 1965, at the Time-Life Auditorium. For pertinent correspondence, see Box 30, MLC. Dr. Tsiang, a Ph.D. in history from Columbia University, wanted to return to Taipei to teach and conduct historical research, but he died at the age of 69 in New York. His obituary in the *New York Times* on October 11, 1965, p. 39, said that Dr. Tsiang had adopted a different transliteration of his family name, Chiang, to avoid confusion with Chiang Kai-shek, to whom he was not related.

42   Letter, Chow Shu-kai to Marvin Liebman, February 4, 1966, Box 9, MLC. He had enjoyed his chat with Liebman the other day, the ambassador added, and would contact him about "the manuscript" when he returned from Texas.

43   Hearings, U.S. Senate, Committee on Foreign Relations, *U.S. Policy With Respect to Mainland China,* 89C2 (1966).

44   See the *New York Times,* March 9, 1966, pp. 1, 7; March 10, 1966, pp. 1, 19; March 11, 1966, pp. 1, 4; and March 14, 1966, pp. 1, 2.

45   *New York Times,* March 21, 1966, pp. 1, 12. A sidebar on p. 12 said that three members of the Association for Asian Studies (the group from whom the 198 were drawn) dissented from the document: Professor Frank N. Trager, New York University; A. Sabin Chase, a former Department of State official; and Stanley K. Hornbeck. Six weeks after this story appeared, Liebman reminded Ben Mandel of the Senate Committee on the Judiciary of an earlier letter he said he had written on behalf of Colonel Harold Riegelman, identified as a longtime Committee friend who wanted to know how many of the 198 signers previously had been associated with the Institute of Pacific Relations. In the interests of time, Liebman asked Mandel to contact Riegelman (whose law firm was registered in 1965 as a foreign agent for the Republic of China—see chapter 4, note 40) directly. See Marvin Liebman to "Ben" Mandel, May 2, 1966, Box 5, MLC.

46   Telegram, William Proxmire to Marvin Liebman, March 21, 1966, and letter, Marvin Liebman to William Proxmire, March 21, 1966, Box 6, MLC.

47   Memorandum, Marvin Liebman to steering committee, March 21, 1966, Box 6, MLC.

48   *New York Times,* March 23, 1966, p. 46.

49   *New York Times,* March 29, 1966, pp. 1, 4. The proposals were totally unrealistic and might have dangerous consequences for the policy of containing Communist China and for the war effort in Vietnam, the *Times* summarized their testimony. Taylor argued there was no advantage to the United States in talking either about recognition of Peking or its admission to the United Nations; Rowe said Peking was ineligible

on "moral, legal and constitutional grounds"; and Judd, who recommended bombing "anything important to North Vietnam's war," said recognition would pull the rug out from America's loyal allies on Taiwan. Rowe also assailed as "pro-Chinese Communist" the statement by 198 academics recommending changes in China policy, attacked the *New York Times* for the space given the statement, deplored the paper's editorial support for changes in China policy, and said equal weight should have been given the Committee's declaration which had been included in a press release the *Times* failed to publish. (The release was written to infer that the declaration had been initiated and endorsed in response to current developments on China policy; actually, however, the 330 signers had been on record as of January 1966.)

50 "Minutes of Policy Meeting of the Steering Committee of the Committee of One Million . . . ," April 6, 1966, Box 6, and letter, Walter H. Judd to Marvin Liebman, April 14, 1966, Box 4, MLC. Judd said he wanted the correction both for historical and psychological reasons.

51 Five years later, after Senator Dodd's death, the Senate Committee on the Judiciary's subcommittee to investigate the administration of the Internal Security Act and other security laws published "The Human Cost of Communism in China," prepared at the request of Senator Dodd. See Committee Print, 92C1 (1971). The study was prepared by Professor Richard L. Walker, University of South Carolina.

52 No such article appeared in *Foreign Affairs* under Acheson's name. In July 1967 the journal published "Mao's China: The Decline of a Dynasty," by L. LaDany, editor of Hong Kong's "China News Analysis." The AAEE distributed reprints of this article.

53 Professor Trager was among the three dissenters quoted in the March 21 article in the *Times*. See note 45, *supra*.

54 See letters, Marvin Liebman to Paul H. Douglas, April 15, 1966, and Paul H. Douglas to Marvin Liebman, April 27, 1966, Box 4, MLC.

55 Letter, Lee Edwards to Marvin Liebman, March 25, 1966, Box 18, MLC.

56 Letter, Lee Edwards to Marvin Liebman, April 19, 1966, Box 1, MLC. See Lee Edwards, *Reagan: A Political Biography* (San Diego: Viewpoint Books, 1967). Edwards began his firm in 1965, according to the book's dust jacket, which also said he was founding editor, in 1961, of a monthly magazine called *The New Guard*.

57 Letter, Marvin Liebman to Lee Edwards, April 28, 1966, Box 1, MLC.

58 Letter, Marvin Liebman to Paul H. Douglas, May 25, 1966, Box 13, MLC. Appropriately, this letter was written on new Committee letterhead listing the 1790 Broadway address.

59 Copy of letter, Paul H. Douglas to Bertram D. Wolfe, July 25, 1966, Box 13, MLC. Liebman had recommmended the additional names after meeting with a Douglas aide, Howard Shuman. See letter, Marvin Liebman to Howard Shuman, June 13, 1966, Box 13, MLC.

60 "Confidential Memorandum," Marvin Liebman to "All Concerned," August 4, 1966, Box 5, MLC.

61   See the *New York Times,* June 10, 1966, p. 4. On June 14, the *Times* ran an article on p. 13 saying the Committee had called on the new group "for a constructive and honest debate." But a spokesman for the National Committee on United States-China relations explained that the organization could not engage in advocative debate because its mission was not to take positions. Members speaking as individuals could and would debate representatives of the Committee.

62   "Most Confidential Memorandum," Marvin Liebman to "All Concerned," June 27, 1966, Box 5, MLC.

63   See Richard Baum, ed., with Louise B. Bennett, *China In Ferment* (Englewood Cliffs, N.J.: Prentice-Hall, 1971), pp. 1–11. Also, see Thomas W. Robinson, ed., *The Cultural Revolution in China* (Berkeley and Los Angeles: University of California Press, 1971).

64   Letter, Marvin Liebman to "Ben" Mandel, July 13, 1966, Box 5, MLC.

65   *Congressional Record,* 89C2 (1966), 112(13):16635–43.

66   Letter, Marvin Liebman to Lee Edwards, July 14, 1966, Box 1, MLC. For Edwards' letter specifying his understanding of the project and terms, see Lee Edwards to Marvin Liebman, August 3, 1966, Box 1, MLC.

67   See letter, Marvin Liebman to Lee Edwards, August 29, 1966, Box 1, MLC. Liebman was inquiring about the status of two as yet undelivered speeches on which he said he was getting some pressure. Also, see Liebman's July 22, 1966 letter to Edwards asking him to arrange inserts in the *Congressional Record* for three communications from the Republic of China's Legislative Yuan and Control Yuan.

68   *Congressional Record,* 89C2 (1966), 112(11):14582–86; *ibid.,* pt. 16, pp. 22252–55.

69   Letter, Lee Edwards to Marvin Liebman, July 11, 1967, Box 1, MLC.

70   Memorandum on Marvin Liebman Associates, Inc. letterhead, Marvin Liebman to F. Clifton White, July 28, 1966, Box 14, MLC.

71   "Confidential Memorandum" on Marvin Liebman Associates, Inc. letterhead, Marvin Liebman to Daniel A. Poling, August 1, 1966, Box 5, MLC.

72   Memorandum on Marvin Liebman Associates, Inc. letterhead, Marvin Liebman to "Don Pemberton and all others concerned," August 11, 1966, MLC.

73   Letters, Tom Charles Huston to Marvin Liebman and Don Pemberton, August 15, 1966, and Tom Charles Huston to Patrick Buchanan on letterhead of World Youth Crusade for Freedom, August 18, 1966, Box 30, MLC. No Buchanan reply was found.

74   Memorandum on Marvin Liebman Associates letterhead, Marvin Liebman to David Keene, Don Pemberton, Toby Solovioff, Tom Charles Huston, October 14, 1966, Box 30, MLC.

75   For the kit, see item #612, Box 28, MLC.

76   The report by the United Nations Association represented the views of 27 prominent persons convened by the association to re-examine American attitudes toward the China seating issue in the United Nations. The panel concluded that representation

by both "Chinas" in the world body would strengthen the position of the United States in the world. See *New York Times,* October 21, 1966, pp. 1, 14.

77 Letter, Marvin Liebman to Walter H. Judd, November 8, 1966, Box 4, MLC.

78 *New York Times,* November 29, 1966, p. 42. A majority of Americans still opposed seating the Chinese Communists, he said, reeling off the Committee's catalogue of congressional declarations, favorable polls, supporting organizations, and administration policy positions. The *Times* obviously felt it had a monopoly of "serious thought," he added, but the Committee's position was the result of at least some "serious thought."

79 Copy of international telegram, Marvin Liebman to Chiang Kai-shek, November 29, 1966. Liebman also sent telegrams to Republic of China Foreign Minister Wei Tao-ming and Ambassadors Liu Chieh and Chow Shu-kai. The latter replied on December 9, enclosing a message from Wei Tao-ming which said President Chiang wanted him to thank Liebman for his telegram and particularly for his tireless efforts which the President hoped would continue for years to come. All materials are in Box 3, MLC.

80 Letters, Walter H. Judd to Marvin Liebman, December 1, 1966, and Marvin Liebman to Walter H. Judd, December 9, 1966, MLC.

81 Letter, Abraham Ribicoff to Marvin Liebman, November 11, 1966, Box 2, MLC.

82 See letter, Marvin Liebman to William A. Rusher, December 30, 1966, Box 3, MLC.

83 Letter, Jacob K. Javits to Marvin Liebman, December 14, 1966, Box 3, MLC.

84 See *New York Times,* December 18, 1966, pp. 1, 8. Also, see letter and enclosures, Jacob K. Javits to Walt W. Rostow, December 20, 1966, General File CO 50-2, Lyndon Baines Johnson Library, Austin, Texas.

85 See memorandum, Marvin Liebman to "Congressional Endorsers of the Declaration in Opposition to any Concessions to Communist China," December 14, 1966, Box 3, MLC.

86 See "Confidential Memorandum," Marvin Liebman to steering committee, December 28, 1966, Box 3, MLC, and "Confidential Memorandum," Marvin Liebman to "All Concerned," January 5, 1967, Box 5, MLC.

87 Letter, Paul H. Douglas to Marvin Liebman, December 22, 1966, Box 4, MLC.

88 "Confidential Memorandum," Marvin Liebman to "All Concerned," January 5, 1967, Box 5, MLC.

89 Memorandum, Marvin Liebman to steering committee, members, and friends, undated report on work and accomplishments covering the January-December 1966 period, Box 4, MLC. A copy of this report was forwarded to I-Cheng Loh, in care of the Chinese Information Office, 1709 Chung Cheng Road, Taipei, Taiwan, with a letter

from Liebman, who said he missed him in New York and looked forward to his return soon. See letter, Marvin Liebman to I-Cheng Loh, December 30, 1966, MLC.

90   "Confidential Memorandum," Marvin Liebman to "All Concerned," January 5, 1967, Box 5, MLC.

91   Letter, Marvin Liebman to Walter H. Judd, April 28, 1967, Box 4, MLC. A new organization, if not exactly a new approach, would come four years later, in 1971, after Liebman had left the Committee, the public relations business, and the country. See chapter 11.

92   See "Report on informal meeting of the Steering Committee of the Committee of One Million on Wednesday, January 18th, 1967, in the office of Senator Peter H. Dominick, Room 140, Old Senate Office Building, Washington, D.C.," January 19, 1967, Box 8, MLC.

93   Letters, Clement J. Zablocki to steering committee, February 17, 1967, Box 8, MLC; and Marvin Liebman to Walter H. Judd, February 28, 1967, Box 4, MLC. Liebman also reported that Senators Lausche and Cooper had turned down membership on the steering committee but would continue to be listed as supporters. The Committee had not yet heard officially from Senator Sparkman, he added, but a telephone call from the Alabamian's office indicated a refusal.

94   Letter, Marvin Liebman to Chow Shu-kai, January 25, 1967, Box 3, MLC. The AAEE decisions: change the name back to the American-Asian Educational Exchange; concentrate solely on Asian affairs; broaden membership in the liberal camp; and encourage greater output of scholarly papers in order to match the opposition.

95   Letters, Courtlandt Otis to "The Committee of One Million," January 25, 1967, and Marvin Liebman to Courtlandt Otis, January 26, 1967, Box 19, MLC.

96   Letters, Marvin Liebman to John Buchanan, March 2, 1967, and John H. Buchanan, Jr. to Marvin Liebman, March 9, 1967, Box 2, MLC.

97   Letter and enclosures, Marvin Liebman to Walter H. Judd, April 11, 1967, Box 4, MLC.

98   Letters and enclosures, Marvin Liebman to B. A. Garside, April 19, 1967; letter, B. A. Garside to Marvin Liebman, April 26, 1967, and letter, Marvin Liebman to Walter H. Judd, April 28, 1967, Box 4, MLC.

99   See letters, Lee Edwards to Marvin Liebman, April 19, 1966; Lee Edwards to Marvin Liebman, June 21, 1967; and Lee Edwards to Marvin Liebman, July 11, 1967, Box 1, MLC.

100   Letter, Marvin Liebman to Gene Loh, August 4, 1967, Box 1, MLC.

101   Letter, Marvin Liebman to Lee Edwards, August 11, 1967, Box 1, MLC.

102   *Congressional Record,* 90C1 (1967), 113(26):35047–050; and *ibid.,* pt. 21, p. 28446.

103   Copy of letter, Lee Edwards to John G. Tower, July 18, 1968, and copy of letter, John G. Tower to Lee Edwards, July 23, 1968, Box 1, MLC.

104   Letter and enclosures, Marvin Liebman to David Martin, September 11, 1968, Box 5, MLC.

105   *Congressional Record,* 90C2 (1968), 114(21):27720–725.

106   Letter, Marvin Liebman to Walter H. Judd, January 24, 1968, Box 4, MLC; and "Confidential Memorandum," Marvin Liebman to steering committee, February 1, 1968, Box 6, MLC.

107   Dodd was censured on one count, that he diverted to his own use $116,000 from testimonial dinners between 1961 and 1965. The censure motion passed 92 to 5 on June 23, 1967. Dodd remained in the Senate until the close of his second term in 1970 and died in May 1971. See the *New York Times,* May 25, 1971, pp. 1, 43, for his obituary. Among the clients listed by Marvin Liebman Associates before the firm dissolved was the National Committee for Justice for Senator Thomas J. Dodd.

108   See "Confidential Memorandum," Marvin Liebman to John Buchanan, Peter H. Dominick, Bourke B. Hickenlooper, Walter H. Judd, and David Martin, February 7, 1968, Box 5, MLC. The memorandum was prepared instead of formal minutes, Liebman said, because of the conference's informal nature.

109   See press release, September 13, 1968, item #803, Box 29, MLC.

11.   Nixon's the Key

1   See memorandum, "Marvin Liebman's Secretary" to steering committee, June 4, 1968, Box 2, MLC. Dr. Judd was not happy about this up-to-date listing of congressional endorsers, according to a penciled note on the file copy.

2   Letter, Marvin Liebman to Walter S. Robertson, July 15, 1968, Box 19, MLC. The steering committee had decided to discontinue circulation of the annual declaration statement to members of Congress, the secretary reported.

3   Letter, Marvin Liebman to Walter H. Judd, June 14, 1968, Box 21, MLC.

4   Letter, Tom Charles Huston to Marvin Liebman, June 18, 1968, Box 21, MLC.

5   Excerpts from the "Huston Plan" were published in July 1974, when four volumes of evidence were released by the House Judiciary Committee investigating the possible impeachment of President Nixon. There was no evidence that the program calling for illegal acts was implemented, but neither was there evidence that the President had withdrawn his earlier approval of the plan. See *Los Angeles Times,* July 19, 1974, pp. 1, 16, 17. For more on Huston, plus a chronology of his work on the domestic security program at the White House, see J. Anthony Lukas, "The Story So Far," *New York Times Magazine,* July 22, 1973, pp. 10–11. Judging from the remaining Committee materials regarding the pre-election period, the policy line Judd and Liebman attempted to pursue in the Nixon camp argued that present policy was "positive" but that suggestions for further concessions were "negative."

6   Letter, Walter H. Judd to Marvin Liebman, September 27, 1968, Box 4, MLC. The offending letter was not discovered.

7   Copy of handwritten letter on personal letterhead, Marvin Liebman to Walter Judd, September 30, 1968, Box 4, MLC.

8   See copy of letter, Lee Edwards to Fulton Lewis, October 1, 1968, and copy of letter, Fulton Lewis III to Lee Edwards, October 4, 1968, Box 19, MLC.

9   See letter, Walter H. Judd to Marvin Liebman, December 17, 1968, and letter, Marvin Liebman to Lee Edwards, December 20, 1968, Box 1, MLC.

10   Letter, Marvin Liebman to William F. Buckley Jr., January 23, 1969, Box 30, MLC.

11   Hutchins, of course, was Robert M. Hutchins, a founder of the Center, long-time president, and today a Life Fellow.

12   Letter, Marvin Liebman to Walter H. Judd, January 23, 1969, Box 4, MLC.

13   Letter, Marvin Liebman to Edward Kemp, February 4, 1969, Box 19, MLC. They had apparently exchanged letters in 1967.

14   These dates were reported to me by an official of the Hoover Institution Archives. Even two of Liebman's former passports were included (see Box 16). Interestingly, Liebman's donation of his papers preceded by five months the July 25, 1969, statutory cut-off date later established by Congress under the Tax Reform Act of 1969 as the legal deadline for tax-deductible gifts of papers by public figures. (This same deadline was involved in the controversy over President Nixon's 1969 tax deductions.)

15   Charles Lam Markmann, *The Buckleys* (New York: Morrow, 1973), p. 201.

16   Lee Edwards was hired on February 26, 1969, according to the Committee's 1971 annual report filed with the New York State Board of Social Welfare (page 5, schedule F). Edwards and the Committee first were located at 1000 Vermont Avenue, N.W., then at 1735 DeSales Street, N.W. All copies of *China Report* are available at the U.C.L.A. Research Library's Public Affairs Service.

17   Marvin Kalb and Bernard Kalb, *Kissinger* (Boston: Little, Brown, 1974), pp. 219–20. The authors provide a fascinating behind-the-scenes account in this and the subsequent section of "The China Breakthrough."

18   Cranston's resolution, S. Res. 205, was debated and passed by the Senate on September 25, 1969. The vote was 77 to 3 with 19 not voting. One of the three dissenters was Senator Dodd. Republican George Aiken joined Cranston as a co-sponsor. See *Congressional Record*, 91C1 (1969), 115(20):27106, 27113–118.

19   *New York Times*, December 21, 1969, section 4, p. 4.

20   *New York Times*, April 26, 1970, p. 14. The decline of the "China Lobby" was underscored, said the non-bylined article, by the restraint of a recent Washington reception for Nationalist China's Deputy Premier Chiang Ching-kuo, the elder son of Chiang Kai-shek. The article pointed to further evidence of a shift in public attitudes: an aide to Hugh Scott, Senate minority leader and a member of the Committee's steering committee, said the senator still opposed admission of the Peking regime to the UN but favored improved relations with the Chinese Communists in the areas of trade and travel. Also, noting that Mrs. Anna Chennault often was referred to in Washington as

"the China Lobby today," the article quoted her as not being a member of the Committee. "That group may have been a good thing in its time, to help Taiwan get established and strong," the widow of World War II General Claire Chennault told the *Times,* "but now something broader and more forward-looking is needed."

21   *Los Angeles Times,* October 18, 1970, section G, p. 6.

22   *Los Angeles Times,* April 16, 1971, p. 6. Correspondent Robert C. Toth said the talks were called off by the Chinese in May following the Cambodian "incursion" by U.S. forces.

23   *New York Times,* May 2, 1971, p. 18.

24   *Department of State Bulletin,* 45, no. 1678 (August 23, 1971):193–96. Asked if the government would work as actively to prevent expulsion of the Chinese Nationalist government as it had in the past to prevent Peking's admission, Rogers replied, "We are not going to speculate at the moment about the tactics we will use." He admitted uncertainty over the outcome of the "dual representation" strategy, as he called it, and indicated the United States would continue to employ the "important question" tactic—only this time as a gambit to prevent the expulsion of a member nation.

25   *Los Angeles Times,* August 16, 1971, pt. II, p. 11.

26   *New York Times,* August 8, 1971, section 4, p. 11.

27   The Committee's 1971 annual report is "unofficial" because the original was sent to the Board without signature, returned, but never resubmitted by the Committee with signature. A photo copy was retained by the Board. Apparently the 1970 report also was submitted without signature by the Committee and returned, but it too was never returned and the Board neglected to make a photo copy, so there is no 1970 report.

28   *New York Times,* October 31, 1971, section 4, p. 1.

29   Every NATO country except the United States, Portugal, Greece, and Luxembourg either voted against the rule or abstained.

30   *New York Times,* October 27, 1971, p. 16.

31   *Los Angeles Times,* February 16, 1972, p. 4.

BIBLIOGRAPHY OF CITED SOURCES

Manuscript Collections

Eisenhower, Dwight D., papers. Dwight D. Eisenhower Library, Abilene, Kansas.
Hornbeck, Stanley K., papers. Hoover Institution on War, Revolution, and Peace, Stanford University, Stanford, California.
Johnson, Lyndon Baines, papers. Lyndon Baines Johnson Library, Austin, Texas.
Kennedy, John F., papers. John F. Kennedy Library, Waltham, Massachusetts.
Liebman, Marvin, papers. Hoover Institution on War, Revolution, and Peace, Stanford University, Stanford, California.

United States Government Documents and Official Publications

Department of the Army. Romanus, Charles F. and Riley Sunderland, *Stilwell's Mission to China*. Office of the Chief of Military History. Washington, D.C., 1953.
Department of State. *Bulletin,* 1953–1971.
—— *Foreign Relations of the United States: Diplomatic Papers, 1942. China.* Washington, D.C., 1956.
—— *Foreign Relations of the United States: Diplomatic Papers, 1944. China.* Washington, D.C., 1967.
—— *Foreign Relations of the United States: Diplomatic Papers, 1945. The Far East and China.* Washington, D.C., 1969.
—— Papers relating to The Committee of One Million Against the Admission of Communist China to the United Nations, Records Services Division.
—— *Register of the Department of State: 1939.* Washington, D.C., 1939.
—— *United States Relations with China: With Special Reference to the Period 1944–1949.* Washington, D.C., 1949. Also cited as *The China White Paper August 1949.* Stanford, California, 1967.

U.S. CONGRESS

Congressional Directory, 1953–1971.
Congressional Record, 1953–1971.
House of Representatives. Committee on Foreign Affairs. *Report on Special Study Mission to Southeast Asia and the Pacific.* 83rd Cong. 2d sess. Washington, D.C., 1954.
—— Committee on Foreign Affairs, Subcommittee on the Far East and the Pacific. *Report: United States Policy Toward Asia.* 89th Cong. 2d sess. Washington, D.C., 1966.
—— Select Committee to Investigate Tax-Exempt Foundations and Comparable Organizations. *Hearings on Tax-Exempt Foundations.* 82d Cong. 2d sess. Washington, D.C., 1954.

Senate. Committee on Armed Services and the Committee on Foreign Relations. *Military Situation in the Far East, Hearings.* 82d Cong. 1st sess. 5 parts. Washington, D.C., 1951.

—— Committee on Foreign Relations, Subcommittee Pursuant to S. Resolution 23. *Hearings on the State Department Employee Loyalty Investigation.* 3 vols. 81st Cong. 2d sess. Washington, D.C., 1950 (Referred to in text as *Tydings Hearings.*)

—— Committee on Foreign Relations, Subcommittee. *Nomination of Philip C. Jessup, Hearings.* 82d Cong. 1st sess. Washington, D.C., 1951.

—— Committee on Foreign Relations. *Activities of Nondiplomatic Representatives of Foreign Principals in the United States, Hearings.* 88th Cong. 1st sess. 12 parts. Washington, D.C., 1963.

—— Committee on Foreign Relations. *Reviews of the World Situation: 1949–1950, Hearings held in Executive Session.* 81st Cong. 1st and 2d sess. Washington, D.C., 1974.

—— Committee on Foreign Relations. *United States-China Relations.* 92d Cong. 1st sess. Washington, D.C., 1971. (Also cited as *Investigation of United States Far Eastern Policy,* December 1945.)

—— Committee on Foreign Relations. *United States Foreign Policy in Asia, Study No. 5.* S. Document No. 24. Washington, D.C., 1961.

—— Committee on Foreign Relations. *U.S. Policy with Respect to Mainland China, Hearings.* 89th Cong. 2d sess. Washington, D.C., 1966.

—— Committee on Foreign Relations. Committee Print. "The United States and Communist China in 1949 and 1950: The Question of Rapprochement and Recognition." A staff study. 93rd Cong. 1st sess. Washington, D.C., 1973.

—— Committee on the Judiciary, Subcommittee to Investigate the Administration of the Internal Security Act and Other Internal Security Laws. *Institute of Pacific Relations, Hearings.* 82d Cong. 1st and 2d sess. 15 parts. Washington, D.C., 1951–1952. (Referred to in text as *McCarran Hearings.*)

—— Select Committee to Study Governmental Operations with Respect to Intelligence Activities. *Alleged Assassination Plots Involving Foreign Leaders, Interim Report.* 94th Cong. 1st sess. Washington, D.C., 1975.

——Select Committee to Study Governmental Operations with Respect to Intelligence Activities. *Foreign and Military Intelligence, Final Report, Book I.* 94th Cong. 2d sess. Washington, D.C., 1976.

——Select Committee to Study Governmental Operations with Respect to Intelligence Activities. *Intelligence Activities and the Rights of Americans, Final Report, Book II.* 94th Cong. 2d sess. Washington, D.C., 1976.

Tensions in Communist China: An Analysis of Internal Pressures Generated Since 1949. S. Document No. 66. Washington, D.C., 1960.

United Nations, Official Documents

United Nations Review. Vol. 2. No. 2. June, 1956.
Yearbook of the United Nations, 1953–1971.

Books and Articles

Acheson, Dean. *Present at the Creation*. New York: Norton, 1969.

Agee, Philip. *Inside the Company*. New York: Bantam Books, 1975.

Barber, Joseph, ed. *American Policy Toward China: A Report on the Views of Leading Citizens in Twenty-Three Cities*. New York: Council on Foreign Relations, 1950.

Barrett, David D. *Dixie Mission: The United States Army Observer Group in Yenan, 1944*. Berkeley: Center for Chinese Studies Research Monograph No. 6, 1970.

Baum, Richard, ed., with Louise Bennett. *China In Ferment: Perspectives on the Cultural Revolution*. Englewood Cliffs, N.J.: Prentice-Hall, 1971.

Bennett, Edward M. "Joseph C. Grew: The Diplomacy of Pacification," Richard Dean Burns and Edward M. Bennett, eds., *Diplomats in Crisis: United States-Chinese-Japanese Relations, 1919–1941*. Santa Barbara, Calif.: ABC-CLIO, 1974.

Berrigan, Darrell. "Uncle Joe Pays Off," *Saturday Evening Post* (June 17, 1944), 20–21.

Borg, Dorothy. *The United States and the Far Eastern Crisis of 1933*–1938. Cambridge: Harvard University Press, 1964.

Bowles, Chester. *Promises to Keep: My Years in Public Life 1941–1969*. New York: Harper & Row, 1971.

Braisted, William R. "The United States and the American China Development Company," *Far Eastern Quarterly*, XI, 2 (February 1952), 147–65.

Buckley, William F. Jr. and L. Brent Bozell. *McCarthy and His Enemies*. Chicago: Regnery, 1954.

Buhite, Russell D. *Patrick J. Hurley and American Foreign Policy*. Ithaca and London, Cornell University Press, 1973.

Burns, Richard Dean. "Stanley K. Hornbeck: The Diplomacy of the Open Door," Richard Dean Burns and Edward Bennett, eds., *Diplomats in Crisis: United States-Chinese-Japanese Relations, 1919–1941*. Santa Barbara, Calif., ABC-CLIO, 1974.

Campbell, Charles S. Jr. *Special Business Interests and the Open Door Policy*. New Haven: Yale University Press, 1951.

Caridi, Ronald J. *The Korean War and American Politics: The Republican Party As A Case Study*. Philadelphia: University of Pennsylvania Press, 1968.

China and U.S. Far East Policy 1945–1967. Washington, D.C.: Congressional Quarterly Service, 1967.

China and U.S. Foreign Policy. 2d ed. Washington, D.C.: Congressional Quarterly Service, 1973.

Clubb, O. Edmund. *The Witness and I*. New York and London: Columbia University Press, 1974.

Cohen, Paul A. *China and Christianity: The Missionary Movement and the Growth of Chinese Antiforeignism 1860–1870*. Cambridge: Harvard University Press, 1963.

Cohen, Warren I. *America's Response to China: An Interpretative History of Sino-American Relations*. New York: Wiley, 1971.

Congress and the Nation 1945–1964. Washington, D.C.: Congressional Quarterly Service, 1965.

Congressional Quarterly Weekly Report, "The China Lobby: A Case Study" (Special Supplement) 9, No. 25-A (June 29, 1951), 939–58.

Dallek, Robert. "The Truman Era," Ernest R. May and James C. Thomson Jr., eds., *American-East Asian Relations: A Survey.* Cambridge: Harvard University Press, 1972.

Davies, John Paton Jr. *Dragon by the Tail: American, British, Japanese, and Russian Encounters with China and One Another.* New York: Norton, 1972.

Davis, Forrest and Robert Hunter. *The Red China Lobby.* New York: Fleet Publishing, 1963.

Donovan, Robert J. *Eisenhower: The Inside Story.* New York: Harper, 1956.

Douglas, Paul H. *In the Fullness of Time: The Memoirs of Paul H. Douglas.* New York: Harcourt Brace Jovanovich, 1971.

—— "Should We Recognize Red China?" *The New Leader,* 41, No. 28 (July 21–28, 1958), 7–8.

Dudman, Richard. "Entrepreneurs of the Right," Robert H. Salisbury, ed., *Interest Group Politics in America.* New York: Harper & Row, 1970.

Dulles, Foster Rhea. *American Policy Toward Communist China 1949–1960.* New York: Thomas Y. Crowell, 1972.

Edwards, Lee. *Reagan: A Political Biography.* San Diego: Viewpoint Books, 1967.

Epstein, Israel. *Unfinished Revolution in China.* Boston: Little Brown, 1947.

Esherick, Joseph W., ed., *Lost Chance in China: The World War II Despatches of John S. Service.* New York: Random House, 1974.

Fairbank, John King. *The United States and China.* 3rd ed. Cambridge: Harvard University Press, 1972. 1948.

Feis, Herbert. *The China Tangle: The American Effort in China from Pearl Harbor to the Marshall Mission.* Princeton: Princeton University Press, 1953.

Flynn, John T. *While You Slept: Our Tragedy in Asia and Who Made It.* New York: Devin-Adair, 1951.

Forman, Harrison. *Report from Red China.* New York: Holt, 1945.

Friedman, Edward and Mark Selden. *America's Asia: Dissenting Essays on Asian-American Relations.* New York: Vintage Books, 1971.

Gardner, John B. *The Image of the Chinese in the United States, 1885–1915.* Ph.D. dissertation, University of Pennsylvania, 1961.

Garside, B. A. *One Increasing Purpose: The Life of Henry Winters Luce.* New York: Revell, 1948.

Gayn, Mark and Edgar Snow. "Must China Go Red?" *Saturday Evening Post* (May 12, 1945), 9–10.

Gilbert, Rodney. "Dope from Red China," *American Legion Magazine,* 57, No. 3 (September 1954), 16–17, 50–53.

Goodno, Floyd Russel. *Walter H. Judd: Spokesman for China in the United States House of Representatives.* Ed.D. dissertation, Oklahoma State University, 1970.

Graebner, Norman. "The Republican Commitment to Chiang: The Truman Years," paper delivered at the Duquesne History Forum, October 30, 1974, Pittsburgh.

Greene, Felix. *A Curtain of Ignorance.* Garden City, N.Y.: Doubleday, 1967.

Grew, Joseph C. *Invasion Alert.* Baltimore: Moran, 1956.

Griffith, Robert. *The Politics of Fear: Joseph R. McCarthy and the Senate.* New York: Hayden, 1970.

Griswold, A. Whitney. *The Far Eastern Policy of the United States*. New Haven: Yale University Press, 1938, 1966.

Hilsman, Roger. *To Move A Nation*. Garden City, N.Y.: Doubleday, 1967.

Hoopes, Townsend. *The Devil and John Foster Dulles*. Boston: Little Brown, 1973.

Hornbeck, Stanley K. *Contemporary Politics in the Far East*. New York: D. Appleton, 1916.

Horton, Philip. "The China Lobby—Part II," *The Reporter*, 6, No. 9 (April 29, 1952), 5–24.

Hunter, Edward. *The Black Book on Red China*. New York: The Bookmailer, 1958.

Huss, Pierre J. and George Carpozi Jr. *Red Spies in the U.N.* New York: Coward-Mc-Cann, 1965.

Kahn, E. J. Jr. *The China Hands: America's Foreign Service Officers and What Befell Them*. New York: Viking, 1975.

Kalb, Marvin and Bernard Kalb. *Kissinger*. Boston: Little, Brown, 1974.

Keeley, Joseph. *The China Lobby Man*. New Rochelle, N.Y.: Arlington House, 1969.

Kennan, George F. "A Fresh Look at China Policy," *New York Times Magazine* (November 22, 1964), 27, 140–47.

—— *Memoirs, 1950–1963*. Vol. II. Boston: Little, Brown, 1972.

Koen, Ross Y. *The China Lobby in American Politics*. New York, Macmillan, 1960.

—— *The China Lobby in American Politics*. Edited with an Introduction by Richard C. Kagan. New York: Harper & Row, 1974.

—— "Two Postscripts to the McCarran Hearings," *Bulletin of Concerned Asian Scholars*. 1, No. 4 (May 1969), 27–31.

Kubek, Anthony. *How the Far East Was Lost: American Policy and the Creation of Communist China, 1941–1949*. Chicago: Regnery, 1963.

Latham, Earl. *The Communist Controversy in Washington From the New Deal to McCarthy*. Cambridge: Harvard University Press, 1966.

Latourette, Kenneth Scott. *The History of Early Relations between the United States and China 1784–1844*. New Haven: Yale University Press, 1917.

Liang, Chin-tung. *General Stilwell in China, 1942–1944: The Full Story*. New York: St. John's University Press, 1972.

Lohbeck, Don. *Patrick J. Hurley*. Chicago: Regnery, 1956.

Lukas, J. Anthony. "The Story So Far," *New York Times Magazine* (July 22, 1973), *passim*.

McCarthy, Joseph R. *America's Retreat from Victory: The Story of George Catlett Marshall*. New York: Devin-Adair, 1954.

McClellan, Robert. *The Heathen Chinee: A Study of American Attitudes Toward China, 1890–1905*. Columbus: Ohio State University Press, 1971.

McCormick, Thomas J. *China Market: America's Quest for Informal Empire 1893–1901*. Chicago: Quadrangle Books, 1967.

McCoy, Alfred W., with Cathleen B. Read and Leonard P. Adams II. *The Politics of Heroin in Southeast Asia*. New York: Harper & Row, 1972.

Mahan, Alfred T. *The Problem of Asia*. Boston: Little, Brown, 1900.

Marchetti, Victor and John D. Marks. *The CIA and the Cult of Intelligence*. New York: Bantam Books, 1975.

Markmann, Charles Lam. *The Buckleys: A Family Examined*. New York: Morrow, 1973.

Marsh, Paul A. "The Macmillan Company and Ross Koen's 'The China Lobby in American Politics'," *The Canadian Far Eastern Newsletter*, 22, No. 218 (April 1970), 4–6.

Masland, John W. "Missionary Influence Upon American Far Eastern Policy," *The Pacific Historical Review*, 10, No. 3 (September 1941), 279–96.

Matusow, Allen J., ed. *Joseph R. McCarthy*. Englewood Cliffs, N.J.: Prentice-Hall, 1970.

May, Ernest R. and James C. Thomson Jr., eds. *American-East Asian Relations: A Survey*. Cambridge: Harvard University Press, 1972.

May, Gary Arthur. *The China Service of John Carter Vincent, 1924–1953*. Ph.D. dissertation, University of California, Los Angeles, 1974.

Moorsteen, Richard and Morton Abramowitz. *Remaking China Policy: U.S.-China Relations and Governmental Decisionmaking*. Cambridge: Harvard University Press, 1971.

Newman, Robert P. "Lethal Rhetoric: The Selling of the China Myths," *Quarterly Journal of Speech*, 61, No. 2 (April 1975), 113–28.

—— *Recognition of Communist China?: A Study in Argument*. New York: Macmillan, 1961.

Nixon, Richard M. *Six Crises*. New York: Doubleday, 1962.

O'Kearney, John. "Lobby of a Million Ghosts," *The Nation*. 190, No. 4 (January 23, 1960), 76–78.

Parenti, Michael. *The Anti-Communist Impulse*. New York: Random House, 1969.

Peck, James. "The Roots of Rhetoric: The Professional Ideology of America's China Watchers," Edward Friedman and Mark Selden, eds., *America's Asia: Dissenting Essays on Asian-American Relations*. New York: Vintage Books, 1971.

Porter, Kirk H. and Donald Bruce Johnson. *National Party Platforms*. Urbana: University of Illinois Press, 1961.

Potter, Charles E. *Days of Shame*. New York: Coward-McCann, 1965.

Remer, C. F. *Foreign Investments in China*. New York: Macmillan, 1933.

Robinson, Thomas W., ed. *The Cultural Revolution in China*. Berkeley and Los Angeles: University of California Press, 1971.

Rosinger, Lawrence K. *China's Crisis*. New York: Knopf, 1945.

Rovere, Richard H. *Senator Joe McCarthy*. New York: Harcourt, Brace & World, 1959.

Scoble, Harry M. *Ideology and Electoral Action: A Comparative Case Study of the National Committee for an Effective Congress*. San Francisco: Chandler, 1967.

Service, John S. *The Amerasia Papers: Some Problems in the History of US-China Relations*. Berkeley, Center for Chinese Studies Research Monograph Number 7, 1971.

Shewmaker, Kenneth E. *Americans and Chinese Communists, 1927–1945: A Persuading Encounter*. Ithaca and London: Cornell University Press, 1971.

Smedley, Agnes. *Battle Hymn of China*. New York: Knopf, 1943.

Snow, Edgar. *Red Star Over China*. New York: Random House, 1938.
—— "Sixty Million Lost Allies." *Saturday Evening Post* (June 10, 1944), 12–13.
Steele, A. T. *The American People and China*. New York: McGraw-Hill for the Council on Foreign Relations, 1966.
Stein, Guenther. *The Challenge of Red China*. New York: McGraw-Hill, 1945.
Stimson, Henry L. and McGeorge Bundy. *On Active Duty In Peace and War*. New York: Harper, 1947.
Swanberg, W. A. *Luce and His Empire*. New York: Scribner's, 1972.
Terrill, Ross. "John Carter Vincent and the American 'Loss' of China," Bruce Douglass and Ross Terrill, eds., *China and Ourselves*. Boston: Beacon Press, 1971.
Thomas, John N. *The Institute of Pacific Relations: Asian Scholars and American Politics*. Seattle and London: University of Washington Press, 1974.
Thomson, James C. Jr. *While China Faced West: American Reformers in Nationalist China, 1928–1937*. Cambridge: Harvard University Press, 1969.
Tsou, Tang. *America's Failure in China 1941–50*. Chicago: University of Chicago Press, 1963.
Tuchman, Barbara W. *Stilwell and the American Experience in China, 1911–45*. New York: Macmillan, 1970.
Urquhart, Brian. *Hammarskjöld*. New York: Knopf, 1972.
Utley, Freda. *The China Story*. Chicago: Regnery, 1951.
Valeo, Francis. *The China White Paper*. Washington, D.C.: Library of Congress Legislative Reference Service, 1949.
Vandenberg, Arthur H. Jr., ed. *The Private Papers of Senator Vandenberg*. Boston: Houghton Mifflin, 1952.
Varg, Paul A. *The Making of a Myth: The United States and China 1897–1912*. East Lansing: Michigan State University Press, 1968.
Vincent, John Carter. *The Extraterritorial System in China: Final Phase*. Cambridge: East Asian Research Center Monograph 30, 1970.
Wedemeyer, Albert C. *Wedemeyer Reports!* New York: Holt, 1958.
Wertenbaker, Charles. "The China Lobby," *The Reporter*, 6, No. 8 (April 15, 1952), 2–24.
Westerfield, H. Bradford. *Foreign Policy and Party Politics: Pearl Harbor to Korea*. New Haven: Yale University Press, 1955.
White, Theodore H., ed. *The Stilwell Papers*. New York: William Sloane, 1948.
White, Theodore H. and Annalee Jacoby. *Thunder Out of China*. New York: William Sloane, 1946.
Whiting, Allen S. *China Crosses the Yalu: The Decision to Enter the Korean War*. New York: Macmillan, 1960.
Young, Kenneth T. *Negotiating with the Chinese Communists: The United States Experience, 1953–1967*. New York: McGraw-Hill, 1968.
Young, Marilyn B. *The Rhetoric of Empire: American China Policy, 1895–1901*. Cambridge: Harvard University Press, 1968.

Newspapers and Periodicals

Chicago Tribune
China Report (published from April 1969 to September–October 1971 by The Committee of One Million and from June 1972 into 1976 by The Committee for a Free China)
Life
Los Angeles Times
National Review Bulletin (June 11, 1960)
Newsweek
New York Times
Time
Washington Post

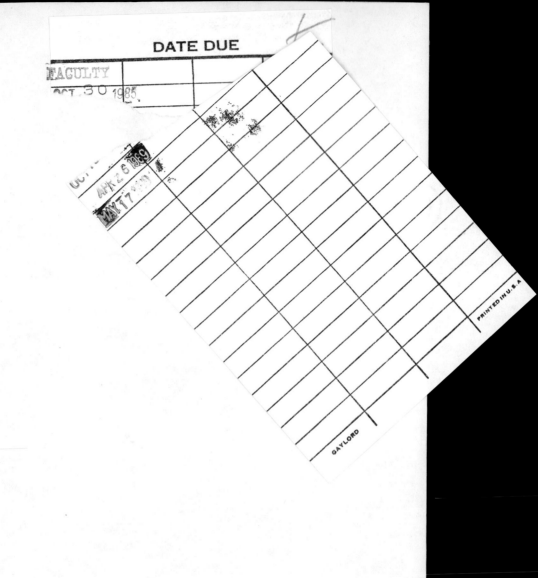